COUNTDOWN

For Mom, my No. 1 fan—

Who was always there, whether it was washing my uniforms, driving me to practice, nursing my wounds, lifting my spirits, or just being my Mom. LaVerne, this hit's for you.

P. E. R.

COUNTDOWN TO COBB

My Diary of the Record-Breaking 1985 Season

By
PETE ROSE

With Hal Bodley

Published by The Sporting News

Published in the United States by THE SPORTING NEWS Publishing Co., 1212
North Lindbergh Boulevard, St. Louis, Missouri 63132.

ISBN: 0-89204-213-3

10 9 8 7 6 5 4 3 2 1

A Times Mirror
Company

First Edition

Contents

Cover Photos

Pete Rose portrait by Stan Denny.
Pete Rose inset action by Richard Pilling.

Contents

FOREWORD

As a lifelong baseball fan and student of the game, I, like millions of others across the United States and Canada this past summer, assiduously followed Pete Rose on his historic quest to become the most proficient batsman ever to play the game. And when he stroked hit No. 4,192 to pass the legendary Ty Cobb on the all-time hit list, I unabashedly cheered.

The 1985 baseball season was a great one for the fans—I called it the Season of the Records—and there was no greater individual achievement than that accomplished by Rose.

A symbolic baton had been passed, and there wasn't a better or more qualified person to carry it forward than Rose. He'd always been a dedicated ambassador of good will for baseball and understood the significance of being a role model for children. Having broken the record and stepped into the ranks of baseball immortality, he recognized that his obligation to our nation's youth would become even greater and more demanding than before, and I'm sure he gladly welcomed the challenge.

Rose was destined for baseball greatness. I wasn't involved with major league baseball when he came to the big leagues in 1963, but, as a fan, I was immediately won over by his spirit, the joy with which he played the game and the wild abandon of youth that has never left him.

Rose was, still is and always will be Charlie Hustle. His brand of ball was never-say-die—whether he was running out a routine ground ball or diving for a sharply hit line drive that had "base hit" written all over it—and it was a throwback to an earlier era, to the St. Louis Cardinals' Gas House Gang of the 1930s. His enthusiasm spread like wildfire to his Cincinnati teammates and by the 1970s, the Reds, with Rose providing the pep, became the dominant team in the National League. And it came as no surprise in 1980, the year after he went to Philadelphia, that the Phillies participated in the World Series for the first time in 30 years— and won.

Over a 23-year major league career, Rose has played for three World Series champions and appeared in 16 All-Star Games. He was National League Rookie of the Year in 1963, the National League's Most Valuable Player 10 years later, the National League batting champion three times, the World Series MVP in 1975, the Hickok Award winner as the best professional athlete of '75 and The Sporting News' Player of the Decade for the 1970s. He holds a host of major league and National League records, but of them all, he will be remembered most for passing Ty Cobb.

Old-timers in baseball had believed that Cobb's record was untouch-able, as unreachable as Joe DiMaggio's 56-game hitting streak. But they had said the same thing about Babe Ruth's career home run record. As the old-timers' generation produced a Babe Ruth and a Ty Cobb, and ours produced a Henry Aaron and a Pete Rose, the next generation will surely produce two hitters who will try to break the records established by Aaron and Rose.

Baseball history is the foundation of the game, and there is no better time than the moment when one of its greatest landmarks falls. That moment belonged to Pete Rose and he deserved it.

Peter V. Ueberroth

4,192: The Rose of Cincinnati Is No. 1 on Baseball's Hit Parade

He uncoiled from his familiar crouch and the ball shot off his bat like it has so many times in 23 beguiling years.

The line drive bounced in front of San Diego left fielder Carmelo Martinez, and the relentless chase of Ty Cobb's ghost had ended.

For Peter Edward Rose, it was major league hit No. 4,192.

At 8:01 p.m. on September 11, 1985, with 47,237 fans cheering wildly at Cincinnati's Riverfront Stadium, this marvelous 44-year-old man had singled to left-center and become baseball's all-time hits leader.

Rose's storied pursuit of Cobb's 57-year-old record was over. The paramount moment had arrived 57 years to the day after Cobb played his last big-league game.

A record many said never would be broken—or even approached—had fallen. Pete Rose cheated not only time, but the experts; he refused to accept the calendar of his years.

Eric Show's first pitch to Rose in the first inning was a fastball, and the Cincinnati Reds' player-manager took it for a ball. Rose then fouled the next pitch back and looked at the third pitch, a slider, which was another ball.

Now, with the count 2-1, the Padres' Show delivered another slider. It was all over.

Rose ran to first base with all his usual vigor and rounded the bag as flashbulbs turned Riverfront Stadium into a light show.

Rose's 15-year-old son Petey led the surge from the Cincinnati dugout. Each of Rose's teammates congratulated him and Show, whose name also will go down in history, elbowed his way through the mob to shake Pete's hand.

A bright red Corvette, with Ohio license "PR 4192," was driven onto the field and presented to Rose.

Marge Schott, owner of the Reds, hugged her hero and planted a kiss or two on his cheek.

Then, Rose became a lonely, confused figure as the ovation swelled.

"I didn't know what to do," he said later. "I've never been on a ball field and not known what to do."

What happened during the next several minutes reduced Peter Edward Rose, born and raised in Cincinnati, to a mere human.

As applause vibrated from one side of Riverfront Stadium to the other, macho man Pete Rose broke down.

First came a tear or two from his bright brown eyes, the eyes so responsible for his uncanny ability to hit a baseball.

Rose tried looking up into the crisp, cool night, shaking his head. It didn't work.

Finally, he gave up. His armor was melting; for once, Pete Rose couldn't handle the situation. He embraced longtime friend Tommy Helms, the Reds' first-base coach, and buried his face in Helms' shoulder.

When Petey returned to first base, Rose was openly crying.

Rose insists that as an adult he hadn't cried since December 8, 1970, the day his father died.

"I'm not smart enough to have the words to describe my feelings," Rose said. "I felt like a man looking for a hole to jump into. I looked around for somebody to talk to and there wasn't anyone.

"Steve Garvey, who said, 'Thanks for the memories,' called this the greatest ovation he's ever seen. It just kept going on and on. I didn't know whether to take my helmet off again or wait for the people in the outfield to clean up all the confetti that had been thrown there.

"I was doing all right until I looked up in the sky and saw my father —he was sitting in the first row, and Ty Cobb was sitting behind him.

"I'm tough, but I couldn't handle it. I didn't have anybody to talk to. Some guy even took the base. I didn't have anything to kick."

Before the night ended, first baseman Rose ripped a triple to the left-field corner, scored two runs and made a game-ending stop on a Garvey grounder. The Reds won, 2-0, as Rose played in his 1,929th winning game (a big-league record).

In the stands, Pete's 70-year-old mother sobbed.

"I knew he'd get the hit tonight," LaVerne Rose Noeth said. "I knew it. He's the greatest. It's his day. I'd like to go down there and give him a great big kiss. Sure, he's crying. He has a soft heart."

Rose's wife Carol, his 11-month-old son Tyler and daughter Fawn were in the stands behind home plate.

"I tried not to cry," Carol said, "but I couldn't hold it in. I looked down at Tyler and said, 'Your Daddy just made history, Smoogie. You're

A jubilant Rose embraces son Petey after collecting hit No. 4,192 on September 11.

too young to know that now, but when you're older, I'll sit down and tell you all about it.' Then, Tyler uttered, 'Daddy,' and I cried some more."

During postgame ceremonies at home plate, President Ronald Reagan telephoned Rose. He talked about what an enduring record Rose had broken and added: "I once rooted for the guy who held the record."

Even the losers tipped their caps, extended their hands and offered words.

"He should bypass the Hall of Fame and go straight to the Smithsonian," Garvey said.

San Diego Manager Dick Williams had mixed emotions.

"It didn't turn out the way I wanted it to," Williams said. "I wanted to see Pete get the record, but not beat us. Tonight, he scored two runs and had two hits.

"He had himself quite a night. I can't see anybody challenging that record. I don't foresee anybody playing that long. It takes a special kind of guy."

Other Padres were moved by the historic night.

Third baseman Kurt Bevacqua: "It was a moment without words; it's the first time I've ever seen Pete break down. As soon as the ball was hit, I was sure it was a hit. I was trying to get the cutoff throw, but (shortstop) Garry Templeton wouldn't let me have it."

Templeton: "I made sure I was the cutoff man; I carried the ball over to Pete Rose personally to make sure he had it in his hand. I congratulated him and handed the ball to him."

Tony Gwynn: "I was very happy for him and when I got to first base (after singling later in the game), Pete said to me that I was the kind of hitter who can get 3,000 or 4,000 hits. I can't comprehend that many hits."

Rose insisted that reaching this pinnacle didn't mean he would soon retire as a player.

"If the season were to end today, I think I'd get another contract," he said. "But I'll never play if I am not having fun and contributing.

"A big milestone has been reached in my life. But I'll come back tomorrow night and continue to do my job. That's the way I approach baseball."

Remaining serious, the usually quick-with-a-quip Rose looked to the future.

"Someday, when things are going bad," Rose said, "I'll be able to reminisce about tonight."

Of course, figure filbert Rose could reminisce about most of his hits—not just the 4,192nd and 4,193rd.

Rose collected the first 3,164 hits of his big-league career with the Reds, the next 826 with the Philadelphia Phillies, the following 72 with the Montreal Expos and the 130 that got him past Cobb with his original club, Cincinnati.

Rose spent his first 16 major league summers with the Reds, toiling for his hometown team from 1963 through 1978. He then signed a free-agent contract with Philadelphia and played for the Phillies from 1979 through 1983. With his career apparently nearing its end, Rose was released by the Phils but caught on with Montreal for 1984.

Two weeks into August of '84, Cincinnati was about to dismiss its manager, Vern Rapp, and Reds President Bob Howsam indicated an in-

Rose, his quest complete, tips his cap to an appreciative crowd at Cincinnati's Riverfront Stadium.

terest in Rose.

Relegated to a part-time playing role with the Expos, Rose made a pitch for the Cincinnati job in a long telephone call to Howsam.

Rose not only convinced Howsam that he could manage the Reds, but that he could still contribute as a player. On August 17, 1984, Rose made his debut as Cincinnati's player-manager. And, carrying the dual workload, he continued his countdown to Cobb—a countdown that ended approximately 13 months later.

"I will never say I was a better baseball player than Cobb," said Rose, well aware that it took him 2,300-plus more at-bats to accumulate 4,191 hits than it did Cobb. "All I'll say is I got more hits than he did."

Rose paused a moment, obviously poised to make a few points of his own.

"But I can say that when Cobb played, few people had heard about relief pitchers. The starters went the entire games most of the time. In my era, relief pitchers come in with fresh arms in the late innings.

"And the travel is fatiguing nowadays. In Cobb's day, the longest trip was on a train from the East Coast to St. Louis. Now, we fly coast-to-coast, many times without a day off. The jet lag gets you sometimes because it's difficult to adjust to the time change.

"Still, Ty Cobb was a great player. I will never say he wasn't."

Tyrus Raymond Cobb's first day in the major leagues was August 30, 1905. He played center field for the Detroit Tigers that afternoon, going 1 for 3 against New York's Jack Chesbro. On September 11, 1928, Cobb made his last big-league playing appearance. Pinch hitting for the Philadelphia Athletics, he popped out against the Yankees' Henry Johnson.

Cobb led the American League in batting 12 seasons and went over .400 three times. He won those hitting titles in a 13-year stretch (1907-1919) and was the A.L. runner-up in 1916, 1921 and 1922. Rose has won three National League batting crowns, and his best average was the .348 mark he compiled in 1969.

Cobb led the American League in runs batted in four times, in runs scored five times, in total bases six times and in slugging percentage eight times.

He topped the league in stolen bases six times, and he held the big-league season and career steals records (96 in 1915, 892 lifetime) until Maury Wills and Lou Brock came along.

Once, Cobb led the A.L. in home runs with nine, although he hit only 118 in the 3,034 games he played. On the day that he broke Cobb's record, Rose had 160 homers.

Cobb's lifetime batting average was .367, more than 60 points higher than Rose's. (Record-keeping discrepancies in 1906 and 1910, uncovered by The Sporting News in 1981, dropped Cobb's career average to .366, his hit figure to 4,190 and his batting-crown total to 11. However, Commissioner Bowie Kuhn and baseball's Official Records Committee rejected the findings of this research. The Sporting News continues to note its discoveries, though, with asterisks being placed alongside appropriate Cobb entries in its Official Baseball Record Book.)

Unlike Rose, Cobb was one of the most hated players in the major leagues. His attitude was "win at any cost" and if that meant trampling or spiking an opponent or shouting nasty remarks at him, Cobb resorted to such tactics.

Detroit's Ty Cobb, known for his take-no-prisoners style of play, slides with spikes high into Philadelphia A's third baseman Home Run Baker in a 1909 game.

When he died on July 17, 1961, at age 74, he was a lonely and angry man.

Rose has played the game with just as much intensity as Cobb, as evidenced by his run-at-all-times enthusiasm, gung-ho belly slides and aggressiveness in all phases of the sport.

Characteristic of the Rose style of play are two episodes forever etched in baseball fans' minds—his home-plate collision with catcher Ray Fosse in the 1970 All-Star Game and his fisticuffs with Bud Harrelson of the New York Mets after Pete's hard slide into second base in Game 3 of the 1973 N.L. Championship Series.

Rose, whose brashness early in his career rubbed some opponents, fans, reporters and even a few teammates the wrong way, has evolved into a baseball favorite—liked by almost everyone connected with the game.

"I like people to like me," Rose said. "You know how some managers always say, 'I don't care if they like me as long as they respect me?' Well, that isn't my philosophy."

Yet the similarities between Rose and Cobb are uncanny.

Both players were driven to excellence by their fathers. And in each case, when the father died, there was a huge void.

Cobb's father was William Herschel Cobb, a Georgia school commissioner who wanted his son to go to college to become a doctor or lawyer.

When Cobb turned his back on those wishes and announced he was going to be a baseball player, the father warned him not to come home a failure.

Cobb's father was shot to death on the night of August 8, 1905, when his wife mistook him for an intruder. Three weeks later, Ty Cobb, at age 18, became a major leaguer with the Tigers, a team for whom he performed for 22 seasons before finishing his career with the Philadelphia A's.

Rose's father, who worked in a Cincinnati bank and died in 1970, wanted his son to be a major leaguer. He taught him, encouraged him and scolded him when his dedication was less than expected.

"I guess not having my father here to share the excitement of this season is one of the unhappy things about this year," Rose said. "He would have loved this because to get this record you have to be consistent. He stressed consistency for as long as I can remember."

Rose has been consistent for the better part of 23 seasons; Cobb played steadily—and spectacularly—for 24 years. Longevity, then, is another bond.

Like Rose, Cobb was a player-manager.

He took over the Tigers in 1921, at age 34, and guided them for six seasons. Detroit had finished seventh in 1920, but under Cobb's direction the Tigers moved as high as second.

After his final managerial season, 1926, Cobb spent his last two seasons in the majors as a player with the Athletics.

Cobb contemporaries said he handled the everyday players well, but had problems with his pitchers. Some gifted players have been known to develop a dislike for teammates who work only every fourth or fifth day.

To Rose's credit, one of his first acts after he took over as Cincinnati's player-manager on August 17, 1984, was to hire Jim Kaat as his pitching coach. The two have become an excellent blend.

Rose, under the expert guidance of attorney Reuven Katz, has been making wise investments for years.

Cobb, a major investor in General Motors and Coca-Cola, reportedly had assets of about $10 million when he died.

Rose has endorsed a large variety of products over the years. Cobb let his name be associated with such products as clothing, cigars and cigarettes.

One of Cobb's passions was his love of powerful automobiles, a love that also hits close to Rose's heart.

Cobb irritated his teammates with what many called his extravagant style of play.

No one, however, ever doubted his dedication to the game. To him, baseball was a science that should be studied daily—and such an attitude helped Cobb dominate the game.

With his hands-apart grip of the bat—he was a lefthanded hitter who threw righthanded—the man they called the Georgia Peach made things happen. He would crowd the plate, hit to the opposite field as adroitly as anyone and race from first to third on a bunt.

Like Rose, Cobb loved the nuances of competition. His bat control enabled him to execute the hit-and-run, hit behind the runner and bunt better than anyone in his generation.

Both players paid the price for their achievements, although Rose's almost singular love for baseball and sports exceeded Cobb's.

"Honestly," Rose said, "I can't think of anything I'd rather be doing in the summertime (than playing ball)."

And this summer, the final chapter was written in the chase of Ty Cobb's ghost, the ghost of 4,191.

It began in true Rose fashion on April 8, 1985.

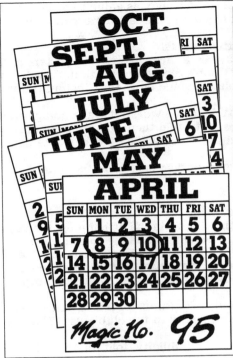

Opening day 1985 was special for Rose, son Tyler and Reds Owner Marge Schott.

MONDAY, APRIL 8........................ ROSE 2 FOR 3

Opening day.

Sure, they're special. For me, they probably mean more than to most people because I grew up in Cincinnati, where the National League opener has always been a happening, a tradition.

As I drove to the ball park for our game against Montreal, I kept thinking about all those other openers—there were 16 of them—with the Reds. I finally came to the conclusion this one best compared to my rookie year in 1963.

So, here I am coming back for my 17th opener—as the Reds' manager and a guy who needs 95 hits to break Ty Cobb's all-time (major league) career record.

Montreal	ab	r	h	rbi		Cincinnati	ab	r	h	rbi
Raines, lf	4	0	0	0		Davis, cf-lf	3	2	1	0
W'n'gham, cf	2	0	0	0		**Rose, 1b**	3	1	2	3
Dawson, rf	4	0	0	0		Milner, pr-cf	0	0	0	0
Driessen, 1b	4	0	1	0		Parker, rf	3	0	2	1
Brooks, ss	4	1	1	0		Cedeno, lf-1b	4	0	2	0
Law, 2b	3	0	0	0		Esasky, 3b	4	0	0	0
Wallach, 3b	3	0	2	1		C'cepcion, ss	3	0	1	0
Fitzgerald, c	3	0	0	0		Oester, 2b	3	0	0	0
Rogers, p	2	0	0	0		Bilardello, c	4	0	1	0
Burke, p	0	0	0	0		Soto, p	3	1	2	0
Dilone, ph	0	0	0	0		Willis, p	1	0	0	0
Roberge, p	0	0	0	0						
Totals	29	1	4	1		Totals	31	4	11	4

Montreal ....0 0 0   0 0 0   1 0 0—1
Cincinnati....................0 0 0   0 3 0   1 0 x—4

Montreal	IP.	H.	R.	ER.	BB.	SO.
Rogers (L. 0-1)	4⅔	8	3	3	1	3
Burke............................	2⅓	2	1	1	3	1
Roberge	1	1	0	0	1	1

Cincinnati	IP.	H.	R.	ER.	BB.	SO.
Soto (W. 1-0)	7	4	1	1	2	5
Willis (Save 1)	2	0	0	0	2	1

Game-winning RBI—**Rose.**
E—None. DP—Montreal 2. LOB—Montreal 5, Cincinnati 8. 2B—Wallach, Driessen, Davis, **Rose,** Cedeno. 3B—Brooks. SB—Davis 2, Milner. T—2:32. A—52,971.

I try not to be too sentimental, but, yes, this was a very important day for me—my 6-month-old son Tyler was going to see me play a regular-season game for the first time.

Peter Ueberroth, the new commissioner of baseball, was going to be here. National League President Chub Feeney was going to be here and our new owner, Marge Schott, was so excited she called me every day for the past three days.

I told her I could get her some free tickets!

Seriously. . . I knew there would be a large group of reporters and everybody would be talking about Cobb's record and all that. I made up my mind I'd discuss it, but the emphasis would be on the Cincinnati Reds and getting off to a good start.

That's what I told my players at Sunday's workout. Sure, going after the record would cause distractions, but I told them to have a lot of fun with it, too. The crowds will be large and there will be a lot of excitement. That electricity should help them.

I also told them I'm just like every other player on the team—two arms, two legs and 4,000 hits!

★   ★   ★

I couldn't have written a better script.

The fact I drove in two runs with a double in the fifth inning, then got a single to drive in another run in the seventh made the opener for me.

Reducing the "magic number" (to break Cobb's record) to 93 was important, but driving in the game-winning runs and helping the team get off to a big start with a 4-1 win over Montreal was even more important.

I got to Riverfront Stadium about 10:30 (a.m., for a 2:05 p.m. game) and there were already some of my players in the clubhouse. That's a good sign—they couldn't wait to get started.

Jim Ferguson, our vice president for publicity, told me there was a chance we could break the Riverfront Stadium attendance record for opening day. As it turned out, he was right—52,971 came to see us beat Montreal, the team I played for almost five months last year.

I still feel uncomfortable sitting behind a desk in the manager's office, but it goes with the territory. I received some telegrams wishing us well and there were some other notes on my desk.

I think there are certain events in your life you always remember. You know—where you were and what you were doing at certain times.

Opening days are like that.

I went to a lot of them at Crosley Field with my father. He'd let me miss school—kids in Cincinnati used to do that—and he'd take me to the games. We'd go early and a lot of times sit in the bleachers. In a sense, we were more than just fans—he'd sit there with me and explain as many details about the game as he could.

I wish he could have been here today. (The elder Rose died in December 1970.)

We had a little team meeting before the game, even though I don't like meetings.

I told the players to forget about where the experts picked us to finish this year. Stranger things have happened than us contending or winning in '85. I told them I'm not going to be surprised; the so-called experts will be surprised.

It was a crazy day, weatherwise.

During batting practice it was cold, but the sun was bright.

But as the game progressed, the weather was like Dr. Jekyll and Mr. Hyde.

— 18 —

Both our Mario Soto and Steve Rogers of the Expos were pitching well. Before the fourth inning started, the skies had darkened and there was a drizzle that turned to snow. Within five minutes the field was covered by snow. Then, after a delay, the sun came out again as we were taking a 3-0 lead in the fifth inning.

But the whole thing happened again. The skies darkened, there was more snow and the game was halted almost an hour.

One minute I thought I was at the beach, and the next thing I knew I was in the middle of a blizzard.

Luckily, the sun came back out and we finished our 4-1 victory.

I told my players Sunday when it was cold during the workout that if they go 0 for 4 in the opener, it was going to seem like it was a lot colder. I told them I wanted them to be aggressive, and they were—running the bases and at bat.

Winning gave me a great deal of satisfaction. We worked hard on fundamentals all spring. In the opener (today), we played solid on defense and got some big hits. I'm talking about the fifth inning when Soto singled with two out. When you get an inning going that way, you have to make the most of it.

After the game, I overheard Dave Parker talking to reporters: "We knew he (Rose) was going to come through today. You can feel it. That is the way he leads. He tells us how he wants it done, then goes out and does it. I don't think there is a better way."

That's going to be my style as manager.

Today was a start.

My job is to keep these guys from accepting losing. I have some young players who need to start playing with positive attitudes. I was always thinking about a double when I hit a single, and even the pitchers on this team will know how to run the bases aggressively.

We're going to steal a game or two here and there. The season's going to be more than me breaking Cobb's career hits record. That's just a matter of time.

TUESDAY, APRIL 9 .... OPEN DATE

I have never liked open dates.

When I was younger, I'd seldom take one. If I could find a coach or somebody else to throw batting practice, I'd go to the park and take some swings.

It has always been my belief when you're swinging the bat well, an open day destroys your momentum, timing or whatever.

But this one might have been good for some of our guys. It gave them a chance to get settled, unpack from spring training and take care of personal business.

It really wasn't a complete open date.

For as long as I can remember, the Cincinnati Club has been holding a luncheon about the time of the season opener. It's something called "Meet the Reds." The players all show up and are introduced.

It's a good public relations thing and gives the fans a chance to learn more about the team.

This year, I was the only one who spoke and I told everybody how good I thought this team could be.

Can you believe there were some people out there who looked like they thought I was just up there talking?

I learned a lot about this ball club last September (upon being named manager) and in spring training.

In September, I got an inkling what kind of character, what kind of backbone this team had. They busted their butts for me the last four weeks. They didn't have to come out there and play three games over .500 (15-12), but they did.

All the feelings I have for this team are based on things I saw. I could care less what happened in April, May, June, July and the first 16 days of August. I wasn't here.

I knew Tom Browning was going to be a good pitcher. I knew Jay Tibbs is a good pitcher and that Johnny Franco can pitch.

That's why they're all on this team. I saw a lot of them the last six weeks of 1984.

I knew that Dave Parker could do the same thing for this team that Dale Murphy does in Atlanta, Pedro Guerrero does in Los Angeles and Mike Schmidt does in Philadelphia.

This is a weak division (N.L. West), and I've told everyone, including Marge Schott and (Reds President) Bob Howsam, we can win it. I honestly believe that.

WEDNESDAY, APRIL 10 .... ROSE 1 FOR 4

When I was with Montreal in 1984, I kept telling Tim Raines how much talent he had. He is the kind of player who can be an MVP.

In today's game, he gave us a little show on how good he really is and he looks like he's off to a fine start.

I got a single off Bill Gullickson, who pitched seven strong innings (allowing only four hits, walking none and striking out five), but we really couldn't do much against the Expos and Montreal won, 4-1.

To me, the Expos played with a new spirit. They didn't show that when I was there last year. I'm going to have to watch them closely because unless I miss my guess, I think they're going to cause some trouble in the National League's Eastern Division this year.

Montreal	ab	r	h	rbi	Cincinnati	ab	r	h	rbi
Raines, lf	4	2	3	0	Davis, cf	4	0	0	0
W'n'gham, cf	4	0	0	0	**Rose, 1b**	4	0	1	1
Dawson, rf	4	1	2	0	Parker, rf	4	0	1	0
Schatzeder, p	0	0	0	0	Cedeno, lf	3	0	1	0
Reardon, p	0	0	0	0	Esasky, 3b	3	0	0	0
Driessen, 1b	3	0	1	0	C'cepcion, ss	3	0	1	0
Brooks, ss	3	0	2	3	Oester, 2b	3	0	0	0
Law, 2b	3	1	0	0	Bilardello, c	3	0	0	0
Wallach, 3b	4	0	1	0	Tibbs, p	1	0	0	0
Fitzgerald, c	3	0	0	0	Kr'chicki, ph	1	0	0	0
Gullickson, p	3	0	1	1	Hume, p	0	0	0	0
Johnson, rf	1	0	0	0	Power, p	0	0	0	0
					Milner, ph	1	1	1	0
Totals	32	4	10	4	Totals	30	1	5	1

Montreal .... 1 1 0   0 0 1   0 1 0—4
Cincinnati........................ 0 0 0   0 0 0   0 0 1—1

Montreal	IP.	H.	R.	ER.	BB.	SO.
Gullickson (W. 1-0)....	7	4	0	0	0	5
Schatzeder	1	0	0	0	0	1
Reardon	1	1	1	1	0	1
Cincinnati	IP.	H.	R.	ER.	BB.	SO.
Tibbs (L. 0-1).............	6	7	3	3	1	1
Hume...........................	2	2	1	1	2	2
Power..........................	1	1	0	0	0	1

Game-winning RBI—Brooks.
E—Esasky. DP—Montreal 1, Cincinnati 2. LOB—Montreal 5, Cincinnati 2. 2B—Milner. 3B—Raines. SB—Raines 2, Concepcion. SF—Brooks. WP—Reardon. Balk—Gullickson. T—2:19. A—10,491.

Although (Montreal infielder) Dougie Flynn is a close friend, I think the addition of Hubie Brooks as their shortstop is going to help the Expos.

Hubie drove in a run with a single in the first inning, hit a sacrifice fly in the sixth and had another run-scoring single in the eighth.

Raines had three hits and two stolen bases today.

I'm a little concerned about my catcher, Dann Bilardello. Raines is going to steal on anybody, but at this point I'm going to have to pay close attention to my catching.

We tried all winter to make a trade for a front-line catcher and couldn't do it.

Bill Bergesch, our general manager, is still talking to clubs, but I don't know if we're going to be able to get one.

I was involved in what could have been our best threat of the game in the seventh inning.

With the Expos leading 3-0, I singled and eventually ended up on third base and I tried to score on a fly to outfield. I beat the throw to catcher Mike Fitzgerald, but third-base umpire John Kibler said I left the base too early and called me out.

We did score a run off Montreal's reliever, Jeff Reardon, in the ninth inning. I sent up Eddie Milner to pinch hit and he ripped a double to center.

Eric Davis—he's swinging like he's trying to hit every ball over the fence—struck out. With me batting, Reardon threw a wild pitch and Eddie went to third. I hit a grounder to first for an out, but Milner scored. Parker popped out and the game was over.

It was the kind of loss you try to forget. That's what I keep telling my players. We didn't have very many chances and that happens when you go up against somebody throwing as well as Gullickson did.

One thing about being manager I am finding difficult. When you're a player, if you've done your best and had a good game—not made any errors or struck out with runners on base—you can forget a loss pretty quickly, maybe by the time you get home.

But when you're the manager, the game stays with you longer. You wonder if you should have made this move or that move, if you did everything you could to help your team win.

One thing I liked today—and my pitching coach, Jim Kaat, agrees with me—is the way Jay Tibbs is throwing. Montreal got three earned runs off him, but if he continues to pitch the way he did today, he's going to win a lot of games for the Cincinnati Reds.

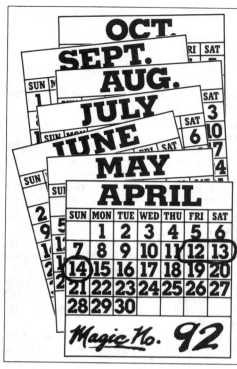

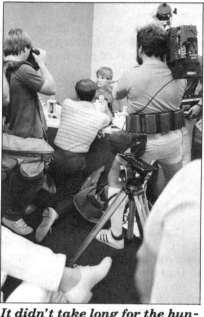

It didn't take long for the hun-
gry media to descend upon the
cooperative Rose.

FRIDAY, APRIL 12 .... ROSE 2 FOR 4

The first day in New York is always difficult and today was no different.

There is so much media attention.
Everyone has a microphone and tape
recorder. They wanted me to do this
TV interview, talk to this reporter. It
seems like it never ends.

And, of course, I always do the
pregame show with Marty Brennaman, who broadcasts the Reds games
over our radio network.

You know, I've always cooperated
with the press. It's just my nature and,
besides, in the long run they help put
money in my pocket. A lot of the
young players do not realize this.

This is the beginning of our first
road trip. We flew here last night.

Cincinnati	ab	r	h	rbi	New York	ab	r	h	rbi
Davis, cf	4	0	0	0	Backman, 2b	4	0	1	0
Rose, 1b	4	0	2	0	Wilson, cf	3	0	0	0
Redus, pr	0	0	0	0	Hern'dez, 1b	4	0	0	0
Parker, rf	4	0	0	0	Carter, c	4	1	1	1
Cedeno, lf	4	0	0	0	Strawb'ry, rf	4	0	2	0
Esasky, 3b	3	0	0	0	Foster, lf	3	0	2	0
C'cepcion, ss	2	0	0	0	Johnson, 3b	4	0	0	0
Oester, 2b	3	0	0	0	Santana, ss	2	0	1	0
Bilardello, c	1	0	0	0	Berenyi, p	1	0	0	0
Milner, ph	1	0	1	0	Blocker, ph	1	0	0	0
Van Gorder, c	0	0	0	0	Sisk, p	0	0	0	0
Soto, p	1	0	0	0					
Walker, ph	1	0	0	0					
Willis, p	0	0	0	0					
Totals	28	0	3	0	Totals	30	1	7	1

Cincinnati ....0 0 0   0 0 0   0 0 0—0
New York ....0 0 0   1 0 0   0 0 x—1

Cincinnati	IP.	H.	R.	ER.	BB.	SO.
Soto (L. 1-1)	7	6	1	1	3	2
Willis	1	1	0	0	0	1
New York	IP.	H.	R.	ER.	BB.	SO.
Berenyi (W. 1-0).........	7	1	0	0	1	6
Sisk (Save 1)..............	2	2	0	0	1	1

Game-winning RBI—Carter.
E—None. DP—New York 2. LOB—Cincinnati 4,
New York 9. HR—Carter (2). SB—Strawberry 2, Wilson. SH—Berenyi. HBP—By Berenyi (Bilardello). T—
2:24. A—31,120.

We'll play three games here, then go to Atlanta for three.

So, with all the interest in the Cobb record, my first time into each
city is going to be busy. The writers and radio-TV guys all want to interview me. I seldom do live TV interviews because they usually come

when I'm taking batting practice.

I've never let the media interfere with my preparation for a game. When it's time for me to take ground balls, I take ground balls. When it's time to take batting practice, I will walk away from the guys. Some of my close friends are members of the media.

I knew when I became player-manager there were certain things I would have to do to represent the ball club. All managers are expected to do that, but I'm not your normal manager. I'm a player, too. Some of the things the Reds may have done with (recent managers) Russ Nixon or Vern Rapp, they may not ask me to do. Jim Ferguson meets with me every two or three days and we go over the requests—do I want to do it or do I not want to do it.

If he's got a group that wants me to do something that may sell 5,000 tickets, I cooperate with them because my interest is the Reds.

The New York media is tough.

There's one question I'm getting tired of answering. A writer came up to me today and said, "You know, Hall of Fame players have never made good managers."

I looked him straight in the eyes and said, "Who are we talking about?"

He said Ted Williams and Frank Robinson.

"Did you ever stop to think neither one of those guys had enough good players to win with?" I asked. "You're putting me in a group of everybody who has been a good ballplayer and become a manager because of Ted Williams and Frank Robinson."

I don't know where people get all those things. I tell them I'm different because everything I've gotten out of baseball I've had to work extra hard for. Not that they didn't work, but I was a self-made player. They had all the natural talent in the world. Ted Williams could swing his bat and the ball was gone. He had great eyes. Frank Robinson didn't have problems doing things. I don't know if Ted Williams expected his players to hit like him or not. I don't know.

There is a lot of hype around the Mets this year; a lot of people are picking them to win the Eastern Division. I don't know.

They sure did get good pitching tonight. Bruce Berenyi gave up only one single in seven innings and that was my liner to left field with one out in the first inning.

I also got another single—that leaves me 90 short of breaking the record—but we just couldn't get anything started.

Mario Soto pitched well for us. It was the kind of game where you wish you could score some runs because you hate to see such a good performance go to waste.

Gary Carter led off the fourth inning with a home run and that was all the Mets needed. They beat us, 1-0. Doug Sisk pitched the last two innings and gave up two hits—my other single and one by Eddie Milner.

So now we're 1-2 and have our work cut out for us the next two days.

SATURDAY, APRIL 13 .... ROSE 1 FOR 4

It was only the fourth game, but today I became a little concerned that we're not getting the key hits.

I had a single off the Mets' starter, Ed Lynch, but we lost our third straight game, 2-1.

We scored a run in the second inning when Davey Concepcion doubled home Nick Esasky, but a 1-0 lead is like walking a tightrope when you're having trouble getting key hits and scoring runs.

Just like Mario Soto on Friday night, Tom Browning pitched a good game for us. I like Tom a lot. He's a gamer, a fighter. Anybody who has a screwball as his best pitch is going to be real tough.

Tom gave up just three hits in seven innings, but our defense let him down. Dave Parker, Eric Davis and Concepcion made errors. Davey had two.

The Mets scored their only run off Browning in the sixth inning.

I had to take him out for a pinch-hitter in the top of the eighth and brought in John Franco, and that's a tough thing for a rookie (Browning) who's pitching well in a close game.

In the bottom of the ninth, Darryl Strawberry led off with a homer and it was over.

These two losses to the Mets were tough. My pitching has given up only three runs in two games and has nothing to show for the effort but two losses.

Jim Kaat, my pitching coach, is good for the young players. When they lose games like this, he emphasizes the positive things. He tells them if they continue to pitch like they have, they're going to win a lot of games.

As far as the hitting was concerned, getting a clutch hit with men on base . . . I don't think you can teach that. No way. You just have to get guys who develop consistency.

If they develop consistency day in and day out, it should come in stride to get base hits with runners in scoring position.

I have always thought a good athlete thrives on competition. If the winning run is on second base, I want to be the hitter. Or, if I am the pitcher and the bases are loaded, give me the ball. I'll get the guy out. I've been in enough situations like that you sort of expect them. If we've got a man on second, I'm not going to bunt for a base hit and leave it up to the next guy. A lot of guys leave it up to the next guy.

If you've got a guy who is a .300 hitter year in and year out, day in and day out, month in and month out, you know he's going to get a lot of clutch hits because he gets a lot of hits overall.

If he's on a good team, there are usually guys in scoring position when he gets those hits.

That's what I'm hoping my guys will start doing, but you can't teach it.

Cincinnati	ab	r	h	rbi	New York	ab	r	h	rbi
Davis, cf	4	0	0	0	Wilson, cf	3	0	2	0
Franco, p	0	0	0	0	Chapman, 2b	3	1	0	0
Rose, 1b	4	0	1	0	Hern'dez, 1b	2	0	0	1
Redus, lf	0	0	0	0	Carter, c	4	0	1	0
Parker, rf	3	0	1	0	Strawb'ry, rf	4	1	2	1
C'deno, lf-1b	4	0	2	0	Foster, lf	3	0	0	0
Esasky, 3b	3	1	1	0	Blocker, lf	0	0	0	0
C'cepcion, ss	3	0	1	1	Johnson, 3b	3	0	0	0
Oester, 2b	3	0	0	0	Santana, ss	3	0	0	0
Bilardello, c	2	0	0	0	Lynch, p	2	0	0	0
Milner, ph-cf	1	0	0	0	Gard'hire, ph	1	0	0	0
Browning, p	2	0	0	0	McDowell, p	0	0	0	0
Walker, ph	1	0	0	0					
Van Gorder, c	0	0	0	0					
Totals	30	1	6	1	Totals	28	2	5	2

Cincinnati ....0 1 0   0 0 0   0 0 0—1
New York ....0 0 0   0 0 1   0 0 1—2
None out when winning run scored.

Cincinnati	IP.	H.	R.	ER.	BB.	SO.
Browning	7	3	1	0	1	5
Franco (L. 0-1)	1*	2	1	1	1	0

New York	IP.	H.	R.	ER.	BB.	SO.
Lynch	7	4	1	1	1	2
McDowell (W. 2-0)	2	2	0	0	0	1

*Pitched to one batter in ninth.

Game-winning RBI—Strawberry.
E—Parker, Davis, Concepcion 2. DP—Cincinnati 1, New York 2. LOB—Cincinnati 4, New York 6. 2B—Esasky, Concepcion. HR—Strawberry (1). SB—Wilson. SH—Esasky, Chapman. SF—Hernandez. T—2:24. A—26,212.

SUNDAY, APRIL 14 .... ROSE 1 FOR 4

My 44th birthday. Got a lot of cards and letters, and my wife Carol called to wish me a happy birthday.

This time last year we were celebrating my 4,000th hit. I got it April 13 off Jerry Koosman of the Philadelphia Phillies.

Little did I know a year later I would be back with the Cincinnati Reds as their player-manager.

A birthday gift I'll never forget was given to me today by Barry Halper, a baseball artifacts collector. It's a metal bust of Ty Cobb.

The other gift wasn't as memorable —the New York Mets pitched Dwight Gooden against us today.

In the first two games of this series, we just couldn't come up with key hits. Today, that was part of the problem, but Dwight Gooden was even more.

Cincinnati	ab	r	h	rbi	New York	ab	r	h	rbi
Milner, cf	4	0	0	0	Backman, 2b	3	1	1	0
Rose, 1b	4	0	1	0	Wilson, cf	4	1	2	1
Parker, rf	3	0	1	0	Hern'dez, 1b	4	0	0	0
Cedeno, lf	4	0	0	0	Carter, c	2	1	2	2
Kr'chicki, 3b	3	0	1	0	Strawb'ry, rf	3	1	0	0
C'cepcion, ss	4	0	0	0	Foster, lf	4	0	1	0
Oester, 2b	3	0	0	0	Johnson, 3b	3	0	0	0
Bilardello, c	3	0	1	0	Gard'hire, ss	3	0	1	1
Tibbs, p	2	0	0	0	Gooden, p	4	0	1	0
Price, p	0	0	0	0					
Foley, ph	1	0	0	0					
Hume, p	0	0	0	0					
Totals	31	0	4	0	Totals	30	4	8	4

Cincinnati ....0 0 0   0 0 0   0 0 0—0
New York ....0 0 0   0 0 2   2 0 x—4

Cincinnati	IP.	H.	R.	ER.	BB.	SO.
Tibbs (L. 0-2)	6*	8	4	4	4	2
Price	1	0	0	0	0	1
Hume	1	0	0	0	1	2

New York	IP.	H.	R.	ER.	BB.	SO.
Gooden (W. 1-0)	9	4	0	0	2	10

*Pitched to two batters in seventh.

Game-winning RBI—Carter.
E—Bilardello. DP—Cincinnati 1. LOB—Cincinnati 6, New York 8. 2B—Wilson 2. 3B—Backman. HR—Carter (3). SB—Parker, Strawberry, Johnson. SF—Carter. T—2:26. A—30,456.

I got a third-inning single to right field off him, but that was just one of four hits we managed. He struck out 10 batters and the Mets beat us, 4-0.

The loss was our fourth straight and we fell to 1-4. The Mets, the talk of the National League, are 5-0, but it's early. Very early.

I'm 88 hits from breaking the Cobb record, but right now there are more important things to think about. I've got to get this team turned around.

I'm still more convinced than ever we are going to be contenders in the National League Western Division, but we're just not scoring runs. In our three games here at Shea Stadium, we scored just one run and were shut out twice.

I had to feel sorry for Jay Tibbs. He pitched well (today), but Gary Carter homered to left field in the sixth inning to end a scoreless tie.

My bullpen did fine. Joe Price and Tom Hume blanked the Mets in two innings, so I think we're going to be OK there.

The New York reporters are excited about Dwight Gooden, and they should be. They think I am the only active player who has batted against both Sandy Koufax and Gooden. (Rose is, in fact, the only player—active or inactive—who has hit against both pitchers, although other players' careers have spanned the Koufax and Gooden eras. Rose's teammate, Tony Perez, for example, batted against the Dodgers' Koufax 20 years ago but didn't face Gooden in the Met pitcher's rookie season of 1984 and wasn't used against him today.)

They (the writers) keep asking me to compare. What I told them was that at this stage of Dwight's career, he probably has better all-around stuff than Sandy—or than most people who ever pitched in the majors.

They tell me he (Koufax) was very wild as a kid. I know when he pitched for the University of Cincinnati, he couldn't keep the ball within the backstop and that's why the Cincinnati Reds never pursued him. The first couple of years in the majors, he was very wild and inconsistent.

After three losses to the Mets, I'm happy to be getting out of New York. It's on to Atlanta and back to our division for three games against the Braves. Maybe we can get something started there.

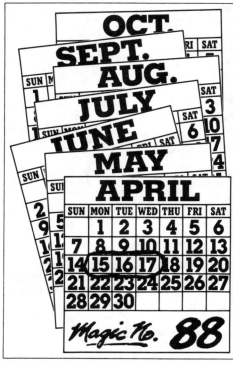

Relief ace Ted Power chalked up save No. 1 with a big strikeout April 15.

MONDAY, APRIL 15....................... ROSE 1 FOR 4

It was bad enough we lost three games to the Mets, but when we got to the airport after Sunday's game our flight was delayed.

We were supposed to leave for Atlanta at 20 after 5, but because of mechanical problems with the airplane we didn't take off until 20 minutes to 10. There's nothing worse than waiting around an airport after you've lost four games in a row, plus being swept in a three-game series with the Mets.

I'm told there was a lot of bickering (among the Reds) last year and before that because of some of the team rules.

Well, I've always thought you treat major league baseball players like men.

I got them two cases of beer for each of our flights. And I got them new-style socks this year. What people don't understand is that I know the

Cincinnati	ab	r	h	rbi	Atlanta	ab	r	h	rbi
Davis, cf-lf	6	1	1	0	Wash'gton, rf	4	1	1	0
Rose, 1b	4	1	1	0	Ramirez, ss	4	1	1	0
Milner, cf	0	0	0	0	Komminsk, lf	5	2	2	1
Parker, rf	5	0	1	1	Murphy, cf	5	2	2	3
C'deno, lf-1b	4	2	2	1	Horner, 3b	5	1	1	1
Esasky, 3b	4	3	3	2	Perry, 1b	5	0	1	0
C'cepcion, ss	4	2	1	0	Cerone, c	5	1	4	2
Oester, 2b	4	0	1	2	Hubbard, 2b	5	0	1	0
Van Gorder, c	5	0	3	3	Perez, p	0	0	0	0
Stuper, p	2	0	0	0	McMurtry, p	1	0	0	0
Price, p	0	0	0	0	Smith, p	1	0	0	0
Willis, p	0	0	0	0	Chambliss, ph	1	0	0	0
Power, p	0	0	0	0	Forster, p	0	0	0	0
					Oberkfell, ph	1	0	0	0
					Garber, p	0	0	0	0
Totals	38	9	13	9	Totals	42	8	13	7

Cincinnati .... 5 0 2   2 0 0   0 0 0—9
Atlanta .... 1 0 3   1 0 0   0 0 3—8

Cincinnati	IP.	H.	R.	ER.	BB.	SO.
Stuper (W. 1-0)	5⅓	9	5	5	1	2
Price	⅓	0	0	0	1	0
Willis	3	3	3	0	0	1
Power (Save 1)	⅓	1	0	0	0	1
Atlanta	IP.	H.	R.	ER.	BB.	SO.
Perez (L. 0-1)	⅓	4	5	5	2	0
McMurtry	2⅔°	5	4	4	2	2
Smith	3	1	0	0	0	3
Forster	2	2	0	0	1	0
Garber	1	1	0	0	0	2

°Pitched to two batters in fourth.

Game-winning RBI—Parker.
E—Parker, Esasky, Concepcion. LOB—Cincinnati 10, Atlanta 9. 2B—Murphy 2, Horner, Esasky. HR—Esasky (1), Cerone (1). SH—Stuper, Willis. HBP—By McMurtry (Cedeno). T—2:51. A—7,404.

players more than any manager because I'm a player.

I know they don't want a damn dictator going around telling them they can't do this, they can't do that, you gotta wear your hair like this.

I don't give a damn how a player wears his hair. All that stuff is the front office; it's not me.

I care whether or not a guy is on time. I care if a guy does a good job and works hard. I don't care about the other stuff.

Rules. I have a list of rules that was sent down from the last manager and the manager before him. You have to have a set of rules to protect you from the players' association and grievances. If a guy misses a plane, you have to have a rule on how much the fine can be.

We have a curfew rule; it's 2½ hours from the time the team bus gets back to the hotel. But you think I'm going to lose my sleep by going out and knocking on doors to see if guys are in their rooms? No way.

If the players aren't smart enough to realize they're going to get paid on what they do and the only way they can do it is to be in good shape, they've got problems.

If they want to go out drinking all night, that's their business because I will find out soon enough.

How are 40 men going to get drunk on two cases of beer on an airplane?

Why should you tell them they can't have beer on airplanes? Do that and they'll start sneaking it in their briefcases. Then, they'll start bringing on the hard stuff and you've got a big problem. If people want to drink, they're going to drink one way or the other.

Even though we've lost four games in a row, I had a good feeling about the team flying here. We've got some hitters on this team and it's just a matter of waiting for them to get started.

When I'm in Atlanta, I always spend some time with Tom and Evelyn Kirkland, friends for a long time. And Mario Nunez, the "Cuban," always drives that wreck of his up from Tampa when I'm here. I've known the Cuban for a long time also; he goes to the dog track with me in spring training.

★　　★　　★

There's one thing about playing in Atlanta Stadium. No lead is ever safe.

We were up 9-5 after four innings tonight, but the Braves scored three runs in the ninth to make it close.

With Gerald Perry on third base and two out, (reliever) Ted Power struck out Glenn Hubbard to end it.

I singled to right field in the first inning, leaving me 87 short of breaking the record.

It seems like anything can happen in this ball park—and usually does. Tonight, our defense fell apart at the wrong time. We made two errors in the ninth. Three of their runs were unearned.

But we ended the losing streak, we hit the ball well and scored nine runs. Maybe this is the start of something good.

TUESDAY, APRIL 16....................... ROSE 0 FOR 4

Tonight, we made the most of four hits and beat the Braves, 2-1.

These low-scoring games are becoming a way of life. But as I look at box scores of other National League games, I see the Cincinnati Reds are not alone.

I don't really know what's causing it because the season's early. Maybe it's just because there are a lot of good, young pitchers in this league.

When you get strong pitching like we did tonight from Mario Soto, you don't expect the opposition to do much scoring. The problem is, the Braves got seven hits and we got only four.

Eric Davis hit a leadoff homer in the sixth inning to win it for us. That was his first homer and first game-winning RBI. I hope that relaxes him a little because he has been pressing lately and striking out too much. I would really like to see him get in a good groove because he has the talent to help this ball club.

Cincinnati	ab	r	h	rbi	Atlanta	ab	r	h	rbi
Davis, cf-lf	4	1	1	1	Wash'gton, rf	3	0	0	0
Rose, 1b	4	0	0	0	Ramirez, ss	4	0	1	0
Milner, cf	0	0	0	0	Komminsk, lf	4	0	1	0
Parker, rf	4	0	0	0	Murphy, cf	4	1	2	1
Cedeno, lf-1b	3	0	0	0	Chambliss, 1b	4	0	0	0
Esasky, 3b	4	0	1	0	Oberkfell, 3b	4	0	1	0
C'cepcion, ss	3	1	1	0	Cerone, c	4	0	2	0
Oester, 2b	3	0	1	1	Hubbard, 2b	2	0	0	0
Van Gorder, c	3	0	0	0	Barker, p	1	0	0	0
Soto, p	3	0	0	0	Hall, ph	1	0	0	0
					Camp, p	0	0	0	0
					Perry, ph	1	0	0	0
					Forster, p	0	0	0	0
Totals	31	2	4	2	Totals	32	1	7	1

Cincinnati .... 0 1 0 0 0 1 0 0 0—2
Atlanta .... 0 1 0 0 0 0 0 0 0—1

Cincinnati	IP	H	R	ER	BB	SO
Soto (W. 2-1)	9	7	1	1	2	8

Atlanta	IP	H	R	ER	BB	SO
Barker	5	3	1	1	0	6
Camp (L. 0-2)	2	1	1	1	0	1
Forster	2	0	0	0	1	0

Game-winning RBI—Davis.
E—None. DP—Cincinnati 2. LOB—Cincinnati 3, Atlanta 6. 2B—Oester. HR—Murphy (5), Davis (1). T—2:14. A—15,175.

When Soto's pitching, you have to manage for a low-scoring game. You scratch out one or two runs and go from there. Tonight, Davis got us the big run.

It's difficult to say just what Mario Soto means to the Reds. He's to this team what Dwight Gooden is to the Mets, Rick Sutcliffe is to the Cubs, Nolan Ryan is to the Astros, Fernando Valenzuela is to the Dodgers.

When we send Mario out there, we expect to win. We should win. Tonight, he got his first complete game of the season, which gave the bullpen a big lift.

There has been a lot of pressure on the pitching staff because we have not been scoring many runs.

Mario told me whenever he pitches he tries to pitch a shutout. That is always his game plan and it's a good one because you're not depending on the offense outscoring the other team.

It looks to me like Dale Murphy is off to an MVP year. He hit his fifth homer of the season in the second inning to tie the game.

I'm a little concerned about Dave Parker. He's got a gum problem that's causing him a lot of pain. He's had a dentist look at it and has been told it needs minor surgery. He's going to get it taken care of Thursday when we get off this road trip.

I went into the trainer's room tonight and Parker had an ice pack on his jaw. He said the pain is brutal, that it starts down around the jaw and goes all the way up to his eye.

He was trying to laugh and said, "If I don't get this taken care of, you are going to have one big crying outfielder. I've never had pain this bad."

I'm learning a lot about this ball club.

We went to New York and lost three tough games we could have—no, make that should have—won. They beat us the first two games with their gloves; they picked us. We didn't play badly, they just beat us. We lost Friday, lost Saturday and Dwight Gooden shut us out Sunday.

We have plane problems and are late getting here. We go right to the ball park (Monday) and beat them.

And tonight, we did the same thing.

I think a lot of teams would have had trouble here after losing like we did in New York, but we bounced back. To me, that's character.

WEDNESDAY, APRIL 17 .... ROSE 1 FOR 5

The first thing I learned this morning when I got out of bed was that Mario Soto had a scuffle in a nightclub after the game last night.

I'm sure it will be in the newspapers, but as far as I'm concerned it's no big deal.

Bill Bergesch is on this trip and went to Atlanta Municipal Court with Mario, who was charged with hitting a waiter.

Bergesch says he thinks Mario, who was with catcher Dave Van Gorder and Rafael Ramirez, the Braves' shortstop, was irritated by some remarks the waiter made.

Anyway, Van Gorder said Mario didn't even hit the guy, that he just laid his hand on his face to push him back. From the facts I've gotten, I'm 100 percent behind Mario.

I don't get worked up about things like this. No big deal.

Cincinnati	ab	r	h	rbi	Atlanta	ab	r	h	rbi
Davis, cf-rf	5	1	1	1	Wash'ton, rf	4	0	0	0
Rose, 1b	5	1	1	0	Ramirez, ss	4	0	0	0
Parker, rf	3	1	2	0	Komminsk, lf	4	0	0	0
Milner, cf	2	0	1	0	Murphy, cf	4	1	2	0
Cedeno, lf	5	1	1	0	Horner, 3b	4	0	0	0
Esasky, 3b	4	2	3	2	Chambliss, 1b	4	0	1	0
C'cepcion, ss	4	0	1	1	Cerone, c	3	0	2	1
Oester, 2b	2	0	1	0	Hubbard, 2b	3	0	0	0
Van Gorder, c	2	0	1	1	Bedrosian, p	2	0	0	0
Browning, p	4	0	0	0	Smith, p	0	0	0	0
					Harper, ph	1	0	0	0
					McMurtry, p	0	0	0	0
Totals	36	6	12	5	Totals	33	1	6	1

Cincinnati ....0 0 0 2 0 3 0 0 1—6
Atlanta ....0 0 0 1 0 0 0 0 0—1

Cincinnati	IP.	H.	R.	ER.	BB.	SO.
Browning (W. 1-0)......	9	6	1	1	0	3

Atlanta	IP.	H.	R.	ER.	BB.	SO.
Bedrosian (L. 0-1)......	5*	8	5	4	1	4
Smith.....................	3	3	0	0	1	1
McMurtry.................	1	1	1	1	0	0

*Pitched to four batters in sixth.

Game-winning RBI—Esasky.
E—Horner. DP—Atlanta 1. LOB—Cincinnati 7, Atlanta 5. 2B—Murphy, Parker. HR—Davis (2). SH—Oester. SF—Van Gorder. WP—Bedrosian. T—2:08. A —13,513.

★   ★   ★

Some of the writers were talking to Henry Aaron, the Braves' director of player development, before the game. They were asking him about the pressures I will be under when I get close to Cobb's record.

Aaron broke Babe Ruth's career home run record 11 years ago, so he knows what it's like to go after a record people never thought would fall.

He said it was very difficult for him, that people hounded him so much he had to have two different hotel rooms, one in his name, one in somebody else's that he actually stayed in.

I really don't think there's going to be any pressure. I really don't.

I've always been open with the media and available. As long as they let me do my work, I will cooperate.

Hank Aaron had some problems with the press over the years, so I guess there was a little resentment there. I'm not sure, but I'm just not putting any pressure on myself about the record. It's going to come, it's a matter of time.

★   ★   ★

I've been talking since spring training about Tom Browning, our rookie lefthander. He can pitch.

We had a 5:40 game today because of Braves' television and we beat them, 6-1. Nick Esasky was 3 for 4 and drove in two runs.

I led off the fourth inning with a single to start a two-run rally against Steve Bedrosian. That hit leaves me 86 short of breaking the record.

We've had pretty good pitching all season, but today's was excellent. Browning gave us another complete game and you won't see a better-pitched game.

In his two starts, Browning has given up just one earned run and only nine hits (in 16 innings).

Jim Ferguson, our PR director, told me that since Browning reported to the Reds last September, he has an ERA of 1.14. Just five earned runs in $39\frac{1}{3}$ innings.

He's a gamer, a real fighter. Tonight, when their catcher, Rick Cerone, bunted on him, I thought there might be a little problem. I wouldn't have been surprised if there had been some chin music the next time Cerone batted. Browning's like that. My kind of player.

Eric Davis hit his second homer in two days, and Esasky is really starting to swing the bat good.

Esasky told Billy DeMars (batting coach) he's a lot more comfortable at the plate compared to when spring training started. Billy has worked hard with Nick, teaching him to make good contact and hit in the clutch. They're trying to build consistency.

After three losses in New York, we've turned it around and swept the Braves in their ball park.

We're at .500 now and go home for four games with the Giants.

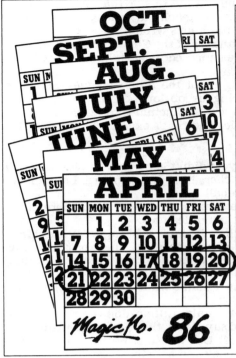

Magic No. **86**

Rose and coach Tommy Helms (above in 1966) were roommates as Reds players.

THURSDAY, APRIL 18 .... ROSE 1 FOR 4

When I first came back last August, I went to Bob Howsam's office every day and talked with him.

I don't do that nearly as much this year, but he keeps me posted on what's going on. I fill him in on field things he may not know about.

He's been concerned somewhat with our fundamentals. We made three errors last Monday night in Atlanta, two in the ninth inning when they came within a run of tying us.

Tommy Helms, my first-base coach, and I go a long way back. Early in my career in Cincinnati, he was my roommate.

Bob told me he didn't especially like Tommy's approach to fundamentals. I disagreed.

I said, "Hey, wait a minute. Tommy Helms learned fundamentals the same place I did. He knows fundamentals as well as anyone."

San Fran.	ab	r	h	rbi	Cincinnati	ab	r	h	rbi
Gladden, cf	4	1	1	1	E. Davis, cf	5	1	0	0
Trillo, 2b	4	0	2	0	**Rose, 1b**	4	1	1	0
C. Davis, rf	4	0	1	1	Walker, rf	4	0	2	0
Leonard, lf	4	1	1	0	Redus, pr-lf	0	1	0	0
Brenly, c	3	0	0	0	C'deno, lf-rf	3	0	2	2
Th'mpson, 1b	5	0	0	0	Esasky, 3b	3	0	0	0
Brown, 3b	4	1	2	1	Parker, ph	1	0	1	1
Uribe, ss	5	0	2	0	Foley, pr-3b	0	0	0	0
Krukow, p	2	0	0	0	C'cepcion, ss	4	1	1	0
Rajsich, ph	0	0	0	0	Oester, 2b	3	0	1	1
LeMaster, pr	0	0	0	0	Van Gorder, c	3	0	0	0
Garrelts, p	0	0	0	0	Kr'chicki, ph	1	0	0	0
Minton, p	1	0	0	0	Bilardello, c	0	0	0	0
					Tibbs, p	1	0	0	0
					Milner, ph	1	0	0	0
					Willis, p	0	0	0	0
					Perez, ph	1	0	1	0
Totals	36	3	9	3	Totals	34	4	9	4

```
San Francisco..........0 0 1  0 0 0  0 0 1—3
Cincinnati................0 0 0  0 1 0  0 0 1—4
One out when winning run scored.
```

San Francisco	IP.	H.	R.	ER.	BB.	SO.
Krukow	8	5	1	0	1	6
Garrelts	⅓	1	1	1	0	0
Minton (L. 0-1)	1	3	2	2	3	0

Cincinnati	IP.	H.	R.	ER.	BB.	SO.
Tibbs	8	4	1	1	4	4
Willis (W. 1-0)	2	5	2	2	1	1

Game-winning RBI—Cedeno.
E—Krukow, Brenly, Esasky. DP—San Francisco 1. LOB—San Francisco 12, Cincinnati 8. 2B—Walker, Leonard. 3B—Brown. SB—Cedeno, Foley, E. Davis 2, **Rose.** SH—Krukow, Trillo, Tibbs, Cedeno, Brenly. SF—Gladden. WP—Tibbs 2. T—2:59. A—12,410.

I told Bob he could sit there and tell me this or that about Tommy Helms, but when Tommy and I have to teach major leaguers the right and wrong way to play baseball, something's wrong.

If I'm not mistaken, I'm the manager of the Cincinnati Reds, not the Cedar Rapids Reds. These guys are supposed to learn how to play baseball by the time they get to me.

This is the big show here. This is not the minor leagues. Someone other than Tommy Helms is not doing his job down there.

If you're going to bring the players to Cincinnati to teach them how to play baseball, we're all in trouble. And that's exactly what I told Bob Howsam.

And he understands, too.

The problem is a lot of our players didn't learn how to play baseball in the minor leagues. We're not teachers here in Cincinnati. I don't have time to teach guys how to play baseball.

I'll tell you the truth. My 15-year-old son, Petey, knows more about baseball than a lot of players in the major leagues.

I sometimes don't know what they (today's big-leaguers) are thinking about. At times, I think they regard baseball, their profession, as secondary and that's wrong because I've got too many players making under $150,000.

I told all the guys at a meeting I didn't want to hear all that crap about going to arbitration for $10,000.

"Go have a good year and get a half-million-dollar raise," I told them. "But don't hit .230 or .220 and say, 'Well, this guy's also hitting .230 and making $200,000, why can't I?' Don't be a little person, be a big person. Go out and make a lot of money and help the team."

★   ★   ★

I've always felt Cesar Cedeno had great talent. When I was with the Phillies, he used to have a condo below mine in Clearwater, Fla. I always used to tease him. I like Cesar.

Tonight, he got a bases-loaded single and drove in two runs in the 10th inning to give us a 4-3 victory over San Francisco, our fourth straight win.

I got one hit and scored a run, including the winner in the 10th. I now need 85 to break the record.

Dave Parker had his gum problem operated on this morning and was still in a lot of pain. I didn't start him, but he told me before the game he could pinch hit.

I called on him in the ninth inning and he gave us a single off the Giants' ace reliever, Greg Minton, to drive in the tying run.

FRIDAY, APRIL 19 .... ROSE 1 FOR 4

People often ask me how I manage.

Well, my theory is you build a strong coaching staff, then delegate authority.

I'll listen to my coaches, but the final decision is always mine.

Jim Kaat handles the pitchers and he's good with them. He'll offer his opinion and I'll either agree or disagree.

I talk strategy with George Scherger, who helped Sparky Anderson here for years. George gives me the options, and I make the decisions.

I've got Tommy Helms, who works with the infielders and coaches first base. Billy DeMars, who was with the Phillies when I was there, is my batting instructor and coaches third base, and Bruce Kimm is my bullpen coach.

Jimmy Stewart does most of the advance scouting.

So far, the system's working well.

★   ★   ★

We're on a roll now, I think. We beat the Giants, 4-2, for our fifth straight win tonight.

Now, we have two more games with them at Riverfront before we hit the road again. For some reason, we play a lot more road games early in the season than we do home games.

San Fran.	ab	r	h	rbi	Cincinnati	ab	r	h	rbi
Gladden, cf	4	1	1	0	E. Davis, cf	4	1	2	1
Trillo, 2b	3	0	1	1	**Rose, 1b**	4	0	1	1
C. Davis, rf	3	1	1	0	Parker, rf	4	0	0	0
Leonard, lf	4	0	2	1	Cedeno, lf	4	1	2	0
Brenly, c	4	0	0	0	Esasky, 3b	3	0	1	1
Green, 1b	4	0	0	0	C'cepcion, ss	4	0	0	0
Brown, 3b	4	0	1	0	Oester, 2b	4	2	3	0
Uribe, ss	3	0	0	0	Van Gorder, c	3	0	0	0
M. Davis, p	0	0	0	0	Stuper, p	1	0	1	0
Williams, p	0	0	0	0	Milner, ph	0	0	0	0
Rajsich, ph	1	0	0	0	Perez, ph	1	0	0	0
Laskey, p	2	0	0	0	Hume, p	0	0	0	0
LeMaster, ss	1	0	0	0	Walker, ph	1	0	0	0
					Power, p	0	0	0	0
Totals	33	2	6	2	Totals	33	4	10	3

San Francisco .... 1 0 1   0 0 0   0 0 0—2
Cincinnati .... 2 0 0   1 0 1   0 0 x—4

San Francisco	IP.	H.	R.	ER.	BB.	SO.
Laskey (L. 0-1)	5⅓	9	4	4	1	3
M. Davis	1⅔	0	0	0	0	3
Williams	1	1	0	0	1	0

Cincinnati	IP.	H.	R.	ER.	BB.	SO.
Stuper (W. 2-0)	6	6	2	2	2	3
Hume	2	0	0	0	0	1
Power (Save 2)	1	0	0	0	0	0

Game-winning RBI—E. Davis.
E—Trillo. LOB—San Francisco 6, Cincinnati 8. 2B —Leonard, Cedeno, Esasky, **Rose**, Oester 2. 3B—E. Davis. SB—C. Davis, Stuper, Gladden, E. Davis. SH— Stuper. Balk—Stuper, M. Davis. T—2:14. A—24,839.

I had a double tonight and drove in a run. That hit left me 84 short of breaking the Cobb record.

John Stuper was the winning pitcher. Tom Hume and Ted Power did a good job out of the 'pen.

Stuper has worked real hard.

He was the winning pitcher in the sixth game of the 1982 World Series for St. Louis, but last year they apparently gave up on him. They sent him to Vancouver (in July, on loan) and he said the two months he spent there were the toughest of his life.

We got him in September (via a trade), and I've never seen anyone work harder. He does something like 2,000 situps a week and works hard in the Nautilus room.

When his earned-run average reached 6.19 in the spring, somebody asked me about that. I told the reporter I wasn't worried about ERAs, that I want guys who can win.

★   ★   ★

As I've said so often, I enjoy cooperating with the media. By the same token, I get disturbed when they are careless. That happened after tonight's game.

One guy asked me a question and I answered it the best I could. Within the next two minutes, he said three different things wrong.

I told him I thought Dale Murphy was the best player in the National League and he started talking about the American League.

Then he said, "You said he is better than Eddie Murray of Baltimore."

I didn't say that. I said Rick Cerone, the Atlanta catcher, said Murphy is better than Murray.

"Didn't you listen to me?" I asked. "You asked me one question and you screwed it up. And you don't even have your tape recorder on."

Is it that difficult to be accurate? After all, reporting is his job just like baseball is mine.

— 33 —

SATURDAY, APRIL 20 .... ROSE 1 FOR 2

Six in a row!

We're beginning to get our act together. Earlier, we were getting good pitching, but weren't coming through with key hits.

Eddie Milner scored the winning run today in the ninth inning on an error and we beat the Giants, 2-1.

What can I say about Mario Soto? He gave us another complete game to get his third win. He's lost just once.

Dave Parker is really cooking. He had a double and a single today. He's right around .300 (11 for 37, .297) and says the biggest thing that has helped him is Billy DeMars' advice to relax. Billy thinks the Cobra has been trying too hard.

San Fran.	ab	r	h	rbi	Cincinnati	ab	r	h	rbi
Gladden, cf	3	0	1	0	E. Davis, cf	3	1	0	0
Wellman, 2b	4	0	1	0	**Rose, 1b**	2	0	1	0
Leonard, lf	4	0	0	0	Parker, rf	3	0	2	0
C. Davis, rf	3	1	1	0	Cedeno, lf	3	0	1	1
Brown, 3b	3	0	0	0	Esasky, 3b	4	0	1	0
Th'mpson, 1b	4	0	0	1	C'cepcion, ss	3	0	0	0
Trevino, c	3	0	1	0	Oester, 2b	3	0	0	0
Uribe, ss	3	0	0	0	Foley, ph-2b	1	0	0	0
Gott, p	1	0	0	0	Van Gorder, c	2	0	0	0
Garrelts, p	1	0	0	0	Milner, ph	1	1	1	0
Y'ngblood, ph	1	0	0	0	Soto, p	3	0	0	0
Williams, p	0	0	0	0					
Totals	30	1	4	1	Totals	28	2	6	1

San Francisco.................0 1 0 0 0 0 0 0 0—1
Cincinnati.......................0 0 1 0 0 0 0 0 1—2
None out when winning run scored.

San Francisco	IP.	H.	R.	ER.	BB.	SO.
Gott............................	4⅔	4	1	1	3	1
Garrelts......................	2⅓	1	0	0	2	1
Williams (L. 0-1).........	1*	1	1	0	0	2
Cincinnati	IP.	H.	R.	ER.	BB.	SO.
Soto (W. 3-1).............	9	4	1	1	3	11

*Pitched to two batters in ninth.

Game-winning RBI—None.

E—C. Davis, Williams. LOB—San Francisco 5, Cincinnati 10. 2B—Parker, Esasky, Milner. SB—C. Davis, Gladden. SH—Concepcion, Soto. SF—Cedeno. Balk—Gott. T—2:27. A—18,115.

Billy told him he was too tense, that when he went to the plate he was acting like he was in trouble. Billy said to reverse that, meaning that when the Cobra goes up there the pitcher is in trouble.

Dave is relaxing and swinging a lot better.

I don't know what his problems were during his last year or so in Pittsburgh, but I am glad he is with us. (After spending 11 seasons with the Pirates, Parker became a free agent and signed with the Reds in December 1983.)

It's difficult to teach players how to relax. The best thing you can do is try to tell them how you approach situations. Lecturing doesn't work, but I've found that by citing some of my experiences they relate better.

I don't get nervous. Not about anything. I get butterflies on opening day, or the opening day of a World Series, or the opening game of the playoffs. But once the game starts, they leave.

It's OK to get butterflies before the action starts, but you can't get them once the game starts.

A lot of players worry about the crowds, about boos and all that. I think the crowd used to get on Mike Schmidt pretty good in Philly.

I play the crowd. I don't shut the fans out at all. I hear everything that goes on. I don't miss much. I honestly like it when the crowd boos me. All that makes me do is try harder to get a base hit so they will boo me louder.

A lot of guys go into a shell when they're booed. I have always been taught—my father told me this—and I believe it, when you're playing sports the home team is supposed to be rooted for and the visiting team is supposed to be booed. That doesn't bother me. Not in the least.

I always have enough to worry about . . . without worrying about what 45,000 people are doing.

Most fans want a good, honest effort; they want you to try to win the game. They don't want you to loaf. You're going to strike out and they understand that. You're going to make errors and they understand that, too.

But give 'em a good effort and they won't get on your back. I hit .245 in Philly my last year and they didn't boo me because they knew I was busting my butt.

That's what I tell my guys. Give 110 percent and you'll be OK.

They've been doing that during this winning streak and they know how much fun this game can be.

When you win.

SUNDAY, APRIL 21 .... DID NOT PLAY

We made it seven in a row today (beating San Francisco, 1-0). I didn't play for the first time this season because the Giants started a lefthander, Atlee Hammaker. I moved Cesar Cedeno to first base.

In the early part of the season, I'm not going to start myself against lefthanders, but if I'm in a real good groove and Cedeno and Tony Perez aren't hitting, I'll put myself in. (Entering the 1985 season, Rose had a .311 lifetime batting average against righthanded pitching and a .292 career mark against lefthanders. Last year, though, he slumped to .211 against lefthanders while hitting .310 against righthanders.)

The win put us over .500 with me as manager (27-26 record), going back to last August 17 when I took over. We're in first place (with an 8-4 mark), 1½ games ahead of San Diego and Los Angeles in the Western Division.

The Giants—it's hard to believe they're not hitting better—have lost six straight overall and dropped four one-run games in their last five. And they've lost 16 of their last 18 games at Riverfront.

After there were two out in the bottom of the third, Eric Davis tripled to the right-field corner off Hammaker. When the count went to 3-and-1 to Gary Redus, Davis broke for home.

Their catcher, Bob Brenly, saw what was happening and moved in front of the plate to the left side before Hammaker threw the ball.

It looked like a steal of home, but after a long discussion, umpires Eric Gregg and Doug Harvey agreed Brenly interferred, so Davis was denied the steal of home (but was waved across the plate as a balk call against Hammaker accompanied the interference ruling).

There were nearly 30,000 at Riverfront today and they loved it.

Eric is so fast, I've been giving him the green light almost every time he's on base. He bluffed before that pitch and I thought he might go then. You've got to create something and make something happen. Eric did a good job.

Tom Browning pitched a whale of a game. He gave up just five hits in eight innings, but it was so hot out there that I decided to bring Teddy Power in for the ninth.

Browning has not allowed a run in 13 innings and just one earned run in 24 innings. He has an earned run average of 0.38. Not too bad for a rookie.

We left for Houston after the game. I just want to keep this streak going. The one thing that concerns me a little is the fact we've scored only 19 runs in the last six games (of the seven-game streak), but we've held the opposition to eight.

My second baseman, Ron Oester, missed the game because he sprained his left shoulder Saturday while making a catch.

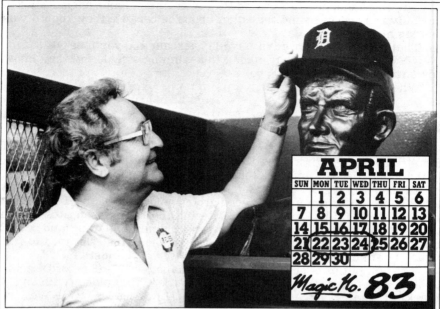

Reds equipment manager Bernie Stowe keeps a watchful eye on the bronze bust of Ty Cobb that was given to Rose on his birthday.

MONDAY, APRIL 22....................... ROSE 0 FOR 3

I like to come to Houston because you know you're going to play.

Besides, I have a lot of pleasant memories about the Astrodome. It was here in 1980 when I was with the Philadelphia Phillies that we beat the Astros in the playoffs to win the National League pennant.

That was probably the most exciting playoff since they were started in 1969. I had eight hits in the five games, and four of the games were extra innings.

The Astrodome is a nice place to play. When you come here, you know there are not going to be any rainouts. There are other places I'd rather play in, but it's kinda interesting here. I don't mind the fences where they are now (10 feet closer down the foul lines and in the power alleys after an off-season stadium renovation). And they've built new clubhouses that are nice.

Houston has some pretty good pitchers and it seems like the team is always tailored for the Astrodome.

Cincinnati	ab	r	h	rbi	Houston	ab	r	h	rbi
Milner, cf	3	0	1	0	Doran, 2b	4	1	1	0
Rose, 1b	3	0	0	0	Bass, rf	4	1	1	1
Parker, rf	4	0	1	0	Walling, 1b	4	1	1	1
Cedeno, lf	4	0	0	0	Cruz, lf	4	0	1	0
Kr'chicki, 3b	4	0	1	0	Mumphrey, cf	3	1	1	1
C'cepcion, ss	3	1	1	0	Garner, 3b	3	0	1	0
Foley, 2b	4	0	1	0	Ashby, c	2	0	0	0
Bilardello, c	3	0	1	0	Reynolds, ss	2	0	1	1
Tibbs, p	2	0	0	0	Scott, p	3	0	0	0
Walker, ph	1	0	0	0	Smith, p	0	0	0	0
Price, p	0	0	0	0					
Totals	31	1	5	1	Totals	29	4	7	4

```
Cincinnati ......................0 0 0   0 1 0   0 0 0—1
Houston ........................0 0 0   0 1 2   0 1 x—4
```

Cincinnati	IP.	H.	R.	ER.	BB.	SO.
Tibbs (L. 0-3)	7	6	3	2	2	4
Price............................	1	1	1	1	0	1

Houston	IP.	H.	R.	ER.	BB.	SO.
Scott (W. 1-0)	8⅓	5	1	0	3	5
Smith (Save 2)............	⅔	0	0	0	0	0

Game-winning RBI—Walling.
E—Mumphrey, Foley. DP—Cincinnati 1, Houston 1. LOB—Cincinnati 6, Houston 3. 2B—Reynolds, Doran. 3B—Mumphrey. HR—Bass (1). T—2:04. A—10,197.

I have a tendency to have a little trouble picking up the rotation of the ball the first couple of games (here). It looks fuzzy to me.

Most of the players are excited about the seven-game winning streak and the fact we were able to bounce back after losing three games in New York.

I was surprised when I walked out of my office to see that bronze bust of Ty Cobb that was given me for my birthday sitting near the clubhouse entrance to the field. I later found out since we won seven in a row, the guys told Bernie Stowe, our equipment man, to bring it on the trip.

Jimmy Stewart is our advance scout. He turned in a report to George Scherger, my bench coach, that we went over at a meeting before the game. All the teams do this now. The report tells how we should try to play them (the Astros) on defense, how to pitch them, what they're hitting and what they're not, what the pitchers are throwing—stuff like that. Jimmy got to see them play four or five times before we arrived.

I changed the lineup for tonight's game, putting Wayne Krenchicki at third instead of Nick Esasky and deciding to let Eric Davis sit in favor of Eddie Milner. Chick (Krenchicki) hasn't played in a while, and since Eric has played every day (11 of 12 games) I thought I'd give Eddie a shot.

The fact we haven't been hitting and scoring runs—even though we won seven in a row—caught up with us in this game.

Mike Scott, a righthander, allowed only five singles in 8⅓ innings and they beat us, 4-1.

I went 0 for 3 with a walk and our big guys, Dave Parker, Cesar Cedeno and Krenchicki, just couldn't do the job with runners on base.

Our best chance came in the fourth when there was no score. Scott had retired nine straight when Eddie Milner singled to right. I walked. That gave us two on and no outs, with the meat of our order coming up.

Parker popped out to the catcher, Cesar struck out and Chick hit a hot liner to the gap in left-center, but Jose Cruz made a good running catch. He took two runs away from us.

Still, you've got to score more than one run. You can't win every night scoring just one run.

Jim Kaat came into my office after the press left and said, "Skip, I'll be glad when we start hitting. It's unrealistic to think our pitching will continue to shut people down."

Jay Tibbs pitched well, but lost his third game.

Our team earned-run average is 2.13, which is best in the league, but the team batting average is .224, eighth in the league.

We've had to play our last two games without Ron Oester, our second baseman. He has a sprained left shoulder he got diving for a ball Saturday afternoon against the Giants. My trainer, Larry Starr, says he's going to be out for several more days.

I told the coaches after the game to schedule a workout for tomorrow afternoon. We gotta get some batting practice.

TUESDAY, APRIL 23 .... DID NOT PLAY

I decided to sit this one out.

Since April 14, I've had five hits in 26 at-bats, so I thought I would let some of my younger players start.

I put Eric Davis back in the outfield and used Cesar Cedeno at first base. Cesar likes to play against the Astros because he spent so many years (12) with them.

As far as the young players are concerned, with (Houston's) Ron Mathis making his third appearance in the majors, I thought they would be able to hit the young righthander.

A lot of your young hitters who aren't established have a tendency to do all right against guys just up from Triple-A. The guys are their own age and they feel more comfortable. Their lack of experience shows sometimes when they're hitting off experienced pitchers.

I was wrong. We got just three hits off Mathis—two through seven innings—and they beat us, 6-4, even though we scored four runs in the eighth inning. Mathis pitched even better than the numbers show. When he left in the eighth, he hadn't given up any runs, but there were two Reds on base. He struck out five batters and gave up only three hits.

Mathis had retired 11 in a row when Dann Bilardello singled in the eighth inning with one out. After Mathis walked my pinch-hitter, Wayne Krenchicki, (Houston Manager) Bob Lillis went to his bullpen. We scored four times and had runners on first and third, but Nick Esasky grounded into a double play. If Nick gets a hit there, it might have been a different ball game.

★   ★   ★

I've had something on my mind today that has really been bugging me. It seemed even more important after we got beat. I mentioned it to the coaches before we went back to the Shamrock Hilton Hotel.

Maybe I'm from the old school, but one thing I was always taught, going back to when my dad was teaching me baseball, is you've got to be prepared.

Tonight, I sat on the dugout bench for 20 minutes when Ron Mathis was warming up. I knew every pitch he was throwing. I studied his velocity and his motion.

I looked down the bench and I'm the only guy sitting there and I'm not even playing!

I said to myself, "Where the hell are all my players who have never seen this guy before?" Once the game starts, they're going to be wanting to know what pitches Ron Mathis throws. I'll tell you the truth, I'm not sure they all knew which hand he throws with.

This is not an easy game. To be a champion, you have to invest a little extra. Like my father said—and I've tried to do—you have to always give 110 percent because the other guy is going to give 100 percent.

WEDNESDAY, APRIL 24 .... ROSE 1 FOR 5

It's always a good battle when Nolan Ryan and I face each other. He gets a kick out of pitching to me and I always rev myself up against him. It's a good confrontation.

In 1981 (on the next-to-last night of play before the players' strike started), I got a single the first time up against Ryan to tie Stan Musial as the guy with the most hits in the National League—3,630. Nolan then struck me out the next three times and I only swung once (on the third strike).

In the nine seasons Ryan has been in the league, I've gotten 15 singles and two doubles off him.

Today, he got me four times. One was a called third strike on a low, bad pitch. The home-plate umpire, John McSherry, lost it and I had some words with him. (Rose also grounded out twice and flied out against Ryan.)

We won the game, 8-3, with five runs in the ninth, but when Nolan left it was 3-3, a good match between him and Mario Soto.

Ryan can still pitch real good. The radar gun was clocking his fastball at 97, but I'm not big on the radar gun. Some of them are four or five miles an hour different from others. I don't think they're legitimate because I don't care how hard a guy's throwing on a radar gun, if his ball is straight you're going to hit it.

Radar guns are fine for velocity, but I think a pitcher throwing 85 miles an hour who moves the ball in and out is more effective than a guy who throws hard and straight.

Cincinnati	ab	r	h	rbi	Houston	ab	r	h	rbi
Milner, cf	5	0	1	2	Doran, 2b	3	0	0	0
Rose, 1b	5	0	1	1	Bass, rf	4	1	0	0
Parker, rf	5	1	1	0	Walling, 1b	3	0	1	0
Power, p	0	0	0	0	Cruz, lf	4	0	1	2
Walker, lf	3	1	1	2	Mumphrey, cf	4	0	1	0
Davis, ph-rf	0	1	0	0	DiPino, p	0	0	0	0
Esasky, 3b	3	1	1	1	Dawley, p	0	0	0	0
C'cepcion, ss	3	1	1	1	Calhoun, p	0	0	0	0
Foley, 2b	4	1	1	0	Garner, 3b	3	1	1	0
Van Gorder, c	3	0	0	0	Ashby, c	3	0	1	1
Kr'chicki, ph	0	1	0	0	Reynolds, ss	4	0	1	0
Bilardello, c	0	0	0	0	Ryan, p	1	0	0	0
Soto, p	3	0	0	0	Gain'y, ph-cf	1	1	0	0
Perez, ph	0	1	0	0					
Cedeno, lf	0	0	0	0					
Totals	34	8	7	7	Totals	30	3	6	3

Cincinnati ....0 0 0   0 0 0   3 0 5—8
Houston ....0 0 0   1 0 0   0 2 0—3

Cincinnati	IP.	H.	R.	ER.	BB.	SO.
Soto (W. 4-1)	8	6	3	3	4	3
Power	1	0	0	0	2	0

Houston	IP.	H.	R.	ER.	BB.	SO.
Ryan	8	3	3	2	1	7
DiPino (L. 0-2)	⅔	2	3	3	1	0
Dawley	0*	2	2	2	2	0
Calhoun	⅓	0	0	0	0	0

*Pitched to four batters in ninth.

Game-winning RBI—Esasky.
E—Garner, Gainey. DP—Cincinnati 2. LOB—Cincinnati 4, Houston 8. 2B—Garner, Ashby. HR—Walker (1), Concepcion (1). SB—Concepcion, Davis. SH—Ryan. SF—Esasky. HBP—By Power (Gainey). Balk—DiPino. T—2:38. A—8,513.

I had a hunch about today's game and it paid off. Somebody told me Duane Walker got two home runs off Ryan in a game August 16, 1982. I figured it was worth starting him (in the outfield) for the second time this season even though after he got those two homers, he struck out seven times in his next nine at-bats against Ryan.

Ryan was leading 1-0 and working on a no-hitter when Dave Parker singled with one out in the seventh. Nolan then hung a changeup to Duane and he hit it over the right-field fence. That got us started. Phil Garner made an error to let the third run score and we were up 3-1.

They tied Mario with two in the eighth, but I like the way we battled back with the five-spot in the ninth.

I got a single to right-center off their reliever, Bill Dawley, to drive in the fifth run.

We were tied with the Astros for first place in the Western Division before the game and didn't want to get swept.

Eric Davis got the big inning started. I sent him up to bat for Walker with Frank DiPino, a lefthander, pitching.

Eric walked, stole second and, with Esasky batting, was balked to third.

Nick then hit a pop to shallow right. It really wasn't deep enough—only about 80 feet behind first base—but Eric took off and scored to put us ahead. I had an inkling he was going.

Teddy Power saved it for Mario in the ninth even though he made it exciting (by walking two batters).

It was a good win because you never want to get swept. Even though we fell two runs short, we scored four times in the eighth inning Tuesday night. And we came back with five in the ninth today.

I think that's a good sign. I think our hitting is coming around. We'll find out in San Francisco.

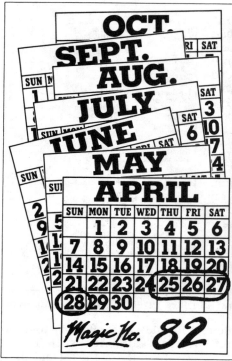

Magic No. **82**

Rose, a bat in each hand, prepares for battle.

THURSDAY, APRIL 25 .... ROSE 0 FOR 4

It was a good flight to San Francisco last night. When you score five runs in the ninth inning to win, it gives everybody on the team a lift.

We got in about 9 p.m., so everybody could get a good night's sleep for today's game.

On plane trips, I regard myself as just one of the players. I sit with the guys, play cards and have a lot of fun. There's a lot of joking because it keeps everybody loose. On yesterday's flight, I played cards with Davey Concepcion, Ron Oester, Wayne Krenchicki and Tony Perez.

Our president, Bob Howsam, and our general manager, Bill Bergesch, are on the trip.

Before we left Houston, I told my coaches I probably wouldn't play the Friday and Saturday games in Frisco because we're facing two lefthanders, Atlee Hammaker and Dave LaPoint. I don't have any hits off a lefthander yet this year. I'll go against

Cincinnati	ab	r	h	rbi	San Fran.	ab	r	h	rbi
Milner, cf	3	0	0	0	Gladden, cf	4	2	2	0
E.D'vis, ph-cf	1	0	0	0	Trillo, 2b	3	0	1	0
Rose, 1b	4	0	0	0	C. Davis, rf	3	2	2	4
Willis, p	0	0	0	0	Leonard, lf	4	1	1	0
Parker, rf	4	1	1	0	Th'mpson, 1b	4	0	1	0
Cedeno, lf-1b	3	1	1	0	Brenly, c	3	1	1	2
Esasky, 3b	3	1	1	3	Wellman, 3b	3	0	2	0
C'cepcion, ss	4	0	1	0	Uribe, ss	4	1	0	0
Foley, 2b	3	0	0	0	Gott, p	2	0	0	0
Perez, ph	1	0	0	0	M. Davis, p	1	0	0	0
Van Gorder, c	4	0	0	0					
Pastore, p	2	0	1	0					
Hume, p	0	0	0	0					
Redus, ph-lf	0	0	0	0					
Totals	32	3	5	3	Totals	31	7	10	6

Cincinnati .... 0 0 0 0 0 0 3 0 0—3
San Francisco .... 1 0 0 0 0 2 1 3 x—7

Cincinnati	IP.	H.	R.	ER.	BB.	SO.
Pastore	6	7	3	3	1	5
Hume (L. 0-1)	1	0	1	0	0	0
Willis	1	3	3	3	0	1

San Francisco	IP.	H.	R.	ER.	BB.	SO.
Gott	6*	4	3	3	1	2
M. Davis (W. 1-1)	3	1	0	0	2	4

*Pitched to three batters in seventh.

Game-winning RBI—None.
E—Wellman, **Rose**, Van Gorder. DP—Cincinnati 2, San Francisco 1. LOB—Cincinnati 5, San Francisco 4. 2B—Pastore. HR—C. Davis 2 (2), Esasky (2), Brenly (2). SB—Wellman, Gladden 2, Leonard. SH—Trillo. SF —C. Davis. HBP—By Hume (Wellman). Balk—Hume. PB—Brenly. T—2:16. A—4,056.

Mike Krukow on Sunday.

I don't like to play in Candlestick Park, but I don't make a big thing of it because if I do my players will be thinking about it. But I can't ever remember playing a series here when something weird didn't happen. It's one of those ballparks where you lose a lot of games you would win if you were playing at home. The conditions are terrible.

We lost today, 7-3, and fell out of first place. I was 0 for 4, but hit a couple of balls hard. I also made an error.

I started Frank Pastore in place of Tom Browning. Browning—he's got a 0.38 ERA—split the fingernail on the middle finger of his left hand yesterday in Houston shagging fly balls. He'll probably miss two starts.

In the Giants' six previous games, no San Francisco player had hit a home run, but Chili Davis hit two today and drove in four runs.

The one he hit off Carl Willis in the eighth inning, when they scored three times, would have gone out of Yellowstone Park—and I haven't even seen Yellowstone Park.

Jose Uribe, their shortstop, scored the go-ahead run in the seventh inning when I dropped an infield popup.

We scored three times in the top of the seventh to tie the score against Jim Gott, who had not allowed a hit until Pastore doubled to left-center in the sixth.

I brought in Tom Hume in the seventh and he hit their first batter, Brad Wellman. Uribe hit a grounder to me and I forced Wellman with a good peg to Davey Concepcion, who was covering second.

Mark Davis, their pitcher, was trying to move the runner with a bunt, but popped out. I figured we were in good shape now.

But Dan Gladden hit a pop about 40 feet from home plate.

I think I have dropped three popups in my whole career and all of them have been at Candlestick Park. It's the high sky. After the game, Manny Trillo, an old buddy from my Philadelphia days, told me in the past week there were five of them lost in the sun between home and first base and three of them fell for doubles.

But, no excuses.

I lost the ball going up. When I finally picked it up coming down, it got in the wind and fluttered away from me. I was on the dead-run and it hit off my glove. With two out, Uribe was running and scored.

I made the error, but it wasn't completely my fault. The pitch before that to Gladden was 0-2 and I flashed the pitchout sign. Uribe was going; I know he was. But Hume balked and he took second.

If Hume doesn't balk, the guy doesn't score from first on a short pop.

There wasn't much I could say to my teammates, but I learned a long time ago whenever the ball goes up in the daytime in Frisco, nobody wants it. It's an adventure. But anytime you make an error and a run scores—the go-ahead run—it hurts and you feel bad.

It was an honest error.

The big problem is we're still not getting enough key hits. On this trip, we've not scored in 31 of 36 innings.

FRIDAY, APRIL 26 .... DID NOT PLAY

This was a long day.

Bob Howsam and Bill Bergesch called me early to talk about some deals they've been trying to make.

We're still looking for a catcher, but at this point it's not going to be easy. The teams willing to part with one want some of our young players. Even though he's been struggling, I'm not going to give up Eric Davis. I feel the same way about Gary Redus.

We did make a minor league deal this morning that could help us in the future.

During spring training we sent Skeeter Barnes, a young infielder, to Denver (Cincinnati's Triple-A affiliate). The Montreal Expos have been interested in him, so what we did was trade him to their Indianapolis farm club for outfielder Max Venable, a lefthanded hitter who was batting .358 with nine RBIs. Venable's got a lot of speed and might be able to help us down the road.

Barnes, who grew up in Cincinnati, criticized some of us over the winter for playing too many veterans.

★   ★   ★

My marketing agent, Bill Hayes, has worked out a deal with Wheaties for me to be on their cereal boxes for three or four months this summer. Mary Lou Retton is on there right now.

I usually don't do too many things like this during the season because they take so much time.

This one worked out fine. They rented a hotel room near Candlestick Park. I went to the ball park, got my uniform on and they picked me up at 3 o'clock and took me to the room where all the lights and everything were set up. They were done by quarter to 4 and I was back at the ball park getting ready for the night game shortly after that.

It's important for me to always get to the ball park before the players. For that reason, I never take the team bus which leaves the hotel 2½ hours before the game. I feel it's my obligation to get the lineup posted before anyone gets there. I don't want the guys sitting around wondering.

★   ★   ★

This was not a very good game for us.

There's no easy way to lose, but when you're leading 6-1 heading into the ninth inning you're supposed to win. No, you gotta win.

We hit well against Atlee Hammaker, who lasted only five innings.

Jay Tibbs, who had lost his first three decisions, had pitched fine until the ninth. Then, the Giants really busted loose.

They had scored three runs when Dan Gladden hit a home run (off reliever Ted Power) with two guys on base and they win, 7-6.

Just like I've always said, something always happens in this ball park. But when you're leading 6-1 in the ninth, you gotta win.

SATURDAY, APRIL 27 .... DID NOT PLAY

I didn't play for the second straight day, and I'm thinking about sitting Pete Rose down tomorrow, too.

We beat the Giants, 2-1, today. It was the kind of game where the manager does very little. But it was also the kind of game managers love.

John Stuper, who had a 2-1 record and a 6.19 earned-run average before today, was outstanding. We're still not hitting, but he gave the

Giants just two hits and went the distance.

Eric Davis hit a home run in the first inning and Dann Bilardello singled home Davey Concepcion—he had doubled—with the winning run in the sixth. Just enough offense.

Before today, I didn't think Stuper was really aggressive enough when he was on the mound. He had worked on that in spring training and pitched well, but once the season started he seemed to fall back to his old habits.

Jim Kaat was a teammate of Stuper's when both were on the Cardinals in 1982 (and 1983). Kitty told me the way Stuper pitched today was the way he did for the Cardinals down the stretch in '82. And everybody knows they were world champions that year.

The Giants tied us in the bottom of the first inning when Danny Gladden walked and Chili Davis doubled down the right-field line.

From that time on, Stuper settled down and at one point retired 18 of 19 batters.

★   ★   ★

I've learned one thing managing I probably knew all along, but never really paid much attention to. In baseball today, one thing that hurts young players—and some of the veterans, too—is they don't prepare themselves right for a game.

They just don't get ready. The game starts and they don't know where in hell their bats are. They don't know where their batting gloves are. I'm serious.

I just hope they watch me. You can ask anybody on this team who in this league knows at all times where his bats are. Pete Rose. I do.

Because everywhere I go, I've got that bat with me. I take my ground balls and I put it right by the screen near first base. When I'm through with ground balls, I take my glove and my hat and I get my batting helmet and I have my bat in my hand.

I'm the only guy on the team who after the game takes his bats out of the dugout rack and puts them in his locker, or next to my desk in my office when we're home.

I've seen guys go on road trips and they're ticked off they don't have their bats. I say, "Where are they?"

"The batboy was supposed to pack them in the bags," they say.

"What do you mean the batboy is supposed to put your bats in the bags? You have to pick your own bats out and put them in the bags yourself. That's your responsibility."

I had a guy this year in a spring-training game who couldn't find his glove when I put him in.

Today, we take the field in the first inning and Davey Concepcion calls time out. He came to the dugout and said he needed sunglasses.

How many day games do you think Davey Concepcion has played in Frisco? Umpteen hundred and he doesn't know you need sunglasses here?

We had a game the other day and Davey was getting ready to go up and hit and his bat was in his locker in the clubhouse.

Over the years there have probably been people who think I'm rude, but when it gets close to game time, it's my responsibility to get ready to play. Nothing else is important. This is something I want everybody on my team to learn.

We lose, 2-1, in 11 innings to the Giants and it was another one of those games we should have won.

I hate to keep saying that, but we ended this road trip today winning two and losing five. For April, we're 5-8 (on the road). Not too good, not too bad. I can honestly say we should have won at least two more games in Frisco.

What we've got to do is stop saying we should've done this or should've done that and start doing it!

I didn't start today for the third game in a row. I did send Pete Rose up to pinch hit in the ninth inning, but I grounded out. I still need 82 hits to break the record.

I had a hunch today. I figured with Mario Soto pitching for us, it would be a low-scoring game—and it was. Mario was trying to become the first Reds pitcher since Jim Merritt, in 1970, to win five games in April.

Cincinnati	ab	r	h	rbi	San Fran.	ab	r	h	rbi
E. Davis, lf	5	0	0	0	Gladden, cf	3	0	0	0
Milner, cf	4	1	2	0	Trillo, 2b	4	1	1	1
Parker, rf	5	0	1	0	Leonard, lf	4	0	0	0
Cedeno, 1b	3	0	1	1	C. Davis, rf	4	0	1	0
Esasky, 3b	4	0	0	0	Green, 1b	5	0	1	1
C'cepcion, ss	5	0	3	0	Trevino, c	4	0	1	0
Oester, 2b	4	0	1	0	Wellman, 3b	4	0	2	0
Bilardello, c	3	0	0	0	Uribe, ss	3	1	1	0
Rose, ph	1	0	0	0	Krukow, p	1	0	0	0
Van Gorder, c	1	0	0	0	LeMaster, ph	0	0	0	0
Soto, p	3	0	0	0	Th'mpson, ph	1	0	0	0
Walker, ph	1	0	0	0	Garrelts, p	0	0	0	0
Power, p	0	0	0	0	Rajsich, ph	1	0	0	0
Kr'chicki, ph	1	0	0	0	Minton, p	0	0	0	0
Hume, p	0	0	0	0					
Totals	40	1	8	1	Totals	34	2	7	2

Cincinnati	0 0 0	0 1 0	0 0 0	0 0—1
San Francisco	0 0 0	0 0 1	0 0 0	0 1—2

Two out when winning run scored.

Cincinnati	IP.	H.	R.	ER.	BB.	SO.
Soto	8	4	1	1	1	7
Power	2	2	0	0	1	1
Hume (L. 0-2)	⅔	1	1	1	1	1

San Francisco	IP.	H.	R.	ER.	BB.	SO.
Krukow	8	7	1	1	3	7
Garrelts	2	0	0	0	0	1
Minton (W. 1-1)	1	1	0	0	1	0

Game-winning RBI—Green.

E—Wellman, Esasky, Green. DP—Cincinnati 2, San Francisco 1. LOB—Cincinnati 11, San Francisco 7. 2B —Uribe, Trillo, Concepcion 2. SB—Milner. SH—Krukow, Esasky, Uribe. SF—Trillo. HBP—By Hume (Gladden). WP—Hume. PB—Van Gorder. T—3:04. A— 32,963.

In a low-scoring game, you need speed and defense in the outfield. That's why I put Eric Davis in left and let Cesar Cedeno play first base.

I've always hit Mike Krukow, the Giants' starter, well. So if I had it to do over again, I'd probably have played.

Krukow did a nice thing today.

It's nothing-nothing in the fifth when Eddie Milner singled and stole second. Cedeno then singled Milner home. It was Cesar's 2,000th career hit.

When they flashed 2,000 on the scoreboard, Krukow tipped his cap to Cedeno. Now Krukow hadn't allowed an earned run in 27 innings and here we were taking the lead, but he showed me a lot of class doing that.

The Giants tied us in the sixth and that's the way it stayed until we played some sloppy baseball in the 11th.

We left 11 runners (on base) today, the most we've stranded all year, and six of those were in scoring position.

Mario gave up only four hits in eight innings and pitched perfect baseball until there were two out in the fifth.

It was a tough day for reliever Tom Hume. In the 11th, he hit Danny Gladden with a pitch, then let him go to second on a wild pitch.

Manny Trillo bunted and we cut Gladden down at third, but Hume then walked Jeff Leonard, putting Trillo in scoring position.

We were in good shape, I thought, but we continued to play sloppy baseball. Hume struck out Chili Davis with a good curve, but Dave Van Gorder, our catcher, let the ball get by and there were runners on second and third.

Hume threw David Green a sinker and he drilled it for a single and they win.

Pitching coach Jim Kaat (background) shares a moment with pitcher Jay Tibbs.

TUESDAY, APRIL 30........................ ROSE 2 FOR 4

It's always good to be home.

We didn't leave San Francisco until late Monday morning, so we didn't get back in Cincinnati until around 5 p.m. yesterday.

I was anxious to see Tyler, my son who was born last October 1. Carol told me over the phone he hasn't been feeling too well and that worries me, so I wanted to see firsthand.

He can't keep his food down. Seems like five or 10 minutes after he eats, it all comes up. She's had him to one doctor, but if he isn't OK in a day or two, I want her to take him to a specialist.

When I got home last night, Carol told me she found a new car she's fallen in love with. It's a Ferrari Testarossa, bright red. I went to look at it this morning and after driving it, I'll tell you, it's one of the smoothest cars I've ever driven.

Atlanta	ab	r	h	rbi	Cincinnati	ab	r	h	rbi
Wash'gton, rf	3	2	2	2	Milner, cf	4	1	2	0
Ramirez, ss	5	1	0	0	**Rose, 1b**	4	1	2	0
Komminsk, lf	5	1	1	1	Parker, rf	4	0	1	1
Murphy, cf	5	0	1	2	Cedeno, lf	4	1	1	1
Chambliss, 1b	4	0	0	0	Esasky, 3b	3	0	1	0
Cerone, c	4	0	0	0	C'cepcion, ss	4	0	1	1
Oberkfell, 3b	4	1	2	0	Oester, 2b	4	0	0	0
Hubbard, 2b	3	1	1	0	Bilardello, c	3	0	0	0
Bedrosian, p	1	1	1	0	Willis, p	0	0	0	0
Garber, p	0	0	0	0	Franco, p	0	0	0	0
Perry, ph	1	1	1	1	Kr'chicki, ph	1	0	0	0
Smith, p	0	0	0	0	Price, p	0	0	0	0
Runge, ph	0	0	0	0	Tibbs, p	2	0	0	0
Sutter, p	0	0	0	0	Van Gorder, c	2	1	2	0
Totals	35	8	9	6	Totals	35	4	10	3

Atlanta	.0 0 0		0 3 0		5 0 0—8			
Cincinnati	.0 0 0		0 0 3		1 0 0—4			

Atlanta	IP.	H.	R.	ER.	BB.	SO.
Bedrosian	5⅓	6	3	3	3	4
Garber (W. 1-0)	⅔	0	0	0	0	1
Smith	1	3	1	1	0	1
Sutter	2	1	0	0	0	2

Cincinnati	IP.	H.	R.	ER.	BB.	SO.
Tibbs (L. 0-4)	6⅓	7	6	6	3	5
Willis	⅔	2	2	1	0	0
Franco	1	0	0	0	1	1
Price	1	0	0	0	0	1

Game-winning RBI—Perry.
E—Washington, Oester, Parker, Willis. DP—Atlanta 2, Cincinnati 1. LOB—Atlanta 5, Cincinnati 7. 2B—Oberkfell, Hubbard, Murphy. 3B—Washington. SB—Esasky, Concepcion. SH—Bedrosian. WP—Bedrosian. T—2:29. A—14,356.

It also has a big price tag—about $115,000!

If we get it, we'll have to sell our BMW M-1 and the red Porsche turbo Carol drives. Otherwise, it just won't fit in the budget that Reuven Katz, my attorney, and our accountants have us on.

But, I'll tell you, that Ferrari is some kind of car.

The first day back from a road trip there's a lot of catching up to do at the ball park. There's mail I have to go through and there'll be a lot of people waiting to see me.

Bob Trumpy, a former pro football player, is now a sportscaster at WLW and a good friend. We do a long interview once or twice a week when we're home and he edits them down into little daily sports shows.

Plus, Jim Ferguson, publicity vice president, always has a long list of requests.

Before tonight's game with Atlanta, Wayne Krenchicki came into my office and wanted to know why he's not been playing much.

"Chick," I said, "you're not in there because Nick (Esasky, the Reds' third baseman), is leading the team in RBIs and is just about the hottest player we've got."

I'm not sure he accepted that, but it was the truth.

A little later, Jim Kaat, my pitching coach, came in. He wanted to know if we're going to have a workout Thursday, which is an open date. He wants to go to New York for some promotional thing. I told him the way we've been hitting we've got to work out, but that he can go ahead and go. He works hard.

I've found that in being a manager of a baseball team, 90 percent of the time all you have to use is common sense to get by. I'm not looking for authority and all that, but the players must understand I have to make out the lineup card. I have to make the pitching changes. And sometimes they don't like it.

Carol says sometimes it's difficult being the manager's wife.

"Occasionally, some of the players' wives snub me," she's said.

Well, to me that's the dumbest thing in the world for some wife to snub her. Especially if they do it in an obvious way. How can somebody be that stupid? Carol knows about as much about what I'm doing with those players on the field as the man in the moon.

"I really don't feel any different," she has said, "but people try to make me feel different. 'Oh, you're the manager's wife now,' they'll say."

What she should say when they throw that at her is, "Yeah, but I'm still the first baseman's wife, too."

★　　★　　★

We lose tonight, 8-4, to Atlanta.

It wasn't pretty because we made three errors. I got two singles, leaving me 80 short of topping Cobb, but I'd much rather see us win.

Jay Tibbs blanked them for four innings, but they scored three in the fifth and came back with five in the seventh.

And Dale Murphy—I think he's the best player in the National League now—tied the league record for RBIs in April. He got his 29th to go even with Ron Cey, who had that many with the Dodgers in 1977.

One of the good things about tonight's game was the fact we battled back. Scored three times in the sixth to tie, but couldn't overcome their five in the seventh.

Tibbs is 0-4 now and I'm getting a little worried about his confidence.

I'll talk to Kitty about that tomorrow.

I went home, had a nice steak dinner, spent some time with my co-author, Hal Bodley, then watched the end of the Los Angeles-at-St. Louis game on my satellite TV.

The more I watch the Cardinals, the more I think they're going to have a better season than most people think.

WEDNESDAY, MAY 1 .... ROSE 0 FOR 2

Atlanta bombed us, 17-9. The faster I put this game out of my mind, the better I'll be.

I think I could've brought Walter Johnson back, sent him out there to pitch today and they still would have gotten hits.

I've seen some pretty big innings in my time, but I don't think I've ever seen 15 hits after two innings. Fifteen hits! I have a good memory, but I can't even remember who got all the hits over there. They came in bunches.

When I stopped for breakfast at Bob Evans (restaurant) not too far from my home, I didn't see any way we'd be able to play the 12:35 business day special. It was raining hard, just like it had been since late last night.

After I got to the ball park and put my uniform on, I went to Bob Howsam's office. He filled me in on some of the conversations he and Bill Bergesch have been having with other teams. We're still looking for a catcher, al-

Atlanta	ab	r	h	rbi	Cincinnati	ab	r	h	rbi
Wash'gton, rf	6	1	2	3	Milner, cf	4	2	1	0
Ramirez, ss	6	1	3	2	**Rose, 1b**	2	0	0	0
Komminsk, lf	6	2	3	1	Willis, p	0	0	0	0
Murphy, cf	5	4	3	3	Davis, ph	1	1	1	1
Hall, cf	0	0	0	0	Oester, 2b	1	0	0	0
Chambliss, 1b	6	1	4	1	Parker, rf	5	2	3	4
Cerone, c	6	2	3	1	Es'sky, 3b-1b	5	1	1	1
Oberkfell, 3b	5	2	2	3	C'cepcion, ss	4	1	2	1
Hubbard, 2b	5	2	2	2	Franco, p	0	0	0	0
Mahler, p	4	1	2	1	Foley, 2b-ss	4	0	0	0
Garber, p	1	1	1	0	Van Gorder, c	4	0	2	1
					Stuper, p	0	0	0	0
					Pastore, p	0	0	0	0
					Price, p	0	0	0	0
					Redus, ph	1	1	1	0
					Hume, p	0	0	0	0
					K'cki, ph-3b	3	0	0	0
Totals	50	17	25	17	Totals	39	9	13	9

Atlanta .... 6 6 1 0 0 0 2 2 0—17
Cincinnati .... 0 0 2 0 0 3 2 0 2— 9

Atlanta	IP.	H.	R.	ER.	BB.	SO.
Mahler (W. 6-0)	5⅓	8	5	4	2	1
Garber	3⅔	5	4	4	0	1
Cincinnati	IP.	H.	R.	ER.	BB.	SO.
Stuper (L. 3-2)	⅓	5	5	5	0	0
Pastore	1⅓	10	7	7	0	1
Price	1⅓	1	1	1	1	2
Hume	2	3	0	0	0	2
Willis	2	2	2	2	0	0
Franco	2	4	2	2	1	1

Game-winning RBI—Murphy.
E—Chambliss, Walker. DP—Atlanta 1, Cincinnati 1. LOB—Atlanta 9, Cincinnati 5. 2B—Chambliss 2, Hubbard, Washington, Ramirez, Concepcion 2, Parker 2, Van Gorder. 3B—Walker. HR—Murphy (10), Davis (4), Parker (1). SF—Oberkfell. WP—Garber. T—2:47. A—6,412.

though there is some sentiment to bring Alan Knicely up from Denver. He's been hitting pretty good down there.

I think we're going to have to make a move one way or the other.

I learned a long time ago you should always be prepared to play, regardless of the weather. With AstroTurf, once the rain stops the field can be ready for a game in 20 or 30 minutes.

Some of my guys didn't think we'd play, but when I came back from Mr. Howsam's office I told them the weather report was encouraging. With luck, the game would start on time and we had a chance to get it in.

There hadn't been a rainout in the majors this year, so you knew they were going to give it their best shot.

My starting pitcher was John Stuper, who pitched so well last Saturday in San Francisco. Today, he didn't have it.

He lasted only a third of the first inning, giving up five runs on five hits. Then, when I brought in Frank Pastore, he gave up seven runs on 10 hits in an inning and a third. We were down 12-0 before you could blink an eye. The Braves sent 21 batters to the plate in the first two innings and they got 15 hits.

Stuper told our catcher, Dave Van Gorder, he never got in a groove. Because it rained so hard all morning, everyone was telling him there wouldn't be a game, so I'm not sure he was mentally ready to pitch.

I know for a fact he's the kind of pitcher who must get his rhythm going if he is going to be effective.

This is the kind of game you try to forget about. You're going to win once in a while like this and you're going to stink up the joint like this once in a while. You can't put too much weight on either one.

What did bother me, though, was the fact we almost got away without losing (but didn't).

With one out in the fifth and (Atlanta's) Chris Chambliss and Rick Cerone on base, umpire Bob Engel stopped play and had the field covered. That was a little after 2 o'clock.

We waited almost two hours and it continued to rain hard. Engel told Jim Kaat at about 4 o'clock he was going to call the game. If that had happened, it would have been a rainout (since five innings hadn't been completed) and we would have started all over again later in the year.

But when Engel went out on the field after he talked with Kitty, the rain stopped. Can you believe that?

So, they waited another 41 minutes and started the game even though it was raining a little.

In the bottom of the fifth inning, Van Gorder got a hit and went to second on Wayne Krenchicki's infield out. Now, up comes Eddie Milner.

We're all anticipating a heavy rain because a light rain was already falling. Billy DeMars, our third-base coach, is thinking rain. So, we have to buy some time. If they stop now, it's still not an official game.

The first pitch to Milner is a ball. He looks down at Billy and Billy gives him the take sign because their pitcher, Rick Mahler, is wild.

The next pitch is almost bounced up there and Milner swings at it. He hits a topper to shortstop. The thing is, Eddie wasn't even thinking there might be a cloudburst and we could save a loss.

Eddie was so far away from the game, he's hacking at a bad pitch 1-0. You think he's worried about not getting five innings in!

And just like all the fans out there yelling, "Play ball! Play ball!" We're getting beat 13-2 and if they call it, we save a loss. I wonder what guys are thinking about half the time.

By the seventh inning, the conditions were dangerous and I just can't understand why they continued. We're going to lose anyway now, so I think the smart thing would have been to call it. I hate to lose, but I don't want to get a player hurt. It's not worth it.

My trainer, Larry Starr, got so upset about the conditions that he yelled something about stopping it before somebody got hurt to umpire Jim Quick and he got ejected. When was the last time a trainer got thrown out of the game?

★   ★   ★

When I got home, the good news was that Tyler's feeling a lot better. We sent out for some ribs and watched some games on television.

About 9 o'clock, Marge Schott called. She was worried about today's game. I told her not to worry, that we'll be OK. I also told her if she gets me a catcher, I'll win the division for her.

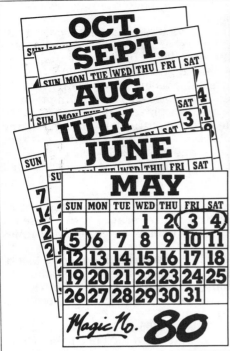

A columnist's suggestion that the Reds might be better off without Rose in the lineup stirred up the Reds' clubhouse.

FRIDAY, MAY 3 .... ROSE 1 FOR 5

It rained hard yesterday, but we still had a good workout at Riverfront Stadium. That's one of the great things about today's modern stadiums. Most of them have batting cages underneath, so the weather doesn't matter.

It wasn't much of a workout for the pitchers, but they were able to use the Nautilus equipment and loosen up. I always try to schedule off-day workouts around 10 o'clock so the guys can have the whole afternoon to do other things.

★   ★   ★

I wasn't very happy when I got up yesterday morning and read Tim Sullivan's column in the Cincinnati Enquirer. It's still on my mind.

Sullivan wrote that the team would be better off if Pete Rose was not the first baseman. Here are some of his comments:

"... After a week of deliberation and several hours of lineup scrib-

New York	ab	r	h	rbi	Cincinnati	ab	r	h	rbi
Dykstra, cf	5	2	2	2	Milner, cf	5	1	2	0
Backman, 2b	2	0	1	0	**Rose, 1b**	5	1	1	1
Ch'p'n, ph-2b	2	0	0	0	Parker, rf	4	2	4	3
Hern'dez, 1b	5	2	1	1	Cedeno, lf	4	0	1	0
Carter, c	3	2	0	0	Esasky, 3b	3	0	0	0
Strawb'ry, rf	3	2	1	0	C'cepcion, ss	4	0	0	0
Heep, lf	4	0	2	5	Oester, 2b	4	0	1	0
Johnson, 3b	2	0	0	0	Van Gorder, c	4	0	1	0
Knight, ph-3b	1	0	0	0	Soto, p	1	0	0	0
Santana, ss	4	1	1	0	Foley, ph	1	0	0	0
Lynch, p	4	0	0	0	Price, p	0	0	0	0
					Willis, p	0	0	0	0
					Kr'chicki, ph	1	0	0	0
					Pastore, p	0	0	0	0
					Power, p	0	0	0	0
					Walker, ph	1	0	0	0
Totals	35	9	8	8	Totals	37	4	10	4

New York........................1 0 2 1 2 0 3 0 0—9
Cincinnati.........................0 0 2 0 0 1 0 1 0—4

New York	IP.	H.	R.	ER.	BB.	SO.
Lynch (W. 1-1)	9	10	4	4	1	3

Cincinnati	IP.	H.	R.	ER.	BB.	SO.
Soto (L. 4-2)	5	7	6	6	4	6
Price	1⅓	1	3	2	3	1
Willis	⅔	0	0	0	0	1
Pastore	1	0	0	0	0	0
Power	1	0	0	0	0	0

Game-winning RBI—Hernandez.
E—Cedeno, **Rose.** DP—Cincinnati 1. LOB—New York 7, Cincinnati 7. 2B—**Rose,** Heep. 3B—Strawberry. HR—Hernandez (1), Dykstra (1), Parker 2 (3). SB—Backman, Johnson, Dykstra, Heep. SF—Heep. WP—Willis, Pastore. T—2:50. A—21,062.

bling, I have come to the appalling conclusion the Reds might be a better team with their manager in the dugout.

"This amounts to heresy, of course, particularly with Pete poised just 80 hits away from (breaking) Ty Cobb's record. But Reds President Bob Howsam thinks Rose could break the record eventually without playing regularly, and there is some evidence to suggest that he should.

"Simply put, Rose is not the hitter he was even as recently as 1980 and is not nearly hitter enough to play first base on a contending team."

Sullivan went on to say I hustle and I inspire my players, but that I don't get enough extra-base hits. He said the outfielders play me in and that, in effect, has made for a smaller field of play. He pointed out that after I went 0 for 2 Wednesday, my average fell to .246.

He said I hit 42 doubles for the Phillies in 1980 to lead the National League.

He also wrote:

"From 1974 through 1980, a period in which Rose won three world-championship rings and five doubles titles, he averaged a two-base hit every 15 at-bats. Since then, he has slowed to one double every 27 times up.

"Accordingly, Rose fell to .271 and .245 seasons following the last of his 15 .300 years in 1981. He was hitting .259, and a lot of folks thought Cobb's record was secure, when Montreal sent him back home (to the Reds) last summer. The Reds made a point of referring to Rose as a manager-player instead of a player-manager.

"What followed was wonderful. Rose hit .365 in 26 games with the Reds and made all his critics dive headfirst for cover. At one point, Howsam inquired why Rose wasn't putting himself in the lineup more often.

"But you can't help wondering now if the real Rose isn't the one who keeps hitting harmless grounders to second base. He does this sometimes to advance baserunners, the burden of the fellow who hits second. But lately there haven't been many baserunners to advance. Were Eric Davis finding his way on base more regularly, the Reds could make good use of Rose's bat-handling skills."

Sullivan talked about all the outfielders we have and made mention of a Sports Illustrated story that said I might be a burden to the Reds (as a player) as I chase Ty Cobb's record.

Sullivan also quoted Howsam in his article:

" 'I think he's a definite asset to a lineup when he wants to play,' " Howsam said of me. " 'If he feels he's not hitting, he takes himself out of the game.

" 'When he came here, we had a long talk about the situation. I talked to him on the basis of not playing. I talked with him about becoming as fine a manager as was possible. After talking to him, I became convinced in my mind that it was not a problem. I feel when the time comes he'll not only know what to do, but he'll do it.' "

Sullivan finished with this gem: "Perhaps it's time to consider the possibility. I hope I'm wrong."

A lot of the guys were talking about the article in the clubhouse yesterday and there was still some mention of it today as they arrived for our game against New York.

What really disturbed me was that Tim wrote the article, then took off for the Kentucky Derby. They say he won't be back until Sunday.

I'm going to talk with him then and make some points. About the only thing I can say now is that it was written by somebody who has not seen very many of our games and who doesn't travel with the team.

This is not a dead issue. Not yet.

★   ★   ★

We lost to the Mets, 9-4. Our ace, Mario Soto, was the loser and it was just not his night. Keith Hernandez hit his first home run of the year in the first inning and Mario never got straightened out. They got six runs and seven hits off him before I sent a pinch-hitter up for him in the bottom of the fifth. Danny Heep, who played left field, drove in five runs for them.

Sullivan wasn't around to see it, but I had a double down the right-field line in the third inning to score Eddie Milner from first. Dave Parker hit a single to score me.

That made the score 3-2, but that's as close as we could come.

Ed Lynch pitched a good game, although we got 10 hits off him.

SATURDAY, MAY 4 .... ROSE 1 FOR 1

I got a big kick out of comments by our owner, Marge Schott, in today's Enquirer. She's still fuming about Wednesday's game when we had all the rain.

I like her spirit.

"I just want to know who I should contact about those umpires Wednesday," Schott said. "I suppose it's the commissioner, Peter Ueberroth. That game shouldn't have been played. It wasn't fair to the fans and it wasn't fair to the players. So what if we have to hand out a few thousand rainchecks. It wasn't right."

I didn't have the heart to tell Marge the club makes the decision on whether or not to start a game. Once it starts, it is in the umpires' hands.

You'll be hearing more from her later. You can book on that.

New York	ab	r	h	rbi	Cincinnati	ab	r	h	rbi
Dykstra, cf	3	0	1	0	Milner, cf	3	2	1	0
Backman, 2b	3	0	0	0	Rose, 1b	1	2	1	1
Hern'dez, 1b	2	1	1	0	Davis, rf	1	0	1	2
Christ'sen, lf	1	0	0	0	Parker, rf	4	1	2	3
Carter, c	3	1	1	2	Walker, lf	1	0	0	0
Schiraldi, p	0	0	0	0	C'deno, lf-1b	4	1	2	1
Staub, ph	1	0	0	0	Esasky, 3b	5	2	2	4
Strawb'ry, rf	4	0	0	0	C'cepcion, ss	5	2	2	0
Heep, lf-1b	3	0	1	0	Oester, 2b	4	2	3	2
Johnson, 3b	4	0	0	0	Van Gorder, c	3	1	0	0
Santana, ss	3	0	0	0	Tibbs, p	3	1	0	0
McDowell, p	1	0	0	0					
Sisk, p	0	0	0	0					
Sambito, p	0	0	0	0					
Hurdle, c	1	0	0	0					
Totals	29	2	4	2	Totals	34	14	14	13

New York .... 0 0 0   0 0 2   0 0 0— 2
Cincinnati .... 0 0 0   0 2 10   2 0 x—14

New York	IP.	H.	R.	ER.	BB.	SO.
McDowell (L. 2-1)	5*	6	6	6	3	3
Sisk	⅓	3	4	4	1	0
Sambito	0*	2	2	2	2	0
Schiraldi	2⅔	3	2	2	1	5

Cincinnati	IP.	H.	R.	ER.	BB.	SO.
Tibbs (W. 1-4)	9	4	2	2	4	2

*Pitched to four batters in sixth.

Game-winning RBI—Parker.
E—McDowell. DP—New York 2, Cincinnati 1. LOB —New York 5, Cincinnati 4. 2B—Parker, Oester, Davis. 3B—Concepcion. HR—Carter (4), Esasky (4). SB—Backman. SH—Dykstra. HBP—By McDowell (Rose). WP—Schiraldi, Tibbs. T—2:42. A—16,634.

★   ★   ★

I have lived only 90 miles from the Kentucky Derby most of my life and have never gone to Louisville to see one. I love horse racing and that is something (attend the race) I want to do someday, but as long as I'm in baseball, it won't be possible.

People have often asked me if I ever will be able to walk away from this game. I always tell them when the time comes, sure. Then, I point out I have never been to the Kentucky Derby, never been to the Indianapolis 500. There are things I would like to do.

★   ★   ★

Today's game was what Dallas Green, who managed the (World Series champion) 1980 Phillies, used to call a no-brainer. You just turn your horses loose and they do their thing.

It didn't start out that way, though.

Gary Carter hit a two-run homer off Jay Tibbs in the top of the sixth to tie the score 2-2.

Then, Darryl Strawberry hit a high fly and I'll tell you the truth, I thought it was another homer. It could have been devastating for Tibbs, who has been struggling of late.

But today, he no-hit the Mets until there were two out in the sixth. Keith Hernandez was safe on a shot back to the mound and then Carter hit his fourth homer of the year.

When Strawberry's ball left the bat, Eddie Milner was playing him in deep center. He ran to the wall, jumped and, with his glove extended, hauled in the ball. The TV replay showed his glove hitting the yellow line at the top of the fence, which is eight feet high.

Quite a catch. That seemed to fire us up.

We scored 10 runs in the bottom of the sixth and Dave Parker extended his hitting streak to 13 games with a tie-breaking double in the inning. But the big blow was Nick Esasky's third (career) grand slam in that inning.

I had a single and walked twice, then took myself out and moved Cesar Cedeno from left field to first base.

The clubhouse was as happy as I've seen it after the game. We had lost eight of our previous 10, so this win was a big lift.

I keep telling people Parker is going to have a great year and he sure hasn't disappointed me.

In his last 13 at-bats, he has gotten nine hits—three homers, three doubles, three singles—and 10 RBIs.

Billy DeMars, our batting coach, said he had a talk with Dave during Wednesday's rain game. Billy said he just told him to relax a little more and if you'll remember, Dave got his first home run (of the year) that day.

Reporters are still wondering if we're going to make any trades. They cornered General Manager Bill Bergesch, and he told them there was nothing to a story we're going to deal Cedeno to the Toronto Blue Jays. I don't know where they come up with that stuff.

There was another rumor we've talked with the Dodgers about getting their relief pitcher, Tom Niedenfuer, for an outfielder. Bob Howsam told them he hadn't talked to the Dodgers in quite some time.

There was another one, that we were trying to get Ozzie Virgil, the Phillies' catcher. Well, I can tell you I'd love to have Ozzie Virgil over here, but they're not about to give him up, not while Bo Diaz is on the disabled list.

★　　　★　　　★

Most of us watched Spend A Buck win the Kentucky Derby on television today.

And that brings up another point.

When I came back here last year, one of the first things I discovered was there wasn't a television set in the players' lounge. I asked our clubhouse manager (and equipment man), Bernie Stowe, where the TV was. He said Vern Rapp (the Reds' manager for three-fourths of the '84 season) didn't want a TV.

I said what happens if the Saturday Game of the Week is on and our game doesn't start until 7:35. So, I got the guys a television.

Bernie, or his son Mark, knows that at 7:30 if our game is not on TV, the set is turned off. There won't be any basketball game or anything like that on. If I come into the clubhouse from the dugout at quarter to 8 and the TV set is on and somebody is in there watching something else, like basketball, the TV is gone. The players know that. Gone, adios.

You've got to treat men like men. Maybe I relate to them better because I'm a player—I'm one of them.

SUNDAY, MAY 5 .... ROSE 3 FOR 5

We just got outpitched today. There's nothing else I can say except if this game had been played at night, we might have won.

I had three hits and am now 75 short of breaking Cobb's record. I'm swinging the bat real good right now; I feel like I'm in a good groove.

And anytime you get three hits— the team had only seven—off Dwight Gooden, you have to be happy.

On second thought, I'm never happy when we lose, especially by a run (the Mets were 3-2 winners).

We loaded the bases with two outs in the bottom of the fourth inning. We were trailing 3-0, but I had a good feeling.

Dave Van Gorder hit a 1-2 fastball to the gap in left-center. The ball took a bounce in front of the warning track and went over the fence.

New York	ab	r	h	rbi	Cincinnati	ab	r	h	rbi
Dykstra, cf	4	0	2	1	Milner, cf	4	0	0	0
Chapman, 2b	4	0	1	0	Perez, ph	0	0	0	0
Hern'dez, 1b	4	0	0	0	Parker, rf	5	0	3	0
Carter, c	4	0	1	0	**Rose, 1b**	5	0	3	0
Reynolds, c	0	0	0	0	Walker, lf	1	1	0	0
Strawb'ry, rf	3	1	1	0	Davis, ph-lf	1	0	0	0
Knight, 3b	4	1	1	0	Kr'chicki, 3b	3	1	2	0
Orosco, p	0	0	0	0	Es'sky, ph-3b	1	0	0	0
Christ'sen, lf	3	0	1	1	Oester, 2b	4	0	2	0
Santana, ss	3	1	1	0	Foley, ss	2	0	0	0
Gooden, p	2	0	0	0	C'cpc'n, ph-ss	1	0	0	0
Johnson, 3b	1	0	0	0	Van Gorder, c	4	0	1	2
					Tibbs, pr	0	0	0	0
					Browning, p	1	0	0	0
					Cedeno, ph	1	0	0	0
					Price, p	0	0	0	0
					Redus, ph	1	0	0	0
					Franco, p	0	0	0	0
					Soto, ph	1	0	0	0
Totals	32	3	8	2	Totals	35	2	8	2

```
New York....................0 0 1  2 0 0  0 0 0—3
Cincinnati..................0 0 0  2 0 0  0 0 0—2
```

New York	IP.	H.	R.	ER.	BB.	SO.
Gooden (W. 4-1).........	7	7	2	2	3	9
Orosco (Save 3).........	2	1	0	0	1	1

Cincinnati	IP.	H.	R.	ER.	BB.	SO.
Browning (L. 2-1)......	4	6	3	3	1	1
Price........................	3	2	0	0	1	0
Franco......................	2	0	0	0	1	2

Game-winning RBI—Dykstra.
E—Chapman 2, Walker. DP—Cincinnati 2. LOB— New York 6, Cincinnati 10. 2B—Knight, Carter, Van Gorder. SH—Gooden. WP—Orosco. T—2:48. A— 20,179.

It was a ground-rule double and only two runs could score. Ron Oester, who had to stop at third, said he could have made it home with the tying run easy.

On a sunny day like today, the AstroTurf dries out and balls bounce a lot higher. That same hit at night would not have gone over the fence.

In the ninth, with Tony Perez on first base, I hit a liner to center, but rookie Len Dykstra made a diving catch. It could have been a double. Dave Parker popped up for the final out and his 13-game hitting streak ended.

★   ★   ★

Tim Sullivan, the Enquirer writer, was back from the Derby and came in to see me.

"You speaking to me?" he asked as he poked his head into my office.

"Why not?" I asked. I didn't look him straight in the eyes.

We talked for 20 minutes and I think he understands some things now.

I said, "Well, I'm a little disappointed in the story because I thought you were smarter than that."

He said, "What do you mean?"

"Obviously you haven't seen us play many games this year. Very conservatively speaking, I can have six or seven more hits and if I had those—even four more—I would be batting .315 or so and you wouldn't have written that article."

He said I was probably right.

When he said that, I said: "Well, that's how much the article meant to you. It was the difference of four guys making good plays on me and I should sit down?"

He said he really didn't mean it that way.

"I wasn't talking about average," he said. "I was thinking about power production."

I shook my head.

"I've always been a singles hitter, the first singles hitter to make $100,000," I said. "You know that. I can't get away from that. Now if you want me to take guys and put them at first base who've never played there before, you're not going to strengthen the team."

Then he started talking about the outfielders cheating in on me. I told him I hadn't really noticed that.

"But if they are, and you're a smart defense, you probably do cheat in on me because how many times do you see me hit fly balls? I don't hit fly balls. That's why outfielders can play in on me because I don't hit many balls in the air."

He then asked me what the difference is now compared to five years ago.

"Sure, my stats are going to be down," I told him. "My games played are going to be down, my at-bats are going to be down. I don't play as much. I'm not going to lead the league in doubles because I don't play as much."

He said, "Yeah, but you used to get a double every 15 at-bats or something like that. The last couple of years you've done it every 27 at-bats."

I pointed out to him I was injured last year "and I could very easily have four or five doubles now; I have only three, but I could have five and if I had five you wouldn't have written the article. That's two good catches in the outfield guys made, like in the ninth inning today."

"Maybe I was a little too premature," he interrupted.

I eventually said the whole thing boils down to a case of a guy who doesn't travel with the team and not seeing enough games making a judgment. There are too many things to write about without writing about that.

MAGIC No. **75**

Reds ace Mario Soto jumped off to a quick start, winning his fifth game on May 7.

TUESDAY, MAY 7 .... ROSE 0 FOR 3

We played an exhibition game in Detroit last night and lost, 7-4.

I spent some time with my old manager, Sparky Anderson, who did such a fine job winning the World Series last year with the Tigers.

I used the exhibition game as a chance to get work for some of my guys who haven't been playing much.

Sparky and the Tigers will come to Cincinnati for a rematch Thursday.

Right after the game we flew to Philadelphia. My wife Carol arrived there earlier Monday so we could be together for her birthday today.

Coming back to Philadelphia is a homecoming of sorts. I had five years here and all but part of 1983 were great. The fans are super in Philly. They demand a good effort and when they don't get it, they let you know. But I can honestly say the whole time I wore a Philadelphia Phillies uniform I was never booed once.

We won the World Series in 1980 over Kansas City, lost to Montreal

Cincinnati	ab	r	h	rbi	Phila'phia	ab	r	h	rbi
Milner, cf	3	1	1	0	Samuel, 2b	3	0	0	0
Rose, 1b	3	0	0	0	Stone, lf	4	0	0	0
Parker, rf	4	0	0	0	Hayes, cf	3	0	1	0
Cedeno, lf	4	0	1	1	Schmidt, 3b	4	0	1	0
Esasky, 3b	4	1	1	0	Corcoran, 1b	3	0	1	0
C'cepcion, ss	4	0	0	0	Wilson, rf	4	0	0	0
Oester, 2b	2	0	1	1	Virgil, c	2	0	1	0
Van Gorder, c	4	0	0	0	Jeltz, pr	0	0	0	0
Soto, p	3	0	1	0	Aguayo, ss	3	0	0	0
Franco, p	0	0	0	0	Wock'fuss, ph	1	0	0	0
Power, p	0	0	0	0	K. Gross, p	1	0	0	0
					G. Gross, ph	1	0	0	0
					Hudson, p	0	0	0	0
					Daulton, ph	1	0	0	0
					Rucker, p	0	0	0	0
					Maddox, ph	1	0	1	0
Totals	31	2	5	2	Totals	31	0	5	0

Cincinnati ....0 0 0   1 1 0   0 0 0—2
Philadelphia ....0 0 0   0 0 0   0 0 0—0

Cincinnati	IP.	H.	R.	ER.	BB.	SO.
Soto (W. 5-2)	7	4	0	0	5	6
Franco	1⅔	1	0	0	1	2
Power (Save 4)	⅓	0	0	0	0	1

Philadelphia	IP.	H.	R.	ER.	BB.	SO.
K. Gross (L. 2-3)	5	5	2	2	3	2
Hudson	2	0	0	0	0	2
Rucker	2	0	0	0	1	2

Game-winning RBI—Oester.
E—None. DP—Cincinnati 1. LOB—Cincinnati 6, Philadelphia 10. 2B—Virgil. 3B—Oester. SB—Oester, Esasky, Milner, Samuel. T—2:48. A—21,902.

in the mini-playoffs the next year (the strike season that featured an additional tier of postseason play) and in 1983 made it to the World Series before Baltimore beat us. That's not too bad for five years.

Carol and I had a late lunch in the hotel. I think it was a good day for her. A friend, Bruce Selig, who is in the limousine business, made one of his big Lincolns available for Carol and a couple of her close friends from this area. I gave her some money and they all went on a shopping trip to the King of Prussia mall.

I didn't expect her to bring any change back!

I got to Veterans Stadium by midafternoon, the first time back as manager of the Reds.

Veterans Stadium is fun. The Phillies do a great job as far as making the game fun for the fans, and it's fun for the players. The atmosphere is good.

Plus, I'm coming in here swinging the bat pretty good.

I called Herbie (Mike Schmidt) about two weeks ago (April 19), the day the Phillies were going to face Dwight Gooden. I could see by the newspapers where Schmitty was struggling and I just wanted to pep him up a little bit—not that I am playing favorites. But the week before that, on my birthday, we had faced Gooden.

I gave Herbie a rundown on how Dwight was pitching. Not that I dislike Dwight Gooden. I like him, but I have always been close to Schmitty and I think he is one of the best ballplayers around. I kept telling him that when I was here and he won two MVPs.

This time, I was trying to relax him, but it didn't help because Dwight still pitched a shutout. (Gooden, in fact, got last-inning relief help from Jesse Orosco in a 1-0 game in which Schmidt went 0 for 3.)

Philadelphia has always been one of the best media towns, and they were all out tonight.

Larry Shenk, the Phillies' publicity vice president whom everybody calls The Baron, came down to my office early. He had numerous requests for live television interviews.

I told him Howard Eskin of KYW-TV had called me in Cincinnati and that I promised him one, but that I really didn't like to do live shots close to batting practice.

It seemed like every sportswriter in Philly came out. They all wanted to talk about the Cobb record, managing the Reds and all that.

An hour before the game a bulletin came over the news wires that Peter Ueberroth, the commissioner, was introducing a mandatory drug-testing program for everyone in baseball except the players. The reporters wanted to know what I thought of that. There really wasn't much I could say because it doesn't involve me.

There was a good crowd on hand (21,902), and they gave me an ovation when the game started.

I didn't get any hits, but we shut them out, 2-0, and Mario Soto won his fifth game.

Cesar Cedeno's single and Ron Oester's triple drove in the runs, but as far as I was concerned the game boiled down to a great play by Nick Esasky in the sixth inning.

We were up 2-0, but Mario walked Juan Samuel and Von Hayes. Herbie was the batter with one out.

Now Schmitty is only hitting .219 and has just two homers, but he's still one of the best hitters in the league.

On a 2-2 pitch, he hit a smash down the third-base line that Nick made a diving stop on (preventing the ball from going into left field).

The infield then was drawn in (Schmidt's single had loaded the bases) and Tim Corcoran hit a grounder to me. I made a weak throw to the plate that took a bounce, but Dave Van Gorder held onto it (for a forceout). Soto then struck out Glenn Wilson and we were out of trouble.

After the game, we all went to my favorite Chinese restaurant and celebrated Carol's birthday, complete with cake.

It was a good day, start to finish.

WEDNESDAY, MAY 8 .... ROSE 1 FOR 3

We beat John Denny and the Phillies, 8-2, tonight. It was a good win because it got us to .500 (13-13).

Plus, Jay Tibbs, who has been struggling some and has had some bad luck, was the winning pitcher.

It was a good game for him because I think he gained some confidence by pitching out of a couple of jams. Now, he'll know he can do that when he gets in trouble in the future.

Joe Price did a nice job coming out of the bullpen.

I had a double off Denny and scored three times, but what really pleased me was the fact we were behind 2-1 after the second inning, came back to tie 'em, then scored four times in the sixth and twice in the seventh.

I hit that double to center hard and it left me needing 74 hits to break Cobb's record.

Cincinnati	ab	r	h	rbi	Phila'phia	ab	r	h	rbi
Milner, cf	5	0	0	0	Samuel, 2b	4	1	2	0
Rose, 1b	3	3	1	0	Stone, lf	3	1	1	0
Redus, lf	0	0	0	0	Zachry, p	0	0	0	0
Parker, rf	5	0	2	1	Tekulve, p	0	0	0	0
Davis, rf	0	0	0	0	Hayes, cf	2	0	1	1
C'deno, lf-1b	4	1	0	0	Schmidt, 3b	4	0	0	1
Esasky, 3b	4	1	1	0	Corcoran, 1b	2	0	1	0
C'cepcion, ss	4	1	1	0	R'sell, ph-1b	1	0	0	0
Oester, 2b	4	1	2	1	Wilson, rf	4	0	1	0
Van Gorder, c	4	1	2	3	Virgil, c	4	0	1	0
Tibbs, p	2	0	0	0	Jeltz, ss	4	0	0	0
Price, p	0	0	0	0	Denny, p	2	0	0	0
					Carman, p	0	0	0	0
					G. Gr's, ph-lf	1	0	0	0
					Maddox, ph	1	0	0	0
Totals	35	8	9	5	Totals	32	2	7	2

```
Cincinnati .......................1 0 1   0 0 4   2 0 0—8
Philadelphia ...................2 0 0   0 0 0   0 0 0—2
```

Cincinnati	IP.	H.	R.	ER.	BB.	SO.
Tibbs (W. 2-4)	6⅔	7	2	2	4	2
Price	2⅓	0	0	0	0	6

Philadelphia	IP.	H.	R.	ER.	BB.	SO.
Denny (L. 1-3)	6⅓	8	7	6	2	1
Carman	⅔	0	1	0	1	0
Zachry	1	1	0	0	1	0
Tekulve	1	0	0	0	0	0

Game-winning RBI—Oester.
E—Wilson, Schmidt. DP—Cincinnati 2, Philadelphia 1. LOB—Cincinnati 5, Philadelphia 7. 2B—Hayes, **Rose**, Parker. HR—Van Gorder (1). SB—**Rose**. SH—Tibbs. T—2:25. A—22,416.

I honestly wasn't thinking about that article Tim Sullivan of the Enquirer wrote last week when I got the double, but one of the reasons I've always been able to get along so well with the media is the fact I'll always talk to them.

Sure, I wasn't happy with the article he wrote, but we talked and I think I convinced him he was wrong.

At least he came back the other day and in so many words said so. He wrote:

"(Debating the issue) was a fascinating exercise, one few people in Rose's position would indulge. When asked for enlightenment on various decisions, many major league managers react bitterly and complain about being 'second-guessed.' But you can second-guess Rose, even about playing himself, and he will conduct a reasoned debate without resorting to hysterics.

"This is not a very important skill in a first baseman, but it is nearly essential in a manager, who must get along not only with the press but 25 players of varying temperaments. There is no place to second-guess Rose here."

He satisfied me with that.

★ ★ ★

Reporters are still asking a lot of questions about the commissioner's drug program.

I'm convinced we don't have a problem. As far as baseball goes, I don't think we've got any worse a drug problem than lawyers or doctors do. I'll say this: I've never seen a guy in a Cincinnati uniform I thought had a problem.

I make up the lineup card, not the medical report. But I can tell you this: If I see a guy acting differently, doing things or not doing things he has been consistent about, then I'd wonder. I really don't think about those things, but maybe I should, in my position.

I'm going to keep my eyes open.

★ ★ ★

Before the game tonight, I talked with Bill Giles. He's the Phillies' president.

We're still looking for a catcher and I wanted to see about Ozzie Virgil or Bo Diaz. Ozzie is their No. 1 guy now, so they're not going to trade him. Bo broke a bone in his wrist in April and is on the disabled list.

Giles said the Phillies need a lefthanded hitter.

I think we have to make a decision about Alan Knicely soon. He hit .333, had 33 homers and drove in 126 runs for Wichita last year. In 15 games with Denver this year, he's hitting .380.

We returned to Cincinnati after the game, so tomorrow (Thursday) morning I'll be talking with Bob Howsam and Bill Bergesch.

Rookie Tom Browning seems to become more poised every time he pitches.

FRIDAY, MAY 10 .... ROSE 0 FOR 1

Today's game showed me a lot about this team.

I didn't get any hits—I walked three times—but we beat the Astros, 5-2.

It seems like every time Tom Browning, my rookie lefthander, goes out there he gets more poise.

They scored two runs off him in the fifth inning, but Browning hung in there.

Then, in the eighth, we scored five times to win. That's the sign of a good team. A lot of teams, when they're down a couple of runs late in the game, just don't come back. We've struggled off and on getting key hits, but today—even though Houston outhit us 8-6—we made the most of what we got.

Houston	ab	r	h	rbi	Cincinnati	ab	r	h	rbi
Doran, 2b	3	0	1	0	Milner, cf	3	1	1	0
Cabell, 1b	4	0	0	0	**Rose, 1b**	1	0	0	0
Garner, 3b	4	0	0	0	Davis, pr	0	1	0	0
Cruz, lf	4	0	0	0	Bilardello, c	0	0	0	0
Bass, cf-rf	4	1	3	1	Parker, rf	4	1	1	2
Puhl, rf	3	1	0	0	Cedeno, lf	4	1	2	1
Smith, p	0	0	0	0	Esasky, 3b	4	0	1	0
Ashby, c	4	0	2	0	Power, p	0	0	0	0
Thon, ss	3	0	1	0	C'cepcion, ss	4	0	1	0
Reynolds, ph	1	0	0	0	Oester, 2b	3	0	0	0
Niekro, p	2	0	1	1	Van Gorder, c	2	0	0	0
DiPino, p	0	0	0	0	Redus, ph-lf	1	0	0	0
Mumphrey, cf	1	0	0	0	Browning, p	2	0	0	0
					Kr'cki, ph-3b	0	1	0	0
Totals	33	2	8	2	Totals	28	5	6	3

Houston...........................0 0 0   0 2 0   0 0 0—2
Cincinnati.......................0 0 0   0 0 0   0 5 x—5

Houston	IP.	H.	R.	ER.	BB.	SO.
Niekro	7⅓	4	2	2	5	5
DiPino (L. 1-4)	0*	1	2	1	1	0
Smith	⅔	1	1	0	0	0

Cincinnati	IP.	H.	R.	ER.	BB.	SO.
Browning (W. 3-1)	8	8	2	2	2	5
Power (Save 5)	1	0	0	0	0	0

*Pitched to two batters in eighth.

Game-winning RBI—Cedeno.

E—Concepcion, Garner, Cruz. DP—Houston 2, Cincinnati 2. LOB—Houston 7, Cincinnati 5. 2B—Concepcion, Thon. HR—Bass (3). SB—Milner. SF—Niekro. PB—Ashby. T—2:07. A—22,097.

Dave Parker drove home two runs with a single and Cesar Cedeno—he always likes to hit against his old teammates—followed with a tie-breaking single.

I brought in Ted Power to pitch the ninth and he did a solid job for his fifth save. It was our third straight win, putting us a game over .500 at 14-13.

With those three walks tonight, I have been on base 19 times in the last eight games. In those games, I've scored seven runs, had eight hits, walked 10 times and been hit by a pitch once.

I almost did something tonight that would have raised a few eyebrows in the press box.

I seriously considered pinch hitting for Pete Rose in the eighth inning when we scored our five runs. Joe Niekro was pitching for Houston and we had two runners on and two out. That's when Bob Lillis, the Astros' manager, brought in Frank DiPino, their lefthanded reliever.

Now, I don't have any hits off lefthanders this year, so I asked George Scherger, who helps me manage a lot when I'm playing, if I should send up a pinch-hitter.

"No," Scherg said. "Go ahead and hit."

That's what I did, and DiPino walked me.

But the minute I got to first, I called on Eric Davis to pinch run. Eric eventually scored the winning run when Cesar singled.

I don't mind pinch running for a guy—any guy—if it's the winning run. I was that guy and that was the winning run—the run we played this game for tonight.

Parker is really doing a job for us. He has had 12 hits in his last 31 at-bats (.387).

He has a great attitude. People who a couple of years ago said his career was on the downside were totally wrong.

SATURDAY, MAY 11 .... ROSE 1 FOR 3

I've got a little bit of a problem today, but I'm going to nip it in the bud.

It seems that Eric Davis and Gary Redus, who haven't been playing much lately, have decided they aren't going to shag fly balls.

I got upset when I found out they told one of my coaches about this a day and a half ago and he didn't tell me until today.

I thought the best way to handle this was to call in my bench coach, George Scherger. He can really get through to Davis and Redus.

I said, "Hey, Scherg, go have a talk with those guys. I don't want to get into a big fuss about shagging. Just tell them if they want to take batting practice they can take it, but they have to go pick up the balls after they hit them. You know, get their butts out there shagging. Tell them if Dave Parker and Pete Rose can shag,

Houston	ab	r	h	rbi	Cincinnati	ab	r	h	rbi
Doran, 2b	5	2	2	0	Milner, cf	2	0	1	1
Puhl, rf	4	1	2	0	Redus, ph-cf	1	0	0	0
Walling, 1b	3	1	1	1	**Rose, 1b**	3	1	1	1
C'bell, ph-1b	1	1	0	1	Davis, pr	0	0	0	0
Cruz, lf	4	2	3	3	Franco, p	0	0	0	0
Mumphrey, cf	3	1	0	1	Parker, rf	5	0	1	0
Garner, 3b	4	1	1	3	Cedeno, lf-1b	5	1	2	0
Bailey, c	4	0	1	1	Esasky, 3b	5	1	2	2
Reynolds, ss	4	0	0	0	C'cepcion, ss	5	0	2	0
Scott, p	0	0	0	0	Oester, 2b	5	2	3	0
Bass, ph	1	0	0	0	Van Gorder, c	2	1	1	1
Solano, p	1	0	0	0	Foley, ph	1	0	0	0
Dawley, p	1	1	0	0	Bilardello, c	0	0	0	0
DiPino, p	0	0	0	0	Soto, p	2	0	1	0
Smith, p	0	0	0	0	Kr'chicki, ph	1	0	1	0
					Price, p	0	0	0	0
					W'ker, ph-lf	1	1	1	2
Totals	35	10	10	10	Totals	38	7	16	7

Houston ....0 0 0   1 0 5   2 0 2—10
Cincinnati ....1 2 2   0 0 0   0 2 0— 7

Houston	IP.	H.	R.	ER.	BB.	SO.
Scott	2	5	3	3	1	0
Solano (W. 1-0)	3	5	2	2	1	1
Dawley	2⅓	4	2	2	0	1
DiPino	⅓	1	0	0	1	1
Smith (Save 4)	1⅓	1	0	0	0	0

Cincinnati	IP.	H.	R.	ER.	BB.	SO.
Soto (L. 5-3)	6	4	6	6	2	2
Price	2	4	2	2	1	2
Franco	1	2	2	2	2	1

Game-winning RBI—Bailey.
E—Concepcion 2, **Rose**. DP—Houston 2, Cincinnati 1. LOB—Houston 6, Cincinnati 9. 2B—Cedeno, Esasky, Oester, Puhl, Walling. 3B—Garner. HR—Cruz (3), Walker (2). SB—Cruz. SH—Bailey, Puhl. SF—Milner, **Rose**, Mumphrey. WP—Scott, Price. T—3:00. A—26,098.

they are going to shag, too."

I just don't know what some players are thinking. If they don't want to shag here, they are going to shag someplace else.

What some of these players don't seem to understand is I can do a lot for them behind the scenes. I can pull a few strings around here for their benefit.

I don't know whether I'm your everyday manager or not. I don't know whether guys like John Felske in Philadelphia or Buck Rodgers in Montreal have the same rapport with their owners.

I don't want to get in a situation where this (manager's office) becomes a Gestapo. But, I'll tell you, if a guy is going to give me problems that make my job harder, his butt is going to be out of here. I don't care who he is.

★　　★　　★

This was a good night and a bad night for Davey Concepcion.

Davey got his 2,000th career hit in the fifth inning when he singled up the middle off the Astros' Julio Solano on a 1-2 pitch. He would have been a lot happier had we won and if he hadn't made two errors.

I also made an error on a ground ball Mark Bailey hit to me. I just blew it.

I really thought we had something going tonight. I singled in the first inning off their starter, Mike Scott, and went to third when Cesar Cedeno singled. Nick Esasky drove me home with a hit to right field.

We scored two runs in the second and two more in the third.

When you're up 5-0 and Mario Soto is pitching, you should win. Mario did not allow a hit until there were two out in the fourth. That's when Jose Cruz—he's a good hitter—homered.

In the sixth, they scored five times on three hits, two walks and a squeeze bunt.

They went on to win, 10-7, and I wasn't very happy. You just shouldn't blow five-run leads.

SUNDAY, MAY 12 .... ROSE 0 FOR 1

We're trying to do everything we can to get Jay Tibbs untracked.

Jay can pitch. I'm convinced of that, but it seems like whenever he makes a mistake, the opposing batters jump on it.

I didn't start because Bob Knepper, Houston's lefthander, was pitching. I batted for Tom Hume in the eighth inning and grounded out against lefthanded reliever Jeff Calhoun, who replaced Knepper in the sixth.

We got a 2-0 lead in the first inning against Knepper, but Tibbs couldn't hold it.

We had errors today by Davey Concepcion, Ron Oester and Dave Van Gorder.

Houston	ab	r	h	rbi	Cincinnati	ab	r	h	rbi
Doran, 2b	6	1	3	2	Redus, cf	5	1	2	0
Pankovits, 2b	0	0	0	0	Cedeno, lf	4	1	0	0
Puhl, rf	4	1	1	0	Parker, rf	4	1	3	2
Walling, 1b	5	2	2	2	Perez, 1b	5	0	2	2
Cruz, lf	4	1	1	0	Esasky, 3b	4	1	1	0
Mumphrey, cf	4	0	0	0	C'cepcion, ss	4	0	3	1
Garner, 3b	5	2	2	1	Oester, 2b	5	0	2	0
Bailey, c	5	2	2	2	Van Gorder, c	4	0	0	0
Reynolds, ss	5	1	1	1	Tibbs, p	1	1	0	0
Knepper, p	3	0	0	0	Davis, ph	1	0	0	0
Calhoun, p	1	0	0	1	Hume, p	0	0	0	0
					Rose, ph	1	0	0	0
					Willis, p	0	0	0	0
Totals	42	10	12	9	Totals	38	5	13	5

Houston	.0 0 1	2 2 0	0 2 3—10
Cincinnati	.2 0 0	1 0 1	0 0 1— 5

Houston	IP.	H.	R.	ER.	BB.	SO.
Knepper (W. 4-0)	5	8	3	3	4	5
Calhoun (Save 2)	4	5	2	2	1	1

Cincinnati	IP.	H.	R.	ER.	BB.	SO.
Tibbs (L. 2-5)	5	7	5	3	1	2
Hume	3	2	2	2	3	2
Willis	1	4	3	3	0	0

Game-winning RBI—Garner.
E—Knepper, Concepcion, Oester, Van Gorder. DP—Houston 2. LOB—Houston 10, Cincinnati 11. 2B—Cruz, Reynolds, Redus 2, Concepcion, Parker, Esasky. HR—Doran (1), Bailey (1), Walling (2), Parker (4). SB—Puhl. SF—Calhoun. T—2:58. A—15,749.

Tibbs gave up five runs on seven hits (in five innings), but two of the runs were unearned. The Astros got two runs off Hume and three off Carl Willis, who has been struggling lately.

You just don't picture Houston as a power team. In their first 28 games, they hit 12 home runs. Today, Bill Doran, Mark Bailey and Denny Walling hit the ball out (as the Astros romped, 10-5).

Tony Perez, who had two hits and drove in two runs as my first baseman, said Houston looked like the Boston Red Sox today.

Still, we just didn't play very well.

We scored first and even after they went up 3-2, we came back to tie when Doggie (Perez) singled home Tibbs from second base in the fourth.

Joe Morgan, my old teammate and buddy, does commentary on our television network and talks to me when he's in town to do the games.

I have to agree with one thing he feels is very important. When you're in a tight game and you score to either tie or go ahead, the next half inning is very important.

He says it could be the most important inning in the whole game and I'm not going to argue with him.

That's when you have to shut the other guy down. You can't afford to let him get up off the deck. If you do, the momentum and confidence swings and more times than not, you're in trouble.

That's what happened today.

We tie in the fourth inning, but Houston came right back to go up by two runs and they had the momentum.

Maybe Tibbs was tired because he was running the bases. I'm not sure, but I do know that's when you have to keep the opponent from getting the upper hand.

★   ★   ★

Interest is beginning to increase in the Cobb record even though I need 73 hits to break it.

Jim Ferguson has received requests from Newsweek, Time, Inside Sports and ESPN during this homestand. They all want to spend time with me. The 10- or 15-minute interview is not enough. They want several hours, and a lot of them want to come to my home.

If I can work them in my schedule, I do it. They're helping me in the long run. I turned down Inside Sports for some personal reasons, but I'm going to do the others.

Newsweek and Time are going to take pictures for possible use on their covers.

Lou Palmer, a good friend at ESPN, wants to come to my home and spend two hours taping a documentary of sorts. They'll use it when I get close to the record. I told him to come on Monday, June 24, because we're off that day.

Earlier today, before the game, photographer Stan Denny came here to take a picture you'll see on the cover of this book.

It's always hectic at home, especially when you're only here for six days, then hit the road again.

'Good Morning America' host David Hartman suited up and impressed Rose with his hitting ability.

MONDAY, MAY 13......................... ROSE 2 FOR 4

This was a long day, but I never care about the hours when the results are satisfying.

I was out of the house early to meet David Hartman and his crew of ABC-TV's "Good Morning America" at the stadium.

I never mind spending time with David because he has been very good to me over the years. And there aren't many guys on TV as enthusiastic about what they do as he is.

David spent some time with us in spring training and while the crew was in Tampa, Fred Farrar, the producer, suggested it would be interesting if—after the season opened—David came to Cincinnati and I gave him some hitting tips.

David suited up. We got him uniform No. 85 with his name on the back.

Phila'phia	ab	r	h	rbi	Cincinnati	ab	r	h	rbi
Samuel, 2b	4	0	1	1	Milner, cf	3	1	1	0
Stone, lf	4	0	0	0	**Rose, 1b**	4	1	2	0
Schmidt, 3b	4	1	1	1	Franco, p	0	0	0	0
Hayes, cf	3	1	1	0	Power, p	0	0	0	0
Corcoran, 1b	3	0	1	1	Parker, rf	4	0	1	2
Wilson, rf	4	0	0	0	Cedeno, lf	4	0	0	0
Daulton, c	3	1	1	0	Esasky, 3b	4	0	0	0
Aguayo, ss	3	0	1	0	C'cepcion, ss	3	2	1	0
G. Gross, ph	1	0	0	0	Oester, 2b	3	1	1	0
Denny, p	2	0	0	0	Van Gorder, c	4	1	2	1
Rucker, p	0	0	0	0	Stuper, p	1	0	0	0
Russell, ph	0	0	0	0	Kr'chicki, ph	0	0	0	0
Andersen, p	0	0	0	0	Perez, ph-1b	2	1	1	4
Totals	31	3	6	3	Totals	32	7	9	7

Philadelphia ....0 0 1   2 0 0   0 0 0—3
Cincinnati..........................2 0 0   1 0 4   0 0 x—7

Philadelphia	IP.	H.	R.	ER.	BB.	SO.
Denny (L. 1-4)	5*	8	6	6	3	0
Rucker	1	1	1	1	0	0
Andersen.....................	2	0	0	0	0	1

Cincinnati	IP.	H.	R.	ER.	BB.	SO.
Stuper (W. 4-2)	6	6	3	3	1	1
Franco.........................	1	0	0	0	1	1
Power..........................	2	0	0	0	2	0

*Pitched to three batters in sixth.

Game-winning RBI—Perez.
E—None. DP—Cincinnati 2. LOB—Philadelphia 5, Cincinnati 5. 2B—Daulton, Hayes, Samuel. 3B—Parker, **Rose**. HR—Schmidt (3), Perez (1). SH—Stuper. T—1:58. A—12,068.

I did an instructional book on hitting, so we used some of the examples from that. Jim Kaat threw some "heat" to David and he did pretty well.

"When I was a kid," David said later, "my dad told me to very carefully watch people who do whatever they do well. It was one of those lessons that has stuck with me—and I mean in my immediate consciousness all my life. And it's been one of those great pleasures, if you will, on a moment-to-moment basis just to watch anybody do anything well, whether it's watching somebody flying a jet bomber or a man on the docks cleaning fish.

"I feel that way about Pete. Watching him in a ball game is like watching a surgeon. I have felt like that about him since I became aware of him in the middle '60s. It was like he's not playing with a baseball bat. It's like he's playing with a lacrosse stick, catches the ball and says, 'I think I'll put it there or hit it over there, a gapper to right-center.'

"Somehow, everything turns to slow motion in a funny way when he goes after the ball. That's aside from the enthusiasm, that spirit, that fire.

"When we were together today, all of that focused or crystalized in those three minutes we did the segment. He was saying, 'If the pitch is here, put your hands here. If the pitch is there, put your hands here.' In rapid-fire order, he instructed me. It was just really fun being with somebody who does something better than anybody. It's an unusual kind of opportunity I have from time to time. It's very exciting."

Thanks, David, but you've got to work on that swing a little before we put you in the lineup.

Seriously, he's a good athlete and probably could've made it to the majors had he not decided to give up baseball after college.

★   ★   ★

I said in spring training that if I needed a younger first baseman, I would use Tony Perez—he turns 43 tomorrow. I'm 44.

Doggie, as we all call him, gave us a big lift as we beat the Phillies tonight, 7-3.

With the score tied 3-3 in the sixth inning, I sent Doggie up to bat for Wayne Krenchicki with the bases loaded. He'd only had nine at-bats, but Doggie's a good clutch man. He likes for the game to be on the line when he's up there.

John Felske (Phillies manager) had just brought Dave Rucker in and Perez hit the ball over the left-field fence.

Doggie became the oldest player ever to hit a grand slam. Cap Anson was 42 years, 3 months old when he hit one in 1894. It was Tony's sixth career slam, but it was the first pinch-hit slam by a Cincinnati player since Hal King's in 1973. I remember that one.

I had my first triple of the year tonight and a single to leave me 71 hits short of topping Cobb.

TUESDAY, MAY 14......................... ROSE 0 FOR 4

Today, we had another one of those 12:35 business day specials at Riverfront. We haven't won one yet (in three attempts, with the Phillies winning this game, 7-1).

When I was with Philadelphia, I liked a young pitcher we had by the name of Charles Hudson. We used to call him Charlie when he first came up in '83, but when his mother read some of the stories about him, she told everybody his name is Charles.

He always reminded me of Fergie Jenkins the way he pitches. He even looks a little bit like Fergie.

I'll tell you one thing, Charles can pitch.

We were playing the Astros one night (July 20) in '83 and he had a no-hitter until Craig Reynolds got a bloop single to center with one out in the ninth inning.

And in our playoffs that year, he beat the Dodgers, 7-2, in the third game. He gave 'em just four hits and went nine.

When the Phillies and I parted company after that season, I tried to sell him my condo in New Jersey, but we couldn't work out the details.

I mention all this because today Charles Hudson did a number on our batters.

Phila'phia	ab	r	h	rbi	Cincinnati	ab	r	h	rbi
Samuel, 2b	5	1	2	5	Milner, cf	4	1	1	0
Hayes, lf	5	0	2	1	Rose, 1b	4	0	0	0
Schmidt, 3b	4	1	1	1	Parker, rf	4	0	2	0
W'k'fuss, 1b	3	0	1	0	Cedeno, lf	3	0	0	1
Corcoran, 1b	2	0	0	0	Esasky, 3b	3	0	0	0
Wilson, rf	3	0	0	0	C'cepcion, ss	3	0	0	0
Virgil, c	4	0	2	0	Oester, 2b	2	0	0	0
Maddox, cf	3	2	1	0	Van Gorder, c	2	0	0	0
Aguayo, ss	3	2	1	0	Kr'chicki, ph	1	0	0	0
Hudson, p	2	0	0	0	Bilardello, c	0	0	0	0
Stone, ph	1	1	0	0	Browning, p	1	0	0	0
Carman, p	0	0	0	0	Walker, ph	1	0	0	0
					Willis, p	0	0	0	0
					Pastore, p	0	0	0	0
Totals	35	7	10	7	Totals	28	1	3	1

Philadelphia............0 0 0   0 3 1   0 0 3—7
Cincinnati.............0 0 0   0 0 0   0 0 1—1

Philadelphia	IP.	H.	R.	ER.	BB.	SO.
Hudson (W. 1-2)	8	1	0	0	3	7
Carman	1	2	1	1	0	2
Cincinnati	IP.	H.	R.	ER.	BB.	SO.
Browning (L. 3-2)	8	7	4	4	2	5
Willis	0*	1	3	3	2	0
Pastore	1	2	0	0	0	0

*Pitched to three batters in ninth.

Game-winning RBI—Samuel.
E—None. DP—Philadelphia 1, Cincinnati 1. LOB—Philadelphia 6, Cincinnati 4. 2B—Parker. HR—Samuel (2), Schmidt (4). SH—Hudson. SF—Cedeno. T—2:19. A—10,079.

For some reason, he's had trouble getting going over there. John Felske used him in relief until today, but Charles made his first start and through eight innings allowed just one hit.

And Sammy (Juan Samuel, Philadelphia's second baseman) drove in five runs. The Phillies have been having a lot of problems, but they didn't show it today.

I didn't get any hits in four at-bats, so I need 71 now to break the Cobb record. But I wasn't the only guy on my team not hitting (the Reds managed only three hits overall, two by Dave Parker).

My old buddy Herbie, Mike Schmidt, hit his fourth homer for the Phillies. He's been in a slump, but his mom and dad always drive over from their home in Dayton when he plays here, so I know he made them happy.

Neither team had scored when Sammy hit a homer with two guys on in the fifth inning. Our Tom Browning had pitched well until then and settled down after that. I took him out after the eighth for a pinch-hitter and in the ninth they got three runs off Carl Willis. Willis pitched to three batters and didn't get anybody out before I brought in Frank Pastore.

I was a little surprised Felske took Hudson out for a pinch-hitter after the eighth. Charles wasn't very happy, either. He was shooting for a complete-game shutout.

We got our only run in the ninth off Don Carman when Cesar Cedeno's sacrifice fly brought home Eddie Milner.

We left after the game for Montreal, where we're supposed to play two.

Ron Robinson was summoned from Denver to help the Reds in middle relief.

WEDNESDAY, MAY 15 .... ROSE 2 FOR 4

This is my first time back to Montreal since I returned to the Reds last August.

Actually, the last time I was here was on August 12, 1984, because that was the Sunday night I had the long talk with Mr. Howsam.

We (the Expos) left the next day on a road trip to San Francisco and I never returned. I went right from Frisco to Cincinnati and that big press conference (at which Rose was introduced as the Reds' new manager).

There's nothing special for me coming back here. I really wasn't with the Expos that long. I couldn't think too much about it because we had to make some important roster changes during the past 24 hours.

Cincinnati	ab	r	h	rbi	Montreal	ab	r	h	rbi
Milner, cf	4	1	1	1	Raines, lf	4	0	0	0
Rose, 1b	4	0	2	0	Law, 2b	4	0	0	0
Davis, lf	0	0	0	0	Dawson, cf	4	0	1	0
Parker, rf	4	0	1	1	Wallach, 3b	4	0	0	0
C'deno, lf-1b	3	0	0	0	Driessen, 1b	4	1	1	0
Kr'chicki, 3b	3	0	0	0	Wohlford, rf	2	0	0	0
C'cepcion, ss	4	0	0	0	Wash'gton, ss	3	0	1	1
Oester, 2b	4	1	2	0	Fitzgerald, c	2	0	0	0
Van Gorder, c	4	0	1	0	Smith, p	2	0	0	0
Price, p	3	0	0	0	Dilone, ph	1	0	0	0
Walker, ph	1	0	0	0	Roberge, p	0	0	0	0
Power, p	0	0	0	0					
Totals	34	2	7	2	Totals	30	1	3	1

Cincinnati				0 0 0	0 2 0	0 0 0—2
Montreal				0 1 0	0 0 0	0 0 0—1

Cincinnati	IP.	H.	R.	ER.	BB.	SO.
Price (W. 1-0)	8	3	1	1	2	8
Power (Save 6)	1	0	0	0	0	0

Montreal	IP.	H.	R.	ER.	BB.	SO.
Smith (L. 5-1)	8	6	2	2	2	6
Roberge	1	1	0	0	0	1

Game-winning RBI—Parker.
E—None. LOB—Cincinnati 7, Montreal 4. 2B—Washington, Dawson, Oester 2. T—2:10. A—23,198.

I've been talking about our catching problem since spring training. Dave Van Gorder is hitting .217 and Dann Bilardello only .125.

We sent Bilardello and Carl Willis, a middle reliever, to Denver and called up Alan Knicely and Ron Robinson, who had been pitching pretty good down there.

It's never easy to send guys back to the minors, but it's part of my job and I try to do it the best I know how. I told both Bilardello and Willis to go to Denver and work so hard I'd be forced to bring them back up.

It was hard for me to believe, but Knicely was used as the designated hitter at Wichita last year and that really hurt him. If he had caught like he was supposed to instead of just being the DH, he probably would have been my opening-day catcher.

Knice was the Minor League Player of the Year last year. We have a lot of hope for him.

At Denver, he was batting .446 with seven homers and 29 RBIs.

He's going to do a lot of catching for me. You don't bring a guy up hitting .446 and sit him. I think we're better with Knice catching and Van Gorder in the dugout ready to come in for defense in the eighth and ninth.

Our minor league reports indicate Knicely has made a lot of progress in his catching. One thing he'll do is work hard. That day I told him he was going back in spring training, he wasn't ticked off or anything like that. He said he was going to go to Denver and bust his butt and that's what he has done.

He's not Gary Carter yet, but who is?

I was happy the way Van Gorder took the news today. He agreed with me that if we can win more games with Knice catching, go for it. I gave him (Van Gorder) a month back there, the best chance he's ever had. He had 12 RBIs in 69 at-bats, and that's not too bad.

Robinson should help us in middle relief. He took it pretty hard when I sent him down in spring training. He'd been called up in mid-August (of 1984) and expected to make the club this spring.

He's a righthander who made six starts for Denver. He won two games (lost one) and his earned-run average was 2.72.

★　　　★　　　★

There was a good crowd (23,198) at Olympic Stadium for a night game in May and they gave me a nice ovation.

I had two singles and one was in the fifth inning when we scored two runs to go ahead. And that's how the game ended (2-1, Cincinnati).

I started Joe Price at the last minute because Mario Soto has had some tenderness in his right elbow. It was Joe's first start of the year and he gave me eight strong innings. I took him out for a pinch-hitter in the ninth and Teddy Power got his sixth save.

THURSDAY, MAY 16 .... ROSE 1 FOR 3

It's still early, but as I wrote earlier, I'm going to be surprised if Montreal doesn't have a good year. I think they're going to be a team to reckon with in the Eastern Division.

When I came back here yesterday, I didn't have any special vengeance or anything like that. I was hurt last year and things didn't go that well for me, but I don't think about it.

I don't look around and say to myself, "Boy, am I glad I'm not still here." No, nothing like that. I just come back here to play the game.

I think the Expos are playing with the type of attitude I thought they would play with last year. It's an all-around different attitude, and it's good.

That's why they are doing so well. I think they got rid of the people on the team who were negative. Plus, they changed managers and brought in Buck Rodgers. They also made some other changes. All this can do nothing but help them.

I don't think they have changed the fans yet, though. They're still very quiet. They're getting more and more knowledgeable, but not that much knowledgeable right now.

They really don't understand the game. They're getting better, but they still don't know the little intricacies of baseball like they should. The game just hasn't been here on the major league level long enough.

They seem to just sit back and wait for something to happen, then they get excited, but they don't anticipate things as the game goes along.

Cincinnati	ab	r	h	rbi	Montreal	ab	r	h	rbi
Milner, cf	4	1	1	0	Raines, lf	2	1	1	0
Rose, 1b	3	0	1	0	Wash'gton, ss	2	1	1	1
Davis, pr-lf	0	1	0	0	Dawson, rf	4	0	1	0
Parker, rf	3	1	1	2	Driessen, 1b	4	0	1	1
C'deno, lf-1b	4	0	1	0	Wallach, 3b	4	0	1	0
Esasky, 3b	4	0	0	0	Law, 2b	3	0	0	0
Oester, 2b	4	1	2	0	W'n'gham, cf	3	0	1	0
Foley, ss	4	0	2	1	Fitzgerald, c	4	0	0	0
Van Gorder, c	4	0	0	0	Dilone, ph	1	0	0	0
Tibbs, p	3	0	0	0	Roberge, p	0	0	0	0
Hume, p	1	0	0	0	Francona, ph	1	0	0	0
Totals	34	4	8	3	Totals	30	2	6	2

Cincinnati .... 0 0 0 2 0 0 1 1 0—4
Montreal .... 0 0 2 0 0 0 0 0 0—2

Cincinnati	IP.	H.	R.	ER.	BB.	SO.
Tibbs (W. 3-5)	6⅔	6	2	2	6	2
Hume (Save 1)	2⅓	0	0	0	0	2

Montreal	IP.	H.	R.	ER.	BB.	SO.
Gullickson (L. 4-4)	7	8	3	3	1	3
Roberge	2	0	1	0	1	1

Game-winning RBI—Foley.
E—Wallach. DP—Cincinnati 3, Montreal 2. LOB—Cincinnati 5, Montreal 7. 3B—Foley, Raines. HR—Parker (5). SB—Washington, Milner, **Rose**, Davis. T—2:09. A—18,128.

I really didn't notice that too much until I played here last year. It will take some time, but it will come.

We came from behind for the second night in a row and won, 4-2.

I was happy for Jay Tibbs. He pitched a good game and got his third win. He got in a little trouble in the seventh inning, but Tom Hume came in and shut them down and got his first save.

I got one hit, but it was a big game for Tom Foley. I started him at shortstop in the place of Davey Concepcion, who has not been swinging too good.

Before tonight, Foley had no RBIs, no extra-base hits and a .071 batting average.

He gave us some fire tonight. He had two hits, including a triple (which netted the game-winning RBI) in the seventh inning when we took a 3-2 lead.

Dave Parker is swinging a good bat. He hit his fifth homer in the fourth off Bill Gullickson after Eddie Milner had singled.

We've won two in a row and now go to Pittsburgh.

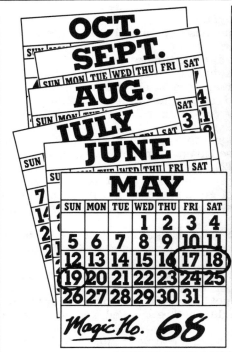

Magic No. 68

A May 17 rain delay didn't stop John Stuper from earning his fifth victory.

FRIDAY, MAY 17 .... ROSE 2 FOR 3

This three-game series is important.

Every one of the 162 games you play is important. We swept Montreal, which is a pretty good team. Now, we're in Pittsburgh and the Pirates are having a tough time of it. There's always a tendency to slack off some when you do well against a tough team, then play a weaker one.

My father drilled into my head the key to success in anything is consistency. When I was named Player of the Decade for the 1970s (by The Sporting News), the reason I got that award was because I was consistent. If you check my stats, they're fairly even. There weren't many highs and lows. That's consistency.

So, to prove we are a consistently good team we must do well against the Pirates.

I know (Pirates Manager) Chuck Tanner is having a tough time of

Cincinnati	ab	r	h	rbi	Pittsburgh	ab	r	h	rbi
Milner, cf	4	0	0	0	Wynne, cf	4	0	0	0
Rose, 1b	3	2	2	0	Ray, 2b	4	0	2	1
Cedeno, 1b	1	0	0	0	Madlock, 3b	3	0	0	0
Parker, rf	5	2	3	2	Th'mpson, 1b	2	1	0	0
Knicely, c	5	2	2	2	Hendrick, rf	3	0	0	0
Power, p	0	0	0	0	Pena, c	4	0	0	0
Walker, lf	1	0	0	0	Kemp, lf	3	1	0	0
Davis, ph-lf	2	0	0	0	Almon, ss	4	1	3	1
Esasky, 3b	3	0	0	1	DeLeon, p	1	0	0	0
Oester, 2b	3	0	1	0	Foli, ph	1	0	1	0
Foley, ss	4	0	0	0	Scurry, p	0	0	0	0
Stuper, p	3	0	0	1	Guante, p	0	0	0	0
Franco, p	0	0	0	0	Mazzilli, ph	1	0	1	1
V. Gorder, c	0	0	0	0	Holland, p	0	0	0	0
Totals	34	6	8	6	Totals	30	3	7	3

Cincinnati	0	0	0	1	3	0	2	0	0—6
Pittsburgh	0	0	0	0	0	1	2	0	0—3

Cincinnati	IP.	H.	R.	ER.	BB.	SO.
Stuper (W. 5-2)	6⅔	5	3	3	4	2
Franco	⅔	2	0	0	1	1
Power (Save 7)	1⅔	0	0	0	0	1

Pittsburgh	IP.	H.	R.	ER.	BB.	SO.
DeLeon (L. 0-6)	6	5	4	3	6	8
Scurry	⅓	2	2	2	1	1
Guante	⅔	1	0	0	0	0
Holland	2	0	0	0	1	1

Game-winning RBI—Stuper.
E—Ray, Hendrick, Parker. DP—Cincinnati 3, Pittsburgh 1. LOB—Cincinnati 10, Pittsburgh 5. 2B—Parker, **Rose**, Knicely. HR—Parker (6). SB—Milner. SF—Esasky. WP—Franco. T—2:53. A—7,239.

it. They've lost seven of their last nine games and the trades they made since last year just aren't working yet.

But we're not looking down our noses at them because the Pirates still have an excellent pitching staff.

It was a dreary night. It was rainy and foggy and I'll tell you, with the weather the way it was it was difficult to get up for the game. But that kind of attitude separates winners from losers. There are going to be days when it's too cold, too hot, too rainy or too something. You can't let the elements bother you because if you do, the other guy might be playing over them and beat you.

We made the most of our opportunities and beat them, 6-3. By the time the game finally ended, Three Rivers Stadium was almost empty. (The paid attendance was only 7,329.)

The start was held up 2 hours, 15 minutes because of the rain. I thought they would probably just go ahead and call it off, but there haven't been any rainouts in the majors yet, so I think they were willing to wait forever.

The delay didn't bother John Stuper. He gave up just one hit in the first five innings and pitched almost as well as he did in San Francisco three weeks ago.

He got tired in the seventh when they scored two runs, so I brought in John Franco, my lefthanded reliever. He gave up a single to Lee Mazzilli that drove in their second run, but got Marvell Wynne on a fly for the last out. Franco got one out in the eighth before I called Teddy Power to finish it.

I got a single and double and scored a couple of runs. I feel like I'm swinging the bat real good now.

I gave Alan Knicely his first start behind the plate and he hit a two-run double, had a single and scored twice. He caught a good game, too. I think he's going to be the answer to our catching problem.

The Cobra, Dave Parker, continued on his hot streak. He hit a two-run homer and had three hits.

SATURDAY, MAY 18 .... ROSE 2 FOR 4

I've been concerned about Cesar Cedeno.

Today, he came into my office. We aired out his problems and I feel a lot better.

When I came back here last August, I talked about Cesar's talent and how much he can help the ball club. He seemed to come to life last September and has had some good games this spring.

But several days ago when he came into the clubhouse, he was very quiet. That's not Cesar Cedeno. Plus, he hadn't been swinging the bat very good.

I called him in after the game—he and I were the last ones in the club-

Cincinnati	ab	r	h	rbi	Pittsburgh	ab	r	h	rbi
Milner, cf	4	2	1	0	Almon, ss	3	0	0	0
Rose, 1b	4	1	2	2	Morrison, 2b	4	0	1	0
Foley, 2b	0	0	0	0	Madlock, 3b	4	0	0	0
Parker, rf	3	2	3	1	Hendrick, rf	4	0	1	0
Knicely, c	4	0	2	2	Th'mpson, 1b	4	0	1	0
Redus, lf	3	1	1	0	Pena, c	3	0	0	0
C'cepcion, ss	5	0	0	0	Lezcano, lf	3	0	0	0
Esasky, 3b	4	1	1	0	Wynne, cf	3	0	2	0
Oester, 2b	4	1	1	0	Bielecki, p	1	0	0	0
Cedeno, 1b	1	0	1	2	Foli, ph	0	0	0	0
Browning, p	3	0	0	0	Guante, p	0	0	0	0
					Belliard, ph	1	0	0	0
					Robinson, p	0	0	0	0
Totals	35	8	12	7	Totals	30	0	5	0

Cincinnati			0 0 1	3 0 1	0 1 2—8
Pittsburgh			0 0 0	0 0 0	0 0 0—0

Cincinnati	IP.	H.	R.	ER.	BB.	SO.
Browning (W. 4-2)	9	5	0	0	2	5

Pittsburgh	IP.	H.	R.	ER.	BB.	SO.
Bielecki (L. 1-3)	6	8	5	5	5	4
Guante	2	2	1	1	2	1
Robinson	1	2	2	2	2	0

Game-winning RBI—Knicely.
E—None. DP—Cincinnati 1, Pittsburgh 1. LOB—Cincinnati 11, Pittsburgh 5. 2B—Parker, **Rose**, Cedeno. HR—Parker (7). SH—Browning 2. WP—Guante.
T—2:28. A—9,708.

house.

I said, "Ceeze, what's going on? There's something wrong with you. You can tell me it's none of my business, but there's something going on. I can tell because your personality isn't the same; you're not acting like Cesar Cedeno. If you want me to shut up, I will. You're a friend of mine and I like you. You can help my team, but you can't help my team if you're not Cesar Cedeno. Right now, you're not playing like Cesar Cedeno."

He said, "Yeah, I've got some things on my mind."

He stumbled around. He thanked me and said no one had ever done that with him before.

I said, "Well, I just feel you're a big part of the Cincinnati Reds and, if nothing else, I want you to feel good when you go out of here."

We left the stadium and he didn't say anything else.

When he came in today, he said, "Skip, I really appreciate your calling me in the other day. No one has ever taken time like that with me, but I really lied to you."

I said, "What's the matter?"

He said, "I do have a problem and it's been bothering me quite a lot."

He told me what the problem was—I don't want to go into details here—and we went over two or three different ways of coping with it. After that conversation, he started being himself a little more.

He's not getting to play very much, but he says he's not bitter.

He said, "Hey, Skip, the other guy (Gary Redus) is doing a good job in front of me. Don't forget, I'm in the dugout over there and if you need me to do anything, I am there."

Being the manager, you not only have to take care of yourself, but also 24 other guys. It's not the most pleasant thing, but I can handle it. I don't mind.

I told the guys they aren't going to do anything on or off the field I haven't been through myself.

I said, "I'm going to try to help you solve your problems just by knowing the right way to do it."

I think being player-manager allows me to see things like Cedeno being quiet because I know him.

If I just know him like, "Hey, how you doin', Cesar? Good morning" —it's not enough.

★   ★   ★

I had a double, single and drove in two runs today as we beat the Pirates, 8-0, for our fourth straight win. It was my second straight two-hit game.

Chuck Tanner's a good manager, but he's got some problems with that Pittsburgh team. Only 9,000-plus came out for tonight's game—on a Saturday night. And there were only 7,000-plus here last night.

Tom Browning got his first big-league shutout, giving the Pirates only five hits. He's really coming. Alan Knicely drove in two runs with two singles and Dave Parker hit his seventh homer.

SUNDAY, MAY 19 .... ROSE 0 FOR 3

After getting two hits each of the last two days, I went 0 for 3 today.

That doesn't bother me too much because I swung the bat good and we beat Pittsburgh, 7-1.

We swept them in their ball park and Mario Soto won his sixth game. Like I was saying, the Pirates have some problems. They've lost 10 times in their last 12 games and their 10-24 record is the worst in the National League.

They've had a lot of distractions. There's the drug thing (an ongoing investigation in the major leagues, with Pittsburgh reportedly being a focal point) that all the reporters want to talk about, and the team's for sale. There's even some talk it might be moved out of Pittsburgh after it's sold.

That would be a shame.

I have a lot of respect for John and Dan Galbreath, who own the Pirates. When I was a free agent in 1978, I visited their Darby Dan Farm (thoroughbred racehorse stable) in Columbus, Ohio. One of the things they offered me as part of the deal was the service of some of their top stallions.

That could have been the best offer I got before I signed with the Phillies, but what bothered me about that was I would've had to wait so long to see how good the thoroughbreds would become.

Anyway, it's a shame this franchise is having problems because over the years it has been a great one. But to see the stadium almost empty Friday and Saturday nights, then only about 12,000 here today, it's depressing.

But we're winning.

Davey Concepcion hit a homer, his third, in the fourth inning after Nick Esasky singled. That gave us a 4-0 lead and we added three more in the ninth off reliever John Candelaria.

Davey also had a single. His homer ended a 0-for-13 slump, and it came just in time (Concepcion was hitting .240 entering the game).

After the game, he said he has been so down he'd even considered quitting. I don't believe that, but Davey is such a competitor it bothers him when he's not contributing. And don't forget, he's our captain.

He told some of the reporters that he woke up this morning staring at the ceiling in his hotel room.

"I was thinking about quitting," he said. "I almost hung my glove up, I was feeling so down. I wasn't used to it. I didn't want it. I decided to go to the ball park, to put the uniform back on. I know I can still play and I proved that to myself today."

That's Davey. When he gets down, he gets real down.

But like all of us, there's nothing like a couple of base knocks to forget about all that.

Davey's got 2,000 hits (through today, actually 2,007 career hits in the majors), so he's been doing something right all these years. And they don't give all those Gold Gloves (five) to guys who can't pick it.

It's off to Chicago and three day games in Wrigley. We'll have to sleep fast tonight.

Cincinnati	ab	r	h	rbi	Pittsburgh	ab	r	h	rbi
Milner, cf	4	0	0	0	Wynne, cf	4	0	0	0
Rose, 1b	3	0	0	0	Ray, 2b	4	0	1	0
Davis, lf	1	1	1	2	Madlock, 3b	4	0	0	0
Parker, rf	3	0	1	1	Th'mpson, 1b	4	0	0	0
Knicely, c	5	0	0	0	Hendrick, rf	4	1	3	0
C'deno, lf-1b	4	0	0	0	Kemp, lf	3	0	1	0
Esasky, 3b	3	1	1	0	Foli, ss	4	0	1	0
C'cepcion, ss	4	2	2	2	Ortiz, c	3	0	0	0
Foley, 2b	4	2	3	0	Mazzilli, ph	0	0	0	1
Soto, p	4	1	2	2	Tunnell, p	1	0	0	0
					Frobel, ph	0	0	0	0
					Guante, p	0	0	0	0
					Orsulak, ph	1	0	0	0
					Candelaria, p	0	0	0	0
					Morrison, ph	1	0	0	0
Totals	35	7	10	7	Totals	33	1	6	1

Cincinnati .... 0 0 2 2 0 0 0 0 3—7
Pittsburgh .... 0 0 0 0 0 0 0 0 1—1

Cincinnati	IP.	H.	R.	ER.	BB.	SO.
Soto (W. 6-3)	9	6	1	1	3	6

Pittsburgh	IP.	H.	R.	ER.	BB.	SO.
Tunnell (L. 0-5)	5	6	4	4	3	3
Guante..........................	3	1	0	0	2	3
Candelaria	1	3	3	3	0	1

Game-winning RBI—Soto.
E—None. LOB—Cincinnati 6, Pittsburgh 8. 2B—Foley. 3B—Soto. HR—Concepcion (3), Davis (5). SB—Milner, Ray. T—2:20. A—11,990.

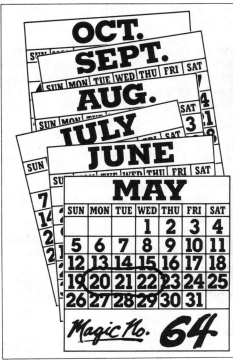

Rose has a lot of respect for Cubs G.M. Dallas Green, his manager in Philadelphia.

MONDAY, MAY 20..................... ROSE 1 FOR 4

I always like to come to Chicago, although playing three day games in Wrigley Field messes up my normal schedule. I can see where it's difficult for the Cubs, playing all their home games in Wrigley in the daytime.

I have a lot of friends on the Cubs. Larry Bowa, Keith Moreland, Warren Brusstar and Dick Ruthven all were with the Phillies when we won the World Series in 1980. (And Chicago's Gary Matthews and Bobby Dernier were teammates of Rose on the 1983 National League champion Phils.)

Gary Matthews was always a take-charge guy with the Phillies. He was a leader in his own way. A few years ago, I decided he should be named Sarge. I went out one day and had a lot of T-shirts printed up with Sarge on them and passed them out in the clubhouse.

The nickname stuck, just like Herbie for Mike Schmidt and Pee Wee for Bowa. You look at a guy and you just know what he should be called.

Vuk—John Vukovich—has been a friend for a long time. He's now

Cincinnati	ab	r	h	rbi	Chicago	ab	r	h	rbi
Milner, cf	4	0	0	0	Dernier, cf	4	2	2	0
Rose, 1b	4	1	1	1	Sandberg, 2b	4	2	1	0
Parker, rf	3	0	1	0	Lopes, 3b	3	1	2	2
Knicely, c	3	0	0	0	Moreland, rf	3	0	1	1
E. Davis, lf	4	0	1	0	Hebner, 1b	3	1	0	0
Esasky, 3b	4	0	1	0	Dayett, lf	4	0	1	0
C'cepcion, ss	3	0	0	0	Lake, c	4	0	1	2
Foley, 2b	3	0	0	0	Bowa, ss	3	0	1	0
Robinson, p	0	0	0	0	Sanderson, p	2	0	0	0
Tibbs, p	2	0	0	0					
Hume, p	0	0	0	0					
Kr'chicki, 2b	1	0	1	0					
Totals	31	1	5	1	Totals	30	6	9	5

Cincinnati ....0 0 0 1 0 0 0 0 0—1
Chicago ....1 0 2 0 0 3 0 0 x—6

Cincinnati	IP.	H.	R.	ER.	BB.	SO.
Tibbs (L. 3-6)	5⅓	8	6	6	1	1
Hume	⅔	0	0	0	0	2
Robinson	2	1	0	0	0	4

Chicago	IP.	H.	R.	ER.	BB.	SO.
Sanderson (W. 3-1) ...	9	5	1	1	2	5

Game-winning RBI—Lopes.
E—Rose. DP—Cincinnati 1, Chicago 1. LOB—Cincinnati 5, Chicago 4. 2B—Dernier. HR—**Rose** (1). SB—Dernier, Sandberg, Lopes. SH—Sanderson. SF—Lopes, Moreland. T—2:22. A—21,231.

named Sarge. I went out one day and had a lot of T-shirts printed up with Sarge on them and passed them out in the clubhouse.

The nickname stuck, just like Herbie for Mike Schmidt and Pee Wee for Bowa. You look at a guy and you just know what he should be called.

Vuk—John Vukovich—has been a friend for a long time. He's now first-base coach with the Cubs. He played for the Reds for a while and also was with the Phillies.

And, of course, there's Dallas Green.

Dal and I go way back. He was our manager in 1980 (at Philadelphia) and did a super job. I've always felt he should have gotten Manager of the Year then (The Sporting News honored Houston's Bill Virdon instead). He did as much pulling that team together as anybody. Had he not handled some of the guys the way he did, I'm not sure we would've won it.

Now, he has come over here to Chicago (Green is president and general manager of the Cubs) and put together a championship outfit. Nobody expected them to win last year (the Cubs ruled the N.L. East), but they played well and fooled some people. Dallas Green made some clever deals, getting Rick Sutcliffe (in June 1984) and trading with the Phillies for the Sarge and Bobby D just before the season opened last year. You've got to give Dallas a lot of credit.

I always like to tease him.

A lot of people don't know it, but I got the only grand slam of my career off Dal when he was pitching for the Phillies on July 18, 1964. It was at Crosley Field and we beat them, 14-4.

Speaking of home runs, I got one today, but it didn't mean much because we lost to the Cubs, 6-1, and our five-game winning streak ended.

Jay Tibbs got roughed up and I made an error.

That home run was my first since September 18, 1982.

We just couldn't do too much with Scott Sanderson today. We got only five hits.

The home run was the 2,107th run of my career and let me tie Henry Aaron for the all-time National League lead in runs scored.

I wasn't trying to hit a home run. I just went up there trying to hit the ball hard. It sure didn't make much difference because it was just one run.

People have always asked me why I never hit more home runs—I've got 159 for my whole career and 151 of them have come with the Reds. I've had only nine homers since 1978.

I always felt I was strong enough to hit 'em, but if I had gone for home runs, I wouldn't have gotten all the singles and doubles I have. I would have been swinging for the fences instead of placing the ball.

I became a singles-type hitter a long time ago, and that has certainly worked for me.

TUESDAY, MAY 21 .... DID NOT PLAY

Dave Parker came through again for us today. He got a tie-breaking double in the eighth inning and we scored three runs to beat the Cubs, 5-2.

There was a good lesson in this game, something my pitching coach, Jim Kaat, and I talk about all the time.

Walks can kill you. There were 12 walks and 12 hits in this game. That's the same as 24 hits.

I can't remember the statistics, but somebody came up with one that says if a batter leads off an inning with a walk, the odds are in that team's favor they're going to score.

I told my pitchers to let the Cubs hit the ball today. We gave up five walks and we got seven off them.

After Parker got his double, we got two bases-loaded walks to score two more runs.

I didn't play today because they started a lefthander, Ray Fontenot.

Doggie—Tony Perez—started in my place at first base and hit a (bases-empty) homer in the fourth inning that put us up 2-0. Doggie also got another RBI when he got one of those walks with the bases full.

★   ★   ★

Jim Ferguson, our publicity director, has figured out that I should break the Cobb record at home on August 7 against San Diego. Fergie took all my stats for the first six weeks of the season and multiplied them over the rest of the year. That's how he arrived at August 7.

In February, I picked August 26 at home against St. Louis as the date.

I was up in New York for a press conference with the Mizuno sporting goods people, the Japanese firm I represent.

They set up this big calendar for the month of September. When they asked me to circle a date for the record, I crossed out September and made it August.

To tell the truth, I did it without much thought. We're on a long road trip that starts in Los Angeles on August 8 and ends in Pittsburgh on August 22. We play a weekend series with Chicago at home (August 23-25), then the Cards come in on August 26. I just circled the 26th.

Fergie says his formula assumed I'll play in 80 percent of the games and hit .280.

Through Monday's game, which was our 37th, I've played in 32 and have 32 hits. My home run was my 4,129th hit, leaving me 63 short of breaking Cobb's record.

I've never been one to predict things like this. It's just something that'll happen and there's no pressure at all.

A hitting streak is different because you've got to get a hit every day.

WEDNESDAY, MAY 22 .... ROSE 2 FOR 4

We've been having a lot of discussions lately about our roster. We're trying to decide whether or not Eric Davis should be sent to Denver.

Eric has been having a tough time of it here and there is some sentiment he'd be better off back in the minors for a while. I don't know.

We have an outfielder, a kid named Kal Daniels, who's just sitting at Denver waiting to come up to the big leagues. But as long as Gary Redus is hitting OK, he's going to have to stay down there.

This kid (Daniels) is a tremendous left fielder. He can hit better than any outfielder I've got, except for Parker. He's going to be a leadoff hitter. He can hit; the kid can just flat out hit. (Through Sunday, Daniels was batting .336 in American Association play with five home runs and 21 runs batted in.)

We had him in spring training; he's only been in pro ball three summers.

We've got an infielder, Tommy Runnells, they're trying to sell me on. Now Wayne Krenchicki is doing a good job, but Runnells can play second, short and third. The way he's playing down at Denver, he could give my team more flexibility than, say, a Krenchicki. Krenchicki can really do a good job only at third base.

Runnells can switch hit and play three infield positions. (The latest American Association statistics show him with a .312 batting mark, two homers and 17 RBIs.)

I get a lot of help from Bob Howsam and Bill Bergesch, but these are tough decisions. When you've got good kids like this, sometimes they're better off playing every day at Denver than coming up here and sitting.

I think we're going to do something in a few days, but at this point everything's up in the air.

★　　　★　　　★

I had two singles today, but we got beat by the Cubs, 7-4. We lose two out of three to them and now go home for six games, starting Friday against St. Louis.

I'm looking forward to seeing that kid they've got, Vince Coleman. He's been stealing a lot of bases.

Today, we had a 4-2 lead in the bottom of the sixth inning, but they sent up a pinch-hitter, Brian Dayett, and he hit a home run with the bases loaded off Tom Browning.

I thought we had a chance to get out of the inning when Larry Bowa hit a grounder to third and we got the force at the plate. But Browning made a mistake to Dayett and they got four runs.

We started this trip by taking five in a row. We should get back on the winning side Friday night because I've got Mario Soto going. The Cardinals are going to start a lefthander, John Tudor, so I won't play.

It will be good to get back home and see my little boy, Tyler. And my wife, Carol, too.

Cincinnati	ab	r	h	rbi	Chicago	ab	r	h	rbi
Milner, cf	5	1	1	0	Dernier, cf	4	1	2	0
Rose, 1b	4	1	2	0	Woods, ph-cf	1	0	0	0
Parker, rf	4	1	2	0	Sandberg, 2b	3	1	1	0
Knicely, c	4	1	2	3	Lopes, lf	3	0	1	1
Redus, lf	4	0	2	0	Moreland, rf	4	0	0	0
Esasky, 3b	4	0	0	0	Cey, 3b	3	0	1	0
C'cepcion, ss	3	0	0	0	Smith, p	0	0	0	0
Foley, 2b	4	0	0	0	Davis, c	3	1	1	1
Browning, p	2	0	0	0	Durham, 1b	2	2	1	1
Hume, p	0	0	0	0	Bowa, ss	4	1	1	0
Kr'chicki, ph	1	0	1	0	Eckersley, p	2	0	0	0
Robinson, p	0	0	0	0	Dayett, ph	1	1	1	4
Walker, ph	1	0	0	0	Brusstar, p	0	0	0	0
					Speier, 3b	1	0	0	0
Totals	36	4	10	4	Totals	31	7	9	7

Cincinnati .... 0 0 1　0 0 3　0 0 0—4
Chicago .... 2 0 0　0 0 4　0 1 x—7

Cincinnati	IP.	H.	R.	ER.	BB.	SO.
Browning (L. 4-3)	5⅓	7	6	6	5	2
Hume	⅔	0	0	0	0	0
Robinson	2	2	1	1	0	2

Chicago	IP.	H.	R.	ER.	BB.	SO.
Eckerlsey (W. 5-3)	6	7	4	4	1	9
Brusstar	1	1	0	0	0	1
Smith (Save 10)	2	2	0	0	0	2

Game-winning RBI—Dayett.
E—Knicely, Bowa. DP—Cincinnati 1. LOB—Cincinnati 6, Chicago 6. 2B—Dernier, Parker. HR—Knicely (1), Dayett (1), Durham (4). SB—Lopes, Milner, Redus, Sandberg. SF—Davis. WP—Browning. T—2:33. A—27,863.

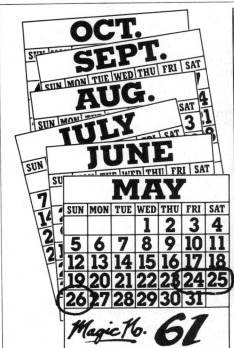

Rose thinks it's time for Gary Redus to tap his enormous potential.

FRIDAY, MAY 24 .... ROSE 0 FOR 0

We haven't been playing as well at home as we should. In fact, at times this year we've played poorly at Riverfront (while building an 8-8 home record entering tonight's game).

But tonight we faced St. Louis for the first time and won, 7-6, in 12 innings. That pushed them a game under .500 (and improved the Reds' record to 22-18).

Dave Van Gorder, who came into the game late as my catcher, singled with one out in the 12th to score Eric Davis. The game took almost four hours, but when you win one like this nobody complains about a long night.

And when I got home after midnight, I still had to feed my three horses. Nobody said it was going to be easy!

I pinch hit for the third time this year and walked (in the eighth inning).

When we got our scouting report from Jimmy Stewart, he said the whole thing about beating the Cardinals is to keep those rabbits—Vince Coleman and Willie McGee—off the bases. They're what's making this Cardinals team go. They're getting on, and Tommy Herr and Jack Clark are driving them in.

Well, Herr did drive in two runs, but both of them were on sacrifice flies. We kept Coleman off base—he was 0 for 5—and McGee got on only once, with a single, and didn't score.

★　　　★　　　★

Some of the writers covering this team say that as a manager I never like to use the bunt.

That's not entirely true. I think bunting is in order in certain situations, but I don't like to bunt early in the ball game because you've got hitters up there you think can hit. Plus, bunting seems to be a lot more difficult today on AstroTurf.

I think in a lot of cases if you start trying to bunt, you leave it up to the next guy all the time.

But if you're in a tie ball game at home in the eighth or ninth inning and you get the guy leading off on, and the next guy is a good bunter, I believe in bunting. Sure.

But I don't like to take the bat out of Dave Parker's hands—anybody hitting in the three, four or five slot.

There are certain guys who can really bunt. Like I've bunted Nick Esasky a couple of times; Nick's probably the best bunter on our team.

By the same token, when you've

St. Louis	ab	r	h	rbi	Cincinnati	ab	r	h	rbi
Coleman, lf	5	0	0	0	Redus, lf	3	0	0	0
McGee, cf	5	0	1	1	Hume, p	0	0	0	0
Herr, 2b	2	1	0	2	**Rose, ph**	0	0	0	0
Clark, 1b	6	0	0	1	Power, p	0	0	0	0
Van Slyke, rf	4	1	1	1	Walker, ph	1	0	0	0
Pendelton, 3b	3	1	0	0	Franco, p	0	0	0	0
Horton, p	1	0	0	0	C'cepcion, ss	5	1	3	1
Smith, ss	5	0	0	0	Parker, rf	6	1	1	0
Nieto, c	3	1	2	0	Knicely, c	3	0	2	1
Braun, ph	1	1	1	0	Oester, pr	0	1	0	0
Porter, c	1	0	0	0	Kr'chicki, 2b	2	0	0	0
Tudor, p	1	0	0	0	Perez, 1b	3	1	2	1
Campbell, p	0	0	0	0	Milner, pr-cf	2	1	0	0
Lahti, p	0	0	0	0	Davis, cf-lf	6	1	1	1
Dayley, p	0	0	0	0	Esasky, 3b	5	0	1	0
Allen, p	0	0	0	0	Foley, 2b	3	0	1	0
Lawless, 3b	0	0	0	0	V. G'der, ph-c	3	1	2	3
Jorgensen, ph	0	0	0	0	Soto, p	2	0	0	0
DeJ's, pr-3b	1	1	0	0	C'deno, ph-1b	3	0	1	0
Totals	38	6	5	5	Totals	47	7	14	7

St. Louis.........0 0 1 1 0 2 0 0 2 0 0 0—6
Cincinnati.......0 0 0 2 0 0 0 4 0 0 0 1—7
One out when winning run scored.

St. Louis	IP.	H.	R.	ER.	BB.	SO.
Tudor	6⅔	7	2	2	2	2
Campbell	⅔	2	3	0	0	0
Lahti	⅓	0	0	0	0	0
Dayley	0*	2	1	1	0	0
Allen	0*	0	0	0	1	0
Horton (L. 0-1)	3⅔	3	1	1	1	3

Cincinnati	IP.	H.	R.	ER.	BB.	SO.
Soto	7	3	4	4	4	4
Hume	1	0	0	0	1	1
Power	3	2	2	2	2	1
Franco (W. 1-1)	1	0	0	0	0	0

*Pitched to two batters in eighth.
Game-winning RBI—Van Gorder.
E—Knicely, Pendleton. DP—St. Louis 1. LOB—St. Louis 7, Cincinnati 12. 2B—Concepcion, Esasky, Knicely, Cedeno. HR—Perez (3), Van Slyke (4). SB—Pendleton, Herr, Van Slyke, Davis. SH—Tudor 2. SF—Herr 2, Knicely. HBP—By Allen (Concepcion). WP—Soto 2. PB—Nieto. T—3:49. A—20,665.

got guys who can steal bases like Gary Redus and Eddie Milner and they never get a bunt base hit, I just think they're not using all their ability.

I've even told them if they don't want to bunt, to at least fake a bunt once in a while. That makes the third baseman come in and gives them an advantage. (If swinging away, the batter would benefit from the drawn-in positioning of the third baseman; if actually bunting, the hitter would gain an edge because the third baseman—fearing a full swing—figures to be backpedaling, even if only slightly.)

It's amazing to me to watch Redus lead off a game, like tonight's, and see where the infielders play him. They're way in and he doesn't ever try to bunt.

Redus—he was 0 for 3 tonight—can't bunt; he never bunts. I just think in his case if he gets on, he can be all the way to third two pitches from now.

I just hate to see Redus and Milner keep hitting fly balls and popups. It doesn't make sense, and I've talked to them a lot.

What happened to Redus, I think, was that in 1983 he had a good year with 17 home runs. Right away, he thinks he's going to be a home run hitter. He thinks the only way he's going to make money is to hit home runs.

He's got a lot of potential, but it's about time for him to reach that potential. He's 28 years old.

By the time I was 28, I was winning batting titles. Redus should be in a situation now where he's an established hitter, getting 75 stolen bases every year.

SATURDAY, MAY 25 .... ROSE 2 FOR 3

Our plan to keep Vince Coleman and Willie McGee off the bags didn't work tonight.

Before the game, I talked with my pitchers and told them the one thing I didn't want was to have them walk Coleman.

So what happened?

Jay Tibbs walked Coleman to start the game and he ended up scoring on Jack Clark's sacrifice fly.

See how much walks can hurt you?

They kept the lead the rest of the night. We kept coming back, but were unable to close the gap and lost, 6-4.

About the only thing I can say about this game is they didn't get any stolen bases.

Tommy Herr really swung the bat good for them. He had three singles and drove in two runs. He's leading

St. Louis	ab	r	h	rbi	Cincinnati	ab	r	h	rbi
Coleman, lf	3	1	1	0	Milner, cf	5	0	0	0
McGee, cf	5	1	1	1	**Rose, 1b**	3	1	2	0
Herr, 2b	5	0	3	2	Davis, pr	0	0	0	0
Clark, 1b	3	1	1	1	Parker, rf	5	1	1	0
Van Slyke, rf	4	0	0	0	Knicely, c	4	0	2	1
Pendleton, 3b	4	1	2	1	Redus, lf	4	1	2	1
Smith, ss	4	0	0	0	C'cepcion, ss	4	1	1	2
Nieto, c	4	1	1	1	Kr'chicki, 3b	3	0	0	0
Andujar, p	3	1	0	0	Foley, 2b	4	0	1	0
Dayley, p	0	0	0	0	Tibbs, p	0	0	0	0
					Price, p	1	0	0	0
					Esasky, ph	0	0	0	0
					Pastore, p	0	0	0	0
					Oester, ph	1	0	0	0
					Robinson, p	0	0	0	0
					Walker, ph	1	0	0	0
Totals	35	6	9	6	Totals	34	4	9	4

St. Louis.......................1 3 0 1 0 0 1 0 0—6
Cincinnati...................0 0 2 0 0 2 0 0 0—4

St. Louis	IP.	H.	R.	ER.	BB.	SO.
Andujar (W. 8-1)........	8⅔	9	4	4	4	2
Dayley (Save 4)..........	⅓	0	0	0	0	0
Cincinnati	IP.	H.	R.	ER.	BB.	SO.
Tibbs (L. 3-7)	1⅓	3	4	4	3	0
Price...........................	2⅔	3	1	1	3	1
Pastore	2	1	0	0	0	3
Robinson	3	2	1	1	0	1

Game-winning RBI—Clark.
E—None. DP—St. Louis 2. LOB—St. Louis 7, Cincinnati 8. 2B—Clark, Knicely. HR—McGee (2), Concepcion (4). SB—Redus 2. SF—Clark. HBP—By Andujar (Rose). WP—Andujar, Tibbs 2. T—2:50. A—24,846.

the league with a .379 average and, like I said, with those two greyhounds, Coleman and McGee, in front of him and Clark behind him, he's getting a lot of good pitches to hit. You just can't work around him; he's getting a lot of fastballs. He's off to a great start and is playing with a lot of momentum, a lot of intensity.

Joaquin Andujar was a little wild, but pitched well for them. We had some good chances, but were unable to cash in. Both of us had nine hits, but we left eight runners on the bags.

I had a couple of singles, leaving me 59 short of surpassing Cobb. I'm swinging pretty good now and have my average up to .303.

Davey Concepcion hit a home run in the sixth inning, and Dave Parker's single gave him a 16-game hitting streak. I think he is really going to have some kind of year.

We've got to figure out a way to get Tibbs straightened out. Today, he gave up a run in the first inning, then I had to take him out in the second.

Some of the writers have said I'm a little too patient with my pitchers. But I just don't like to yank a guy early in the game, or later on if I think he's got a chance to get out of an inning.

I've always been patient, but Tibbs just wasn't getting the ball where he wanted it. He gave up only three hits, but walked three and had two wild pitches.

SUNDAY, MAY 26 .... ROSE 0 FOR 4

Today was a case of my pitcher, John Stuper, just trying too hard. We got beat, 7-2.

Everybody in the clubhouse knew how important this game was to him. St. Louis sent him (on loan) to Vancouver (Milwaukee's Class AAA affiliate) last July and that's where he stayed until we made a deal for him on September 10.

I think Stuper wanted to get even with the Cardinals in one game. He was so pumped up, I think he felt like he had to throw the ball through a brick wall.

Even Bill Bergesch, our general manager, told him to stay within himself.

Still, you can't take away the fact Stuper was pitching against his old teammates, the team he helped win the World Series for in 1982.

His pitches were all over the place (Stuper walked the game's first batter, Vince Coleman). He was overly strong because he was working with four days rest, instead of three.

St. Louis	ab	r	h	rbi	Cincinnati	ab	r	h	rbi
Coleman, lf	3	2	1	0	Milner, cf	3	0	2	0
McGee, cf	4	2	3	2	**Rose, 1b**	4	0	0	0
Herr, 2b	3	1	2	2	Parker, rf	4	2	1	1
Clark, 1b	5	1	0	0	Knicely, c	3	0	2	1
Van Slyke, rf	2	1	0	0	Cedeno, pr	0	0	0	0
Landrum, rf	1	0	0	0	Van Gorder, c	1	0	1	0
Pendleton, 3b	3	0	0	1	Redus, lf	4	0	0	0
Smith, ss	4	0	3	1	C'cepcion, ss	4	0	0	0
Porter, c	3	0	0	1	Kr'chicki, 3b	3	0	0	0
Cox, p	4	0	0	0	Foley, 2b	3	0	0	0
					Stuper, p	0	0	0	0
					Oester, ph	1	0	0	0
					Franco, p	0	0	0	0
					Walker, ph	1	0	0	0
					Hume, p	0	0	0	0
Totals	32	7	9	7	Totals	31	2	6	2

St. Louis	0	1	2	0	0	0	0	3	1—7
Cincinnati	0	0	0	1	0	0	1	0	0—2

St. Louis	IP.	H.	R.	ER.	BB.	SO.
Cox (W. 5-1)	9	6	2	1	2	6

Cincinnati	IP.	H.	R.	ER.	BB.	SO.
Stuper (L. 5-3)	6	5	3	3	3	2
Franco	2	3	3	1	0	1
Hume	1	1	1	1	2	0

Game-winning RBI—Porter.
E—Coleman, Concepcion. DP—St. Louis 1. LOB—St. Louis 6, Cincinnati 2. 2B—Knicely 2, Herr. 3B—McGee 2. HR—Parker (8). SB—McGee 2, Coleman. SH—Pendleton. SF—Porter, Herr. T—2:22. A—21,349.

We were getting beat 3-1 when I took Stuper out for a pinch-hitter in the bottom of the sixth. He'd given up five hits and three runs. His three walks cost him, too.

I had to pinch hit there because we had to take a shot at getting back into the game. You never like to lose a game, but I think Stuper should have learned a lesson in this one. The next time he faces the Cardinals, he should be more relaxed. He had been telling guys in the clubhouse he has had this game on his mind since the day of the trade.

Still, we were in it after he left, but John Franco gave up three runs in the eighth inning. An error by Davey Concepcion didn't help very much.

The ninth was what I have been talking about for three days.

I brought in Tom Hume to pitch. He got the first two outs and then walked Coleman, who stole second. Willie McGee comes up and gets his third hit of the game and they have another run.

I didn't get any hits in four at-bats, but I hit a liner that Ozzie Smith made a great catch on.

One thing that pleased me today was the way Alan Knicely swung the bat. He had his fourth straight two-hit game and his sixth since we called him up from Denver. He's hitting .343 and has driven in 10 runs.

The first day I saw him take batting practice in Montreal after he was brought up, I knew he was a different hitter from what he was last year. He wasn't hitting the ball to right field like he did then. And you know what I like—everything he hit was hit hard.

Dave Parker hit a home run in the seventh, which gave us a homer in each of our last 10 games. The Cobra has hit in 17 straight games, and according to Jim Ferguson, our publicity director, that's the longest hitting streak in the majors right now. Parker is hitting .380 for the month of May and .335 overall.

After winning Friday night, we thought we had a shot at sweeping these guys, but had to settle for just the one win. We've got to get back on the winning track against Chicago tomorrow night.

Cubs starter Dennis Eckersley beat the Reds for the second time in six days on May 27.

MONDAY, MAY 27 .... ROSE 0 FOR 3

This was the kind of game that stays with you longer than most.

Like I've said before, when you're a player and you have a couple of hits and don't mess up, you usually forget about a loss by the time you get home.

As manager, I think about games more than I did before, but I never dwell on them. What's done is done.

But this was one that bothered me, and I know it was tough on the fans. We had a good Memorial Day crowd tonight of over 20,000.

We had the tying run at third base in the ninth inning with nobody out and couldn't score.

The Cubs won, 4-3, and we've now dropped three in a row.

Anytime you've got the tying run at third, you're playing at home, nobody's out and you can't get him in, you don't deserve to win. Damn!

I guess you have to give their relief pitcher, Lee Smith, some of the credit. He shut us down just when he had to. That's what a guy like him

Chicago	ab	r	h	rbi	Cincinnati	ab	r	h	rbi
Dernier, cf	4	0	2	2	Milner, cf	4	0	0	0
Sandberg, 2b	4	1	1	0	**Rose, 1b**	3	0	0	0
Lopes, lf	3	1	1	0	Parker, rf	4	0	0	0
Woods, lf	1	0	0	0	Knicely, c	4	1	1	1
Moreland, rf	4	0	3	1	Redus, lf	3	1	0	0
Cey, 3b	4	0	1	1	C'cepcion, ss	4	1	2	0
J. Davis, c	4	0	0	0	Esasky, 3b	1	0	1	0
Durham, 1b	4	1	1	0	Kr'cki, pr-3b	3	0	1	1
Bowa, ss	4	1	1	0	Oester, 2b	3	0	1	0
Eckersley, p	3	0	0	0	Robinson, p	0	0	0	0
Smith, p	0	0	0	0	Walker, ph	1	0	0	0
					Browning, p	2	0	0	0
					Foley, 2b	2	0	1	0
Totals	35	4	10	4	Totals	34	3	7	2

Chicago ....0 0 0   0 2 1   0 1 0—4
Cincinnati......................0 0 0   0 0 0   1 0 2—3

Chicago	IP.	H.	R.	ER.	BB.	SO.
Eckersley (W. 6-3).....	8*	6	2	2	0	6
Smith (Save 12)	1	1	1	0	1	1

Cincinnati	IP.	H.	R.	ER.	BB.	SO.
Browning (L. 4-4).......	7⅔	10	4	4	1	4
Robinson	1⅓	0	0	0	0	1

*Pitched to one batter in ninth.

Game-winning RBI—Dernier.
E—J. Davis. DP—Cincinnati 1. LOB—Chicago 5, Cincinnati 6. 2B—Dernier, Moreland, Cey, Concepcion, Krenchicki. HR—Knicely (2). SB—Sandberg 2, Lopes, Redus, Concepcion. HBP—By Eckersley **(Rose)**. T—2:28. A—20,046.

gets paid to do. (Smith relieved Cubs starter Dennis Eckersley after Alan Knicely led off the Reds' ninth with a home run that cut Chicago's lead to 4-2.)

I didn't get any hits (0 for 3), but I hit a rope in the first inning to center that Bobby Dernier had to make a diving catch on.

Eckersley beat us for the second time within six days, but we had our shots at him.

Tom Browning pitched OK for us, but when they scored a run in the eighth, I had to take him out. I brought in Ron Robinson.

That ninth inning. It's hard to believe.

I told Gary Redus (the first batter to face Smith) to get on base, to make them throw his pitch. After he walked, Davey Concepcion singled.

That gave us runners on first and second. I flashed the steal sign and we pulled off a double steal. Jody Davis, their catcher, threw the ball into the dirt and it bounced into left field. Redus scored and Concepcion took third. It looked like we were in business.

The rest was hard to watch.

Wayne Krenchicki grounded out to the second baseman and Davey had to stay put.

I sent up Duane Walker to pinch-hit for Robinson and he struck out on three straight sliders. He didn't even get a swing.

That left it up to Tom Foley. He popped out to shortstop and that was that.

Dave Parker didn't get any hits, so his 17-game streak is over.

I started Ron Oester at second base for the first time in over a week, but he told me after the game the shoulder he jammed in Pittsburgh was still bothering him some. He said it really hurt when he had to reach out and go for a ground ball.

As long as Oester says he is all right, I'm going to let him play.

TUESDAY, MAY 28 .... DID NOT PLAY

I didn't play tonight because the Cubs started a lefthander, Larry Gura.

So, I let Doggie—Tony Perez—play first base and it turned out to be a wise decision.

All he did was homer, double, single and drive in four runs.

But what I liked most about this game was the way we came back. After three innings we were down 6-0 and it would have been easy to say, "We'll get 'em tomorrow."

Then, we were also down 10-5, but kept coming back. Believe me, this team has the ability to keep coming back.

With Doggie leading the way, we scored five in the fourth and six in the sixth and went on to win, 13-11.

There's not much I can say about Doggie that hasn't already been said.

I've always felt when the Reds traded him to Montreal after we won the World Series over New York in 1976, it was the beginning of our downfall. He meant a lot more to the team than some people realized.

If you wanted a key hit, a key RBI, Tony always got it. There's just something about him when there are runners on. He's an RBI man and the ultimate team player. He kept the clubhouse loose and the younger guys looked up to him.

When you have a great team like we had in the mid-1970s, all the parts are important. They traded Doggie so Dan Driessen could play first base. Well, take nothing away from Danny because he is a great player, but once Doggie left something was missing.

Ask Sparky Anderson. He'll tell you the same thing. But somebody thought we could get along without him.

A lot of people thought Doggie, who is 43, should have retired several years ago. I never felt that way because as long as he can swing the bat, he can help you.

A few years ago, I was at the San Francisco airport waiting for a flight to Japan when my attorney, Reuven Katz, phoned me. He also represents Doggie and had just worked out a one-year contract for him with the Phillies for 1983. (Perez, signed as a free agent by Boston in November 1979, had been released by the Red Sox in November 1982.)

That meant Doggie, Joe Morgan (traded from San Francisco to Philadelphia) and I were all going to be on the same team again.

But what it really meant was that we had a guy who could come off the bench as a pinch-hitter, play some first base and help a team.

I'll tell you this right now. Having Doggie caused me some problems because late in spring training in '83 I was asked to switch to right field (so Perez could be inserted into the lineup). I hadn't played the outfield in a long time, but I agreed. I had a sore arm from throwing so much and would have preferred to remain at first base. But had we not had Doggie in the lineup the first part of the season, we wouldn't have made it to the World Series against Baltimore.

He had played winter ball near his home in Puerto Rico and was really swinging good. He almost carried us in the early weeks.

Reuven negotiated a deal with the Reds in December of '83 and Tony came back here. This past winter, we didn't put him on the roster, but I told them to invite him to spring training as a non-roster player. I was pretty sure he was going to make the team.

And tonight, he deserved a chance to start. With those four RBIs, he now has 1,603 and that leads all active players. And the homer was his 375th.

He has made four starts this season and in those starts he has eight hits in 14 at-bats, nine RBIs and three homers.

With tonight's win, we ended our three-game losing streak and now have a shot at taking two out of three from the Cubs by winning tomorrow. I've got to think that way because I've got my ace, Mario Soto, going.

WEDNESDAY, MAY 29 .... DID NOT PLAY

I expected Mario Soto to give us a great game today—and he did.

We scored a run in the third inning and that's all Mario needed. Ryne Sandberg got a single in the first inning and Keith Moreland one in the fourth. That was it. We won, 1-0.

Mario keeps telling everybody around here he pitches better when we don't get runs for him. Maybe he does.

We got our only run in the third when Gary Redus doubled to the left-field corner, went to third when Eddie Milner grounded out and came home on Dave Parker's sacrifice fly. The Cobra got the run home again.

Mario showed me what kind of pitcher he is in the fourth. Zonk (Moreland) got a single with two out and then stole second. Mario lost his concentration and walked Ron Cey. He also walked Leon Durham, who has killed him in the past.

We didn't want to walk Durham intentionally, but we didn't want to give him anything to hit, either. The next batter was Steve Lake and he grounded out.

Mario gives up a lot of home runs, and he said later that's what was worrying him when Durham came up. He said he'd pitch the Bull carefully and take his chances with Lake. It worked out.

He also told me that when Davey Concepcion and Alan Knicely went to the mound, they really settled him down.

Davey gave him a pep talk in Spanish because Mario felt like John McSherry, the home-plate umpire, was squeezing him, not giving him close strikes.

Mario has now won seven games for us and this was his first shutout since September 13, 1983.

So, after dropping the first game in this series, we've come back to take two in a row.

That should give us some momentum for our weekend series in St. Louis.

★   ★   ★

Some of the writers wanted to know what I plan to do with Jay Tibbs.

Sure, he's been struggling (3-7 record, 5.21 earned-run average), but I told them it didn't matter to me if they give up on him because I'm the one who matters. And I ain't gonna give up on him.

I've told Tibbs that.

I'm not about to take him out of the rotation or send him to Denver. I'm not going to do that with a good, young pitcher even though he's not getting anybody out and everything they hit goes in the hole. I'm not going to give up on a good hitter if he goes 0 for 25.

It's just like Kitty (pitching coach Jim Kaat) said. Sometimes you have to look down the road and think about the future. You have to think about what this guy can do for you later on.

And it's not a matter of not having anybody else to take his place in the rotation. I could always use Joe Price. He's a good pitcher and could start if I wanted him to.

Kitty feels sometimes the best thing you can do is just keep sending a guy who's struggling out there and hope he gets straightened out.

Of course, if Tibbs doesn't get straightened out, sooner or later I'll have to make a change. But not right now.

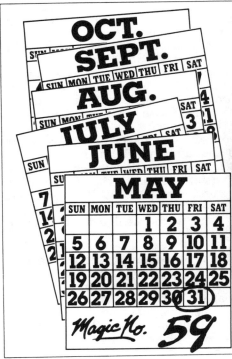

Dave Concepcion's two-out, eighth-inning single ruined Danny Cox's bid for a perfect game on May 31.

FRIDAY, MAY 31 .... ROSE 0 FOR 4

Marge Schott, owner of the Reds, is a little upset with me and, really, it's just a misunderstanding. I'm sure I'll be able to convince her once she hears all the details.

We were supposed to catch our charter flight to Denver yesterday for an exhibition game, then come on here (St. Louis) for three games.

When we got to the airport, Marge was waiting for us. She'd just gotten back from New York and wanted to talk with me and Joe Price, the Reds' player representative.

She asked us not to vote for a strike. She told us to take our time and think about the issues and everything before we took the vote. She even told Joe Price she would open the Reds' books for him.

What she didn't realize was we had the meeting with Don Fehr of the players' association set up for two weeks.

The players, including me, unanimously voted to support the association's executive board. In other words, we gave the board our backing to set a strike date.

Cincinnati	ab	r	h	rbi	St. Louis	ab	r	h	rbi
Milner, cf	4	0	0	0	Coleman, lf	4	2	3	0
Rose, 1b	4	0	0	0	McGee, cf	3	2	2	0
Parker, rf	3	0	0	0	Herr, 2b	4	0	2	3
Knicely, c	3	0	0	0	Clark, rf	5	1	1	2
Redus, lf	3	0	0	0	Pendleton, 3b	5	0	2	0
C'cepcion, ss	3	0	1	0	Jorgensen, 1b	2	0	0	0
Oester, 2b	3	0	1	0	Smith, ss	3	0	1	0
Kr'chicki, 3b	3	0	0	0	Porter, c	3	0	0	0
Stuper, p	1	0	0	0	Cox, p	4	0	0	0
Foley, ph	1	0	0	0					
Pastore, p	0	0	0	0					
Walker, ph	1	0	0	0					
Totals	29	0	2	0	Totals	33	5	11	5

Cincinnati .... 0 0 0   0 0 0   0 0 0—0
St. Louis .... 0 0 3   0 0 2   0 0 x—5

Cincinnati	IP.	H.	R.	ER.	BB.	SO.
Stuper (L. 5-4)	5	6	3	3	6	0
Pastore	3	5	2	2	1	2

St. Louis	IP.	H.	R.	ER.	BB.	SO.
Cox (W. 6-1)..............	9	2	0	0	0	3

Game-winning RBI—Herr.
E—None. DP—Cincinnati 1. LOB—Cincinnati 2, St. Louis 12. HR—Clark (10). SB—Coleman 2, McGee 2. SF—Herr. T—2:05. A—38,910.

Now, Marge is offended. She thought we were slapping her in the face, but we really weren't because the meeting was already set before she came over and talked to Joe and me yesterday.

After the meeting, reporters asked me a lot of questions. They wanted to know if I voted in favor of a players' strike and I said I had.

They brought up 1981. That was the year I tied Stan Musial's record (the National League career hits mark of 3,630) on June 10, then we went on strike. I didn't get the record until we came back on August 10.

They said the same thing might happen with the Cobb record. I told them if they knew the facts, they would vote for a strike, too.

Seriously, don't you ever ask yourself why one team can give a guy $2 million a year, then turn around and say they're losing money?

I happen to think I know a little bit about what's going on. I've talked to Don Fehr. I went through free agency. Much of what I've received from baseball in the way of salary and benefits, I owe to the players' association.

I'm going to sit down with Marge and maybe she'll understand where I'm coming from.

★   ★   ★

The one thing I like about coming to St. Louis is our hotel. The Marriott Pavilion is right across the street from Busch Stadium. You can look out your window and see the ball park. It's so close you can walk to it and because of that, I always go early.

This was just one of those games where we got blown away.

Their pitcher, Danny Cox, who beat us last weekend in Cincinnati, had a perfect game going until Davey Concepcion singled to left with two out in the eighth. Ron Oester came right back with another hit and that's all we got.

We hit some balls hard, but they threw some leather at us. They beat us, 5-0.

I didn't get any hits, but hit a couple of balls hard.

We left only two guys on base and they left 12, so that shows me John Stuper pitched pretty good in some tough spots, but also that he was in trouble a lot.

SATURDAY, JUNE 1 .... ROSE 2 FOR 5

Dave Parker and I had a long talk after last night's game.

He was upset, like I was, about the way we got beat. While we were talking, he suggested something I have been thinking about since last weekend when we played the Cardinals back home.

You know what makes this St. Louis team go?

Well, they've got those two greyhounds (Vince Coleman and Willie McGee) in the first two slots, Tommy Herr hitting third and Jack Clark in the cleanup spot.

The whole key to that is Herr.

We've got the same kind of hitters they do, so what I decided to do was move Gary Redus from the fifth spot to leadoff, drop Eddie Milner to second, bat myself third and drop Parker from third to fourth. And I put Alan Knicely in the fifth spot.

Today, the new lineup really worked. We win, 9-3, and score in six of the nine innings. I ended a 0-for-13 slump with two hits, leaving me 57 short of beating Cobb.

The first inning was a good example of what we can do with this lineup.

Redus walked, then stole second on the first pitch to Milner. Their pitcher, Kurt Kepshire, tried twice to pick Redus off the bag and the second time the ball got past Ozzie Smith and Gary scored.

I think I've been wasting the speed we've got on this team, especially with Redus in the fifth spot. I can handle the bat and make contact, but that was being wasted with me hitting second.

I'm not criticizing Eddie, but I'm limited in what I can do with the bat when he's going 3 for 34 (Milner's figures for May 19 through May 31).

I think we're going to stick with this for a while.

Parker and I are going to see a lot of fastballs because pitchers are going to be concerned about Redus and Milner stealing.

Parker said he doesn't mind moving to cleanup.

"Pete," he said, "they (the Cardinals) have been running us ragged. Gary and Eddie do the same thing for us that Coleman and McGee do for them. And this will give the other pitchers something to think about. I've been saying for nearly two years I think Gary might be the fastest guy in our league, and Eddie can steal a lot of bases, too."

I think Redus and Milner can steal bases just about as good as Coleman and McGee if they get on base. That's the key—they've got to get on base more. And you know I can do a lot of things with the bat when there are runners on base—hit a fly ball, hit to the right side, advance guys to third—you name it.

I want to see Redus use the whole field. He's making contact and getting on base, but he seldom hits the ball to the right side. It seems like he's always pulling the ball, or trying to pull it. If he can start using the whole field, he'll get on base a lot more.

Speaking of Redus, there was a rumor today he was being traded to Detroit. Not true.

Bob Howsam, our president, told reporters he had talked with the Tigers during spring training and that Gary's name might have been mentioned, but there was no deal.

Cincinnati	ab	r	h	rbi	St. Louis	ab	r	h	rbi
Redus, lf	4	1	0	0	Coleman, lf	3	2	1	0
Milner, cf	5	2	3	1	McGee, cf	4	0	0	0
Rose, 1b	5	1	2	0	Herr, 2b	4	1	1	0
Parker, rf	4	1	1	1	Clark, 1b	3	0	2	2
Knicely, c	5	2	2	3	Campbell, p	0	0	0	0
C'cepcion, ss	4	1	2	0	Pendleton, 3b	4	0	0	0
Oester, 2b	4	0	1	1	Landrum, rf	2	0	1	0
Kr'chicki, 3b	3	1	1	1	Braun, ph-rf	1	0	0	0
Browning, p	1	0	1	0	Smith, ss	4	0	1	0
Hume, p	1	0	0	0	Nieto, c	3	0	0	0
					Porter, c	1	0	0	0
					Kepshire, p	2	0	1	0
					Dayley, p	0	0	0	0
					Allen, p	0	0	0	0
					J'g'sen, ph-1b	1	0	0	0
Totals	36	9	13	7	Totals	32	3	7	2

Cincinnati ....1 0 1   1 0 1   2 0 3—9
St. Louis ....1 0 0   0 0 1   0 1 0—3

Cincinnati	IP.	H.	R.	ER.	BB.	SO.
Browning (W, 5-4)......	6	6	2	2	1	6
Hume (Save 2)	3	1	1	0	2	0

St. Louis	IP.	H.	R.	ER.	BB.	SO.
Kepshire (L, 2-5)........	5*	6	4	3	4	1
Dayley	1†	5	2	2	0	0
Allen	2	0	0	0	0	1
Campbell	1	2	3	3	1	0

*Pitched to one batter in sixth.
†Pitched to three batters in seventh.

Game-winning RBI—Milner.
E—Kepshire, Oester. DP—Cincinnati 2, St. Louis 3. LOB—Cincinnati 7, St. Louis 5. 2B—Clark, Landrum, Krenchicki, Concepcion, Oester, Herr. HR—Knicely (3). SB—Redus, Coleman 2, McGee, Milner. SF—Oester, Krenchicki. PB—Nieto. T—2:53. A—35,586.

SUNDAY, JUNE 2 .... ROSE 3 FOR 4

Jay Tibbs hadn't won since May 16, so if there was anything we wanted to do today it was get him turned around.

So, you know what I did? I made an error in the first inning that helped the Cardinals score two times.

When the game finally ended and we won, 8-3, I looked back at that error and it might have helped Tibbs more than anything at the time.

I used the same batting order today, with me in the third hole. I had three hits—the first time I had three since May 5. I knocked in two runs. My big hit was a double in the fourth inning when we scored six runs.

I'm swinging pretty good now and those three hits leave me 54 short of topping Cobb.

Tibbs did just what Kitty (pitching coach Jim Kaat) and I didn't want him to do in the first. He walked leadoff hitter Vince Coleman.

I was holding Coleman on at first when Willie McGee hit a hard grounder to me. The ball hit my glove and shot into right field. Coleman went all the way to third and McGee took second.

Tommy Herr then hit a blooper into short center and both runners scored.

Cincinnati	ab	r	h	rbi	St. Louis	ab	r	h	rbi
Redus, lf	4	2	2	0	Coleman, lf	3	1	1	0
Milner, cf	4	1	0	0	McGee, cf	4	1	1	0
Rose, 1b	4	2	3	2	Herr, 2b	4	0	2	2
C'deno, pr-1b	1	0	0	0	Clark, rf	4	0	0	0
Parker, rf	5	1	1	1	Pendleton, 3b	4	1	1	0
Knicely, c	4	0	2	1	Jorgensen, 1b	3	0	0	0
C'cepcion, ss	4	1	2	2	Smith, ss	4	0	1	0
Oester, 2b	4	1	1	0	Porter, c	1	0	0	0
Kr'chicki, 3b	4	0	2	1	Nieto, c	3	0	2	1
Tibbs, p	3	0	0	1	Forsch, p	1	0	0	0
					Horton, p	0	0	0	0
					Lawless, ph	1	0	0	0
					Allen, p	0	0	0	0
					Braun, ph	1	0	0	0
					Lahti, p	0	0	0	0
					Harper, ph	1	0	0	0
Totals	37	8	13	8	Totals	34	3	8	3

Cincinnati ....0 0 0 6 1 0 1 0 0—8
St. Louis ....2 0 0 0 0 0 0 0 1—3

Cincinnati	IP.	H.	R.	ER.	BB.	SO.
Tibbs (W. 4-7)	9	8	3	2	2	4

St. Louis	IP.	H.	R.	ER.	BB.	SO.
Forsch (L. 4-3)	3⅓	4	5	5	2	1
Horton	1⅔	5	2	2	0	1
Allen	2	3	1	1	0	1
Lahti	2	1	0	0	0	3

Game-winning RBI—Concepcion.
E—**Rose**. DP—Cincinnati 1. LOB—Cincinnati 5, St. Louis 6. 2B—**Rose** 2, Concepcion, Krenchicki, Nieto. 3B—Redus. SB—Redus, Coleman. SH—Tibbs. T—2:29. A—33,774.

After I made the error, I walked toward the mound and yelled: "My fault. Pick me up." What the hell else could I say?

I'm not about to recommend errors for settling pitchers down, but after that he really concentrated.

A lot of guys would have said, "How can I win when I'm not getting any support? What the hell is going on here?"

I couldn't have felt worse when I made the error. It was the worst thing I could do with the kid trying to get back on track.

Kitty and Tibbs have been working on some problems in his delivery and they discovered there was a little hitch in it. He was not extending his arm on his follow-through.

I'm not the kind of manager who's going to try to scare a guy into getting out of a slump. I mean, I'm not going to say in the newspapers if he doesn't come around he'll be out of the rotation. What happened in the first inning today should make Tibbs realize that no matter what happens, he can handle it.

A week, 10 days ago he wouldn't have been able to bounce back after that error. Don't forget, he's only 23.

You've got to give Tibbs all the credit in the world today. He pitched a great game against a very good baseball team. He proved to me he's the kind of pitcher I thought he was because he kept his composure when a lot of guys would have lost it.

In two games, this new batting order has produced 17 runs and 26 hits.

Davey Concepcion is really swinging good, and this is a guy who two weeks ago said he was thinking about quitting.

One thing really helping us is our defense. We've got 51 double plays and that is tops in the league with Houston.

We flew home after the game and tomorrow's an open date, but I intend to take some batting practice with Billy DeMars.

The Pirates come in Tuesday night.

Eric Davis had his moments, but was sent to the minors to get more playing time.

TUESDAY, JUNE 4 .... ROSE 2 FOR 4

I haven't even been home one day and Carol's gone. She flew to New York today to work with Good Housekeeping magazine. They're going to fix her hair, make her up and all that stuff for a story that's going to run in the fall.

Looks like she's getting more publicity than I am! I don't think I've ever had my picture in Good Housekeeping.

★   ★   ★

I took some batting practice yesterday with Billy DeMars because when you're swinging good, you never like an off-day.

I had two hits and drove in a run tonight and we beat the Pirates, 9-3, for our third straight victory. Since I came back last August, I've been on base in 57 of the 62 games I've started.

But for me, it was a tough day. I had to send Eric Davis back to the minors. I've said many times I think

Pittsburgh	ab	r	h	rbi	Cincinnati	ab	r	h	rbi
Ray, 2b	4	0	0	0	Redus, lf	5	2	2	2
Mazzilli, 1b	3	1	1	0	Milner, cf	5	1	1	1
Kemp, lf	2	1	0	0	**Rose, 1b**	4	1	2	1
Hendrick, rf	4	1	1	2	Van Gorder, c	1	0	0	0
Pena, c	4	0	3	1	Parker, rf	4	0	2	0
Madlock, 3b	4	0	1	0	Knicely, c	2	0	1	0
Krawczyk, p	0	0	0	0	E. Davis, ph	1	1	1	1
T. Davis, cf	4	0	1	0	Power, p	0	0	0	0
LeMaster, ss	4	0	0	0	C'cepcion, ss	4	1	1	1
Winn, p	1	0	0	0	Oester, 2b	4	2	2	1
Frobel, ph	1	0	0	0	Kr'chicki, 3b	3	1	2	1
Guante, p	0	0	0	0	Soto, p	2	0	0	0
Holland, p	0	0	0	0	Perez, ph-1b	2	0	1	1
Candelaria, p	0	0	0	0					
Morrison, 3b	1	0	0	0					
Totals	32	3	7	3	Totals	37	9	15	9

Pittsburgh	0	0	0	0	0	2	0	1	0—3
Cincinnati	0	1	0	0	0	1	6	1	x—9

Pittsburgh	IP.	H.	R.	ER.	BB.	SO.
Winn	6	5	2	2	0	1
Guante (L. 1-1)	0*	1	2	2	1	0
Holland	⅔	5	4	4	0	1
Candelaria	⅓	1	0	0	0	0
Krawczyk	1	3	1	1	0	1

Cincinnati	IP.	H.	R.	ER.	BB.	SO.
Soto (W. 8-3)	7	6	2	2	2	7
Power	2	1	1	1	2	2

*Pitched to two batters in seventh.

Game-winning RBI—Concepcion.
E—T. Davis. DP—Pittsburgh 1, Cincinnati 2. LOB—Pittsburgh 6, Cincinnati 6. 2B—Pena, Oester, Milner, Redus. HR—Hendrick (2), Krenchicki (1), Redus (2). SB—Mazzilli, T. Davis, E. Davis. SH—Krenchicki. WP —Krawczyk, Soto 2. T—2:33. A—13,222.

this is the toughest part about managing—when you have to call a kid into the office, close the door, and tell him he's going back.

I'd called Eric in about 2½ weeks ago because they—I'm talking about the bosses, Bob Howsam and Bill Bergesch—were concerned that he wasn't playing enough. They wanted to know what I was going to do with him because they didn't want him to sit.

I said, "Well, give him another couple of weeks because he's really helping the ball club, pinch running and stuff like that."

When Davis came in then, I told him he was going to get a lot of playing time and the reason he hadn't been playing was because Gary Redus and Eddie Milner have been doing so well.

From the time Davis left that office, Redus really got hot. Redus, Milner and Dave Parker were really playing well and I just couldn't get Eric in the lineup.

So, my bosses bring it to my attention again. "What are we going to do with Eric? He's got to play. He's 23 years old."

Neither one of them wanted him to sit around, although he could help us win. But you can ruin a kid like that if he doesn't play. He doesn't have time to get the confidence, he doesn't have time to learn the things he must be able to do. He just has to go to Denver and learn how to make contact.

These things (player demotions) really bother me. Eric called me Pops before the game.

When I called him in, he said he was surprised. I think I made him understand that I think he'll be back real fast. I told him to make me bring him back up.

One thing I learned in spring training was to always have someone in the office with me when I send a guy out.

It's usually Greg Riddoch, our director of minor league clubs, who knows most of our kids. The reason you want someone in there with you is because you don't ever want a player to be able to say you said something to him you didn't. A lot of times players will say this guy promised me I'd be back in a month, or this guy promised me that.

When you send a guy like Eric Davis out, it's not like he doesn't have a chance to get back to the big leagues. Eric had only 90 at-bats, was hitting only .189 and had 31 strikeouts. Like I said, he needs to work on making contact.

We're bringing up Max Venable to replace him. Max can play the outfield positions, can pinch hit and has good speed.

I haven't had anyone yell at me when I sent them out. I guess because they understand.

Ron Robinson had pitched well (for the Reds) late last year and had a great spring training, but we had decided to go with a four-man rotation. He was the most heartbroken of all the players I sent back, but then he showed the kind of character he has.

He got up to leave my office, looked at me and said, "Skip, do me a favor."

I said, "What's that, Ron?"

He said, "Don't beat that record until I get back."

He went down there (Denver), put the numbers on the board and the first time we needed a pitcher, here he was. (Robinson was recalled three weeks ago.)

WEDNESDAY, JUNE 5 .... ROSE 1 FOR 4

We've had some conversations the last couple of days with the Pittsburgh Pirates. They're trying to trade John Candelaria.

They'll let us have him, but they want Gary Redus and Eric Davis. That's too much.

All through spring training we were very interested in a catcher because we didn't know what Alan Knicely was going to do.

But Knicely has come up from Denver and catching is not our biggest problem anymore. Matter of fact, it's not even a problem.

We were interested in Ozzie Virgil or Bo Diaz from the Phillies, but they wanted Ted Power or this guy or that guy.

We thought we had good leverage in spring training because we had a lot of young pitchers who were throwing well—with experience. Then we ran into a situation where teams wanted to wait and go with their own players.

They tell you they're real anxious to make a deal, then when you start talking about giving them what they want, they back off.

When we left spring training, I was really the only one who thought we could win the West. I sold it, talked about it and said it in every interview. I believe Bob Howsam didn't think we could win.

We probably will make some deals, but you can't make too many when you're winning (entering tonight's game, the Reds are in second place with a 27-22 record, 1½ games behind San Diego). You just don't want to change too many things around. I think Howsam wants to continuously strengthen the team. That's all you can do.

Sometimes you're better off with the deal you didn't make than the one you could've made.

★   ★   ★

We won tonight, 11-9, over Pittsburgh and it sure wasn't pretty. I had one hit, so I need 51 to break the record.

But we made a couple of errors and threw the ball around a lot. But when you get 12 hits and score nine runs, that can make up for a lot of things.

We were down two runs in the first inning, but nobody got very upset about that because it was early.

Because San Diego is coming in for a big four-game series this weekend, one of their papers sent a writer, Barry Bloom, here to check us out. I was telling him before the game how good we've been playing, and this was one of the worst games we've played all year. I was thinking about that out at first base.

But we ended up winning because we stayed on the offense and scored when we had the opportunity.

Pittsburgh	ab	r	h	rbi	Cincinnati	ab	r	h	rbi
Ray, 2b	5	2	3	0	Redus, lf	5	0	1	2
Mazzilli, 1b	3	3	2	0	Milner, cf	4	1	1	0
Kemp, lf	4	0	1	0	Rose, 1b	4	3	1	0
Hendrick, rf	5	1	1	2	Parker, rf	4	2	2	2
Pena, c	5	1	4	1	Knicely, c	4	1	1	3
Madlock, 3b	4	0	1	1	C'cepcion, ss	3	1	1	1
T. Davis, cf	3	1	0	0	Oester, 2b	3	1	1	1
Almon, ph-cf	1	0	0	0	Kr'chicki, 3b	4	1	2	1
LeMaster, ss	3	1	1	2	Stuper, p	1	0	0	0
Foli, ph-ss	1	0	0	0	R. Robinson, p	0	0	0	0
Rhoden, p	1	0	0	0	Cedeno, ph	1	0	0	0
Scurry, p	1	0	0	0	Pastore, p	0	0	0	0
D. Rob'son, p	1	0	0	0	Venable, ph	1	1	1	0
Morrison, ph	1	0	0	0	Franco, p	1	0	0	0
Candelaria, p	0	0	0	0					
Totals	38	9	13	6	Totals	36	11	12	10

Pittsburgh ....2 0 6   0 0 0   1 0 0— 9
Cincinnati ....2 3 0   0 2 4   0 0 x—11

Pittsburgh	IP.	H.	R.	ER.	BB.	SO.
Rhoden	1⅓	5	5	5	1	2
Scurry	3	2	2	2	3	2
D. Robinson (L. 2-1)...	2⅔	4	4	0	1	3
Candelaria	1	1	0	0	0	1

Cincinnati	IP.	H.	R.	ER.	BB.	SO.
Stuper	2*	7	7	6	1	3
R. Robinson	2	2	1	1	1	1
Pastore (W. 1-0)........	2	1	0	0	0	1
Franco (Save 1).........	3	3	1	1	1	1

*Pitched to five batters in third.

Game-winning RBI—Knicely.
E—LeMaster, Milner, Knicely. DP—Cincinnati 1. LOB—Pittsburgh 5, Cincinnati 6. 2B—Pena, Mazzilli, Redus, Venable, Parker. HR—LeMaster (1), Parker (9), Knicely (4). T—2:46. A—12,540.

Cesar Cedeno's key homer on June 8 is the kind of feat that earns a postgame chat with broadcaster Joe Nuxhall.

FRIDAY, JUNE 7 .... ROSE 1 FOR 4

Dave Parker had all the players and their families over to his place for a barbecue yesterday afternoon.

Carol and I went and had a good time. Food was great. Outings like this are good for the guys and their wives, to get together socially once in a while. You can have a lot of laughs and relax. It eases some of the tension and brings everybody a little closer together.

On the way to the party, Carol and I rode by the dealership where that red Ferrari Testarossa is for sale. We still want it, but until we sell the BMW M-1, it's out of the question. I've got a guy who says he's interested, so maybe it's just a matter of time.

I've had to have my home telephone number changed again. You can give it out to people you want to

SECOND GAME									
San Diego	ab	r	h	rbi	Cincinnati	ab	r	h	rbi
Flannery, 2b	6	1	2	0	Redus, lf	5	0	1	0
Gwynn, rf	5	2	3	1	Milner, cf	5	0	1	0
Garvey, 1b	6	0	2	2	**Rose, 1b**	4	0	1	0
Kennedy, c	5	0	1	0	Parker, rf	3	0	0	0
McR'nolds, cf	5	0	4	0	Knicely, c	5	0	2	0
Nettles, 3b	5	0	0	0	Cedeno, pr	0	0	0	0
Martinez, lf	4	0	1	0	C'pc'n, ss-3b	5	1	1	0
Templeton, ss	5	0	2	0	Oester, 2b	5	1	0	0
Show, p	4	0	0	0	Kr'chicki, 3b	4	0	1	2
Gossage, p	0	0	0	0	Foley, pr-ss	0	0	0	0
Bumbry, ph	1	0	0	0	Tibbs, p	2	0	0	0
Lefferts, p	0	0	0	0	Venable, ph	1	0	1	0
					Franco, p	0	0	0	0
					Walker, ph	0	0	0	0
					Power, p	0	0	0	0
Totals	46	3	15	3	Totals	39	2	8	2

San Diego........... 0 0 0   0 0 0   2 0 0   0 1—3
Cincinnati............. 0 0 0   0 0 0   0 0 2   0 0—2

San Diego	IP.	H.	R.	ER.	BB.	SO.
Show	7⅓	5	0	0	3	5
Gossage	1⅔	2	2	0	1	1
Lefferts (W. 3-2)	2	1	0	0	0	2

Cincinnati	IP.	H.	R.	ER.	BB.	SO.
Tibbs	8	11	2	2	3	2
Franco	1	1	0	0	0	0
Power (L. 0-2)	2	3	1	1	0	2

Game-winning RBI—Gwynn.
E—Templeton. DP—San Diego 1, Cincinnati 2. LOB—San Diego 13, Cincinnati 8. 2B—Redus, Kennedy, Flannery, Knicely, Garvey, Krenchicki. HR—Gwynn (3). SB—Templeton. WP—Tibbs. T—3:05. A—37,753.

have it, then the first thing you know somebody gets it you don't want to have it and you start getting calls all hours of the day and night. You go on the road and your wife starts getting calls at 1 o'clock in the morning and the person hangs up. You don't know if somebody is robbing you or what.

★   ★   ★

For the first time in three or four years, the Reds have a series that is important. We're going head-to-head with first-place San Diego and there is a lot of excitement around town.

Because of the importance of this series, some members of the national media are here. They keep asking me about the Cobb record.

"When should we pick you up?" somebody asked.

We've got a 10-game homestand beginning August 23, so it could happen then.

I told them to show up when I get within five hits because I've had nine five-hit games in the majors.

But I told 'em not to come if I need 10 because the only way I could do that would be to play a doubleheader, but since I don't play many doubleheaders anymore, I told 'em to pick me up at five.

Speaking of doubleheaders, the one thing you hate about them happened tonight. We lost two games to the Padres and it hurt.

We started this series 1½ games back of the Padres and by dropping two, fell 3½ off the pace. Had we swept, which is hard to do even at home, we would have been a half-game in front.

I sat out the first game and the Padres won, 9-3. They used the long ball to beat us; Kurt Bevacqua hit a grand slam and Carmelo Martinez hit a three-run homer.

The second game was a lot better, but we still got beat, 3-2, in 11 innings. We were down 2-0 but came back to tie in the ninth inning with two unearned runs off Goose Gossage.

Then, in the 11th, Tony Gwynn hit a homer off Teddy Power and that was it. It was a tough loss.

You're going to split more doubleheaders than you're going to win or lose. When you're in a pennant race and you're in September and all of a sudden the team you're chasing has a lot of doubleheaders, you look at each doubleheader as a loss (for that team).

You say to yourself, "Well, they've got four doubleheaders in September. Hell, that's four games we're going to pick up on them."

Most people, especially on the road, approach doubleheaders looking for a split.

Tomorrow's game is very important. We've got to win so the Padres aren't in a position to sweep us.

SATURDAY, JUNE 8 .... DID NOT PLAY

I didn't realize it until today, but I think our guys were a little bit uptight for the doubleheader last night.

The pennant winners from last year were coming in and there was a lot of excitement.

It didn't really hit me until I noticed how loosey-goosey my guys were when they got to the ball park for tonight's game—a big contrast.

I didn't play tonight because the Padres started a lefthander, Dave Dravecky.

Cesar Cedeno hit a three-run homer and Dave Parker drove in two runs and we won, 7-4.

— 93 —

After losing two games, there was a lot of disappointment, but what I liked was the way they bounced back tonight. Our team has been like that ever since I've been back here. Every time we've needed to win a game, we've come right back—after a disappointing loss, or after losing a series. We've bounced back with good enthusiasm and showed what kind of spine we've got.

We came out today and we hit the ball, caught the ball and got good pitching. Joe Price pitched five good innings. He got tired because it's been about two weeks since he was out there.

Tom Hume came in and pitched one-run baseball for three innings and John Franco got the save. Humie is throwing the ball well right now.

Other teams have been getting a lot of "flare" hits off us lately—seeing-eye hits and jammers with guys on base. Everything evens out—I guess.

★   ★   ★

There was some talk in the newspapers today about my strategy in that doubleheader—when the Padres broke a 0-0 tie in the seventh inning of the second game. With runners on second and third, I ordered Tony Gwynn walked and had Jay Tibbs pitch to Steve Garvey. Garvey gets a single and two runs score.

Well, I've got a righthander who was throwing good. Gwynn is a lefthanded batter, and I just think he's one of the best hitters in the league right now. He's on a tear and Garvey (a righthanded hitter) isn't.

I put Gwynn on and Garvey broke his bat with a two-RBI single. The ball was away from him and he hit it on the end of the bat. He very easily could have popped it up or hit it to Ronnie (Oester) at second base, or a ground ball to me. But the pitcher made the pitch and Garvey hit the ball for a base hit.

Now, don't forget Gwynn came up in the 11th inning and beat us with a home run.

Anyway, we won tonight and now I'm thinking that if we can take tomorrow's game, a split with the league champions is not too bad—not after losing a doubleheader Friday night.

Like I told my guys, that wouldn't be bad at all.

SUNDAY, JUNE 9 .... ROSE 2 FOR 5

We got beat today, 5-3. Like I told my players, this isn't the end of the world.

If I remember correctly, the division champion is decided over 162 games, so losing three out of four to the first-place team in our division in June isn't a matter of life and death.

It (the series finale) was just about the kind of game you would expect with Andy Hawkins and Mario Soto pitching.

It's 1-1. Then, all of a sudden with two out in the eighth, they get a couple of infield hits, a wild pitch, a passed ball, a little jammer to right-center and they've got a four-run inning going.

But in the ninth, against Goose Gossage, we came right back. Gary Redus struck out, but Eddie Milner tripled to center and I got a single to center—my second hit of the day—and Milner scores. Dave Parker then doubles to right, with me going to third, and we've got the tying run at the plate.

Alan Knicely just missed a homer. He got under it a little bit. He hit a fly ball to left and I scored. Davey Concepcion grounded out to short to end the game.

This was a great game (one in which Hawkins ran his record to 11-0).

Here's what I really liked today: San Diego had a four-run lead with two innings to go and Gossage out there pitching. You knew (San Diego Manager) Dick Williams was going to go all the way with him.

But we kept coming. That's the attitude our players have—don't quit, don't die and just keep coming.

After the game, the guys were OK. We started the series 1½ games back and now we're 3½ out. We're still in it. That's what they kept telling reporters who were milling around our clubhouse.

San Diego	ab	r	h	rbi	Cincinnati	ab	r	h	rbi
Flannery, 2b	5	0	0	0	Redus, lf	4	0	1	0
Gwynn, rf	5	0	1	0	Milner, cf	3	1	1	0
Garvey, 1b	5	1	1	0	**Rose, 1b**	5	1	2	1
Kennedy, c	4	1	1	0	Parker, rf	4	0	1	0
McR'nolds, cf	4	1	1	1	Knicely, c	3	1	1	1
Nettles, 3b	2	2	1	1	C'cepcion, ss	5	0	2	0
Martinez, lf	3	0	1	1	Oester, 2b	4	0	2	0
Templeton, ss	4	0	3	1	Kr'chicki, 3b	3	0	1	0
Hawkins, p	3	0	0	0	Soto, p	3	0	1	1
Bumbry, ph	1	0	0	0	Robinson, p	0	0	0	0
Gossage, p	0	0	0	0	Walker, ph	1	0	0	0
					Pastore, p	0	0	0	0
Totals	36	5	9	4	Totals	35	3	12	3

San Diego.................0 0 0 0 1 0 0 4 0—5
Cincinnati................0 0 0 1 0 0 0 0 2—3

San Diego	IP.	H.	R.	ER.	BB.	SO.
Hawkins (W. 11-0)	7	8	1	1	6	2
Gossage	2	4	2	2	0	2

Cincinnati	IP.	H.	R.	ER.	BB.	SO.
Soto (L. 8-4)	7⅔	8	5	5	3	3
Robinson	⅓	1	0	0	0	0
Pastore	1	0	0	0	0	0

Game-winning RBI—None.
E—None. DP—San Diego 2. LOB—San Diego 7, Cincinnati 12. 2B—Redus, Parker. 3B—Milner. HR—Nettles (5). SB—Milner. SF—Knicely. WP—Hawkins, Soto. PB—Knicely. T—2:41. A—28,971.

The next time we play them it will be even a bigger series and the next time a bigger one yet. I told the Cincinnati reporters that the last time they've had a big series to talk about was when the Steelers came in here to play the Bengals.

I like what Parker told Greg Hoard of the Enquirer: "This series is not one to get too excited about, losing three out of four. It was the first time they saw us. We're not going to let this get to us."

And it won't.

It's good we don't have an off-day tomorrow. The Dodgers are coming right in and that's a bigger rivalry for the Reds anyway because of the days of the Big Red Machine. Our guys have a tendency to play pretty good against L.A.

The Dodgers are coming in here for a three-game series and we don't have to see Fernando (Valenzuela) and we don't have to see (Orel) Hershiser. We'll face Rick Honeycutt, Jerry Reuss and Bob Welch.

So, that's kind of a break. I mean, these guys are major league pitchers, but they're obviously not as good as Fernando and Hershiser. Anytime you can stay away from those two in a series with the Dodgers, it's got to help you.

I was hoping we could win today because coming back to take two after dropping the Friday night doubleheader would have been a big thing.

But the Padres are starting on a long road trip now and, sure, they beat us three out of four. But I think they realize we're over here.

After the game, I was tired. I went home, fed the horses and watched Houston—Joe Niekro—shut out San Francisco, 5-0, on my satellite TV. That win let Houston tie us for second place. We've got 29-25 records.

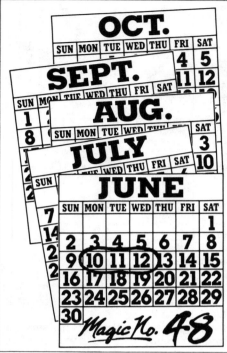

Catcher Alan Knicely hit his fifth home run on June 10, but his error helped the Dodgers score five fifth-inning runs.

MONDAY, JUNE 10 .... DID NOT PLAY

I'm concerned about my starting pitchers, at least in recent games.

I thought coming off the weekend series with San Diego, plus the great rivalry (with Los Angeles), would help us get by the Dodgers, but it didn't happen that way.

I didn't play because they started a lefthander, Rick Honeycutt, so I still need 48 hits to break the record.

When you're playing at home and you score three times in the first inning, I think you should win. Well, we scored three in the first and were on our way, but they came up with two in the fourth and five in the fifth and beat us, 7-4.

It was a sloppy game. Alan Knicely made two errors and the one in their big inning was really costly.

They hit three homers against us—by Pedro Guerrero, Mike Marshall and Greg Brock.

The fifth inning really hurt.

Dave Anderson hit a single past Nick Esasky at third. Now, with Honeycutt coming up, everybody in the ball park knew he was going to bunt. He bunted the ball in front of the plate and Knicely pounced on it.

Al threw the ball to second base, but the throw was short and didn't have much mustard on it. The ball got by Davey Concepcion and both runners were safe.

That's the kind of error Al has been getting down on himself about.

They had runners on first and second and hadn't even hit the ball hard yet. He (Knicely) just took too much time with the throw. If he had just put a little more zip on it, Davey probably would have had it.

The Dodgers didn't really run the bases well. Steve Sax screwed up (he was retired in a rundown after reaching base on a force play), but they still end up scoring five runs. (Brock's two-run homer capped the outburst.)

John Stuper was the losing pitcher; I had to get him out of there in the fifth even though all five of those runs were unearned.

Here's what really has me concerned, and Jim Ferguson, our publicity vice president, was quick to point it out to me: In the last five games, our starting pitchers have a combined earned-run average of 5.76 and have lasted an average of less than six innings per game. In $29\frac{2}{3}$ innings, they've allowed 19 earned runs, 25 runs overall, given up 42 hits and walked 11 batters. (And in the contest preceding this five-game stretch, Stuper yielded six earned runs and seven hits in two-plus innings as the Reds' starter.)

If they're winning, I could care less about statistics, but the problem is we've lost four of our last five games.

I think we're going to have to do some things to correct these problems.

JUNE 11, JUNE 12 .... RAINED OUT

I lost a hit today (Wednesday, June 12), but those things happen. I learned a long time ago not to worry about what might've been. You can't control that.

I had a single in the first inning and drove in a run against the Dodgers. We ended up taking a 2-0 lead but after their pitcher, Bobby Welch, singled in the top of the second, the game was stopped because of rain.

We waited 31 minutes to get the game started in the first place, then after it was stopped in the third inning, we waited another two hours before Harry Wendelstedt, the umpire crew chief, called it. (Tuesday's game also was rained out.)

Funny thing, by the time we got to the airport for the flight to Atlanta, the rain had stopped. Oh, well.

We've never had back-to-back games called off before (at Riverfront Stadium, which has now had only 11 postponements since it opened in 1970).

While we were waiting for the rain to stop, I had a meeting with my coaches. We went over the pitching staff because that really has been bothering us lately.

Also, Bill Bergesch told me we've sold catcher Brad Gulden, who was at Denver, to Tucson. That's the Houston Astros' farm club in the Pacific Coast League.

Gulden was frozen at Denver because when we sent him down this spring, it was his last option. We've been trying all along to get him a big-league job. Maybe he'll work his way up from Tucson.

★　　　★　　　★

I picked up the morning newspaper today and whose picture do I see? Pete Rose the second.

He has a Reds uniform and sits in the dugout with us during games when his American Legion team isn't playing. He usually comes out early and I'll throw him some batting practice and he'll work out with our guys during "BP."

He got his picture in the paper because he went over to Richmond, Indiana, Monday to a Reds tryout camp. He's only 15 and you're supposed to be 16 to try out. He said the scouts asked him to play. In three at-bats, he was safe on an error, flied out and singled.

He wants to be a major leaguer and I think he'll make it.

★   ★   ★

I think we're going to have to put John Stuper in the bullpen for a while. That way, he can work his way back to the starting rotation.

We need something to give us a lift, and I think Frank Pastore can help us as a starter. He pitched well in San Francisco (in his lone start of the season, yielding seven hits and three runs while working six innings on April 25).

Stuper is 0-3 (with one no-decision) in his last four starts. Jim Ferguson says his ERA was 7.13 over that period.

It's like a hitter who is 0 for 20 and struggling a bit ... you give him a rest. You sit him down and hope he gets everything together. Stuper's got the kind of arm where he can pitch every day, an inning or two.

This move might help him.

I'm looking forward to Atlanta. Hitters like to play in Atlanta Stadium because the ball carries so well there.

I'm taking Carol on the trip, so I hope we have a good weekend.

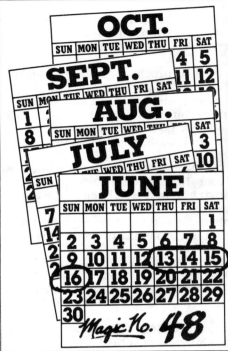

Rose continued to stick with Jay Tibbs, even though the youngster had experienced a tough April and May.

THURSDAY, JUNE 13 .... ROSE 0 FOR 4

I didn't get any hits, but we beat the Braves, 9-2, tonight in 11 innings.

This was a good way to start the trip because on our homestand we'd been scoring early, but not doing much in the late innings.

We got two runs in the fourth, then they got one in the fifth and one in the eighth to tie us.

When you're on the road in a tie game, the home team has every advantage. But our relief pitching was excellent, and we got seven runs in the 11th inning.

I don't know what it is, but sometimes you just have a feeling something's going to happen. That's the way I felt tonight; I just knew we were eventually going to score a lot of runs.

They started a kid named Steve Shields, a righthander, and he pitched a whale of a game. He went eight innings, gave us just one hit—a two-run

Cincinnati	ab	r	h	rbi	Atlanta	ab	r	h	rbi
Redus, lf	4	1	1	2	Wash'gton, rf	5	0	1	1
Milner, cf	6	1	1	1	Komminsk, lf	4	0	1	0
Rose, 1b	4	1	0	0	Murphy, cf	5	0	0	0
Parker, rf	5	2	2	2	Horner, 1b	3	0	0	0
Walker, rf	0	0	0	0	Oberkfell, 3b	4	1	1	0
Knicely, c	3	0	0	0	Ramirez, ss	4	0	0	0
Venable, pr	0	0	0	0	Hubbard, 2b	4	1	1	1
Van Gorder, c	1	1	1	1	Owen, c	3	0	0	0
Oester, 2b	5	1	1	1	Shields, p	2	0	0	0
Kr'chicki, 3b	3	0	0	0	Perry, ph	1	0	0	0
Es'sky, ph-3b	0	1	0	1	Camp, p	0	0	0	0
Foley, ss	3	0	0	0	Forster, p	0	0	0	0
Power, p	0	0	0	0	Dedmon, p	0	0	0	0
Perez, ph	1	0	0	0	Harper, ph	1	0	0	0
Franco, p	1	0	1	1	Garber, p	0	0	0	0
Tibbs, p	2	0	0	0	Schuler, p	0	0	0	0
C'cepcion, ss	3	1	2	0					
Totals	41	9	9	9	Totals	36	2	4	2

Cincinnati .... 0 0 0   2 0 0   0 0 0   0 7—9
Atlanta .... 0 0 0   0 1 0   0 1 0   0 0—2

Cincinnati	IP.	H.	R.	ER.	BB.	SO.
Tibbs	7⅓	4	2	1	2	3
Power.........................	1⅓	0	0	0	1	2
Franco (W. 3-1).........	2	0	0	0	0	2

Atlanta	IP.	H.	R.	ER.	BB.	SO.
Shields.......................	8	1	2	2	1	5
Camp.........................	1	1	0	0	0	0
Forster.......................	⅔	0	0	0	2	0
Dedmon......................	⅓	0	0	0	0	1
Garber (L. 1-3)...........	⅓	2	3	3	1	0
Schuler......................	⅔	5	4	4	1	1

Game-winning RBI—Milner.
E—Foley 2, Ramirez. DP—Cincinnati 1, Atlanta 1. LOB—Cincinnati 5, Atlanta 5. HR—Parker (10). SB—Redus, Venable, Milner. SH—Owen, Redus. WP—Tibbs 2. T—3:06. A—15,814.

homer by Dave Parker—and struck out five.

I had never seen Shields before, but that doesn't bother me as much as it did in the old days. I used to hate to see a pitcher for the first time and if you check my record, I never hit very well against a guy I hadn't seen.

But, like I said, that doesn't give me as much trouble as it used to. I sit on the dugout bench and watch them warm up. That gives me a pretty good idea what pitches they're throwing and how hard they throw.

Still, I didn't get any hits off Shields, but I hit a couple of balls hard. I'll bet you anything this kid won't pitch as good a game for a while.

I've been sticking with Jay Tibbs and some people have been on me for it.

But I think he's pitched three or four pretty good games in a row after not doing very well for about four. He had some problems with his mechanics, but Kitty helped straighten him out. He's back in the groove now.

He's also had a confidence problem. He just went through that for a period of time. I talked with him a lot and told him to go out there and forget what had happened. I stayed with him.

Tonight, he gave up just one earned run in 7⅔ innings, but I had to bring in Teddy Power in the eighth. They tied us when Claudell Washington singled to right field, but Tibbs could have been out of the inning had it not been for Tom Foley's throwing error on Glenn Hubbard's grounder.

After Washington singled, Tibbs walked Brad Komminsk, so I went to my bullpen. Power struck out Dale Murphy on a fastball in tight.

Davey Concepcion got us started in the 11th when he singled off Gene Garber. Davey now has hit in 14 straight games and was the first of 12 batters to come up.

After he singled, I had Gary Redus bunt him to second and Eddie Milner ripped a single to left to give us the go-ahead run. (Cincinnati collected five more hits and six more runs in the inning.)

Concepcion—that's the same guy who was down so low almost a month ago that he said he was going to quit—is on a roll. In his last 17 games, he's got 25 hits in 66 at-bats (.379), has scored 14 times and driven in nine runs.

★   ★   ★

Mario Soto has to go to court tomorrow morning over that problem he had here the first time in. Bill Bergesch mentioned this to me in case I wanted to switch my pitching plans.

I talked to Kitty and we don't want to mess up the rotation. As best I can tell, Mario didn't do anything, so he's going to be my starter tomorrow night.

With him going, we've got a good chance at taking the first two here.

FRIDAY, JUNE 14 .... DID NOT PLAY

There's a place in Atlanta where Carol gets a good deal on shoes. That was one of the reasons she came along on this trip, plus it gave her a chance to rest up. Tyler is growing so fast that he's taking most of her time.

Anyway, this was a good day for her to go shopping because I made arrangements for us to get the field at 3 o'clock for a workout. When we're on the road, this is something I always try to do. It gives everybody a chance to get some extra batting practice, me included.

Before the season started everybody was picking Atlanta as the one team that might beat out San Diego in our division.

Now, with the season two months old, the Braves are really struggling. The newspapers here have been getting on (Manager) Eddie Haas, and everybody wants to know what's wrong with the Atlanta Braves.

Well, the first time we came here, it seemed like their pitching was in chaos and ours was pretty well set.

Len Barker was hurting, Pascual Perez wasn't throwing well and Rick Camp didn't know what his role was going to be. Rick Mahler was the only guy who was really pitching, the only guy who had any wins.

Zane Smith, who pitched tonight's game, was in the bullpen at the time. They just didn't know who they were going to use. That was only like a week and a half out of spring training.

They were getting in trouble early in the ball game and that eliminated Bruce Sutter. We came down here and beat them three games when we started that seven-game winning streak. We eliminated Sutter (the Braves' relief ace didn't appear in the earlier series) by having more than two-run leads most of the time.

If Atlanta's not tied or (as close as) one run behind, Eddie won't bring in Sutter. That's why we beat them; no more, no less.

Tonight, the game was perfect for Sutter and he ended up getting the win.

We got beat, 6-4, in a game we had a good shot at winning.

We've been leading the league—or been near the lead—in double plays, but tonight we butchered one and it cost us.

★   ★   ★

There was some good news today—those charges against Soto (stemming from an April 16 incident in an Atlanta nightclub) were dropped.

SATURDAY, JUNE 15 .... ROSE 0 FOR 3

They gave out beach towels here in Atlanta tonight and the fans really needed them. It rained and rained and rained. Hard.

I'll never know what might have happened had the game not been interrupted by rain, but the bottom line is that Atlanta won, 7-0.

Atlanta Stadium can be miserable when it rains. Well, they delayed starting this game about 10 minutes because of a light rain. The field, which is natural grass, was soggy when we finally started.

I had a hunch Joe Price would crank up a good one for us. And for two innings, he was outstanding. He pitched to seven batters and set four of them down on called third strikes. Terry Harper got the only hit, a single up the middle that Davey Concepcion gloved but couldn't get out of his glove in time to make the throw.

After that, they stopped the game for a little over an hour. When Joe went back to the mound, he wasn't the same pitcher. You always run the risk of your pitcher losing it when there's a long rain delay. That's apparently what happened to Joe. I think he might have stiffened up some and never got loose when he went back out there.

Price started the third by walking Paul Runge, the shortstop. He struck out Steve Bedrosian, their pitcher, but got into more trouble when he threw a wild pitch to Brad Komminsk. That let Runge take second before Komminsk hit a smash to Wayne Krenchicki at third base. The ball hit Wayne's forearm and the scorer called it an error.

That was a tough error on that field tonight. The ball was hit hard and took a bad hop. Even the broadcasters told me after the game it should not have been an error. A lot of the errors here are tough.

Glenn Hubbard doubled in a run and it was 1-0. I put Dale Murphy on to load the bases, hoping we could get a double play. But Bob Horner hit a sacrifice fly and Terry Harper hit a three-run homer.

Cincinnati	ab	r	h	rbi	Atlanta	ab	r	h	rbi
Milner, cf	4	0	0	0	Komminsk, rf	4	1	0	0
Rose, 1b	3	0	0	0	Hubbard, 2b	3	1	1	2
Parker, rf	3	0	0	0	Murphy, cf	3	1	0	0
Knicely, c	4	0	0	0	Horner, 1b	3	0	0	1
Walker, lf	4	0	0	0	Harper, lf	4	2	3	3
C'cepcion, ss	4	0	2	0	Oberkfell, 3b	3	0	2	0
Oester, 2b	3	0	1	0	Owen, c	3	0	0	1
Kr'chicki, 3b	2	0	0	0	Runge, ss	2	2	1	0
Price, p	1	0	0	0	Bedrosian, p	2	0	0	0
Cedeno, ph	1	0	1	0	Perry, ph	1	0	1	0
Robinson, p	0	0	0	0	Dedmon, p	1	0	0	0
Esasky, ph	0	0	0	0					
Stuper, p	0	0	0	0					
Venable, ph	1	0	0	0					
Totals	30	0	4	0	Totals	29	7	8	7

Cincinnati ....0 0 0   0 0 0   0 0 0—0
Atlanta ....0 0 5   0 0 0   1 1 x—7

Cincinnati	IP.	H.	R.	ER.	BB.	SO.
Price (L. 2-1)	4	4	5	1	2	6
Robinson	2	0	0	0	1	1
Stuper	2	4	2	2	1	0

Atlanta	IP.	H.	R.	ER.	BB.	SO.
Bedrosian (W. 3-5)	7	3	0	0	3	4
Dedmon	2	1	0	0	2	2

Game-winning RBI—Hubbard.
E—Runge, Krenchicki. DP—Cincinnati 1, Atlanta 2. LOB—Cincinnati 9, Atlanta 5. 2B—Hubbard, Oester. HR—Harper (5). SF—Horner, Hubbard, Owen. HBP—By Bedrosian (Esasky). WP—Price, Dedmon. T—2:26. A—29,635.

It was our sixth loss in eight games and we fell 4½ games behind San Diego in the Western Division, tied with Los Angeles for third place.

★　　★　　★

Duane Walker has been doing some talking lately to the writers who travel with this team. He told 'em he's fed up because he hasn't gotten to play. So, I started him tonight in left field.

Walker says he's not bitter, but wants us to try to trade him.

I told him his greatest value on this team is as a pinch-hitter. If everybody in my outfield stays healthy, it will be tough to get him into the lineup more often.

It's just like Bill Bergesch, our general manager, told him. We're really not interested in trading him. You need somebody like that coming off the bench and being ready in case somebody gets hurt. If something happened to Dave Parker, Walker would be in there right away.

The trading deadline was tonight and we didn't do anything.

SUNDAY, JUNE 16 .... ROSE 2 FOR 4

This could've been one of those "here we go again" games.

The Braves had us 5-3 in the ninth inning with Bruce Sutter pitching. I'll tell you, that's not a very good predicament for any team to be in, let alone one that has been struggling. We've made a lot of errors lately, and today my pitcher couldn't hold a 3-0 lead.

Tom Browning was real wild. He walked three batters and couldn't get past the third inning. Davey Concepcion, who extended his hitting streak to 17 games, made an error on Brad Komminsk's grounder and they ended up scoring four times in the third.

I've got to figure out a way to get Browning back on track. His screwball wasn't working today and he threw a lot of pitches. He's only a rookie, but still he has given up 23 earned runs, 35 hits and 13 walks in his last 25⅔ innings.

While he had a tough day, I can't say enough for the job my relievers did. After those four runs, they shut down the Braves and that made it possible for us to win, 6-5, in the 10th.

This was a big win for a lot of reasons. We beat the best reliever in the league (Sutter), we split the four games here and the Padres dropped a doubleheader today to the Giants. San Francisco won three out of four in that series. We're tied for second now with the Dodgers, three games back of San Diego.

I had two hits, a single in the first inning off Rick Mahler and a single in the ninth off Sutter that tied the game.

Mahler pitched a good five innings, then Terry Forster pitched well in the sixth and seventh to get them to Sutter. And that's the way they have to use Bruce. The newspapers here have been getting on Eddie Haas for not using him enough, but it takes a situation like today's for Sutter.

The ninth inning today gave us a big lift.

Cincinnati	ab	r	h	rbi	Atlanta	ab	r	h	rbi
Redus, lf	5	2	3	4	Komminsk, rf	5	1	0	0
Venable, cf	4	0	0	0	Hubbard, 2b	3	0	1	0
Rose, 1b	4	0	2	1	Murphy, cf	5	1	1	1
Power, p	0	0	0	0	Horner, 1b	5	2	3	2
Franco, p	0	0	0	0	Hall, pr	0	0	0	0
Parker, rf	4	0	1	0	Harper, lf	3	0	1	0
Knicely, c	5	0	1	0	Oberkfell, 3b	4	0	0	0
C'cepcion, ss	5	1	1	0	Cerone, c	4	0	1	2
Oester, 2b	4	1	1	0	Runge, ss	4	0	0	0
Foley, 2b	1	0	0	0	Mahler, p	0	1	0	0
Kr'chicki, 3b	2	0	0	0	Forster, p	1	0	0	0
Es'sky, ph-3b	1	2	1	1	Sutter, p	1	0	0	0
Browning, p	1	0	0	0					
Robinson, p	1	0	0	0					
Cedeno, ph	1	0	0	0					
Hume, p	0	0	0	0					
Perez, ph-1b	2	0	0	0					
Totals	40	6	10	6	Totals	35	5	7	5

```
Cincinnati ............... 0 3 0   0 0 0   0 0 2   1—6
Atlanta ................... 0 1 4   0 0 0   0 0 0   0—5
```

Cincinnati	IP.	H.	R.	ER.	BB.	SO.
Browning	2⅓	4	5	3	3	4
Robinson	2⅔	1	0	0	1	1
Hume	3	1	0	0	0	2
Power (W. 1-2)	1⅓	1	0	0	2	1
Franco (Save 3)	⅔	0	0	0	0	0

Atlanta	IP.	H.	R.	ER.	BB.	SO.
Mahler	5	6	3	3	3	2
Forster	2	0	0	0	1	0
Sutter (L. 3-2)	3	4	3	3	1	1

Game-winning RBI—Esasky.
E—Concepcion, Runge. DP—Cincinnati 1. LOB—Cincinnati 9, Atlanta 8. 2B—Horner 2, Redus. HR—Redus (3), Esasky (5). SB—Harper. SH—Hubbard. SF—Cerone. Balk—Mahler. T—3:05. A—24,863.

There was one out when Gary Redus hit a double to left to score Nick Esasky. Max Venable grounded out, but Gary went to third and I came up.

Sutter got two strikes on me, then he had me 2-2 when I got a base hit to left to score Redus and tie the game. He threw me a good pitch and I hit it—a split-fingered fastball down and away. That's Sutter's million-dollar pitch, but I got it past Ken Oberkfell at third.

Right now, Sutter's in a little bit of a rut. The bottom's not dropping out of his split-finger like it can. But he can get it back real fast.

Esasky, who lives in Marietta, Georgia, which is not very far from Atlanta, hits well against the Braves. Maybe it's because he always has a lot of family and friends in the stands.

Well, after Sutter got two outs in the 10th, Nick homered to left-center and we had the lead.

This year alone, Nick has 12 hits in 23 at-bats against the Braves.

Teddy Power and John Franco did a good job of relief. Teddy got the win and Franco a save.

My two hits today left me 46 from breaking the record, and the second one meant a lot in the game.

Plus, the win made the long ride (flight) to San Francisco a lot more fun.

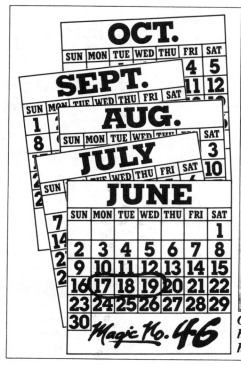

Magic No. 46

Giants lefty Atlee Hammaker handcuffed the Reds on four hits in a June 17 game.

MONDAY, JUNE 17 .... DID NOT PLAY

When the game started today, I thought we were a little bit flat.

I didn't expect that to happen, especially after coming from behind to beat Bruce Sutter yesterday. I don't know why this happens. I've never been able to figure it out.

I don't know whether it's because of the coast-to-coast travel or what. We weren't flat in batting practice or in the clubhouse before the game.

We got here (San Francisco) from Atlanta last night at a pretty decent hour; we had a charter and everybody had time to get a decent night's sleep. But, we had to travel, then get up relatively early for the 1:05 p.m. game. I just don't know.

Maybe the real reason was Atlee Hammaker. He just handcuffed us, 4-0. Gave us only four hits in one of the best ball games pitched against us this year. A lefthander can't do a much better job. Walked two, had six strikeouts. Total control. He has a cut-fastball that is tough on right-handers.

Davey Concepcion went 0 for 4, and his 17-game hitting streak was snapped on his 37th birthday. Not a very good present. He just didn't swing good. He broke three bats and all three that he broke he hit on the end. Atlee was just throwing sinkers away and Davey was getting only the end of the bat on them.

You never expect a guy on a 17-game hitting streak who hits left-handers as good as anybody to break three bats in a game. Usually when

— 104 —

a guy breaks three bats, it's against a hard-thrower and he's not swinging good.

I've never been able to figure out which is tougher, going from the East Coast to the West Coast or vice versa. You gain three hours when you come out here, then lose it when you go home. Usually, when you go home from here, you've got an open date to recuperate.

In the course of the whole season, though, I don't think you're going to run into many days when you're not rested enough to go out there and play. You get used to it; you learn how to rest on the plane and different things like that.

People keep asking me if I'm resting myself more. I'm not. We're just facing a lot of lefthanders, and it's all according to what Doggie (Tony Perez) does. I'll just have to leave it up to my discretion as to whether he's swinging good or not.

TUESDAY, JUNE 18 .... ROSE 0 FOR 3

This was one of those days.

First, I get knocked on my can by old buddy Manny Trillo, then one of my own players throws cold water on me while I'm in the shower.

Well, I'll tell you, I can't complain because we beat the Giants, 6-1, today and Frank Pastore pitched a great game for us. He gave me nine strong innings and allowed only four hits. He struck out three.

I didn't get any hits, but did get an RBI because I walked on five pitches with the bases loaded in the seventh inning. Their third baseman, Ricky Adams, made a couple of great plays on me.

Cincinnati	ab	r	h	rbi	San Fran.	ab	r	h	rbi
Redus, lf	4	1	1	1	Y'ngblood, cf	4	0	0	0
Milner, cf	5	1	3	1	Trillo, 2b	4	0	2	1
Rose, 1b	3	0	0	1	C. Davis, rf	4	0	0	0
Parker, rf	3	1	1	2	Leonard, lf	4	0	0	0
Knicely, c	5	0	1	1	Brenly, c	3	0	0	0
C'cepcion, ss	4	0	1	0	Green, 1b	3	0	0	0
Oester, 2b	4	1	0	0	Adams, 3b	3	0	0	0
Kr'chicki, 3b	3	1	1	0	Uribe, ss	3	1	2	0
Pastore, p	3	1	0	0	Laskey, p	1	0	0	0
					Williams, p	0	0	0	0
					Rajsich, ph	1	0	0	0
					Garrelts, p	0	0	0	0
Totals	34	6	8	6	Totals	30	1	4	1

Cincinnati			0 0 0	0 0 3	3 0 0—6	
San Francisco			0 0 1	0 0 0	0 0 0—1	

Cincinnati	IP.	H.	R.	ER.	BB.	SO.
Pastore (W. 2-0)	9	4	1	0	1	3

San Francisco	IP.	H.	R.	ER.	BB.	SO.
Laskey (L. 1-8)	6⅓	6	6	2	2	2
Williams	1⅔	1	0	0	1	0
Garrelts	1	1	0	0	1	0

Game-winning RBI—Parker.
E—Krenchicki, Youngblood, Trillo. LOB—Cincinnati 8, San Francisco 4. 2B—Redus, Milner. SB—Green, Concepcion. SH—Laskey, Pastore. SF—Redus, Parker. WP—Pastore. T—2:16. A—5,961.

The first time up, I walked. The next time, I hit a ball down the third-base line and Adams made a spectacular play. He backhanded it, jumped up and threw a strike to first base. Later, with a man on second and one out, I hit a line shot right at him. Boom! Boom! He caught it before I was out of the box.

Pastore says he likes to pitch here. He used only 96 pitches, and Kitty told me he was ahead in the count on 17 of the 32 hitters he faced. He retired 10 in a row during one spell and 17 of the last 18 he faced.

I used him in place of John Stuper, who's in the bullpen right now. The reason Pastore got to start was because except for that terrible game against Atlanta (May 1, when he yielded seven runs in 1⅓ innings), he's pitched well. In his last nine relief outings, he had allowed only two runs in 14⅔ innings. Today was his first complete game since May 10, 1984.

The bullpen work helped him throw strikes and gave him confidence. He got the opportunity today and took advantage of it.

We're in a five-man rotation right now, mostly because when we tried to firm up a four-man rotation in the middle of May, Mario Soto got all upset. He said he didn't want any part of it.

You never know how to play popups here, especially when the sky is high—and that's the way it was today at Candlestick Park.

Trillo hit one and when Alan Knicely and I went after it, Manny ran into me and knocked me down. Manny was called out by umpire John McSherry for interference, but I fell and jammed my left wrist.

I didn't know what happened at first. I thought Alan might have hit me. My wrist is not bad. I'll ice it down tonight, and I don't plan to play tomorrow anyway.

Then, when I'm taking my shower—I was scrubbing my hair—all of a sudden, somebody threw a bucket of water on me and it was cold!

When I came out, I asked who did it. Somebody told me it was Gary Redus. I laughed and said, "He ain't going good enough to do that."

But he had a double, drove in a run and scored another today, so I guess he wanted to get my attention. He did.

WEDNESDAY, JUNE 19 .... DID NOT PLAY

I was talking to Rocky Bridges, one of the Giants' coaches, before today's game about the conditions at Candlestick Park.

I told him the grass here is the worst I've ever seen in baseball. It holds balls from going through the infield; it's almost impossible to get a ball through.

I told him in my opinion that's why San Francisco is hitting something like .213 as a team. A lot of that has to do with the grass.

It helps their pitching, and that's one of the reasons they've got the lowest team earned-run average in the league. (Through Monday's games, San Francisco had a team batting average of .216 and a club ERA mark of 2.66.)

I figured we had a good chance to win today because we had our ace, Mario Soto, going. It was a big game for us because if we had won, we'd go home a game over .500 (4-3) on this road trip.

Mario had the same problems today he's been having and we got beat, 5-2. The loss was our eighth in 12 games since we began that big series back home with the Padres.

Mario walked six guys today. He just couldn't control his fastball and changeup, then he started overthrowing and the hitters jumped on him. Bob Brenly hit a couple of home runs, and here's a guy who was 0 for 14 when the game started.

We had Dave LaPoint on the ropes, but almost every time we had a chance to score we just didn't. Then, they brought in Scott Garrelts and he is real good. He's big and throws hard; he throws strikes.

For some reason, we're always down when we don't get hits. I don't know what it is. You can't spot it in infield or batting practice. I've tried to, just like in Monday's game when I said we were flat.

With some clubs, you can just walk into the clubhouse and feel a team's not there. We're one of those ball clubs that looks real good when we win and real bad when we lose. There is no in-between with us.

Brenly tells reporters about getting his hitting stroke back because of psychology. He's been working with the psychologists the Giants have hired. He says because of this, he's seeing the ball better.

I honestly don't believe in any of that stuff. Sure, it looked like it worked today after he hit a couple of homers, but what about next week?

OCT.

SUN	MON	TUE	WED	THU	FRI	SAT
					4	5

SEPT.

SUN	MON	TUE	WED	THU	FRI	SAT
					11	12

AUG.

SUN	MON	TUE	WED	THU	FRI	SAT
1						3
8						

JULY

SUN			WED	THU	FRI	SAT
						10

JUNE

SUN	MON	TUE	WED	THU	FRI	SAT
7						1
14	2	3	4	5	6	7	8
	9	10	11	12	13	14	15
	16	17	18	19	20	21	22
23	24	25	26	27	28	29
30						

Magic No. **46**

Rose always gets his batting-cage swings, even on open dates.

FRIDAY, JUNE 21 .... ROSE 1 FOR 6

It's always good to get back home. I was looking forward to seeing Carol and Tyler.

That boy is really growing. He's so strong that when he grabs you, he can really hurt you if you're not careful. He's not even 9 months old yet, but he's already walking a little bit. He will put his hands on the edge of a table and guide himself around it. He wobbles a little, but I like his determination. When he falls down, he gets right back up and goes at it again.

Yesterday was an open date, but I met Billy DeMars (batting coach) at the ball park at 11 o'clock so I could get some hitting in. After that, he went to play golf and I went to watch my son, Pete, play baseball. He's becoming a good player.

FIRST GAME

Atlanta	ab	r	h	rbi	Cincinnati	ab	r	h	rbi
Komminsk, rf	4	1	1	0	Redus, lf	5	0	0	0
Wash'ton, ph	1	0	0	0	Milner, cf	4	1	2	0
Ramirez, ss	4	1	0	0	Rose, 1b	3	1	0	0
Murphy, cf	4	0	3	0	Parker, rf	3	1	1	3
Horner, 1b	4	0	1	0	Knicely, c	4	0	1	0
Harper, lf	3	0	1	1	C'cepcion, ss	3	1	1	0
Oberkfell, 3b	4	0	1	0	Oester, 2b	4	0	2	0
Hubbard, 2b	3	0	1	1	Kr'chicki, 3b	1	0	1	1
Owen, c	4	0	0	0	Browning, p	3	0	0	0
Shields, p	2	0	0	0	Power, p	0	0	0	0
Dedmon, p	0	0	0	0					
Runge, ph	1	0	0	0					
Garber, p	0	0	0	0					
Perry, p	0	0	0	0					
Totals	34	2	8	2	Totals	30	4	8	4

Atlanta........................0 0 0 0 0 0 0 2 0—2
Cincinnati....................0 0 0 3 0 1 0 0 x—4

Atlanta	IP.	H.	R.	ER.	BB.	SO.
Shields (L. 1-2)	5⅓	7	4	4	5	2
Dedmon	⅔	0	0	0	0	1
Garber	2	1	0	0	2	1

Cincinnati	IP.	H.	R.	ER.	BB.	SO.
Browning (W. 6-5)	7*	6	2	2	4	6
Power (Save 9)	2	2	0	0	2	2

*Pitched to three batters in eighth.

Game-winning RBI—Parker.
E—None. DP—Atlanta 2. LOB—Atlanta 11, Cincinnati 9. 2B—Murphy, Milner, Oester. HR—Parker (11). SB—Milner, Concepcion. T—2:36.

Before tonight's doubleheader with Atlanta, I had to drive to Kings Island, a resort (and amusement-park area) not too far from Cincinnati, to speak at the Associated Press Sports Editors' Convention.

I talked about a lot of things, but they kept asking about a strike and my thoughts on it.

I told the sports editors the same thing I've been saying all along, that I personally don't think there's going to be a strike and if there is, there's nothing I can do about it. The closer you get to a so-called strike date, there's more pressure on and there's more talking.

Marge Schott, owner of the Reds, has made some statements saying she's upset that I voted for a strike and would stand behind the players' association.

I still think the owners have caused some of their own problems by allowing so many big contracts. That's what I told her.

Here's what she told a reporter:

"Pete's a player-manager, but his first priority should be to management. I still love Pete, but it bothers me he would be so quick to vote yes.

"As an older player, Pete should set an example for the younger players. I was hoping he'd influence them not to strike because it would be tragic if they do."

She's owned the club, what, five months. From my standpoint, well, just look at all the things that have happened to me in my career that have been a result of the players' association. How can I not be loyal to them?

Marge gets excited. Her saying those things is nothing negative toward me. She likes me. What I told her today is to stop talking about a strike and talk about the Reds getting into first place.

She said later we should both cool it, and I couldn't agree more.

★ ★ ★

We won the first game of the doubleheader, 4-2, but lost the second, 5-4.

I usually don't play doubleheaders (both games), but they had two righthanders pitching, so it worked out OK. With a lefthander, Zane Smith, going tomorrow for the Braves, I don't plan to play.

I didn't get any hits in the first game, but got a bunt single in the second.

We lost that second game, but what I liked about it was the fact we took Bruce Sutter to the limit. He got a save, but we got four hits and two runs off him in two innings.

In the ninth inning, we were down 5-3. There was one out and a man on third base. Their third baseman, Ken Oberkfell, was playing me deep. He was giving me a bunt and I took it. I got a hit and the run scored to make it 5-4.

The only reason I bunted was because we were two runs down and there was only one out. If there had been two out, I would have tried to hit a double. But with one out, I had to take it.

SECOND GAME									
Atlanta	ab	r	h	rbi	Cincinnati	ab	r	h	rbi
Wash'gton, rf	3	2	2	2	Milner, cf	4	0	1	0
Ramirez, ss	4	0	1	1	Venable, lf	3	1	1	0
Murphy, cf	5	1	2	1	Redus, ph-lf	1	1	1	0
Horner, 1b	5	1	1	0	Rose, 1b	3	1	1	1
Harper, lf	3	0	1	0	Parker, rf	5	0	2	1
Oberkfell, 3b	5	0	2	0	Kr'chicki, 3b	4	1	1	0
Zuvella, 2b	5	0	3	0	Oester, 2b	4	0	1	1
Benedict, c	4	0	0	0	Foley, ss	2	0	0	0
Camp, p	1	0	0	1	C'pc'n, ph-ss	0	0	0	1
Perry, ph	1	0	0	0	Van Gorder, c	3	0	0	0
Forster, p	0	0	0	0	K'c'ly, ph-c	1	0	0	0
Chambliss, ph	1	0	1	0	Tibbs, p	2	0	1	0
Hall, pr	0	1	0	0	Cedeno, ph	1	0	0	0
Sutter, p	0	0	0	0	Hume, p	0	0	0	0
					Perez, ph	1	0	0	0
					Franco, p	0	0	0	0
Totals	37	5	13	5	Totals	34	4	9	4

Atlanta..................0 1 0   0 1 1   0 2 0—5
Cincinnati..............2 0 0   0 0 0   0 1 1—4

Atlanta	IP.	H.	R.	ER.	BB.	SO.
Camp (W. 2-3)	5	5	2	2	4	3
Forster	2	0	0	0	2	0
Sutter (Save 10)	2	4	2	2	0	0
Cincinnati	IP.	H.	R.	ER.	BB.	SO.
Tibbs (L. 4-9)	6	7	3	3	6	2
Hume	2	6	2	2	0	0
Franco	1	0	0	0	0	0

Game-winning RBI—Ramirez.
E—Tibbs, Forster, Zuvella. DP—Atlanta 1, Cincinnati 1. LOB—Atlanta 12, Cincinnati 10. 2B—Venable, Oberkfell, Parker, Oester. 3B—Washington, Redus. HR—Murphy (17), Washington (7). SB—Concepcion, Redus. SF—Ramirez, Concepcion. WP—Tibbs. T—2:35. A—33,248.

My only hit in last night's double-header was a bunt.

My co-author for this book asked me a difficult question after that. Would I bunt for the Cobb record if I had to?

The answer was simple, and I'm being as honest as possible.

My philosophy is I'd never bunt for any kind of record if the play was not in order for the team. I know I did it several times during my 44-game hitting streak in 1978, but that was different (because of the game-to-game, today-or-else nature of a batting streak compared with the cumulative aspects of the assault on Cobb's record).

If it was in order to help the team in a key situation, sure, I'd bunt for the record. Why not?

Atlanta	ab	r	h	rbi	Cincinnati	ab	r	h	rbi
Komminsk, rf	3	0	0	0	Redus, cf	3	0	0	0
Ramirez, ss	4	0	1	1	Robinson, p	0	0	0	0
Murphy, cf	4	0	0	0	Rose, ph	1	0	1	0
Horner, 1b	4	2	2	2	C'cepcion, ss	4	1	3	1
Harper, lf	4	0	0	0	Parker, rf	5	1	3	1
Oberkfell, 3b	4	0	1	0	Perez, 1b	4	0	1	0
Hubbard, 2b	2	0	0	0	Knicely, c	3	0	1	1
Perry, ph	1	0	0	0	Esasky, 3b	4	0	1	0
Zuvella, 2b	0	0	0	0	Cedeno, lf	4	0	0	0
Benedict, c	2	1	0	0	Oester, 2b	3	1	1	0
Chambliss, ph	1	0	0	0	Price, p	2	0	0	0
Owen, c	0	0	0	0	Milner, ph-cf	1	1	1	0
Smith, p	2	0	2	0					
Dedmon, p	0	0	0	0					
Wash'ton, ph	1	0	0	0					
Forster, p	0	0	0	0					
Totals	32	3	6	3	Totals	34	4	12	3

Atlanta...................0 0 1 0 0 1 1 0 0—3
Cincinnati...............0 0 2 0 0 0 1 0 1—4
One out when winning run scored.

Atlanta	IP.	H.	R.	ER.	BB.	SO.
Smith	6⅓	7	3	2	3	5
Dedmon	1⅔	2	0	0	0	0
Forster (L. 0-2)	⅓	3	1	1	1	0

Cincinnati	IP.	H.	R.	ER.	BB.	SO.
Price	7	6	3	3	3	1
Robinson (W. 1-0)	2	0	0	0	0	0

Game-winning RBI—Parker.
E—Murphy 2. DP—Atlanta 1. LOB—Atlanta 6, Cincinnati 10. 2B—Esasky. HR—Horner 2 (9). SB—Redus, Milner. SH—Smith, Milner. PB—Knicely. T—2:31. A—20,428.

Bunting for base hits is part of my game. I see no reason why you cannot bunt if the guy (third baseman) is going to give it to you. I'll take a bunt every time.

If I come up to bat four times and there's one out or less and the third baseman is behind the bag five feet, I'll bunt.

I don't care. I know I can hit. In my situation, with Dave Parker coming up next, I've got that hole opening up there, especially with a pitcher who throws a lot of slow curves and breaking pitches.

I see guys day in and day out giving you the bunt. All you've got to do is take it, but a lot of players won't.

I'll tell you, if I'm in a tight game and a bunt will help us win—even if it is for the Cobb record—I'll take it.

★   ★   ★

In the ninth inning of today's game, we're tied 3-3 with the Braves and Eddie Milner bunts for a base hit. I pinch hit for Ron Robinson and get an infield single, swinging righthanded off Terry Forster. Then, Dave Concepcion walked and Dave Parker got the game-winning hit. Parker had three hits today.

Joe Price really pitched well. He gave up six hits and had the game under control. I brought in Robinson to pitch the last two innings and he didn't give them anything.

Today started out pretty good. I did the pregame TV show with Skip Caray, who broadcasts for Atlanta's WTBS.

Skip's the son of Harry Caray, the Chicago Cubs' popular announcer. I told Skip I was pretty pleased with a lot of things my club has been doing. It's coming. Because of the satellite, the whole country was watching today and then we went out and got beat, 2-1, by the Braves.

And it wasn't very pretty.

Bob Howsam, the Reds' president, is retiring on July 1, so they honored him before the game. A lot of officials said nice things about him, including former Reds owners Louis Nippert and Bill and James Williams. National League President Chub Feeney also was here. The Reds are going to put a bronze plaque on the walkway around Riverfront Stadium to honor Howsam (chief architect of the franchise's Big Red Machine powerhouse of the 1970s).

You had to see this game to believe how many chances we wasted.

It was a case where we had the right people up there many times, but they just didn't execute. All we had to do was hit some fly balls and we would've won.

Losing was bad enough, but then the writers second-guessed me. That's OK, but I still think I was right.

Atlanta	ab	r	h	rbi	Cincinnati	ab	r	h	rbi
Ramirez, ss	5	1	2	0	Redus, lf	3	0	0	0
Oberkfell, 3b	2	0	0	0	Milner, cf	3	1	0	0
Murphy, cf	3	0	0	1	**Rose, 1b**	2	0	1	0
Horner, 1b	5	0	1	0	Parker, rf	3	0	0	1
Harper, lf	5	0	0	0	Knicely, c	1	0	0	0
Komminsk, rf	3	0	2	0	Hume, p	0	0	0	0
Hubbard, 2b	3	1	0	0	Perez, ph	1	0	0	0
Sutter, p	0	0	0	0	Franco, p	0	0	0	0
Owen, c	3	0	1	1	Power, p	0	0	0	0
Bedrosian, p	3	0	0	0	C'cepcion, ss	4	0	0	0
Camp, p	0	0	0	0	Oester, 2b	4	0	1	0
Zuvella, 2b	1	0	1	0	Kr'chicki, 3b	3	0	2	0
					Es'sky, pr-3b	1	0	0	0
					Pastore, p	2	0	0	0
					Van Gorder, c	1	0	0	0
					Walker, ph	1	0	0	0
Totals	33	2	7	2	Totals	29	1	4	1

```
Atlanta....................0 0 1  1 0 0  0 0 0—2
Cincinnati................0 0 0  0 0 0  0 1 0—1
```

Atlanta	IP.	H.	R.	ER.	BB.	SO.
Bedrosian (W. 4-6).....	6⅓	3	0	0	6	4
Camp..........................	⅔	0	0	0	0	0
Sutter (Save 11)........	2	1	1	0	1	0

Cincinnati	IP.	H.	R.	ER.	BB.	SO.
Pastore (L. 2-1).........	6*	6	2	2	4	2
Hume	2	0	0	0	1	1
Franco........................	⅓	1	0	0	1	0
Power..........................	⅔	0	0	0	0	0

*Pitched to one batter in seventh.

Game-winning RBI—Murphy.

E—Owen, Pastore, Franco. DP—Atlanta 2, Cincinnati 1. LOB—Atlanta 12, Cincinnati 8. 2B—Ramirez, Owen, Krenchicki. SB—Komminsk 3, Ramirez, Redus 2, **Rose**. SH—Oberkfell. SF—Murphy. T—2:27. A—24,538.

It happened in the sixth inning, an inning I'd just as soon forget.

It was really hot today, like 90 degrees, and the AstroTurf must have been over a hundred. Their pitcher, Steve Bedrosian, was getting a little tired, I think. We're down 2-0 and he walks Gary Redus to start the sixth.

Now, the count goes full to Eddie Milner. The next pitch is over his head, but he swung at it and hit a weak fly to left field. They walked me, and here is where the writers didn't care too much for my managing.

Redus, running on his own, took third and I went to second on a double steal.

That gave us runners on second and third with one out. Dave Parker was the next batter and the writers said the double steal took the bat out of his hands. He was walked intentionally. Alan Knicely comes up, hits the ball off the end of the bat and bounces into a double play.

At that stage of the game, I didn't think that (the double steal) was a bad move to get your fifth-place hitter up there. If it had been the eighth inning or so, I would've told Gary not to run.

We left eight guys on base and six of them were in scoring position with less than two outs. We had guys on third with one out three times and couldn't score.

Because of that, this game was very frustrating. We lose two to the Braves by one run, games we could have won.

I think what bothered me just as much as wasting all those chances was the fact my pitcher, Frank Pastore, walked Glenn Hubbard after getting two strikes on him. That was in the fourth. Then their catcher, Larry Owen—he hadn't had a hit in 23 at-bats—doubled Hubbard home. That turned out to be the winning run.

I got my only hit today in the eighth, a bunt single. Their third baseman, Ken Oberkfell, was playing like 10 feet behind the bag.

JUNE

SUN	MON	TUE	WED	THU	FRI	SAT
						1
2	3	4	5	6	7	8
9	10	11	12	13	14	15
16	17	18	19	20	21	22
23	24	25	26	27	28	29
30						

Magic No. **43**

Rose joined Olympic gymnastic star Mary Lou Retton for a Wheaties promotion before the All-Star Game in Minneapolis.

TUESDAY, JUNE 25 .... ROSE 0 FOR 1

I've always had a rule that I don't let endorsements and stuff like that interfere with baseball.

To tell you the truth, there have been so many requests for interviews and picture sessions, I'm going to have to back off a little.

I'm going to talk with Bill Hayes, my marketing agent at Taft Merchandising, and Jim Ferguson to see if some of these things can be put on hold or something.

Yesterday was an off-day, but I had to go to Charleston, West Virginia, to do some promotional work. West Virginia has some great Cincinnati Reds fans.

The promotion was from noon to 4 and when I got back to Cincinnati at about 5:30, I had to pick up Lou Palmer of ESPN. He wanted to do a long taping at my home for a special that's going to be shown in early August.

San Fran.	ab	r	h	rbi	Cincinnati	ab	r	h	rbi
Y'ngblood, cf	5	1	0	0	Redus, cf	5	0	1	1
Trillo, 2b	5	2	3	1	Power, p	0	0	0	0
C. Davis, rf	4	0	2	1	C'cepcion, ss	3	1	0	0
Leonard, lf	4	0	2	0	Parker, rf	4	1	2	2
Brenly, c	3	0	0	2	Perez, 1b	3	0	1	0
Rajsich, 1b	4	0	0	0	Knicely, c	4	1	1	0
M. Davis, p	0	0	0	0	Cedeno, lf	4	1	1	2
Minton, p	0	0	0	0	Esasky, 3b	4	2	3	0
Brown, 3b	4	1	1	1	Oester, 2b	4	1	2	1
Uribe, ss	4	1	1	0	Robinson, p	0	0	0	0
LaPoint, p	3	1	1	1	**Rose, ph**	1	0	0	0
Garrelts, p	0	0	0	0	Stuper, p	0	0	0	0
Th'mpson, 1b	1	0	0	0	Milner, ph-cf	1	0	0	1
Totals	37	6	10	6	Totals	34	7	11	7

```
San Francisco................1 3 0  0 0 0  2 0 0—6
Cincinnati.......................2 0 0  0 0 0  1 4 x—7
```

San Francisco	IP.	H.	R.	ER.	BB.	SO.
LaPoint	6*	7	3	3	2	3
Garrelts	⅔	0	0	0	1	1
M. Davis (L, 3-5)	⅔	4	4	3	0	1
Minton	⅔	0	0	0	0	0
Cincinnati	**IP.**	**H.**	**R.**	**ER.**	**BB.**	**SO.**
Soto	6⅔	8	6	4	3	8
Robinson	⅓	0	0	0	0	0
Stuper (W. 6-5)	1	0	0	0	0	1
Power (Save 10)	1	2	0	0	0	0

*Pitched to two batters in seventh.

Game-winning RBI—Redus.
E—Brenly, Thompson, Esasky. DP—San Francisco 1. LOB—San Francisco 8, Cincinnati 7. 2B—Trillo, C. Davis, Esasky. 3B—Uribe. HR—Brown (4), Parker (12), Cedeno (2). SH—Soto. SF—Brenly. T—2:36. A—13,952.

Well, Lou and I are riding along the expressway when my brother, David, pulls up alongside. He saw Lou sitting there and yelled, "Lou Palmer!" He recognized him right away because we both like ESPN—it does such a great job with sports.

When I got home, David called and asked if he could come over and watch the taping. He did, and it lasted until about 9:30.

A lot of the media people like to come to my home to get pictures of the house, Carol and Tyler, the horses and all that. This is the type of thing that is taking so much time. Time magazine sent Neil Leifer out and he got a lot of pictures. They might put my picture on the cover when I break the record. Newsweek did the same thing.

I want to cooperate with everyone, but if I gave all the national media two or three hours, I wouldn't have any time to play baseball.

Before I got to the ball park today, I had to stop at a studio and tape the commercial that Wheaties will use beginning next month. Mary Lou Retton has a three-year deal with them. I will be used mostly for the rest of the summer—on TV and on their cereal boxes. Then, I guess, they will pick her up again.

All I had to do was sit at a table and eat some Wheaties and smile at the camera. That was easy. They used some film clips of my career, so I didn't have to slide on my belly like I've had to do in other commercials.

★　　　★　　　★

I didn't start in tonight's game because the Giants started a left-hander, Dave LaPoint. I did pinch hit for Ron Robinson in the seventh inning and flied out to left field off Scott Garrelts.

We scored a run in that inning, but still trailed 6-3. In the eighth, we scored four times and won, 7-6. (Cesar Cedeno's two-run homer was the big hit in the eighth.)

I liked the way we came from behind because that is what we did in September last year. It was a good sign.

WEDNESDAY, JUNE 26 .... ROSE 2 FOR 4

There's a little uncertainty around the ball club, but it really shouldn't bother us. And that's what I've told anybody who asked me.

With Bob Howsam retiring July 1, there's a lot of speculation about who will become the Cincinnati Reds' president.

Howsam brought Bill Bergesch in as general manager last October, but since then Marge Schott has bought the team. So, I guess you could say Bill is Howsam's man.

There was a rumor the Reds are looking for a baseball executive, but Marge insists that's not true.

Bergesch has told reporters he hasn't talked with Marge and is just waiting.

San Fran.	ab	r	h	rbi	Cincinnati	ab	r	h	rbi
Gladden, cf	5	0	1	0	Redus, lf	3	3	2	1
Trillo, 2b	4	0	1	0	Milner, cf	4	1	2	3
C. Davis, rf	4	0	1	0	Parker, rf	4	0	2	1
Leonard, lf	4	0	0	0	**Rose, 1b**	4	1	2	1
Brenly, c	3	2	1	1	Knicely, c	4	0	0	0
Brown, 3b	3	2	2	1	C'cepcion, ss	4	0	0	0
Green, 1b	1	0	0	0	Oester, 2b	4	0	2	0
Deer, ph-1b	2	0	0	0	Kr'chicki, 3b	3	0	0	0
R'sich, ph-1b	1	0	0	0	Browning, p	3	1	1	0
Uribe, ss	4	0	1	2	Power, p	0	0	0	0
Krukow, p	2	0	1	0					
Y'ngblood, ph	1	0	0	0					
Williams, p	0	0	0	0					
Th'mpson, ph	1	0	0	0					
Totals	35	4	8	4	Totals	33	6	11	6

San Francisco	0	0	0	2	0	0	0	2	0—4
Cincinnati	1	0	3	0	0	0	2	0	x—6

San Francisco	IP.	H.	R.	ER.	BB.	SO.
Krukow (L. 5-5)	6	8	4	4	2	5
Williams	2	3	2	2	0	1

Cincinnati	IP.	H.	R.	ER.	BB.	SO.
Browning (W. 7-5)	7⅔	8	4	4	2	5
Power (Save 11)	1⅓	0	0	0	0	0

Game-winning RBI—Redus.
E—None. DP—San Francisco 1. LOB—San Francisco 6, Cincinnati 5. 2B—Uribe, Brown, Oester. 3B—Browning. HR—Redus (4), Parker (13), Brenly (9), Brown (5). SB—Redus 2, Milner. T—2:10. A—19,777.

On another matter, there was a report today in the Pittsburgh news-papers that we're still trying to get John Candelaria. Well, we've been talking with the Pirates, but nothing's new on that deal.

Bill talked to their general manager, Joe Brown, the other day but was basically just checking back to see if there's anything new. I'd like to have the Candy Man, but we're not close to anything with them.

★   ★   ★

We're starting to play well at home now. For some reason, and I don't know the answer, we've had a better record on the road than at Riverfront.

By beating the Giants, 6-4, tonight, we're over .500 at home (at 18-17, compared with an 18-15 away mark).

I had two singles, leaving me 41 short of breaking the Cobb record. I singled to center in the third off Mike Krukow to drive in our fourth run and third of that inning.

I also had another single and feel like I'm swinging the bat good.

What I really liked tonight was the way Gary Redus and Eddie Milner, my No. 1 and No. 2 hitters, got things going. Redus went 2 for 3, had a homer, two stolen bases, scored three runs and drove one in. Eddie had a 2-for-4 night, drove in three runs, scored once and stole a base.

When the top guys in the batting order start getting a lot of hits, we can score a lot of runs. Seeing that happen tonight was very refreshing.

Redus told the reporters that he and Milner can do this all the time—and I couldn't agree with him more.

I think it's really important we get things cooking because after to-morrow's game, we go to San Diego for a big weekend series.

The Padres took three out of four here early in the month, so I want to see how we react to that.

We've got a chance to sweep the Giants, and I think that's important. There's nothing like momentum when you're about to start a road trip against the team that's leading your division.

THURSDAY, JUNE 27 .... ROSE 0 FOR 5

I had a lot to do today even before I got to the ball park for our 12:35 p.m. game, which we won, 7-6, over San Francisco.

First, I had to stop by the office of my attorney, Reuven Katz. We're going to have to sue a company because they're trying to sell merchan-dise with the old (1970s) "Little Charlie Hustle" caricature on it.

Seems like everybody's got an angle these days. Lord knows how much stuff is being sold out there that I don't even know about.

★   ★   ★

I went 0 for 5 today and hit only one ball real hard.

I'll tell you how ridiculous that game-winning RBI statistic is. I hit a nubber to the shortstop in the *first* inning to score our first run. Didn't even hit the ball hard. But the run scored, I got an RBI and it was listed in the box score as the game-winner.

According to the rule, whoever drives in the run that puts you ahead to stay—regardless of the inning—is credited with the game-winning RBI.

Reporters kept asking me about momentum going into San Diego and what I told them was the three-game winning streak is nice, but the only momentum we need is to see a San Diego uniform.

— 113 —

We've now beaten the Giants 19 out of the last 21 times they've played here and seven times in a row this season at Riverfront.

I kinda felt sorry for my pitcher, Frank Pastore, today. I've tried to be as patient as possible with all my pitchers. One thing is for sure, I don't have a quick hook. Whenever a guy can get a win, I want to do everything I can to help him.

Well, today I had to take Pastore out in the fifth inning with two out. If he'd gotten one more out, he'd have gotten the win.

There isn't one pitcher who has said I haven't been fair. If starters are going to do a good job for you, you've got to give them a shot at trying to win the game. You don't want to take them out every time they get into a little bit of trouble. Hell, they will never be good pitchers for you.

I just couldn't take a chance

San Fran.	ab	r	h	rbi	Cincinnati	ab	r	h	rbi
Gladden, cf	5	0	1	0	Redus, lf	4	1	1	0
Trillo, 2b	4	2	1	0	Milner, cf	3	1	1	0
C. Davis, rf	5	2	3	1	**Rose, 1b**	5	0	0	1
Leonard, lf	5	2	4	3	Parker, rf	4	1	2	0
Brenly, c	4	0	2	1	Knicely, c	5	1	2	1
Brown, 3b	4	0	0	0	Oester, 2b	4	0	1	0
Rajsich, 1b	3	0	0	0	Kr'chicki, 3b	4	2	3	2
Minton, p	0	0	0	0	Foley, ss	3	1	1	2
Uribe, ss	3	0	0	0	Pastore, p	1	0	1	0
Y'ngblood, ph	1	0	0	0	Robinson, p	0	0	0	0
Adams, ss	0	0	0	0	Walker, ph	1	0	0	0
Gott, p	2	0	0	0	Hume, p	0	0	0	0
Garrelts, p	0	0	0	0	Esasky, ph	0	0	0	0
Kuiper, ph	1	0	1	0	Franco, p	0	0	0	0
M. Davis, p	0	0	0	0	Power, p	0	0	0	0
Deer, 1b	1	0	0	0					
Totals	38	6	12	5	Totals	34	7	12	6

San Francisco................0 0 0 2 2 0 2 0 0—6
Cincinnati.....................2 1 0 2 2 0 0 0 x—7

San Francisco	IP.	H.	R.	ER.	BB.	SO.
Gott (L. 3-5)...............	4⅓	9	7	6	2	3
Garrelts.......................	⅔	2	0	0	0	1
M. Davis	1⅔	1	0	0	3	2
Minton	1⅓	0	0	0	1	0

Cincinnati	IP.	H.	R.	ER.	BB.	SO.
Pastore	4⅔	7	4	4	3	2
Robinson (W. 2-0).....	⅓	0	0	0	0	1
Hume	2	4	2	2	0	1
Franco.........................	1⅔	1	0	0	0	3
Power (Save 12)	⅓	0	0	0	0	0

Game-winning RBI—Rose.
E—C. Davis. LOB—San Francisco 8, Cincinnati 10.
2B—Gladden, Trillo, Brenly, Leonard, Krenchicki, Foley. 3B—C. Davis, Leonard. HR—Leonard (8), Krenchicki (2). SH—Pastore. PB—Brenly. T—2:44. A —17,715.

today, so I brought in Ron Robinson. He pitched to just one guy and got the win.

I really don't understand what's going on with the Giants. Whenever you've got a Chili Davis, a Manny Trillo, a Bob Brenly, a Jeff Leonard and a Jose Uribe, you should win a lot of games. Their pitchers have the lowest team ERA in the league.

As I've said, their ball park hurts them and they're terrible on the road (the Reds' sweep left the Giants with a 9-30 record away from home). Just terrible. Some teams are just like that.

We weren't too rushed after the game for our flight to San Diego. Carol and Tyler picked me up and on the way to the airport, we stopped at Walt's Hitching Post in Kentucky for some ribs.

Tyler's a little young for ribs. We got ribs and he got crackers.

Then, it was off to California. I won't see Carol and Tyler again until next week. They'll join me in Philadelphia.

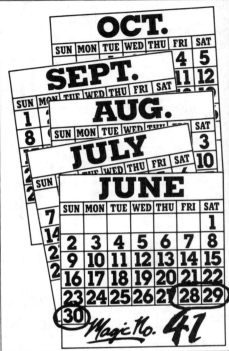

Lefty Joe Price ran out of gas in the fifth inning and failed to get a June 28 victory.

FRIDAY, JUNE 28 .... ROSE 0 FOR 2

There was a lot better atmosphere in the clubhouse before the start of this series than when San Diego came to our place.

Our guys were loose and ready to play. I thought they were a little tight before the first game the last time.

This was one of those games where the team that scored last probably was going to win. It was a little bit like a sandlot softball game.

There were 20 runs scored, 22 hits and six errors.

But—and this is what counts—we won, 11-9. Any time you can win the first game in a series against the division leader in their ball park, it gives everybody a lift. (The victory moved second-place Cincinnati within four games of the Padres in the National League West.)

What was even more important to me was the fact the Padres had won eight of their last 10 games. So, they've been playing good.

I didn't get any hits in the game, but I did something to help us win that might have gone unnoticed.

It was in the fifth inning. I'd walked and was on second base. Dave Parker was on first and Davey Concepcion was hitting with one out.

Eric Show was pitching and got two strikes on Davey. I thought Show was going to throw a curveball, so I broke for third base. When I broke, Kurt Bevacqua took one step toward third and Davey hit the ball right where he had been to left field.

I scored and before the inning was out, Wayne Krenchicki hit a three-run home run. So, we got four runs which we would not have got-

and it would have been a double play. The game was still in doubt then.

I started to go on the pitch before, but didn't. I tried the same thing over in Cincinnati against Show. In that game, I got a great jump, but Alan Knicely hit a ground ball to second. He should have taken the pitch.

The Padres kept coming back tonight, but they were never able to regain the lead (after the Reds slipped ahead 3-2 in the fourth inning).

Joe Price, who grew up near here, pitched as well as he could, but he got tired and I had to take him out in the fifth inning. He had a lot of friends and family in the stands and just ran out of gas. I knew he was tired, but I wanted him to get the win if he could. I decided to let him face one more guy and when he walked him, I brought in Ron Robinson (who wound up getting the decision).

This was a good game for us, considering they handled us so well in Cincinnati. To stay on top of them and outslug them like that was good. That's something a lot of teams don't do in their ball park.

When you win the first one, with our ace (Mario Soto) going tomorrow and Tom Browning on Sunday—I know he'll pitch a good game—a sweep is not out of the question.

We've won four in a row now and things are looking good.

Cincinnati	ab	r	h	rbi	San Diego	ab	r	h	rbi
Redus, lf	2	2	0	1	Royster, 2b	3	1	1	0
Milner, cf	6	0	1	1	Fl'n'ry, ph-2b	1	0	0	0
Rose, 1b	2	1	0	0	Davis, rf	3	1	1	1
Parker, rf	4	2	2	1	Bumbry, ph	1	0	0	1
Knicely, c	5	1	1	0	Lefferts, p	0	0	0	0
C'cepcion, ss	5	1	1	1	Bochy, ph-c	1	1	0	0
Power, p	0	0	0	0	Garvey, 1b	3	0	0	0
Oester, 2b	4	2	2	0	Stoddard, p	0	0	0	0
Kr'chicki, 3b	3	1	2	3	Bevacqua, 3b	4	2	2	1
Es'sky, ph-3b	1	1	1	1	McR'nolds, cf	4	1	1	2
Price, p	3	0	0	0	K'nedy, c-1b	5	0	0	0
Robinson, p	0	0	0	0	Martinez, lf	5	0	1	0
Cedeno, ph	1	0	1	1	Templeton, ss	5	2	2	1
Franco, p	0	0	0	0	Show, p	1	0	0	0
Foley, ss	1	0	1	1	Ramirez, ph	1	1	1	2
					DeLeon, p	0	0	0	0
					Thurmond, p	0	0	0	0
					Brown, rf	1	0	1	0
Totals	37	11	12	10	Totals	38	9	10	8

Cincinnati ....0 0 1 2 4 1 2 0 1—11
San Diego ....0 2 0 0 4 1 1 0—9

Cincinnati	IP.	H.	R.	ER.	BB.	SO.
Price	4⅓	7	6	5	1	3
Robinson (W. 3-0)	1⅔	1	1	2	0	
Franco	1⅔	2	2	1	2	1
Power (Save 13)	1⅓	0	0	0	0	

San Diego	IP.	H.	R.	ER.	BB.	SO.
Show (L. 6-5)	5	6	7	6	5	2
DeLeon	0°	1	1	1	1	0
Thurmond	1	0	0	0	0	0
Lefferts	2	3	2	2	2	1
Stoddard	1	2	1	1	0	1

*Pitched to two batters in sixth.

Game-winning RBI—Redus. E—Show, Bevacqua, Concepcion 2, McReynolds, Milner. DP—San Diego 1. LOB—Cincinnati 9, San Diego 8. 2B—Bevacqua, Knicely, Davis, Cedeno, Oester. HR—Parker (14), Krenchicki (3), Ramirez (1). SB—Redus 3. SH—Esasky. SF—McReynolds. HBP—By Thurmond (Parker). T—3:11. A—30,272.

SATURDAY, JUNE 29 .... DID NOT PLAY

In the early part of May, Kitty (pitching coach Jim Kaat) and I decided the best way to keep the pitching staff sharp was with the four-man rotation.

So, I called the entire starting staff into my office and discussed it.

Mario Soto didn't like it. He was upset.

We were still talking about it, but the showdown finally came on May 15 when we were in Montreal. Mario said his arm couldn't recover from the strain with just three days' rest (and Joe Price was a last-minute replacement that night for Soto, who was scheduled to start against the Expos).

Because he's the senior member of the staff, and our ace, I went along with Mario. I looked him straight in the eyes and told him I was doing him a favor.

I don't like any babies on this team, but he made his points (about a five-man rotation) and sort of convinced me. I still think a four-man rotation would be better.

We'll see.

★   ★   ★

Jay Tibbs was supposed to start tonight's game against San Diego, but he strained his left ankle running in the outfield last week and won't be able to go.

I asked Mario to pitch tonight—with only three days' rest—and he said he would.

I thought Mario pitched a good game even though he got beat, 3-0. He gave up only four hits in six innings, but we couldn't do anything with Dave Dravecky.

We didn't have a lot of opportunities to score. Dravecky's in a good groove right now. He's just throwing strikes. I didn't play tonight because Dave's a lefthander.

★　　★　　★

Soto told reporter Greg Hoard he is troubled about something, and Greg wrote about it in the Cincinnati Enquirer.

Mario told Greg he wants to keep his problems to himself.

Well, I've talked to Mario a lot. He had some strong words a few days ago with a Cincinnati columnist, but the whole episode was blown out of proportion. One story said that Johnny Bench (former Reds star who is now doing some broadcast work) had to keep Mario from hitting the guy with a bat. Not true. Mario just yelled at the guy.

Mario hasn't told me anything about any personal problems. I don't think personal problems have anything to do with his pitching. He was a little wild there for a period of time. He's lost four straight decisions and had a no-decision game. He's just a little bit snakebitten right now.

Every time I talk to him he says he's OK. He's going to turn it around as long as he doesn't start reading in the newspapers that he hasn't lost five in a row since his rookie year (1977) and different stuff like that.

That gets a guy thinking about being in a slump. It weighs on him mentally. The worst thing you can do to a pitcher when he's going bad is talk to him too much. He knows you've got confidence in him because you're sending him out there. You just don't want to get him thinking.

We're 1-1 in this series, so if we can win tomorrow and leave here with two out of three, that would put us in pretty good shape.

SUNDAY, JUNE 30 .... ROSE 2 FOR 5

We beat the Padres, 3-2, today and it might have been the most important game we've played this year.

I got the game-winning hit in the ninth when I singled to left field off Goose Gossage.

We came back after being down 1-0 and 2-1 and we did it against Andy Hawkins, who had an 11-1 record before the game, and against the Goose, who is one of the best relievers in the league.

This was a tricky game because it started at 4:05 in the afternoon. They did that because they had a concert after the game and the musicians said they couldn't play with the sun shining on their instruments.

Cincinnati	ab	r	h	rbi	San Diego	ab	r	h	rbi
Redus, lf	3	0	0	0	Royster, 2b	3	0	1	1
Milner, cf	4	0	1	0	Gwynn, rf	4	0	0	0
Rose, 1b	5	0	2	1	Garvey, 1b	4	0	0	0
Parker, rf	5	1	1	0	Bevacqua, 3b	2	0	0	0
Kr'chicki, 3b	3	0	1	0	McR'nolds, cf	3	0	0	0
Venable, pr	0	0	0	0	Kennedy, c	4	1	0	0
Franco, p	1	0	0	0	Martinez, lf	3	1	0	0
C'cepcion, ss	4	0	1	0	Templeton, ss	4	0	1	1
Oester, 2b	2	0	0	1	Hawkins, p	1	0	0	0
Van Gorder, c	4	1	2	1	Gossage, p	0	0	0	0
Browning, p	3	0	2	0	Davis, ph	1	0	1	0
Esasky, 3b	1	1	1	0					
Totals	35	3	11	3	Totals	29	2	3	2

```
Cincinnati ..................... 0 0 0   1 1 0   0 0 1—3
San Diego ..................... 0 1 0   1 0 0   0 0 0—2
```

Cincinnati	IP.	H.	R.	ER.	BB.	SO.
Browning	7	2	2	1	6	4
Franco (W. 4-1)	2	1	0	0	0	0

San Diego	IP.	H.	R.	ER.	BB.	SO.
Hawkins (L. 11-2)	8⅓	10	3	3	4	3
Gossage	⅔	1	0	0	0	0

Game-winning RBI—**Rose.**
E—Milner. DP—San Diego 1. LOB—Cincinnati 11, San Diego 8. 2B—Milner, Royster. HR—Van Gorder (2). SB—Royster, Venable. SH—Hawkins 2, Redus. SF —Oester. T—2:18. A—26,895.

So they made us go through two-thirds of the game in twilight time. That's the truth. When I hit off Gossage, I couldn't see anything.

You don't mind hitting off Gossage, but nobody likes to hit off him when you can't see. They brought him in to face me with the winning run on second and one out. The first pitch was a strike, the next one was a ball and the next pitch I fouled back. Then I ticked one off the catcher's glove, and the next one I got a base hit in the hole at shortstop and Nick Esasky scored. It was just out of the reach of Garry Templeton and Kurt Bevacqua.

That put us ahead and we got them out in the ninth. John Franco pitched the last two innings and got the win. He gave up just one hit and has been outstanding. Nothing rattles him. He just goes out there and does the job. He wants the ball.

I'll tell you, with Teddy Power from the right side and Franco from the left, we've probably got the best righty-lefty relief combination in the league. Tell me who is better.

I also had a line-drive single to left in the fifth off Hawkins when we tied them at 2-2. With the two hits today, I'm 39 from breaking the Cobb record.

We had a controversial call by umpire Harry Wendelstedt in the fourth inning.

Eddie Milner caught Terry Kennedy's fly ball, but it fell out of his glove and was ruled a two-base error. A lot of people thought Eddie held it long enough for the out, but Harry said that wasn't the case.

I can honestly say I didn't see what happened because I was watching the runner. I did see the replay and it looked to me like Milner caught the ball, but didn't take it out of his glove. It wasn't really obvious, but the rule is you've got to take it out of your glove. When Eddie didn't come in and argue, I knew Wendelstedt must have made the right call.

Although they ended up getting a run in that inning, it really didn't cost us anything.

A long time ago, my father told me not to argue with the umpires when you know they're right, and that's some advice I've tried to follow all my career. For the most part, they all do a good job and I've never been one to try to show them up. It just doesn't pay.

We were able to take two out of three from the Padres and that keeps us in second place, four games back. We've won seven out of our last 10 games and are six games over .500 (with a 39-33 record).

I'm swinging the bat pretty good now, but my right shoulder is really bothering me. At times, it aches like a bad tooth.

I've had our trainer, Larry Starr, take a look at it and I think he wants some doctors to do some tests. It's nothing serious, but it does hurt.

JULY

SUN	MON	TUE	WED	THU	FRI	SAT
1	2	3	4	5	6	
7	8	9	10	11	12	13
14	15	16	17	18	19	20
21	22	23	24	25	26	27
28	29	30	31			

Magic No. **39**

Dodger standout Orel Hershiser was too much for the Reds in a July 1 game in Los Angeles.

MONDAY, JULY 1 .... ROSE 1 FOR 3

We took the bus from San Diego to Los Angeles last night and will play the Dodgers two games before we fly to Philadelphia for the Fourth of July weekend.

Some people told me they were worried we might have a letdown against the Dodgers because we did so well against the Padres, who are ahead of us in the standings. (Entering tonight's game, Los Angeles is in third place, one game behind Cincinnati.)

I don't know about a letdown. Over the years, especially in the 1970s, the rivalry between the Reds and the Dodgers has been one of the best in baseball.

Well, I don't know whether it was a letdown or what, but we stunk up the place tonight and, to make matters worse, we did it on national television.

The Dodgers won, 8-1. Jay Tibbs pitched a horrible game. Plus, he made an error on a pickoff throw that really cost him.

Cincinnati	ab	r	h	rbi	Los Ang.	ab	r	h	rbi
Redus, lf	4	0	0	0	Anderson, 3b	2	2	1	1
Milner, cf	3	0	1	1	Duncan, ss	4	1	1	1
Rose, 1b	3	0	1	0	Landreaux, cf	5	1	2	0
Parker, rf	4	0	0	0	Guerrero, lf	2	2	0	0
Knicely, c	4	0	1	0	Mald'nado, lf	1	0	0	0
C'cepcion, ss	3	0	0	0	Brock, 1b	3	1	2	3
Kr'chicki, 3b	3	1	1	0	Reynolds, rf	4	1	2	1
Oester, 2b	3	0	0	0	Scioscia, c	4	0	1	0
Tibbs, p	1	0	0	0	Sax, 2b	4	0	1	0
Venable, ph	1	0	0	0	Hershiser, p	4	0	0	0
Robinson, p	0	0	0	0					
Walker, ph	1	0	0	0					
Stuper, p	0	0	0	0					
Totals	30	1	4	1	Totals	33	8	10	6

Cincinnati	0 0 0	0 0 0	0 1 0—1
Los Angeles	2 1 0	0 1 1	3 0 x—8

Cincinnati	IP.	H.	R.	ER.	BB.	SO.
Tibbs (L. 4-10)	5	4	4	4	4	1
Robinson	2	5	4	3	2	1
Stuper	1	1	0	0	1	0

Los Angeles	IP.	H.	R.	ER.	BB.	SO.
Hershiser (W. 8-2)	9	4	1	0	2	6

Game-winning RBI—None.

E—Tibbs, Oester, Anderson. DP—Cincinnati 1, Los Angeles 1. LOB—Cincinnati 5, Los Angeles 8. 2B—Duncan. HR—Anderson (3), Brock (12). SB—Landreaux, Walker. HBP—By Hershiser (Concepcion). PB—Knicely. T—2:28. A—23,296.

I've been doing everything I can to help him get straightened out, but now I've got no choice but to put him in the bullpen. Maybe he can get his head on right down there. It's strictly a confidence thing. Nothing more, nothing less.

There's nothing wrong with Tibbs physically. He's throwing the ball good, but he's aiming it and not going at the hitters.

I'm going to put Ron Robinson in the rotation to replace Tibbs. Robinson has real good stuff and he's pitched well in relief for a rookie. He deserves a chance to start. He was nothing but a starter in Denver before we brought him up on May 15.

Tibbs walked three guys in the first inning and he did that on just 13 pitches.

The Dodgers scored two runs in the first, but Tibbs could have been out of the inning. He picked a guy off second base, then had Mariano Duncan picked off first—but threw the ball way wide and the guy went to third. Then, a run scored on a passed ball.

Orel Hershiser was really strong for the Dodgers.

I grounded out the first time up. I got a line drive to left field in the fourth and that was the only hit we got until Wayne Krenchicki led off the eighth with a single.

This was a tough one because we have been telling everybody we've got a good team and now on national television we certainly don't show it.

I really got hot at the umpires in the fifth inning, probably as hot as I've been all year.

We're down 3-0 and I figured we might have a chance to get back in the game even though Hershiser was pitching so good.

With two out, Dave Anderson walked. Duncan lined to those low-level seats that come out near the right-field foul line. The ball hit the ground, then bounced up and I saw a fan grab it.

At first, the umpires appeared to have called it a ground-rule double and said Anderson had to stop at third. Now, (Dodgers Manager) Tommy Lasorda runs out of the dugout and starts yelling and they say the run can score.

I ran over to Joe West, the second-base umpire, and started shouting at him. Honestly, I wasn't that upset—not after Joe and Paul Runge explained it to me. I thought they had called a ground-rule double in the first place and there's no way in the world that guy can score. If he's on first, he gets third.

Then, the third-base umpire, Runge, changed the call. He said the fan reached on the field to get the ball and that nullified the ground-rule double. He said if the guy actually reached underneath the railing, it was the umpire's judgment call where the runner on first would've been. Once he explained that to me, I was OK.

TUESDAY, JULY 2 .... ROSE 0 FOR 1

We wanted to do well against the Padres and Dodgers because Bob Howsam, who is retiring as the Reds' president, is making the final road trip of his career.

He walked through the clubhouse before tonight's game and shook hands with most of the players. He's going to Arizona tomorrow morning to start his second retirement. (Howsam ran the Reds' front office from

1967 to 1978, then became an adviser and consultant to the Cincinnati club. He took command of the front office again in July 1983.)

I wish him well because if it weren't for him, I wouldn't be here as the Reds' player-manager. Bob's still going to serve as a consultant to Marge Schott and Bill Bergesch.

What Bob saw tonight didn't make him very happy. It was too much Fernando Valenzuela. He shut us out, 3-0, on just three hits. I didn't start, but did pinch hit; I grounded out to second base in the eighth inning.

The loss dropped us to third place and we're now five games behind the Padres and one back of the Dodgers.

Cincinnati	ab	r	h	rbi	Los Ang.	ab	r	h	rbi
Redus, cf	4	0	1	0	Anderson, 3b	4	0	1	0
C'cepcion, ss	4	0	0	0	Duncan, ss	4	1	2	0
Parker, rf	3	0	0	0	Reynolds, rf	4	1	1	0
Perez, 1b	4	0	1	0	Guerrero, lf	4	1	3	2
Cedeno, lf	4	0	0	0	Brock, 1b	3	0	1	0
Esasky, 3b	2	0	0	0	Mald'nado, cf	2	0	0	0
Van Gorder, c	3	0	1	0	L'dr'x, ph-cf	1	0	0	0
Oester, 2b	3	0	0	0	Scioscia, c	2	0	0	1
Price, p	2	0	0	0	Sax, 2b	3	0	0	0
Rose, ph	1	0	0	0	Valenzuela, p	3	0	1	0
Hume, p	0	0	0	0					
Franco, p	0	0	0	0					
Totals	30	0	3	0	Totals	30	3	9	3

```
Cincinnati ......................0 0 0   0 0 0   0 0 0—0
Los Angeles ...................0 0 0   2 0 0   0 1 x—3
```

Cincinnati	IP.	H.	R.	ER.	BB.	SO.
Price (L. 2-2)	7	7	2	2	1	3
Hume	⅔	2	1	1	1	1
Franco	⅓	0	0	0	0	0

Los Angeles	IP.	H.	R.	ER.	BB.	SO.
Valenzuela (W. 8-8) ...	9	3	0	0	2	8

Game-winning RBI—Guerrero.
E—Van Gorder. DP—Cincinnati 1. LOB—Cincinnati 5, Los Angeles 6. 2B—Reynolds, Brock. SB—Redus. SF—Scioscia. WP—Hume. T—2:06. A—49,207.

It's hard to believe Fernando has only an 8-8 record the way he pitched, especially since he leads the league in complete games and is among the leaders in several other areas.

★   ★   ★

Joe Morgan, my old teammate, does the Reds' telecasts and he was talking about my philosophy for always bringing the infield in to cut off runs.

I bring the infield in tight a lot when we're down a run or two. My reasoning is I don't like to be down three or four.

Different managers have different philosophies. A lot of managers will stay back and give up a run or two.

If it's early in the game and I figure I can give up a couple of runs, then I'll play it that way.

Say the opponent's got a run in, a man on second and third and one out. You bring the infield in and they get a base hit. Now they've got three runs and the rally's still going.

My feeling here is, stay back, give 'em another run and take your chances. It's according to who's pitching, how your team's swinging and different things like that. A lot goes into the decision.

To say I always bring the infield in to cut off a run is wrong.

★   ★   ★

After the game, we all had a long night ahead of us.

Our traveling secretary, Steve Cobb, does an excellent job moving the team from city to city.

It's always nice to have charter flights, especially when you have to fly all night. But Marge Schott has been watching the dollars and it's much cheaper—although not nearly as convenient—to go commercial.

For our trip to Philadelphia tonight, we took a regularly scheduled flight to Cincinnati, changed planes and went on to Philadelphia. Even though tomorrow's an open date, it is shot because we didn't expect to get to the hotel until 11 o'clock and most of us planned to sleep all day.

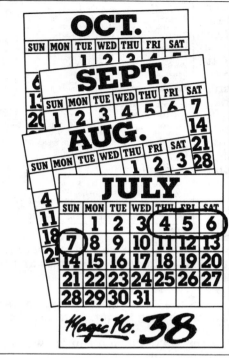

Carol Rose and son Tyler are the leading members of Pete's big fan club.

THURSDAY, JULY 4 .... ROSE 0 FOR 3

It was almost noon by the time I got to bed yesterday after we arrived in Philadelphia from Los Angeles.

Carol and Tyler showed up in a Jeep. She borrowed it from an auto-dealer friend and drove it to Delaware, where she spent Tuesday night with some friends.

Every time I see Tyler, he looks like he's grown and gotten stronger.

I slept most of the day and last night we took some friends to the Garden State Park racetrack in Cherry Hill, N.J.

For me, a night at the racetrack is one of the ways I relax. Have a nice dinner and, if you're lucky, win a few bucks. I wasn't very lucky.

Cincinnati	ab	r	h	rbi	Phila'phia	ab	r	h	rbi
Redus, lf	3	0	0	0	Samuel, 2b	4	1	1	1
Milner, cf	3	0	0	0	G. Gross, 1b	3	0	1	0
Hume, p	0	0	0	0	Corcoran, 1b	0	0	0	0
Rose, 1b	3	0	0	0	Hayes, lf	4	1	1	1
Parker, rf	4	1	1	0	Schmidt, 3b	4	0	1	0
Kr'chicki, 3b	4	0	0	0	Wilson, rf	3	0	0	0
C'cepcion, ss	2	0	0	1	Virgil, c	3	1	2	1
Oester, 2b	3	0	1	0	Maddox, cf	4	0	1	0
Van Gorder, c	2	0	1	0	Thomas, ss	3	0	1	0
Walker, ph	1	0	0	0	Jeltz, ss	0	0	0	0
Knicely, c	0	0	0	0	K. Gross, p	3	0	0	0
Soto, p	2	0	0	0					
V'ble, ph-cf	1	0	0	0					
Totals	28	1	3	1	Totals	31	3	8	3

```
Cincinnati ...................0 0 0   1 0 0   0 0 0—1
Philadelphia .................2 0 0   0 0 1   0 0 x—3
```

Cincinnati	IP.	H.	R.	ER.	BB.	SO.
Soto (L. 8-8)	7	8	3	3	2	6
Hume	1	0	0	0	1	1

Philadelphia	IP.	H.	R.	ER.	BB.	SO.
K. Gross (W. 7-7)	9	3	1	1	3	4

Game-winning RBI—Samuel.
E—Thomas. DP—Cincinnati 1. LOB—Cincinnati 4, Philadelphia 7. 2B—Van Gorder, Maddox. 3B—Parker. HR—Samuel (7), Hayes (8), Virgil (11). SF—Concepcion. T—2:06. A—21,291.

It's always nice to come back to Philly because, as I've said many times, I had some great years here. I know a lot of the people around Veterans Stadium and I enjoy talking with them.

I don't like off-days, especially when I'm so tired from traveling that I stay in bed all day. You get sluggish.

I don't think I've been swinging the bat too well, so an off-day does not help at all.

I got to the ball park about 1 o'clock because the game was early (5 p.m.) and a couple of reporters wanted to spend some time with me. Bill Conlin, who writes for the Philadelphia Daily News, is doing a story about me for when I break the record, and People magazine sent somebody to interview me.

There wasn't the usual number of radio and TV guys here today. I guess it was because of the holiday.

★   ★   ★

The Phillies beat us tonight, 3-1, and I went 0 for 3. Kevin Gross pitched a complete game for them. Gave up only three hits.

I walked the first time up. We had a chance at Gross in the first inning because he walked two guys, but we didn't get anything out of it.

It's tough to win with just three hits. That's why you can't throw furniture or knock over food or get disgusted. When a team goes into a little bit of an offensive slump, there's nothing you can do about it. You just have to ride out the waves, so to speak, and wait for it to turn around. We're hitting only .114 in our last three games.

Orel Hershiser, Fernando Valenzuela and Gross have beaten us and they're good pitchers. But you've still got to get your hits off them.

Mario Soto gave up three home runs and that's what did him in. He's now lost five games in a row and is getting a little uptight about it. The biggest thing is not to let him lose his confidence. He hasn't won since June 4, but I know he'll get himself turned around. He's too good a pitcher not to.

I had Dave Van Gorder catch tonight for the second straight game. The main reason for that is because Alan Knicely has hit under .200 since June 10. (Knicely, a late-game defensive replacement against the Phillies, has managed only 11 hits in his last 59 at-bats—a .186 mark.)

We're six games back of the Padres now. About the only thing I can say, considering we're not hitting, is that it could be a lot worse. We're still close enough.

FRIDAY, JULY 5 .... ROSE 0 FOR 1

I've come to the conclusion that I've got to concentrate on working harder.

I didn't realize this until the other day. All my career I've played every day, but when you don't play every day you don't see that good, live pitching. You can take all the batting practice you want, but it's not the same.

I'm going to work out something with Billy DeMars (Reds' batting coach) so I can get more swings on days I don't play. That will help me keep my stroke.

Yesterday I came to the ball park and I never did get in a groove. I knew I wasn't swinging good in batting practice. I don't like to make excuses, but it takes me time to get over that all-night, red-eye flying. I took a sauna. Thought that would help. Then I drank a couple cups of black coffee. I just had a lot of cobwebs. I just couldn't get the adrenaline flowing; I did everything I know to get loose and it didn't work.

So, what this tells me is that I've got to work a little harder. I've got to concentrate more on days when I don't play.

★   ★   ★

The Phillies beat us tonight, 5-2. I didn't start, but did pinch hit and lined out to right field in the ninth.

This was our fourth loss in a row and it's tough because we haven't been hitting the ball at all since San Diego. We went there and did what we had to do. Then, all of a sudden, we go to L.A. and lose two games and come here and lose two games. Everything we worked hard for in San Diego went right out the window.

Herbie—Mike Schmidt—hit a home run in the first inning off Tom Browning and that's the way it stayed until the seventh when Nick Esasky hit a two-run homer for us off Jerry Koosman.

Cincinnati	ab	r	h	rbi	Philad'phia	ab	r	h	rbi
Redus, cf-lf	4	0	0	0	Samuel, 2b	4	0	0	0
Oester, 2b	4	0	2	0	Schu, 3b	4	0	0	0
Parker, rf	4	0	1	0	Schmidt, 1b	4	2	2	1
Perez, 1b	3	0	1	0	Wilson, rf	4	1	1	1
Milner, cf	1	1	0	0	Virgil, c	3	1	0	0
Esasky, 3b	4	1	1	2	Maddox, cf	3	0	1	0
C'cepcion, ss	3	0	0	0	Russell, lf	3	1	1	2
C'deno, lf-1b	3	0	2	0	Carman, p	0	0	0	0
Van Gorder, c	2	0	0	0	Jeltz, ss	3	0	1	0
Rose, ph	1	0	0	0	Koosman, p	2	0	0	0
Browning, p	3	0	0	0	Andersen, p	0	0	0	0
Hume, p	0	0	0	0	W'k'fuss, ph	0	0	0	0
					G. G'ss, ph-lf	1	0	0	0
Totals	32	2	7	2	Totals	31	5	6	4

Cincinnati ....0 0 0   0 0 0   2 0 0—2
Philadelphia...................1 0 0   0 0 0   4 0 x—5

Cincinnati	IP.	H.	R.	ER.	BB.	SO.
Browning (L. 7-6)	6⅓	6	5	4	0	3
Hume	1⅔	0	0	0	0	1

Philadelphia	IP.	H.	R.	ER.	BB.	SO.
Koosman	6⅔	6	2	2	1	4
Andersen (W. 3-2)	⅓	0	0	0	0	0
Carman (Save 3)	2	1	0	0	1	0

Game-winning RBI—None.
E—Esasky. DP—Philadelphia 1. LOB—Cincinnati 6, Philadelphia 2. 2B—Maddox, Perez, Wilson, Jeltz. HR—Schmidt (10), Esasky (6), Russell (2). SB—Cedeno. HBP—By Koosman (Cedeno). WP—Koosman. T—2:09. A—25,001.

Now, in the bottom of the seventh, Schmidt starts off with a base hit and Glenn Wilson gets a double to left-center to score a run. That puts the go-ahead run at second and then Nick makes an error to let the go-ahead run score. Ozzie Virgil hit a grounder to Nick, who looked Wilson back to second but threw the ball into the dirt at first base. Wilson scored, Ozzie took second and John Russell hits a home run.

Browning pitched a fine game for us. He's a good young pitcher with a lot of poise, a lot of know-how. Like most of today's young pitchers, he's a real pitcher—not a thrower.

We had something going in the ninth off Don Carman, their lefthanded reliever.

We're three runs down, have a man on, two outs. Alan Knicely was available to pinch hit, but I batted for Dave Van Gorder, who hurt his finger in the second inning and was really bothered by it. He couldn't grip the bat.

If I get a hit, I've got the tying run at the plate and I can send Knicely up for the pitcher and hope for a long ball. But I lined out.

★   ★   ★

I had a long talk with my coaches after the game and I think it's time to make a few lineup changes. I told 'em I'd sleep on it. We've got to get some offense.

SATURDAY, JULY 6 .... ROSE 1 FOR 3

Dave Van Gorder has a broken thumb.

We had it checked this morning. Dr. Phillip Marone, the Phillies' orthopedist and a good one, said the X-rays show a little fracture.

So, we're putting Dave on the 15-day disabled list and calling up Dann Bilardello from Denver. Bilardello didn't arrive in time for tonight's game.

It's a shame for Van Gorder, because he's been doing a good job for us. He's the first player we've had to put on the "DL" this year.

They said if the fracture had gone a fraction of an inch more, the thumb would have been broken in two places. It could've been worse.

I decided to make some lineup changes for tonight's game and the move helped us beat the Phillies, 4-2, and end the four-game losing streak.

"True Creature"—Ron Robinson —pitched a good game. It was his first start since we called him up from Denver in mid-May. He gave us six strong innings and is now 4-0.

I nicknamed him "True Creature" because it was just something I thought of. He tells everybody he likes it and takes all the clubhouse teasing in stride.

I got one hit tonight and it ended up being the game-winner. It was a single to right field that put us up 2-1. I even stole a base tonight. I need 37 hits to break the Cobb record.

What we did with the lineup was insert Max Venable and Duane Walk-

Cincinnati	ab	r	h	rbi	Phila'phia	ab	r	h	rbi
V'ble, cf-lf	3	1	1	0	Samuel, 2b	3	0	0	0
Rose, 1b	3	2	1	1	Thomas, ss	3	0	0	0
Power, p	0	0	0	0	W'k'fuss, ph	1	0	1	0
Parker, rf	4	0	2	2	Jeltz, pr-ss	0	0	0	0
Knicely, c	2	0	0	0	Hayes, lf	3	1	1	0
Kr'chicki, 3b	3	0	1	1	Schmidt, 1b	4	1	1	1
Es'sky, ph-3b	1	0	0	0	Wilson, rf	4	0	1	0
C'cepcion, ss	2	0	1	0	Virgil, c	3	0	1	0
Walker, lf	3	0	0	0	Aguayo, pr	0	0	0	0
Franco, p	0	0	0	0	Maddox, cf	3	0	2	1
Perez, 1b	1	0	0	0	Schu, 3b	3	0	1	0
Oester, 2b	4	0	0	0	Corcoran, ph	1	0	0	0
Robinson, p	2	0	0	0	Denny, p	2	0	0	0
Milner, cf	1	1	1	0	Russell, ph	1	0	0	0
					Rucker, p	0	0	0	0
					Andersen, p	0	0	0	0
					G. Gross, ph	1	0	0	0
Totals	29	4	7	4	Totals	32	2	8	2

Cincinnati ....1 0 2 0 0 0 0 1 0—4
Philadelphia ....0 1 0 0 0 1 0 0 0—2

Cincinnati	IP.	H.	R.	ER.	BB.	SO.
Robinson (W. 4-0)	6	5	2	2	0	7
Franco	1⅓	3	0	0	1	0
Power (Save 14)	1⅔	0	0	0	1	1

Philadelphia	IP.	H.	R.	ER.	BB.	SO.
Denny (L. 5-7)	7	5	3	3	3	4
Rucker	⅔	2	1	1	1	0
Anderson	1⅓	0	0	0	1	1

Game-winning RBI—Rose.
E—Krenchicki 2. DP—Cincinnati 1, Philadelphia 1. LOB—Cincinnati 4, Philadelphia 7. 2B—Schmidt, Venable, Parker. 3B—Hayes. SB—**Rose**, Concepcion. SH—Venable, Hayes. SF—Maddox. T—2:28. A—25,161.

er into the outfield (in place of usual starters Eddie Milner and Gary Redus). And I moved myself up to the second slot in the batting order.

Venable hit a third-inning double off John Denny and then I drove him in.

The changes helped, but you can't blame one phase of the team for not winning because we hadn't hit the ball against lefthanders twice and hadn't hit the ball against righthanders twice. So, it's not one or two guys.

I don't believe when you lose four in a row that taking one or two guys out of the lineup is putting the finger on them. That's not the way it is, but there again, I just think every once in a while there are a couple of guys who aren't as strong as other guys and they've been playing an awful lot. They need a day off because it's a grind with the traveling and the intensity of the games lately. Different things like that.

If we have an abundance of anything, it's outfielders. One guy can be the difference in a ball club. If you get a key hit here or a key hit there, you can get everybody going.

SUNDAY, JULY 7 .... ROSE 0 FOR 1

There's one thing I really like about this ball club.

It seems like guys are picking each other up. Today, I grounded out as a pinch-hitter in the 10th inning, but Cesar Cedeno followed with a homer over the left-field fence off Kent Tekulve and we beat the Phillies, 3-2.

The victory gave us a split in this four-game series. Considering the way we were playing when we lost four in a row, that wasn't too bad.

Cedeno got the game-winner, but if it hadn't been for the Cobra, Dave Parker, we might not have been in a position to go extra innings and win.

The Cobra just keeps coming. There's a pretty good chance he and I are going to represent the Reds at next week's All-Star Game in Minneapolis.

Parker deserves it.

In the eighth inning today, we're down 2-1 with one out. The Cobra tripled to right-center and Doggie (Tony Perez) drove him in with a single.

What a lot of people don't know is Parker suffered a hyperextended shoulder on Friday night, but didn't even think of taking a day off.

Davey Concepcion has asked for a couple of games off because he says he's tired and weary.

Well, I really don't think this team is that tired. It's too early. We've played only 78 games and the last time I checked, the schedule called for 162.

Cincinnati	ab	r	h	rbi	Phila'phia	ab	r	h	rbi
Redus, cf	4	0	1	0	Samuel, 2b	4	1	2	1
Hume, p	0	0	0	0	G. Gross, lf	2	0	1	1
Franco, p	0	0	0	0	M'dox, ph-cf	2	0	0	0
Rose, ph	1	0	0	0	Hayes, cf-lf	5	0	1	0
Power, p	0	0	0	0	Wilson, rf	5	0	1	0
C'deno, lf-1b	5	1	1	1	Schmidt, 1b	4	0	0	0
Parker, rf	5	1	2	0	Diaz, c	2	0	0	0
Perez, 1b	4	1	2	1	Thomas, ss	3	1	1	0
Milner, cf	1	0	1	0	Jeltz, ss	1	0	0	0
Esasky, 3b	4	0	1	1	Schu, 3b	4	0	1	0
C'cepcion, ss	3	0	0	0	Rawley, p	2	0	0	0
Knicely, c	3	0	2	0	Corcoran, ph	1	0	0	0
Venable, cf	1	0	0	0	Russell, pr	0	0	0	0
Oester, 2b	4	0	1	0	Carman, p	0	0	0	0
Pastore, p	2	0	0	0	Virgil, ph	1	0	0	0
B'dello, ph-c	2	0	0	0	Tekulve, p	0	0	0	0
Totals	39	3	11	3	Totals	36	2	7	2

Cincinnati ....0 0 0   0 0 1   0 1 0   1—3
Philadelphia ....0 0 0   0 1 0   1 0 0   0—2

Cincinnati	IP.	H.	R.	ER.	BB.	SO.
Pastore	6	4	1	1	4	3
Hume	⅓	2	1	1	0	1
Franco (W. 5-1)	2⅔	0	0	0	1	1
Power (Save 15)	1	1	0	0	0	1

Philadelphia	IP.	H.	R.	ER.	BB.	SO.
Rawley	7	7	1	1	1	6
Carman	2	2	1	1	1	2
Tekulve (L. 4-4)	1	2	1	1	0	0

Game-winning RBI—Cedeno.
E—Thomas, Rawley, Concepcion, Schu. DP—Cincinnati 2, Philadelphia 2. LOB—Cincinnati 8, Philadelphia 9. 2B—Samuel, Esasky. 3B—Parker. HR—Cedeno (3). SB—Cedeno, Schu, Samuel, Thomas. WP—Rawley. T—2:51. A—32,014.

There's only one guy on this team who could justifiably say to me he is tired and that is the Cobra. He's the only guy who's played every day and produced every day. He's been steady and consistent.

Day in and day out, he's done the job. He's having an MVP year if I ever saw one and I've seen quite a lot in my time, what with Joe Morgan and Mike Schmidt (two-time MVP winners while playing with Rose at Cincinnati and Philadelphia, respectively).

I'll tell you something else. He's got a shot at the batting title.

He's hitting .310 and it's going to take somewhere between .325 and .335 to win it. Dave's capable of going that high. The reason I think that is because he doesn't strike out that much. He's got good bat speed to get around on the inside pitch, enough bat speed to beat out toppers in the infield. Plus, he hits lefthanders well. His triple today was off Don Carman, a lefthander.

I just can't say enough about the relief job John Franco and Teddy Power have been doing.

Franco came in today and gave me 2 2/3 innings of shutout ball just when we needed it. He picked up the win, and then Teddy shut the Phillies down in the ninth to get his 15th save. He's had a save in each of his last six appearances.

That's what you've got to get to win a game like this one. We're having trouble scoring runs and you just can't afford to give one up when you're a run down or a run ahead or even.

Now, we go home and play our next seven games at Riverfront before the All-Star break. This is a good chance for us to pick up some ground and be in a pretty good position for the second half.

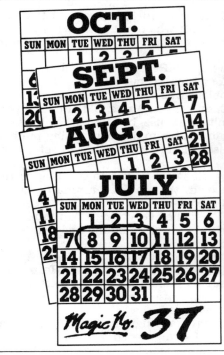

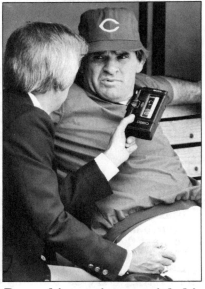

Rose, his patience with his pitching staff wearing a little thin, tapes a pregame show with Marty Brennaman.

MONDAY, JULY 8 ....ROSE 1 FOR 5

Speculation about Bill Bergesch ended today when Marge Schott announced he's going to be our executive vice president and general manager. (Previously, Bergesch carried only the general-manager title.)

Marge is going to take the title of president and have an office at the stadium.

But Bill, in essence, is taking over most of the duties that Bob Howsam had as president and chief executive officer. Bill and I get along good.

Bill will handle most of the day-to-day operations.

★   ★   ★

We were on national TV again tonight and it was another one of those games. The Mets beat us, 7-5, and my patience is wearing a little thin.

I got a double to right field—it was my first extra-base hit in more than a month (since June 2)—in the fifth in-

New York	ab	r	h	rbi	Cincinnati	ab	r	h	rbi
Dykstra, cf	4	1	1	0	Milner, cf	4	2	1	0
Chapman, 2b	3	0	0	0	Venable, lf	3	0	1	1
B'k'n, ph-2b	2	1	1	0	Redus, ph-lf	2	0	1	0
Hern'dez, 1b	5	2	4	3	**Rose, 1b**	5	0	1	1
Carter, c	4	0	0	0	Parker, rf	4	0	0	0
Foster, lf	5	1	2	2	Kr'chicki, 3b	3	0	0	0
Strawb'ry, rf	4	1	1	1	C'pc'n, ph-ss	1	0	0	0
Johnson, 3b	5	1	1	1	Knicely, c	4	2	2	0
Santana, ss	4	0	2	0	Oester, 2b	4	1	3	0
Lynch, p	3	0	1	0	Foley, ss	3	0	2	2
Gorman, p	0	0	0	0	Es'sky, ph-3b	1	0	1	1
Leach, p	0	0	0	0	Price, p	1	0	0	0
Orosco, p	0	0	0	0	Cedeno, ph	1	0	0	0
					Tibbs, p	0	0	0	0
					Franco, p	0	0	0	0
					Perez, ph	1	0	0	0
					Stuper, p	0	0	0	0
Totals	39	7	13	7	Totals	37	5	12	5

```
New York.....................0 0 0   1 2 1   3 0 0—7
Cincinnati...................1 1 0   1 1 0   0 1 0—5
```

New York	IP.	H.	R.	ER.	BB.	SO.
Lynch (W. 6-5)	6	9	4	4	1	2
Gorman	1⅔	3	1	1	0	0
Leach	⅓	0	0	0	0	0
Orosco (Save 8)	1	0	0	0	0	1

Cincinnati	IP.	H.	R.	ER.	BB.	SO.
Price	6	8	4	4	2	4
Tibbs (L. 4-11)	⅓	3	3	3	0	0
Franco	1⅔	1	0	0	0	1
Stuper	1	1	0	0	1	0

Game-winning RBI—Hernandez.
E—None. LOB—New York 9, Cincinnati 7. 2B—Hernandez, Backman, Santana, Foster, Venable, Knicely, **Rose**, Oester 2. HR—Strawberry (7), Hernandez (6), Johnson (4), Foster (13). SB—Dykstra, Redus. SH—Gorman, Price. T—2:52. A—20,391.

níng to drive in a run off Ed Lynch, but our 4-3 lead didn't last very long.

Keith Hernandez had four hits for New York, including a two-run homer and a single that broke a 4-4 tie. It was the seventh win in a row for the Mets, but this was a game that should not have gotten away from us.

I'm upset with two of my pitchers, Joe Price and Jay Tibbs.

Price had a 3-1 lead through four innings, but let it go. He told reporters after the game that his problem was an aching elbow.

Greg Hoard of the Cincinnati Enquirer said Price told him his elbow was killing him. Price said it wasn't an excuse, but that when he went out there he knew he wasn't going to be able to throw breaking pitches.

Everybody knows Joe Price uses his breaking pitch to set up his other stuff.

I think if anybody's got a sore elbow he ought to tell me, or the trainer, or the pitching coach. He owes that to his teammates to tell somebody. What good is it to tell a reporter?

I just don't know about Tibbs. I've done everything I can think of.

I pinch hit Cesar Cedeno for Price in the sixth inning and sent Tibbs out to start the seventh with the score 4-4.

Tibbs faced just four hitters and only got one out.

He gave up a double to Wally Backman and a single to Hernandez before getting Gary Carter to fly out deep to left field. The next guy he faced, George Foster, hit a two-run homer to left.

So, instead of being tied, we were down 7-4.

I think the best thing for Tibbs right now might be to send him down to Denver and see if he can get himself straightened out.

I'm going to talk with Kitty (pitching coach Jim Kaat) when I get to the ball park tomorrow and also see what Bill Bergesch thinks.

I just can't keep sending Tibbs out there until he gets some confidence back. I thought putting him in the bullpen might help, but tonight was the first time I used him in relief and that certainly isn't the answer.

I got irritated with some of the reporters who said they thought I might have stayed with Price too long, that he looked tired.

I told them I would be 3-foot-5 from my pitchers beating me on the head if I took them out when they had a lead. You've got to give a pitcher a chance to pitch his way out of trouble. He's got to get that chance, and I don't care what the reporters say or write.

TUESDAY, JULY 9 .... ROSE 0 FOR 3

We've decided to send Jay Tibbs to Denver.

I had to call him into the office today and tell him the news, but I don't think he was really that surprised.

When we left spring training, we were counting on him being our No. 2 starter. He has pitched in some bad luck, but a lot of his problems have been his own.

In 119⅔ innings, Tibbsie gave up 123 hits and 64 earned runs. He was 4-11 with a 4.84 ERA. I keep wondering if he'd won just five of those 11 games he lost where we might be in the standings.

I just hope pitching at Denver will help him. That should give him a chance to get his confidence back.

We're bringing up Bob Buchanan to take Jay's spot on the roster. Bob is a lefthanded reliever who was 4-3 at Denver with a 2.18 ERA. What I like about him is that in 41⅓ innings, he's walked only 13 batters and struck out 36. That tells me he's throwing strikes.

We'll just have to see what happens.

★   ★   ★

Before I came to the ball park today, I had to speak at the Insiders' Club luncheon, then I went to the Taft Broadcasting studios and taped a show with my old teammate, Johnny Bench (for Major League Baseball Productions).

We sat out on the patio in front of the Taft headquarters and talked about the Cobb record and our careers with the Cincinnati Reds.

New York	ab	r	h	rbi	Cincinnati	ab	r	h	rbi
Dykstra, cf	6	0	1	2	Milner, cf	4	0	0	0
Backman, 2b	6	0	2	0	Venable, lf	4	0	2	1
Hern'dez, 1b	2	3	1	2	**Rose, 1b**	3	0	0	0
Carter, c	3	2	1	0	Parker, rf	3	0	1	0
Reynolds, c	0	0	0	0	Kr'chicki, 3b	4	0	0	0
Strawb'ry, rf	2	2	0	0	Knicely, c	4	0	0	0
Foster, lf	4	3	2	4	Oester, 2b	3	0	0	0
Johnson, 3b	4	0	1	2	Foley, ss	3	1	1	0
Santana, ss	4	0	0	0	Soto, p	2	0	0	0
Gooden, p	4	1	1	0	Hume, p	0	0	0	0
Staub, ph	0	0	0	0	Walker, ph	1	1	1	1
Orosco, p	0	0	0	0	Stuper, p	0	0	0	0
Totals	35	11	9	10	Totals	31	2	5	2

New York .... 0 0 0   1 2 0   0 4 4 — 11
Cincinnati .... 0 0 0   0 0 0   0 2 0 — 2

New York	IP.	H.	R.	ER.	BB.	SO.
Gooden (W. 12-3)	8	5	2	2	2	5
Orosco	1	0	0	0	0	0

Cincinnati	IP.	H.	R.	ER.	BB.	SO.
Soto (L. 8-9)	7*	5	6	5	7	6
Hume	1	0	1	0	1	0
Stuper	1	4	4	4	3	0

*Pitched to three batters in eighth.
Game-winning RBI—Foster.
E—Parker, Hume. DP—Cincinnati 1. LOB—New York 9, Cincinnati 4. 2B—Foley, Walker. HR—Foster (14), Hernandez (7). SB—Backman. SF—Johnson. WP—Soto. T—2:50. A—21,787.

On Thursday night, I don't intend to play (against Montreal lefthander Joe Hesketh), so they're going to wire me for sound to get an idea what I say during a game. Bench was teasing me a little about the fact they've written a country song about me. It was written and recorded by Ken Scott, the same guy in Nashville who did one for Bobby Knight, the Indiana basketball coach.

They call this one, "The Ballad of Pete Rose."

Don't laugh, but it goes like this:

"There's a man in Cincinnati and we all know his name.

"They have a place reserved for him in baseball's Hall of Fame.

"What keeps him going on no one really knows.

"He's got a lot of courage, the man they call Pete Rose."

★   ★   ★

We lost our second straight to the Mets tonight and they really pounded us, 11-2.

Dwight Gooden won his 12th game, although Jesse Orosco pitched the ninth. I didn't get any hits, but hit a couple of balls hard.

Mario Soto lost his sixth straight game, but until the eighth inning he was in a good match with Gooden. In the eighth, Mario got wild and walked the bases loaded before I took him out.

I know Mario's going to come out of this slump and that's what I keep telling everybody.

The thing people don't know is that he's an ace competitor. A lot of people think if he doesn't pitch well, he doesn't care. Well, it bothers him a hell of a lot.

He's such a perfectionist, that's why he gets upset when he doesn't get a strike call. It's not because he's a sorehead or anything.

We've all got confidence in Mario, and that's what should count more than anything else.

WEDNESDAY, JULY 10 .... ROSE 0 FOR 4

I went 0 for 4 tonight and didn't hit the ball very well. I made a point the other day that I don't think I'm concentrating enough on working on days I don't see live pitching.

Well, the Mets beat us tonight, 2-1, and if I'd gotten a hit or two, I might have been able to help us out.

Normally, I'd go home right after the game, but since I'm not planning to play tomorrow, I decided to get in some extra hitting.

It was after 10 o'clock, but I got two of my coaches, Billy DeMars and Bruce Kimm, to go to the batting cage with me. I needed to work on my swing.

My father always told me there's only one way to succeed in anything and that is with hard work. You've got to work harder than the next guy.

New York	ab	r	h	rbi	Cincinnati	ab	r	h	rbi
Dykstra, cf	4	0	1	1	Milner, cf	4	0	0	0
Chapman, 2b	4	1	1	0	Venable, lf	4	0	1	0
Hern'dez, 1b	3	0	2	1	**Rose, 1b**	4	0	0	0
Carter, c	4	0	0	0	Parker, rf	4	1	1	1
Foster, lf	4	1	1	0	Kr'chicki, 3b	4	0	3	0
Strawb'ry, rf	2	0	1	0	Knicely, c	3	0	0	0
Johnson, 3b	4	0	1	0	Oester, 2b	3	0	0	0
Santana, ss	4	0	1	0	Foley, ss	3	0	0	0
Aguilera, p	4	0	0	0	Browning, p	2	0	1	0
					C'cepcion, ph	1	0	0	0
					Franco, p	0	0	0	0
Totals	33	2	8	2	Totals	32	1	6	1

New York....................0 0 0 1 1 0 0 0 0—2
Cincinnati...................0 0 0 1 0 0 0 0 0—1

New York	IP.	H.	R.	ER.	BB.	SO.
Aguilera (W. 3-2)	9	6	1	1	0	3

Cincinnati	IP.	H.	R.	ER.	BB.	SO.
Browning (L. 7-7)	7	7	2	2	3	0
Franco	2	1	0	0	0	0

Game-winning RBI—Hernandez.
E—None. LOB—New York 8, Cincinnati 5. 2B—Hernandez, Krenchicki 2. HR—Parker (15). HBP—By Browning (Dykstra), by Aguilera (Knicely). T—2:25. A—18,958.

Sure, it would have been easy to go home, have Carol fix me dinner and watch TV. But that doesn't help the fact I've had only one hit since last Saturday. I've had only five hits in my last 12 games and that's with 36 at-bats.

The batting cage at Riverfront Stadium is located in a tunnel near our clubhouse. I swung for maybe 20 minutes.

What I like to do is have Billy pitch to me from a short distance. I stand about 30 or so feet from the mound. That way, I can work on contact, seeing the ball and bat speed. Tonight, I started out only 25 feet away, then backed up to about 30.

This is a good exercise for me, especially when I'm not swinging well.

I think the 20 minutes helped me some and I know it let me get rid of some of my frustrations.

I was really beat when I went back to my office to get ready to go home.

We just didn't play well tonight. I sometimes wonder what guys are thinking about out there.

I'm getting tired of people saying, sure, we lost, but because San Diego also lost today (at Chicago), we didn't lose any ground. When the Padres are losing, we should be gaining ground.

I take these losses harder than anyone in this clubhouse. I take it harder because I've made a decision on a pinch-hitter or a relief pitcher that may have contributed to the loss.

I've got that (on my mind) as well as playing in the game. I think about those things. I never want to be a person who loses a game and five minutes later has forgotten about it. I never have gotten used to losing and never will.

Tonight, our only run was a homer by Dave Parker, his 15th of the year. It came in the fourth inning and tied them 1-1.

Tom Browning pitched a pretty good game for us. He went seven innings and gave up seven hits, but we didn't score any runs for him. We just couldn't do anything against their rookie pitcher, Rick Aguilera. He's a righthander and gave us only six hits.

The Mets won in the fifth when Kelvin Chapman singled and Keith Hernandez doubled him home.

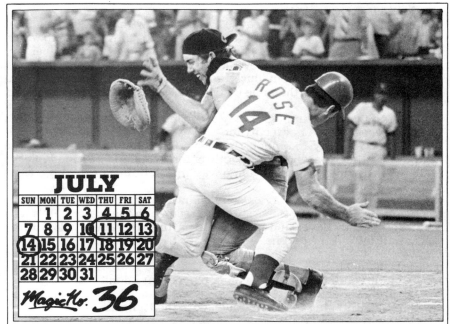

JULY

SUN	MON	TUE	WED	THU	FRI	SAT
	1	2	3	4	5	6
7	8	9	10	11	12	13
14	15	16	17	18	19	20
21	22	23	24	25	26	27
28	29	30	31			

Magic No. **36**

Rose's most memorable All-Star Game was in 1970, when he scored the winning run by bowling over A.L. catcher Ray Fosse.

THURSDAY, JULY 11 .... DID NOT PLAY

Since I didn't play tonight, I was wired for sound to see just what goes on in the dugout during one of our games.

Excerpts from the tape are going to be used in that TV show I did with Johnny Bench. I'm not sure when it's going to be shown, but the big thing tonight was I had to watch everything I said. In a close game, that's not too easy.

The fact they can edit the tape and take anything out that didn't sound too good gave me a chance to relax.

We beat the Expos, 2-0.

Bill Bergesch had some interesting news for me before the game. We've got a chance at getting Buddy Bell, who has demanded that the Texas Rangers trade him.

Our position right now is we're going to continue to negotiate with the Rangers, but Bill thinks they may be asking too much for Bell.

It's like I told columnist Tim Sullivan of the Cincinnati Enquirer. I don't mean any disrespect for Buddy Bell—he's a great third baseman—but if I thought one player could be so dominant that he would make the Reds go from 4 1/2 games behind to 4 1/2 games in front, then I would go to Bill Bergesch and try to tell him to do everything he can to get that player. But there are not a helluva lot of players around like that, are there?

Gus Bell was a favorite when he played for the Reds (1953-1961), and I know Buddy, his son, would like to play for them, too. (Both Bells are Cincinnati residents.)

I never played with Gus because his last year with the Reds was 1961. He then went to the New York Mets—they picked him in the expansion draft after the '61 season—and later to the Milwaukee Braves. When my father used to take me to Crosley Field, I remember seeing Gus play.

To get Buddy, we're obviously going to have to give up some real good players and more than one or two. At least that's what Bill thinks right now.

That's only the beginning. Buddy is getting about $600,000 a year and wants to renegotiate a new contract.

We just can't say too much right now for a couple of reasons. The tampering rules in baseball are strictly enforced, plus if we sound like we really want Buddy, his price will go way up. Not that it's not high right now.

I honestly believe we have a solid chance to win our division and he could help us. He's one of the best third basemen in the majors. He's won six straight Gold Gloves and his lifetime batting average is .286. I think you can throw out the fact he's hitting only .243 this year.

We're not going to make a big thing about this. Buddy has told some people he wants to play for the Reds.

I wouldn't mind giving up a young player, but I don't want to give up two or three who figure in our future.

Bill said he's going to stay in touch with the Rangers.

★ ★ ★

Dave Parker and I got official word from the National League office today that we're going to next Tuesday's All-Star Game at Minneapolis' Metrodome (as reserve players).

A lot of people might not realize this, but I got the first base hit in Metrodome history—on April 3, 1982, when I was with the Phillies. We played an exhibition series there against the Minnesota Twins (who previously had played their home games at Metropolitan Stadium).

FRIDAY, JULY 12 .... ROSE 1 FOR 3

This was a big night for Davey Concepcion.

When he singled in the fourth inning against Montreal, he moved into second place on the Reds' all-time hit list.

I can remember the game in Los Angeles back in 1970 when Davey got his first big-league hit. I think it was a double. Jon Braude, our assistant publicity director, looked it up and that turned out to be correct.

Davey's first hit was in Dodger Stadium on April 8, 1970, in the seventh inning against Fred Norman. I was playing right field then. I had a hit in four at-bats that night, with an RBI and a stolen base.

Now, Davey has 2,049 hits, one more than Johnny Bench had with Cincinnati and 1,210 fewer than I've got with the Reds (3,259).

He said he was disappointed when the fans didn't acknowledge the hit.

"It was like it was just another hit," he said after the game, which we won, 5-4, in 11 innings.

Davey then joked with reporters, saying he doesn't think he has much of a chance to catch me.

We won tonight on an error. I'll take 'em any way I can get 'em.

I got a single in the seventh inning, and also had an RBI. I now need

35 hits to pass Cobb.

There was a lot of talk about how the Expos played the 11th inning.

Eddie Milner got a single to right field in the 11th with one out. He then got his third stolen base of the night and went to third when Max Venable flied out to center field.

Now, with two out, Buck Rodgers, their manager, had to make some decisions.

What he did was walk me and Dave Parker to load the bases.

I then sent up Tony Perez to bat for my pitcher, John Franco.

Doggie hit a chopper to Tim Wallach at third base. Wallach threw to the mound side of second, pulling their second baseman, Al Newman, off the bag. Milner scores and we win.

I thought Rodgers played it absolutely right. He got a ground ball to the infield, which is what he was looking for. And he got it hit to one of his All-Stars. It's one of those plays where Wallach makes a good play, then ends up getting an error and losing the game.

I just think Wallach rushed his throw. He was running when he made the throw.

★　　★　　★

My trainer, Larry Starr, gave me some good news before the game. Dave Van Gorder, our catcher who broke his thumb in Philadelphia on July 5, is coming along faster than they thought he would.

All the swelling has gone down and he can move his thumb without any pain to speak of.

Dave hasn't caught any balls yet and says gripping and swinging the bat is going to give him the most trouble. I'm hoping to get him back after the All-Star Game.

Cesar Cedeno is out of action for a few days with a pulled muscle on the left side of his rib cage. He got hurt during batting practice and Larry says it's going to take a few more days, but that I can use him to pinch hit if necessary. With the All-Star Game break coming up, there's time for Cesar to get healthy.

SATURDAY, JULY 13 .... ROSE 0 FOR 2

It seems like Saturday mornings have been the toughest for outside stuff.

We keep having photographers come to the house to get pictures around the place for future spreads they're planning.

This becomes a little tiring, because each time we have to get up early. Carol has to get herself ready for the pictures and also put some clean clothes on Tyler. I'll tell you one thing, they don't stay clean long.

Montreal	ab	r	h	rbi	Cincinnati	ab	r	h	rbi
Raines, lf	6	0	0	0	Milner, cf	5	2	2	0
Law, 2b-rf	6	2	4	0	Venable, lf	4	1	1	0
Brooks, ss	6	1	2	1	**Rose, 1b**	3	0	1	1
Driessen, 1b	3	1	2	1	Parker, rf	5	0	1	1
Wallach, 3b	4	0	0	0	Kr'chicki, 3b	2	0	1	1
Francona, rf	5	0	2	1	Esasky, ph-3b	2	0	1	0
Newman, 2b	0	0	0	0	Power, p	0	0	0	0
Webster, cf	4	0	1	0	Walker, ph	1	0	1	0
Fitzgerald, c	5	0	2	0	Franco, p	0	0	0	0
Palmer, p	1	0	0	0	Perez, ph	1	0	0	0
O'Connor, p	0	0	0	0	C'pc'n, ss-3b	5	1	1	0
Barnes, ph	1	0	0	0	Oester, 2b	4	0	2	0
Roberge, p	0	0	0	0	Bilardello, c	5	1	2	1
Wohlford, ph	1	0	0	0	Pastore, p	2	0	0	0
Burke, p	0	0	0	0	Hume, p	1	0	0	0
Dawson, ph	1	0	0	0	Foley, ss	2	0	0	0
St. Claire, p	0	0	0	0					
Totals	43	4	13	3	Totals	42	5	13	4

Montreal .... 2 0 0　0 1 0　1 0 0　0 0—4
Cincinnati .... 1 0 1　2 0 0　0 0 0　0 1—5
Two out when winning run scored.

Montreal	IP.	H.	R.	ER.	BB.	SO.
Palmer	3⅔	7	4	4	4	1
O'Connor	1⅓	1	0	0	0	0
Roberge	2	1	0	0	1	0
Burke	2	1	0	0	0	1
St. Claire (L. 3-2)	1⅔	3	1	0	2	0
Cincinnati	IP.	H.	R.	ER.	BB.	SO.
Pastore	5	8	3	3	1	1
Hume	2⅓	2	1	0	1	1
Power	2⅔	3	0	0	0	0
Franco (W. 6-1)	1	0	0	0	0	1

Game-winning RBI—None.
E—Fitzgerald, Wallach. DP—Montreal 2, Cincinnati 1. LOB—Montreal 11, Cincinnati 13. 2B—Law, Driessen, Webster. 3B—Law. SB—Venable, Milner 3. SH—Venable, Palmer, Webster. HBP—By Pastore (Driessen). PB—Bilardello. T—3:32. A—29,372.

Despite the inconveniences, I think all this will be worth it.

For me, breaking Cobb's record will be a once-in-a-lifetime thing, so I have to make the most of it.

I have to give my attorney, Reuven Katz, and my marketing agent, Bill Hayes of Taft Merchandising, a lot of credit. They're sifting through the offers and requests, deciding on what I should do and what I shouldn't do. There are a lot of people out there who want to cash in on the record, so I have to be careful. I don't want to get burned and, by the same token, I don't want to turn this thing into a circus.

Bill told me the other day that he's spending a lot of his time chasing reports and rumors about unauthorized merchandise that has popped up on the market. I guess we can't stop it all, but we're trying.

Montreal	ab	r	h	rbi	Cincinnati	ab	r	h	rbi
W'n'gham, cf	5	2	2	0	Milner, cf	4	1	1	0
Law, 2b	2	2	0	0	Cedeno, ph	0	0	0	0
Brooks, ss	4	1	2	3	Venable, lf	4	0	1	0
Driessen, 1b	4	1	1	0	Perez, ph	0	0	0	0
Wallach, 3b	4	0	0	0	Walker, ph	1	0	0	0
Francona, lf	4	0	2	1	**Rose, 1b**	2	0	0	0
Webster, rf	4	0	0	0	Parker, rf	4	1	2	2
Fitzgerald, c	2	0	1	0	Kr'chicki, 3b	3	0	2	1
Barnes, pr	0	0	0	0	Es'sky, ph-3b	2	0	0	0
Butera, c	1	0	1	0	C'cepcion, ss	5	0	1	0
Gullickson, p	3	0	0	0	Oester, 2b	4	0	1	0
Reardon, p	0	0	0	0	Bilardello, c	4	0	0	0
Lucas, p	1	0	0	0	Soto, p	3	0	0	0
Burke, p	0	0	0	0	Buchanan, p	0	0	0	0
					Redus, ph	1	1	1	0
Totals	34	6	9	4	Totals	37	3	9	3

Montreal ....1 0 3   0 0 0   0 2 0—6
Cincinnati..................0 0 0   0 1 0   0 1 1—3

Montreal	IP.	H.	R.	ER.	BB.	SO.
Gullickson (W. 8-6)	7	6	1	1	2	2
Reardon	0*	1	1	1	0	0
Lucas	1‡	2	1	1	1	0
Burke (Save 4)	1	0	0	0	2	1

Cincinnati	IP.	H.	R.	ER.	BB.	SO.
Soto (L. 8-10)	7⅔	8	6	4	2	6
Buchanan	1⅓	1	0	0	1	1

*Pitched to one batter in eighth.
†Pitched to two batters in ninth.

Game-winning RBI—None.

E—Bilardello 2, Soto, Brooks. LOB—Montreal 6, Cincinnati 12. 2B—Fitzgerald, Milner, Oester. HR—Brooks (6), Parker (16). SB—Brooks, Law, Winningham 3. SH—Law. HBP—By Soto (Fitzgerald). T—3:02. A—31,167.

As for the authorized material, I'm hoping this book by The Sporting News will provide a lasting record of the season.

Also, I did a hitting book last winter and it came out in the spring. That is something that will never really be outdated. I wrote it with Peter Golenbock, who was a big help.

We've also got a lot of other things planned. There will be Pete Rose caps, Pete Rose key chains and Pete Rose T-shirts. We've also been approached about some special baseball cards, but that deal hasn't been finalized yet.

I've been taking a lot of teasing about the painting Andy Warhol is doing of me. This is going to be a limited-edition. Silkscreen prints are going to sell for at least $2,000, but all that money will go to the Cincinnati Art Museum, a charity. There also will be 4,192 (one for each hit) copies of another print that has several pictures of me. That'll go for about $175.

We're doing ceramic plates and figurines, and also some large posters. We also will do silver and gold coins to mark the day when I break the record.

All this has been carefully planned.

In April, Bill Hayes started sending out a monthly Pete Rose Newsletter to about 800 companies and advertising agencies.

And, of course, there's my deal with Wheaties. I'm told there will be some 12 million boxes of the cereal on the shelves by the end of the month with my picture on them. There's also a TV commercial.

It's all exciting, but the one thing I have to guard against is not getting too involved in this stuff—so much so that it affects my hitting.

★   ★   ★

Mario Soto is still having problems. The Expos beat us, 6-3, tonight and Mario lost his seventh straight game.

I was 0 for 2 with three walks.

We had a little problem in the seventh inning when Mario hit Mike Fitzgerald on the batting helmet with a pitch. Earlier, he had thrown a couple pitches inside to Bill Gullickson and when Fitzgerald got hit, umpire Joe West warned both benches and kept Fitzgerald from going at Mario.

Everybody in the ball park remembered those two pitches (to Gullickson). I didn't even think they were that close, but when the Expos' Jeff Reardon threw inside to Wayne Krenchicki, West ejected both Reardon and Buck Rodgers, their manager.

SUNDAY, JULY 14.......................... ROSE 0 FOR 4

Going to the All-Star Game is always enjoyable for me, and beating Montreal, 5-4, in 10 innings today gives me an extra lift.

Dave Parker and I, along with our wives, leave tomorrow morning for Minneapolis and what will be my 16th All-Star Game. (An injury kept Rose out of another All-Star appearance in 1968.)

I finished third in the fan voting at first base with 748,121 votes, trailing Steve Garvey (1,310,111) and Keith Hernandez (841,951).

If you've grown up in the National League like I have, you learn how important the All-Star Game is. It's more than an exhibition.

I'll never forget the years when Mr. Warren Giles, the late National League president (whose reign lasted through 1969), would visit our clubhouse and give all the N.L. players a little pep talk. I think he's a big reason why the National League has been so successful.

Montreal	ab	r	h	rbi	Cincinnati	ab	r	h	rbi
Raines, lf	4	0	1	0	Milner, cf	4	0	2	1
Law, 2b	5	0	0	0	Venable, lf	4	0	1	0
Lucas, p	0	0	0	0	Cedeno, ph	1	1	1	0
Brooks, ss	3	2	1	0	Rose, 1b	4	0	0	0
Wallach, 3b	4	1	2	0	Parker, rf	5	1	2	1
Driessen, 1b	4	0	1	0	Kr'chicki, 3b	0	1	0	0
Wohlford, rf	3	0	1	1	Redus, pr	0	1	0	0
Webster, rf	0	0	0	0	Knicely, c	0	0	0	0
W'n'gham, cf	3	1	1	2	C'pc'n, ss-3b	4	1	2	2
Fitzgerald, c	3	0	0	0	Oester, 2b	4	1	1	0
Roberge, p	0	0	0	0	Bilardello, c	3	0	0	0
Burke, p	0	0	0	0	Foley, ph-ss	0	0	0	0
Francona, ph	1	0	1	0	Browning, p	2	0	1	1
Newman, 2b	0	0	0	0	Walker, ph	1	0	0	0
Smith, p	2	0	1	0	Franco, p	0	0	0	0
Nicosia, c	1	0	0	0	Perez, ph	1	0	0	0
					Power, p	0	0	0	0
Totals	33	4	9	4	Totals	36	5	11	5

```
Montreal .................0 0 1  2 0 1  0 0 0  0—4
Cincinnati...............0 1 0  0 2 0  0 0 1  1—5
```
One out when winning run scored.

Montreal	IP.	H.	R.	ER.	BB.	SO.
Smith	6	6	3	3	0	3
Roberge	2⅓	3	1	1	0	2
Burke	⅔	0	0	0	1	0
Lucas (L. 3-2)	⅓	2	1	1	1	1

Cincinnati	IP.	H.	R.	ER.	BB.	SO.
Browning	7	7	4	4	1	4
Franco	2	1	0	0	1	1
Power (W. 2-2)	1	1	0	0	1	0

Game-winning RBI—Parker.
E—Winningham. DP—Montreal 1, Cincinnati 2. LOB—Montreal 4, Cincinnati 7. 2B—Wallach, Driessen, Parker. 3B—Milner. HR—Winningham (3). SB—Redus, Cedeno. SH—Krenchicki, Nicosia. SF—Winningham, Milner. T—2:32. A—19,824.

My most memorable All-Star Game was 1970 here at Riverfront Stadium. It was the last All-Star Game my father saw me play. He died the following December.

We were tied 4-4 in the 12th inning. With two out, I got a single off Clyde Wright of the Angels and went to second when Billy Grabarkewitz of the Dodgers singled. The Cubs' Jim Hickman then singled to center and I took off for home.

Ray Fosse had positioned himself on the third-base side of home plate a couple of feet up the line, waiting for the throw from Amos Otis.

I hit Fosse standing up with my left shoulder. He lost both his glove and the ball. I was safe and the National League won, 5-4.

That turned out to be one of the most memorable plays in any of the All-Star Games.

Everybody talks about how I knocked Fosse out of action, but they forget I was the one who missed three games after the All-Star Game (because of a leg bruise). Fosse didn't miss any playing time right after the All-Star Game, and it wasn't until much later that they discovered the full extent of his shoulder injuries.

The odd thing about the '70 All-Star Game was that the night before the game, I ran into Fosse and Sam McDowell (both members of the Cleveland Indians) at the banquet. I invited them over to my house and we stayed up much of the night talking baseball.

I gave Ray a baseball many years later and when I signed it, I wrote: "To Ray. Thanks for making me famous."

★   ★   ★

By winning today—I didn't get any hits—we hit the All-Star break with a 44-41 record and are in third place, four games behind Los Angeles. The Padres are second, a half-game back.

I still think this team has a good chance to win the division. The only thing that concerns me a little is the possibility of a strike.

I've said all along I don't think there will be a strike and I still mean it. We've got a lot of things going for us, and I'd hate to see something happen to interrupt it.

I'm happy Parker has been picked to go to the All-Star Game with me. He certainly deserves the chance. USA Today is announcing All-Star teams picked through a survey of big-league players, and Parker is one of the starting outfielders. He sure gets my vote.

Today, he singled to right field in the 10th inning to score Cesar Cedeno from second base with the winning run. That's the 10th game-winning RBI for the Cobra.

This was a good game to win because we got great relief pitching and hung with them. It looked as if we were going to lose, but we came back (to tie in the ninth inning). I look for this team to do a lot of that after the All-Star Game.

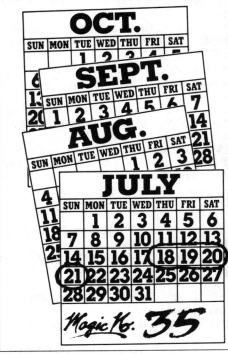

Third baseman Buddy Bell was acquired July 19 and got his first hit in a Reds uniform.

THURSDAY, JULY 18 .... DID NOT PLAY

I had a nice three days at the All-Star Game in Minneapolis.

I batted for Fernando Valenzuela in the eighth inning of the game and grounded out to second base.

Peter Ueberroth asked pitcher Nolan Ryan (the major leagues' all-time strikeout leader) and me to throw out the first ball because we're both involved in records. It was a nice gesture on the commissioner's part.

Tuesday morning, Wheaties held a press breakfast for Mary Lou Retton and me. They showed my TV commercial that will start running right away and gave everybody a copy of the cereal box with my picture on the front.

I told the media I am very happy to be associated with Wheaties and Mary Lou. She's a winner, no question about that.

She's so young, but when she walked into the room she seemed to light it up.

In 1962, I played for the Macon Peaches in the Sally League. The New York Yankees had a team at Augusta, Ga., and the shortstop's name was Ronnie Retton.

Tommy Helms, now my first-base coach and a teammate of mine in '62 (and later with the Reds), and I didn't realize Ronnie Retton was the father of Mary Lou Retton until we watched the Olympics and they said she was from West Virginia. Tommy checked it out and, lo and behold, Ronnie's her father!

He was a good ballplayer. Very aggressive player. I can see where she gets a lot of her athletic ability.

Mary Lou's brother, Ronnie, who attended the breakfast, was born in 1961. I got a laugh when I told the writers that Ronnie remembers what I looked like in '62.

It was good to see the National League win again Tuesday night at the Metrodome and from where I sat, the game didn't look as close as the 6-1 final score.

My first All-Star Game was in Minneapolis (actually in the suburb of Bloomington) in 1965. I went 0 for 2 at Metropolitan Stadium. Struck out both lefthanded and righthanded.

Not many guys have played in two All-Star Games in the same city 20 years apart. That shows you how old I am. (Only four other players have appeared in All-Star Games 20 years apart regardless of the sites— Ted Williams, Stan Musial, Hank Aaron and Carl Yastrzemski. And only Aaron, an All-Star participant at County Stadium in Milwaukee in 1955 and 1975, can match Rose's same-city oddity.)

Carol had a good time in Minneapolis. She and Kellye Parker, the Cobra's wife, went shopping and sat at the game together.

Carol hates to be away from Tyler, but a break like this is good for her.

★　　★　　★

Tonight, we started back up again and I didn't play because the Phillies started a lefthander, Jerry Koosman.

We just couldn't get Juan Samuel out. He had three hits and drove in two runs. They won, 6-3.

Mario Soto was the losing pitcher. He's lost eight in a row, and we've got to get him straightened out somehow. They scored two runs off him in the first inning and we were never able to catch up.

★　　★　　★

Everyone is talking about the possibility of a players' strike.

Joe Price, our player rep, attended the meeting in Chicago on Monday when they set August 6 as a strike deadline. I didn't think it would be that soon, but maybe that's good. If there is a strike—and I don't think there will be one—there will be enough time to get it settled and still salvage the season.

I just feel with Peter Ueberroth behind the scenes, something will be done to keep it from happening. Both sides are too smart to let this happen again for a second time in four years.

FRIDAY, JULY 19 .... ROSE 0 FOR 2

The Buddy Bell deal became official this morning. All the pieces were in place last night, but Bill Bergesch had some details to work out.

So, we're getting one of the best third basemen in baseball. Not only that, but Bell is a Cincinnati resident and is coming home. I've talked to him a couple of times and he says he couldn't be happier.

He was in the lineup tonight and got a hit as we beat the Phillies, 3-2.

Buddy is one outstanding fielder and he's a good hitter. No matter what anybody says, he's going to help this club.

To get him, we had to send outfielder Duane Walker and Jeff Russell, a minor-league pitcher, to the Texas Rangers. Plus, we're negotiating a new contract with Buddy.

The guys I feel sorry for are Nick Esasky and Wayne Krenchicki. By platooning, they've given us the best third-base production in the National League. Together, they've got 88 hits, 48 runs batted in, an on-base percentage of .369 and 44 runs scored.

I plan to use Nick as my left fielder and I also told him there will come a time when I'm not playing first base. After I explained to him my plans for left field, he seemed to be OK.

Chick wasn't as happy.

After the deal was announced and Buddy put on his uniform—he wears the same No. 25 that his father wore with the Reds—Krenchicki told reporters how unhappy he is. He thinks we haven't treated him fairly.

I can understand a guy's feelings when this type of thing happens. The fact remains, we had a chance to get Buddy Bell and went for it. Somebody had to get hurt, but Bill Bergesch and I have to think about the team first.

And as I've said many times, that's the toughest thing about this job. Nobody's ever happy when he doesn't get to play, but Krenchicki's going to be OK. He gives me a lefthanded bat coming off the bench. And he also can be a backup at third base.

I didn't get any hits in tonight's game, but did have two sacrifice flies against the Phils.

We won in the bottom of the ninth when Gary Redus drove in a run that gave John Franco his seventh victory.

It seems like Franco gets into the tight ball games and always gets the win. At this point, I think he's thinking less about saves than he is victories.

Despite all the confusion tonight (caused by the trade and the reaction to it), I made a decision I wanted to make back in May. I'm going with a four-man pitching rotation. I went to a five-man earlier because Mario Soto complained that his arm needed the extra day's rest. Well, he lost his eighth straight game Thursday night and has not won since June 4.

I think this decision will help our staff; everyone will be able to stay sharper.

Phila'phia	ab	r	h	rbi	Cincinnati	ab	r	h	rbi
Samuel, 2b	5	0	0	0	Milner, cf	3	1	0	0
Hayes, lf	5	0	1	2	Venable, lf	3	0	1	0
Tekulve, p	0	0	0	0	C'deno, ph-1b	1	0	1	0
Schmidt, 1b	2	0	0	0	Rose, 1b	2	0	0	2
Wilson, rf	4	0	0	0	Franco, p	0	0	0	0
Virgil, c	4	0	2	0	Parker, rf	3	0	0	0
Maddox, cf	4	0	0	0	Bell, 3b	4	0	1	0
Schu, 3b	2	1	1	0	C'cepcion, ss	4	0	1	0
Jeltz, ss	1	0	0	0	Oester, 2b	3	1	2	0
Russell, ph	1	0	0	0	Bilardello, c	3	0	0	0
Carman, p	0	0	0	0	Browning, p	1	1	1	0
T'mas, ph-lf	1	0	1	0	Hume, p	0	0	0	0
K. Gross, p	2	0	0	0	Redus, ph-lf	1	0	1	1
W'k'fuss, ph	1	0	1	0					
Ag'yo, pr-ss	0	1	0	0					
Totals	32	2	6	2	Totals	28	3	8	3

Philadelphia .... 0 0 0   0 0 0   2 0 0—2
Cincinnati .... 1 0 0   0 1 0   0 0 1—3
One out when winning run scored.

Philadelphia	IP.	H.	R.	ER.	BB.	SO.
K. Gross	6	4	2	1	2	1
Carman	2	2	0	0	1	1
Tekulve (L. 4-5)	⅓	2	1	1	0	0

Cincinnati	IP.	H.	R.	ER.	BB.	SO.
Browning	6⅔	5	2	2	4	2
Hume	⅓	0	0	0	1	0
Franco (W. 7-1)	2	1	0	0	0	2

Game-winning RBI—Redus.
E—Schu, Schmidt. DP—Philadelphia 2. LOB—Philadelphia 9, Cincinnati 8. 2B—Virgil, Hayes, Redus. SB—Venable. SH—Aguayo, Browning, Bilardello. SF—Rose 2. HBP—By K. Gross (Parker). T—2:18. A—28,929.

SATURDAY, JULY 20 .... DID NOT PLAY

A reporter for Cincinnati Magazine is working on a cover story about marriage the second time around. Five couples are being interviewed.

Carol, Tyler and I are supposed to be on the cover.

Carol and I have both been married before.

Carol told the writer she was scared because her first marriage didn't work out.

"It was frightening to go into another one and to go into a marriage with someone like Pete, with everyone wanting him," she said. "I have to accept the fact that there are women out there who don't care that he's married.

"But, just because Pete is who he is and is in the limelight doesn't make us any different. We walk and talk like everyone else, and we're going to have the same kind of problems and enjoy ourselves like anyone else."

For me, a lot of things are different.

I think I have a better understanding of what marriage is all about. I'm more settled, and I think that comes with age.

Take fatherhood. I watched the delivery of Tyler on October 1, 1984. When I had my first kids, it was unheard of for a father to be in there with a mask. It certainly makes you appreciate what women have to go through.

Carol thinks she knows me better than I know myself. I laugh about that, but she might be right.

We have a comfortable home, with plenty of ground. I enjoy the horses and all the time I can spend with Tyler. He's only 10 months old, but we sit there and watch sports on TV.

I also like to see and spend time with my children from my first marriage, Fawn and Petey.

One of the reasons I got the horses in the first place was so Fawn could come here and ride. She loves horses.

We all get along well. Life is too short to be arguing and worrying. You only live once—and if you live right, once is enough.

★ ★ ★

Juan Samuel continued to haunt us in tonight's game. He had a homer, a double, a single and drove in five runs as the Phillies beat us, 10-6.

I didn't play and still need 35 hits to break Ty Cobb's career record of 4,191.

SUNDAY, JULY 21 .... ROSE 1 FOR 3

We went from spring training to early July without getting anybody seriously hurt. But on July 5 in Philadelphia, Dave Van Gorder fractured his thumb and had to go on the disabled list.

Now, the injuries are piling up a little.

I had to put Frank Pastore on the disabled list today and there's a pretty good chance one of my other pitchers, Joe Price, is going to have to be shut down.

Pastore has an inflammation of his right elbow. He hasn't pitched since July 12. The elbow swelled up almost twice its size. The swelling went down, but Frank cannot pitch.

We're putting him on the 15-day disabled list and reactivating Van Gorder.

Price started today's game, but had to leave after just two innings. He's got an inflamed left elbow.

X-rays on Joe showed he's got a calcium deposit that may be causing the trouble. He said the elbow's been bothering him for almost two weeks.

I discussed the situation with Bill Bergesch and Kitty (pitching coach Jim Kaat). I told them if Joe's as bad as he appears to be, we can't have him sitting around. We'd have to go for someone down at Denver.

From what I hear, Andy McGaffigan is pitching good (11-5 record and 2.95 ERA, with 91 strikeouts and only 37 walks in 106⅔ innings) and is the logical guy. I don't think we'll make a decision until we get to New York (where the Reds will open a three-game series Monday night) because Joe's not scheduled to pitch again until Thursday. That gives us some time to see how serious he is and to make some plans.

I'm a little concerned about our starters. Mario Soto has not won since June 4. Price hasn't gotten a win since June 8, and John Stuper—he is now in the bullpen—last won as a starter on May 17 (although he posted a relief victory on June 25). Tom Browning last won on June 26.

Phila'phia	ab	r	h	rbi	Cincinnati	ab	r	h	rbi
Samuel, 2b	4	1	2	1	Milner, cf	3	0	2	1
Hayes, cf	4	0	0	0	Redus, ph-cf	0	0	0	0
Schmidt, 1b	4	0	0	0	Venable, lf	3	0	1	0
Wilson, rf	5	1	2	1	C'deno, ph-lf	1	0	0	0
Diaz, c	3	1	1	0	**Rose, 1b**	3	1	1	0
Thomas, pr	0	1	0	0	Parker, rf	4	2	2	2
Carman, p	0	0	0	0	Bell, 3b	4	1	1	1
G. Gross, ph	1	0	0	0	C'cepcion, ss	3	0	0	0
Russell, lf	0	0	2	1	Oester, 2b	4	1	1	0
Schu, 3b	4	0	2	1	Power, p	0	0	0	0
Jeltz, ss	3	0	1	1	Bilardello, c	4	2	2	2
Ag'yo, ph-ss	1	0	0	0	Price, p	0	0	0	0
Denny, p	3	0	1	1	Stuper, p	0	0	0	0
Virgil, c	0	0	0	0	Foley, ph	1	0	1	0
					Buchanan, p	1	0	0	0
					Franco, p	0	0	0	0
					Kr'chicki, 2b	0	0	0	0
Totals	36	6	11	6	Totals	31	7	11	6

Philadelphia .... 1 2 0   0 0 1   2 0 0—6
Cincinnati .... 0 0 1   2 0 2   2 0 x—7

Philadelphia	IP.	H.	R.	ER.	BB.	SO.
Denny	6	9	5	5	2	2
Carman (L. 2-3)	2	2	2	2	1	3

Cincinnati	IP.	H.	R.	ER.	BB.	SO.
Price	2	3	3	3	3	1
Stuper	3	3	0	0	0	2
Buchanan	1⅔	4	3	3	0	0
Franco (W. 8-1)	1⅓*	1	0	0	2	3
Power (Save 17)	1	0	0	0	0	1

*Pitched to one batter in ninth.

Game-winning RBI—Parker.
E—None. DP—Philadelphia 2, Cincinnati 2. LOB—Philadelphia 8, Cincinnati 4. 2B—Foley. 3B—Diaz, Bell. HR—Samuel (10), Schu (1), Wilson (9), Bilardello (1), Parker (17). SB—Venable. SH—Stuper. T—2:24. A—30,327.

★   ★   ★

Gary Redus is somewhat upset by my plan to put Nick Esasky in left field. He's been talking to reporters, which is typical for guys in his situation.

In today's Cincinnati Enquirer, Gary said:

"If Nick does a good job, I just say where does that leave me? If he plays every day in left field, they're not leaving any place for me. If there's not a place for me here, why do I want to stay around?

"But . . . there's nothing I'm really upset about. I know it's part of the game. You've got to make changes and people move to different places. It comes down to wanting Nick in the lineup, and he's got to play somewhere. Left field is probably the easiest position to play.

"We still have a long way to go and it's no time to panic. It's no time for players being mad. It's time for everyone to pull together. If things happen, things happen."

I had a long talk with Gary and I think he understands where I'm coming from. What I try to tell everyone is that they can help this team. I learned a long time ago it takes 25 guys to win a division. That's what I told him.

★   ★   ★

I got a hit today, leaving me 34 short of surpassing Cobb. It was a big one because it helped us win over Philadelphia, 7-6.

With two out in the seventh and the Phillies ahead 6-5, I singled up the middle off Don Carman, a lefthander. Dave Parker then homered to right field and we were on top.

After the game, we flew to New York. On the flight, a lot of the guys were talking about the possibility of a strike. I think some of them plan to attend Monday's negotiating session in New York.

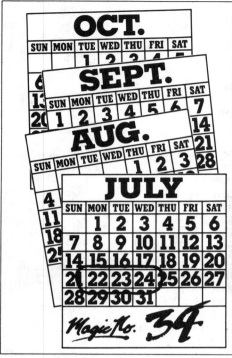

Joe Price's bad elbow resulted in Andy McGaffigan (above) being promoted to Cincinnati.

MONDAY, JULY 22 .... DID NOT PLAY

My co-author, Hal Bodley, and I were guests today with Phyllis George on the "CBS Morning News."

Phyllis is no stranger because several years ago I used to fill in on "NFL Today" when she worked on that show. I became friends with Brent Musburger, Jimmy the Greek and Phyllis. A couple of times, I took the Greek's spot and talked about each of the NFL games.

I get a lot of invitations to go on the morning television shows, but I usually don't accept because you have to get up so early.

We flew to New York last night and I had to get up at 6:30 this morning because the limo picked us up at the Grand Hyatt at 7 o'clock. Now, that's early when it's the day of a game. But I didn't play tonight (because the Mets started a lefthander, Sid Fernandez).

The show gave us a chance to talk about this book and how we're putting it together.

The segment opened with me getting that single in yesterday's game against Philadelphia. I could hear Harry Kalas, the Phillies' announcer, in the background because they borrowed the tape from a Philadelphia station.

Phyllis asked us about the possibility of a strike in two weeks.

I told her the same thing I've been saying—I don't think there'll be one. She asked about what some people think is a disagreement between Reds Owner Marge Schott and me, and I explained that situation like I did earlier in this book.

Hal Bodley doesn't think there's going to be a strike, but he's concerned about how far apart the owners and players are on the pension issue. I think that can be resolved. There can be a compromise. Both sides are too smart to let a strike happen again.

Since the Reds are in contention, Phyllis asked if the strike would hurt me more as a player or a manager.

I told her I had more to lose as a player. When the strike hit in 1981, I was swinging the bat real good. Somebody projected if I had played the whole year and hit at the pace I was going, I would have had 214 hits—something like that. So, if that's true, I lost 74 hits.

I've never complained about that, and I'm not going to now. There are too many people affected to worry about it. I think if there is a strike this time, it will be short.

★   ★   ★

Joe Price was examined today by our team physician, Dr. George Ballou, and Dr. Robert Heidt, an orthopedic specialist.

We're going to bring up Andy McGaffigan tomorrow and put Joe on the disabled list. He has that inflamed left elbow and won't be able to pitch Thursday.

Bill Bergesch also told me today that Frank Pastore's tender elbow might be more serious than we originally thought. Frank's going to Los Angeles to get the arm examined by Dr. Frank Jobe, the specialist a lot of players go to.

★   ★   ★

We beat the Mets tonight, 5-1, but it was more than just a victory. Mario Soto, who had lost eight straight, went nine innings and gave up only six hits.

I've been telling everyone we can't win without him and I'll be very disappointed if he doesn't go on a roll now. I think he's mentally turned around.

You could really see Mario reach back for something special in those last couple of innings.

TUESDAY, JULY 23 .... ROSE 1 FOR 3

We won, 4-0, tonight to make it two in a row over the Mets, who were red-hot when we got here.

I doubled off Ron Darling on a 3-2 pitch in the seventh inning, driving in a run. That hit leaves me 33 short of breaking the record.

Dave Parker hit the 200th home run of his career, and I just can't think of ways to keep explaining how much he means to this team.

Tom Browning pitched a fine game. Gave up just five hits. Anytime you shut out the Mets, you've done something. They hit some balls hard late in the game, but right at people. That's why we've got gloves on.

Cincinnati	ab	r	h	rbi	New York	ab	r	h	rbi
Milner, cf	5	0	1	0	Dykstra, cf	4	0	0	0
Venable, lf	4	2	0	0	Chapman, 2b	4	0	0	0
Rose, 1b	3	0	1	1	Hern'dez, 1b	4	0	1	0
Parker, rf	3	1	1	2	Carter, c	4	0	1	0
Bell, 3b	4	1	1	0	Strawb'ry, rf	4	0	1	0
C'cepcion, ss	4	0	3	0	Foster, lf	3	0	0	0
Oester, 2b	4	0	2	1	Johnson, 3b	3	0	0	0
Bilardello, c	2	0	0	0	Santana, ss	3	0	2	0
Browning, p	4	0	0	0	Darling, p	0	0	0	0
					Sisk, p	0	0	0	0
					Backman, ph	1	0	0	0
					Gorman, p	0	0	0	0
Totals	33	4	9	4	Totals	30	0	5	0

Cincinnati .... 0 1 2   0 0 0   1 0 0—4
New York .... 0 0 0   0 0 0   0 0 0—0

Cincinnati	IP.	H.	R.	ER.	BB.	SO.
Browning (W. 8-7)	9	5	0	0	0	5

New York	IP.	H.	R.	ER.	BB.	SO.
Darling (L. 10-3)	7	9	4	4	5	5
Sisk	1	0	0	0	0	1
Gorman	1	0	0	0	0	0

Game-winning RBI—Oester.
E—Darling. DP—New York 1. LOB—Cincinnati 7, New York 5. 2B—Oester, Rose. HR—Parker (18). SB —Venable. SH—Darling 2. T—2:22. A—34,720.

Browning's a good pitcher; he's a lot better than 8-and-7. He's very consistent. As I've said before, he's your typical young pitcher who comes into the National League today. He pitches with the confidence of a seasoned veteran. That's because they've been taught right. They've had so much instruction on how to pitch by the time they get to the big leagues. Pitching is dominating, and that's why there are only three .300 hitters in the league right now.

The way the Mets have been flying high (15 victories in 17 games preceding this series), I hoped their bats might get a little tired by the time we got here.

If everything goes right, we should have another good pitching match tomorrow—our Ron Robinson against Rick Aguilera. "True Creature" (Robinson) is another one of those youngsters who can pitch.

I told my guys there's no sense in playing good here, then going up to Montreal and not playing well. You could lose everything you've done here in Montreal.

I just want to play consistent baseball.

We've played very well against Montreal this year (6-2) and bad against the Mets (1-8 until winning the first two games of this series). Now we're playing good against the Mets, so I don't want to go up there and reverse it.

★   ★   ★

Before we left the clubhouse, Keith Hernandez's father, visiting from California, stopped by to say hello to Jim Kaat and me. Keith (the Mets' first baseman) and Kitty were teammates on the St. Louis Cardinals. I told John Hernandez that he should be proud of Keith because he's one of the best players in the majors.

When we got back to Manhattan from Queens, I stopped by the Stage Delicatessen on Seventh Avenue to have some dinner. Artie, the night manager, has been a good friend over the years and even has a "Pete Rose" sandwich on the menu.

While we were eating, Ray Knight, his wife Nancy Lopez and their little girl Ashley came over to our table. Ray is the Mets' third baseman, but has been unable to play recently because of a thigh injury.

Nancy, a great golfer, is skipping this week's LPGA tournament in Canada.

When I left the Reds after the 1978 season to sign with Philadelphia, Ray took my place at third base for Cincinnati. I teased him tonight. I said his wife brings home a check every week and pretty big ones.

We had to sleep fast tonight because we've got a day game tomorrow, then go on to Montreal.

WEDNESDAY, JULY 24................... ROSE 2 FOR 4

This was a big day for John Franco, my lefthanded reliever.

We beat the Mets, 3-2, and he got the victory, his ninth straight. In his last 20 appearances, he's allowed just one earned run. You can't do much better than that.

Franco was born in Brooklyn and still lives there. A group of his relatives and friends were at Shea Stadium today, so I knew he would be pumped up when I brought him in after I lifted Ron Robinson for a pinch-hitter in the seventh.

I had two singles today, which leaves me 31 hits short of breaking the

Cobb record. We've got 70 games to go.

I singled to right in the first inning off Rick Aguilera to give us a 1-0 lead.

He threw me the same pitch that I had swung on and missed before. I just choked up on the bat a little more the second time. Made the bat lighter and quicker. He was throwing a little harder than I thought.

I feel like I'm swinging good right now.

Maybe it's coincidental and has nothing to do with the four-man rotation, but we're getting great pitching.

Tom Browning and Mario Soto pitched back-to-back complete games and did not walk anybody. I can't remember the last time that happened.

Cincinnati	ab	r	h	rbi	New York	ab	r	h	rbi
Milner, cf	4	2	2	1	Dykstra, cf	5	0	0	0
Venable, lf	5	0	2	1	Backman, 2b	4	0	0	0
Rose, 1b	4	0	2	1	Hern'dez, 1b	3	1	1	1
Redus, pr	0	0	0	0	Strawb'ry, rf	4	0	1	0
Cedeno, 1b	0	0	0	0	Heep, lf	3	0	1	0
Parker, rf	3	0	0	0	Foster, ph-lf	0	0	0	0
Bell, 3b	3	0	0	0	Hurdle, c	2	0	0	0
C'cepcion, ss	3	0	1	0	Carter, ph-c	1	0	0	0
Oester, 2b	4	0	0	0	Johnson, 3b	3	1	2	0
Bilardello, c	4	1	0	0	Santana, ss	3	0	2	1
Robinson, p	2	0	0	0	Aguilera, p	2	0	1	0
Foley, ph	0	0	0	0	Chapman, ph	1	0	0	0
Franco, p	0	0	0	0	McDowell, p	0	0	0	0
Kr'chicki, ph	0	0	0	0	Staub, ph	1	0	0	0
Power, p	0	0	0	0					
Totals	32	3	7	3	Totals	32	2	8	2

Cincinnati	1 0 1	0 0 0	0 0 1—3
New York	0 0 0	0 1 1	0 0 0—2

Cincinnati	IP.	H.	R.	ER.	BB.	SO.
Robinson	6	8	2	2	2	3
Franco (W. 9-1)	2	0	0	0	1	1
Power (Save 18)	1	0	0	0	1	0

New York	IP.	H.	R.	ER.	BB.	SO.
Aguilera	7	5	2	2	4	6
McDowell (L. 5-4)	2	2	1	0	2	1

Game-winning RBI—Milner.
E—Santana. DP—New York 1. LOB—Cincinnati 8, New York 8. 2B—Milner, Venable 2, Santana 2, Heep, Johnson. HR—Hernandez (8). SB—Milner, Strawberry. SH—Santana. WP—McDowell. T—2:42. A—30,154.

We're playing pretty well and that's good because the first-place Dodgers and second-place Padres are both at home. I really don't know who to root for at this stage in the season, the Dodgers or the Padres.

We have a lot of games left with both of them, so we'll be able to choose our own destiny, so to speak.

We've got to improve a little in some areas—not getting picked off, not missing signs. You can't make mistakes like that against good teams.

Davey Concepcion got thrown out at home plate last night, trying to score from first on Ron Oester's double. I was half-serious after the game when I told him if he hadn't slowed down to spit out some chewing tobacco, he wouldn't have been out.

★　　★　　★

Sure, we're thinking about the August 6 strike date. I want to get as close to the top as I possibly can by then. I didn't take this job to have this team come in third.

I don't think there's going to be a strike, but in case there is, what happens if we come back for only two weeks and we're eight games out? (Entering tonight's games, the Dodgers lead the N.L. West by 1½ games over the Padres, 3½ over the Reds and 9½ over the Astros.)

I'd rather be in our position right now than Houston's.

We'll be playing the people who are ahead of us in the last couple of days before the strike, the Dodgers and the Padres.

If we're a half-game out August 5 and they don't have an agreement, I'm going to play it like the last game of the season. I'd bring a pitcher back with two day's rest.

I know negotiations are going to go right to the deadline. There's always the possibility we could come back and go right to the playoffs.

If you want to look at a strike, which I don't want to do, we could have an advantage. We're at home before August 6, then we're supposed to go to the West Coast for the start of a 14-game road trip. If there's a two-week strike, that's got to be a benefit for us. It's hard to go out there and win series.

Magic No. 31

Second baseman Ron Oester enjoyed the first five-hit game of his career on July 26.

THURSDAY, JULY 25 .... ROSE 0 FOR 1

Since we have friends in Montreal, my wife Carol decided to fly here last night and spend the weekend.

She arrived earlier than I did and was met at the airport by some friends, who picked me up after the ball club got here from New York. Then, we all went to the racetrack.

It was a fun evening.

Tonight wasn't as great.

Our bats went silent against the Expos and our four-game winning streak ended, 1-0. We managed only four singles off Bill Gullickson (who worked 7⅔ innings before giving way to Jeff Reardon) and I didn't get any of them. Even though Gullickson walked seven batters, we couldn't score and left eight runners on base.

Andy McGaffigan made his first start for us and pitched a good game. He gave up just four hits in six innings and struck out five.

They got their run off Tom Hume in the seventh when Herm Win-

Cincinnati	ab	r	h	rbi	Montreal	ab	r	h	rbi
Milner, cf	3	0	1	0	Raines, lf	4	0	1	0
Venable, lf	4	0	0	0	Law, 2b	4	0	1	0
Rose, 1b	1	0	0	0	Dawson, rf	4	0	0	0
Redus, pr	0	0	0	0	Brooks, ss	3	0	1	0
Cedeno, 1b	0	0	0	0	Driessen, 1b	3	0	1	0
Parker, rf	3	0	1	0	Wallach, 3b	2	0	0	0
Bell, 3b	4	0	2	0	W'n'gham, cf	2	1	1	0
C'cepcion, ss	2	0	0	0	Fitzgerald, c	2	0	0	0
Oester, 2b	3	0	0	0	Shines, ph	1	0	1	1
Bilardello, c	2	0	0	0	Butera, c	0	0	0	0
Foley, ph	1	0	0	0	Gullickson, p	3	0	0	0
Van Gorder, c	0	0	0	0	Reardon, p	0	0	0	0
Esasky, ph	1	0	0	0					
McG'figan, p	2	0	0	0					
Kr'chicki, ph	1	0	0	0					
Hume, p	0	0	0	0					
Totals	27	0	4	0	Totals	28	1	6	1

Cincinnati	0 0 0	0 0 0	0 0 0—0
Montreal	0 0 0	0 0 0	1 0 x—1

Cincinnati	IP.	H.	R.	ER.	BB.	SO.
McGaffigan	6	4	0	0	0	5
Hume (L. 1-3)	2	2	1	1	1	2

Montreal	IP.	H.	R.	ER.	BB.	SO.
Gullickson (W. 10-6)	7⅔	4	0	0	7	3
Reardon (Save 25)	1⅓	0	0	0	0	1

Game-winning RBI—Shines.
E—None. DP—Cincinnati 2, Montreal 2. LOB—Cincinnati 8, Montreal 5. 2B—Brooks. 3B—Winningham. SB—Winningham, Redus 2, Parker. SH—Concepcion. HBP—By McGaffigan (Wallach). T—2:22. A—22,366.

ningham walked, stole second and scored on Razor Shines' single to right field—all with two out. They just called up Shines a day or two ago.

I had thought about starting Nick Esasky in left field because he's got to get his feet wet there sooner or later.

George Scherger, who helps me in the dugout so much, has been working with Nick every day in the outfield since we got Buddy Bell. I'm confident Esasky can make the transition from the infield to left field.

I explained to Nick how I did it (Rose was moved from second base to the outfield in 1967) and that a lot of other players have done it. Nick is an excellent athlete, and good athletes adjust quickly.

When Don Heffner was managing the Reds in 1966, he moved me from second base to third base. I told Esasky how unhappy I was with the switch. I didn't like it because I thought it hurt our ball club at two positions. Plus, he didn't ask me to make the change like Sparky Anderson did when he brought me in from left field to third base in 1975.

Nick can be outstanding in the outfield. He's got good speed, a strong arm, an accurate arm and good eyes. I see no reason why he shouldn't be a tremendous outfielder, and there's no question he gives me some power.

With Esasky in the lineup every day, we could have the kind of power to generate home runs like some of the other lineups in the National League.

My plans right now are to start him in left on Sunday (Max Venable got the call tonight). That gives him a few more days to get comfortable out there, working with Scherger.

Nick surprised me a little when he asked about all the good, young outfielders we have in the minors.

I told him Kal Daniels has a broken ankle with a big cast on it, Eric Davis is playing center field and that Paul O'Neill is playing first base now. (All are with Denver.)

★   ★   ★

Carol and I have been lucky enough to find a lady who has agreed to be Tyler's nanny, baby sitter, or whatever.

The woman has agreed to live at our house on certain occasions, plus be there every day when she doesn't stay over. Getting her will give Carol some freedom.

FRIDAY, JULY 26 .... ROSE 0 FOR 1

I never try to show up umpires. They've got a tough job to do and for the most part, they do it well.

That doesn't stop me from getting hot when I think I'm right.

Tonight I got ejected from a game for the first time since I came back as player-manager. It was Pete Rose the player, not Pete Rose the manager, who got run.

It happened in the top of the 10th inning.

We had taken a 6-1 lead into the bottom of the eighth, but Montreal jumped on John Franco for four runs and got another off Ted Power to tie.

I didn't start tonight because the Expos started a lefthander, Dan Schatzeder, but in the 10th I batted for Power with the bases loaded. I hit a grounder to Tim Wallach at third. He came home to get a forceout, then catcher Steve Nicosia threw to first. As I was nearing first base, I threw my arms up and deflected the ball.

Harry Wendelstedt, the home-plate umpire, called me out for interference.

I thought Nicosia made a bad throw on the play. As far as I'm concerned, I ran to first the way I always have after hitting a ball down the line. I saw Terry Francona (the Expos' first baseman) reaching inside—and also that my helmet had come off. So, I just put my arms up so it wouldn't hit me in the head.

I guess I used some profanity when Wendelstedt and I went at it, so he ejected me.

I wasn't going to continue to play anyway, so it didn't matter. George Scherger handled the team the rest of the way and we won, 7-6, when Nick Esasky, who came in as a late replacement for Buddy Bell at third base, homered over the left-field fence on Jeff Reardon's first pitch in the 11th inning.

Cincinnati	ab	r	h	rbi	Montreal	ab	r	h	rbi
Redus, cf-lf	5	1	2	0	Raines, lf	5	2	1	0
C'cepcion, ss	5	0	1	1	Law, 2b	5	1	2	1
Parker, rf	5	0	2	2	Dawson, rf	5	1	3	0
Bell, 3b	5	1	1	0	Brooks, ss	5	1	1	2
Power, p	0	0	0	0	Driessen, 1b	3	0	0	0
Rose, ph	1	0	0	0	Wohlford, ph	0	0	0	0
Buchanan, p	0	0	0	0	F'cona, ph-1b	2	1	2	2
Perez, 1b	2	2	1	0	Wallach, 3b	5	0	2	1
Franco, p	0	0	0	0	W'n'gham, cf	5	0	0	0
Esasky, 3b	2	1	1	1	Butera, c	2	0	0	0
Cedeno, lf-1b	6	0	0	0	Roberge, p	0	0	0	0
Oester, 2b	6	1	5	2	Wash'gton, ph	1	0	0	0
Bilardello, c	4	0	0	0	Burke, p	0	0	0	0
Kr'chicki, ph	1	0	0	0	Webster, ph	1	0	0	0
Van Gorder, c	1	0	0	0	Reardon, p	0	0	0	0
Soto, p	3	0	1	0	Schatzeder, p	1	0	0	0
Milner, cf	2	1	1	0	Shines, ph	1	0	0	0
					St. Claire, p	0	0	0	0
					Nicosia, c	3	0	0	0
Totals	48	7	15	6	Totals	44	6	11	6

Cincinnati .... 0 1 1 0 0 2 1 1 0 0 1—7
Montreal .... 0 0 0 0 0 1 0 5 0 0 0—6

Cincinnati	IP.	H.	R.	ER.	BB.	SO.
Soto	6	3	1	1	2	8
Franco	1⅓	3	4	4	1	0
Power	1⅔	3	1	1	0	2
Buchanan (W. 1-0)	2	2	0	0	0	0

Montreal	IP.	H.	R.	ER.	BB.	SO.
Schatzeder	5	4	2	0	3	2
St. Claire	2	5	3	2	1	1
Roberge	1	2	1	1	0	0
Burke	2	2	0	0	2	1
Reardon (L. 2-4)	1	2	1	1	0	0

Game-winning RBI—Esasky.
E—Butera, Winningham, Schatzeder, Wallach. DP —Montreal 3. LOB—Cincinnati 14, Montreal 8. 2B— Redus, Oester 2, Bell, Milner, Francona. HR—Esasky (8). SB—Redus, Dawson, Raines. T—3:39. A— 23,047.

Ron Oester, my second baseman, had one of the biggest nights of his career. He had five hits in one game for the first time—three singles and two doubles in six at-bats. He also drove in two runs.

I don't ever worry about Ron Oester. I put him in the lineup and let him play. He's a throwback. He plays the game the way it used to be played.

Ron, Dave Parker, Buddy Bell and myself were all raised in Cincinnati.

Ron says he grew up watching the Reds play at Crosley Field (which gave way to Riverfront Stadium in mid-1970). He kids me that when he was about 8 years old he had his picture taken with me on the field at Crosley. He's telling the truth because I remember the day he had me autograph it. (Oester was 8 in 1964, Rose's second season in the majors.)

When something like that happens, you know you're getting a little older.

SATURDAY, JULY 27 .... ROSE 3 FOR 4

I had three hits tonight, the first three-hit game I've had since June 2.

But the important thing is we beat the Expos, 7-6. That means we've won six out of our last seven games overall.

I need 28 hits now to break the Cobb record and I feel like I'm swinging good.

In my book, "Pete Rose on Hitting/How to Hit Better Than Anybody," I talked about the mental approach to this game. I think that is one of the things I've been able to help my players with this year because, for one thing, I'm one of them.

I've said a hundred times that pressure can ruin the best hitters. And yet, in my experience, there really is no such thing as pressure. It doesn't exist—unless you think it does.

I never get nervous. Oh, I might have butterflies from time to time, but that is natural. I always want to be relaxed because that's the only way you can hit a thrown ball. When I go up to the plate, I joke and talk with the umpire and the catcher. I do the same kind of thing when I'm playing first base.

There's also a chance that if I keep this up, the other guy will lose some of his concentration and that gives me an edge.

Concentration. When I step into the batter's box, I have absolutely nothing else on my mind but hitting the ball.

Cincinnati	ab	r	h	rbi	Montreal	ab	r	h	rbi
Milner, cf	5	2	2	0	Raines, lf	4	1	2	1
Venable, lf	4	2	1	0	Wash'ton, 2b	5	1	1	2
Rose, 1b	4	2	3	0	Dawson, rf	5	1	0	0
Parker, rf	5	0	2	3	Brooks, ss	4	1	1	1
Bell, 3b	4	1	1	1	Wallach, 3b	4	1	1	0
C'cepcion, ss	5	0	1	0	Law, 1b	3	0	2	0
Oester, 2b	2	0	1	0	Webster, cf	2	0	0	1
Franco, p	0	0	0	0	Francona, ph	1	0	0	0
Hume, p	0	0	0	0	W'n'gham, cf	0	0	0	0
Bilardello, c	5	0	2	1	Butera, c	3	0	0	0
Browning, p	3	0	0	0	St. Claire, p	0	0	0	0
Power, p	0	0	0	0	Shines, ph	1	0	0	0
Foley, 2b	0	0	0	0	Palmer, p	0	0	0	0
					Lucas, p	1	0	0	0
					Nicosia, ph	1	0	0	0
					Roberge, p	0	0	0	0
					Fitzgerald, c	1	0	0	0
					Driessen, ph	0	1	0	0
Totals	37	7	13	5	Totals	35	6	7	5

Cincinnati ....3 3 0 0 1 0 0 0 0—7
Montreal ....0 0 0 2 0 0 0 3 1—6

Cincinnati	IP.	H.	R.	ER.	BB.	SO.
Browning (W. 9-7)	7⅓	6	5	4	1	6
Power	1	1	1	1	2	1
Franco	⅓	0	0	0	0	0
Hume (Save 3)	⅓	0	0	0	0	1
Montreal	IP.	H.	R.	ER.	BB.	SO.
Palmer (L. 6-9)	1⅓	6	6	6	4	1
Lucas	3⅔	4	1	0	1	0
Roberge	2	2	0	0	0	1
St. Claire	2	1	0	0	1	0

Game-winning RBI—None.
E—Butera, Brooks, Law, Concepcion, Bell. DP—Montreal 3. LOB—Cincinnati 10, Montreal 6. 2B—Milner, Law. HR—Brooks (7), Raines (5), Washington (1). SB—Venable. SH—Browning. SF—Webster. T—2:40. A—25,422.

You just have to leave your away-from-the-park problems at home. I see how teammates can be affected by everyday problems. If something is on your mind, you are not going to do as well at the plate as you would if your mind were free.

After I've talked to the catcher and the umpire, my mind is clear of everything by the time the pitcher is ready to go into his windup. The only thing I'm thinking about is the baseball.

When I'm in a good groove like tonight, I feel I wouldn't mind if I started each at-bat with a 0-2 count. My concentration is so good I don't worry about having two strikes.

I think pitchers have a tendency to relax a little when they get ahead 0-2. That's when I'm waiting for the pitch.

I'd love to know just how many hits I've gotten with two strikes.

My bats this year have a black finish, with "PR-4192" on them. When I get a new bat, I put some tape grips on the handle, then sand the paint off the barrel. I clean the bat with rubbing alcohol so that when I take batting practice, I can check the smudges on the bat to see where the ball is hitting it.

I've done this for as long as I can remember because if you're swinging good, the ball must hit the bat in the proper place every time.

When I went to Japan in the fall of 1980 to sign a deal with the Mizuno Corp. to use its bats, Hal Bodley (co-author of this book) suggested that my bats carry the numerical designation "PR-3631." His idea was that I'd surely break Stan Musial's N.L. career hits record of 3,630 in 1981 and that "3631" would be fitting. Since then, the number has been changed to "PR-4000" and now "PR-4192" for the obvious reason.

As I've said, I don't stick my bats in the cart with all the others. I take them with me to my office after a game and always know where they are. I just never let my bats get very far away from me. Especially this year, because a lot of people are trying to get them for souvenirs.

SUNDAY, JULY 28 .... DID NOT PLAY

This was one of those games we were never in.

Montreal scored three times in the third inning, then went on to win, 6-0.

We had only four singles and you just can't win with only four hits. No way.

Their pitcher, Joe Hesketh, walked four batters in the first two innings, but we just couldn't get a key hit.

Still, we won five of seven games on this road trip, which is as good as can be expected. Except I want to win every game.

★   ★   ★

People talk about what a grind traveling is today, and they're probably right. Sometimes it's tough, but winning makes it a lot easier.

We have a pretty good traveling party. It usually numbers about 45.

There are the players, coaches, the trainer, equipment manager, traveling secretary, publicity director or his assistant, plus the media.

There are only three newspapers that cover the Reds on the road.

Greg Hoard is the regular beat writer for the Cincinnati Enquirer, and Bruce Schoenfeld does the same thing for the Cincinnati Post. The Dayton newspapers alternate on the road between Hal McCoy and Paul Meyer. Both cover us at home.

I would have to say that for the most part, the players and the newspaper reporters have an excellent relationship. This is not the case in some cities.

There are some instances where the players don't like something that has been written. The same thing has happened to me a few times, but usually when you sit down with the writer and explain your side, the air is cleared. That isn't to say you always agree, but at least the relationship remains good.

Joe Nuxhall is the dean of our radio-TV crew. He pitched for the Reds in 1944 when he was only 15 years old. I think that still might be a record. (Nuxhall ranks as the youngest player in big-league history, having pitched against the St. Louis Cardinals on June 10, 1944, when he was 15 years, 10 months and 11 days old.)

Nux, who turns 57 Tuesday, is an Ohio native and has been broadcasting our games for 19 years. He's a lefthander who won 135 games in the majors and still throws batting practice.

Nux also does a pregame show following the one I do with Marty Brennaman.

Marty is in his 12th season as the Reds' play-by-play announcer. We've all had some good times together.

WLW in Cincinnati is the flagship radio station for our broadcasts, which also are carried by about 70 stations in Ohio, Kentucky, Indiana, Virginia, West Virginia, Florida and Tennessee.

WLWT is the flagship TV station. The announcers are Ken Wilson, who is in his third season, and my old buddy Joe Morgan, who is in his first.

It's basically a good group. And we all get along with each other.

★   ★   ★

We flew back to Cincinnati after today's game. Tomorrow's an open date, but on Tuesday we start a homestand against West Division teams Houston, Los Angeles and San Diego by playing the Astros at Riverfront.

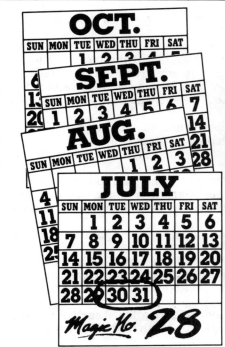

A hit against Houston and Nolan Ryan on July 30 cut Rose's magic number to 27.

TUESDAY, JULY 30 .... ROSE 1 FOR 4

We beat Houston and Nolan Ryan, 4-1, tonight at Riverfront Stadium and I got a single in four at-bats.

We've now got 65 games to go and I need 27 hits to break the Cobb record. If I can't get 27 hits in that many games, we're not going to be as high in the Western Division standings as I think we'll be.

Marge Schott, our owner, says she hopes I break the record on the last day of the season. Well, if it takes me that long, I'm not going to be helping the team win very much.

I got my single in the seventh inning when we scored two times. It was an infield hit and loaded the bases.

On the next play, Eddie Milner was forced out at the plate, but Buddy Bell then singled to left, scoring Max Venable and me.

Houston	ab	r	h	rbi	Cincinnati	ab	r	h	rbi
Doran, 2b	5	0	0	0	Milner, cf	3	1	2	0
Reynolds, ss	4	0	2	0	Venable, lf	3	1	0	0
Bass, cf	3	0	0	0	Rose, 1b	4	1	1	0
Cruz, lf	3	0	2	0	Parker, rf	4	1	2	1
Mumphrey, rf	3	0	0	0	Bell, 3b	4	0	2	2
Davis, 1b	4	0	0	0	C'cepcion, ss	3	0	1	1
Bailey, c	1	1	0	0	Oester, 2b	3	0	1	0
Mizerock, c	2	0	0	0	Bilardello, c	4	0	0	0
Rivera, 3b	2	0	1	0	Soto, p	4	0	0	0
Jones, ph	1	0	1	0					
Ryan, p	1	0	0	1					
Walling, ph	1	0	1	0					
Calhoun, p	0	0	0	0					
Dawley, p	0	0	0	0					
Spilman, ph	1	0	0	0					
Totals	31	1	7	1	Totals	32	4	9	4

Houston		0	1	0	0 0 0	0 0 0—1
Cincinnati		2	0	0	0 0 0	2 0 x—4

Houston	IP.	H.	R.	ER.	BB.	SO.
Ryan (L. 8-9)	6	7	2	2	2	7
Calhoun	⅓	1	2	1	1	0
Dawley	1⅔	1	0	0	0	1

Cincinnati	IP.	H.	R.	ER.	BB.	SO.
Soto (W. 10-11)	9	7	1	1	5	8

Game-winning RBI—Parker.
E—Calhoun. DP—Cincinnati 1. LOB—Houston 9, Cincinnati 8. 2B—Rivera, Walling, Reynolds, Cruz, Milner. 3B—Milner. SB—Oester. SH—Venable. SF—Ryan. T—2:40. A—26,822.

Mario Soto won his second straight decision after that dry spell he had. He went nine innings and gave up only seven hits. He's back where he should be.

He's got a 10-11 record and I just wonder where we'd be if he'd won only half of the games he lost.

★   ★   ★

A lot of people are making something out of the fact we had a 5-2 road trip last week and failed to make up any ground in our division.

We're 7-3 in our last 10 games, which gives us a 52-45 record. We're in third place, 5½ games behind Los Angeles and only a half-game behind the Padres.

I just don't think the Dodgers are going to stay as hot as they are right now. However, if Pedro Guerrero continues to hit home runs the way he has lately (a total of 19 in June and July, 23 overall), nobody's going to catch them.

They'll come back down. They're just going real good right now (16 victories in their last 20 games). They really don't have that much daylight on us, and you have to remember that we're home for over a week now.

We've got two more games with Houston, four against the Dodgers and three with the Padres.

If there's a strike, it's going to happen a week from today—just before we play the Padres in the second game of that series at Riverfront.

Reporters have been asking me a lot about how I'm going to manage this "last" week.

I really don't plan to change much—as I mentioned earlier, we're in a four-man rotation now. The closer we can get to first place by August 6, the better it will be.

★   ★   ★

Yesterday was an open date. I went to Charleston, West Virginia, for another promotional appearance. When I got home, I fed the horses and watched some TV.

Taking care of four horses is getting a little bit too much for me. I've worked out a deal for my brother to come over every two or three days and clean out the stalls and keep the stable in shape. I'll keep on feeding the horses when we're home.

WEDNESDAY, JULY 31 .... ROSE 2 FOR 4

This was a tough day all the way around.

First, I had to do the one thing as manager that bothers me the most. I had to call Alan Knicely into my office and tell him he's going back to Denver.

It's never easy. There's no way to handle something like this, but I thought he took it good.

Frank Pastore, who has been on the disabled list since July 21, is going to have surgery in Los Angeles next week on his right elbow. Dr. Frank Jobe, who's done a lot of these operations, is going to perform the surgery.

So, we've decided to bring Jay Tibbs back. He won't be here until Friday and it's our plan to start him in the second game of that night's doubleheader against the Dodgers at Riverfront.

I told Knicely that even though he's going to Denver, I want him to stay around Thursday in case we need him to pinch hit or something.

We can get by with two catchers, Dave Van Gorder and Dann Bilardello. Besides, there's a chance we might get Bo Diaz from the Phillies. Bill Giles, the Phils' president, says they're willing to trade Bo and you know how much I want him.

I told Knicely we'll bring him back up on September 1 when we can expand the roster to 40 players.

Knicely told reporters that getting sent down for a few weeks might be a blessing in disguise, especially if there's a strike. If he's at Denver, he'll get full pay.

Knice started the season at Denver and we brought him up on May 14. He hit well at first, but his average fell to .253 and he had a lot of trouble throwing runners out.

★   ★   ★

Even though the news from New York isn't encouraging (regarding the baseball contract negotiations), I still don't think there's going to be a strike.

Houston	ab	r	h	rbi	Cincinnati	ab	r	h	rbi
Doran, 2b	4	0	1	0	Milner, cf	4	0	0	0
Thon, ss	5	0	1	0	Cedeno, ph	1	0	0	0
Bass, cf	5	1	1	0	Venable, lf	4	1	2	0
Cruz, lf	5	3	3	0	**Rose, 1b**	4	0	2	1
Mumphrey, rf	5	0	0	0	Parker, rf	4	1	1	1
Davis, 1b	3	2	2	4	Bell, 3b	4	0	2	0
Rivera, 3b	4	1	2	0	C'cepcion, ss	3	0	0	0
Mizerock, c	4	1	1	3	Oester, 2b	4	0	2	0
Scott, p	3	1	2	2	Bilardello, c	4	0	1	0
Jones, p	1	0	0	0	Browning, p	1	0	0	0
DiPino, p	0	0	0	0	Buchanan, p	0	0	0	0
					Hume, p	0	0	0	0
					Foley, ph	1	0	0	0
					Stuper, p	0	0	0	0
					Redus, ph	1	0	0	0
Totals	39	9	13	9	Totals	35	2	10	2

Houston....................0 0 0   3 1 4   1 0 0—9
Cincinnati..................0 0 1   0 1 0   0 0 0—2

Houston	IP.	H.	R.	ER.	BB.	SO.
Scott (W. 10-5)	7	10	2	2	1	4
DiPino	2	0	0	0	0	1

Cincinnati	IP.	H.	R.	ER.	BB.	SO.
Browning (L. 9-8)	5⅓	8	7	7	1	1
Buchanan	0*	2	1	1	1	0
Hume	⅔	1	0	0	0	0
Stuper	3	2	1	0	0	1

*Pitched to three batters in sixth.

Game-winning RBI—Davis.
E—Browning, Oester. DP—Houston 1, Cincinnati 1. LOB—Houston 5, Cincinnati 8. 2B—Mizerock, **Rose**, Bell. 3B—Venable. HR—Davis (8), Scott (1), Parker (19). SH—Browning. WP—Buchanan, Stuper. T—2:33. A—20,758.

I just think Peter Ueberroth will do something at the last moment. I don't think he'd want the mark of a strike on his record. The commissioner told me at the All-Star Game that he was going to be like a hen and keep both sides negotiating every day. Whatever he can do, he'll do, plus a few other things.

★   ★   ★

I got two hits tonight, but we lost to the Astros, 9-2.

One hit was a double to the left-field corner that scored Max Venable in the third inning.

Tom Browning pitched pretty well in the beginning, but they scored four runs in the sixth and that kind of took the wind out of our sails.

My hits left me 25 short of breaking the Cobb record.

★   ★   ★

The Reds have trained in Tampa, Fla., for 52 years. But we've been told by the city that we've got to move after next March. They're planning to tear down Al Lopez Field. A domed stadium is going to be built so they can try to get a big-league team.

Bill Bergesch told me today that Pompano Beach and Port St. Lucie, both on the east coast of Florida, are the most likely choices for our relocation. Both of those cities would like to have the Reds.

THURSDAY, AUGUST 1 ....DID NOT PLAY

Rick Reilly of Sports Illustrated has been spending a lot of time with me the last few days.

I even invited him to spend a night at my house, to get an idea what my routine is like.

Rick is a nice guy, but I'm not sure just what kind of a story he's planning to write about me.

He spent an afternoon at my first wife's home and asked a lot of questions about me—at least that's what I've heard.

Then, he interviewed Carol and asked her some questions that I don't think anybody really cares about.

I'm always a little suspicious of this type of thing.

After the game tonight, Rick asked me how much money I spend at the track each year. I told him it was nobody's business, but that it was not nearly as much as a lot of people think it is.

Now, what does that kind of stuff have to do with me going after Ty Cobb's record? I guess everybody has an angle or is trying to find something out about me that hasn't been written before.

As far as going to the track is concerned, one of the ways I relax—as I've said many times—is to go to dog races in spring training and to horse races on off-nights during the season. Like, when I was with the Philadelphia Phillies, Carol and I would drive to Brandywine Raceway in Wilmington, Delaware, on Sunday nights when the team was home.

I enjoy that. I love horses and I like the competition. To me, I'm right up-front with the fans. I think this is a lot better than sitting in a bar drinking. I don't drink.

But I told Rick nobody has ever seen me at a window at a racetrack because I don't place my own bets or cash them.

I like to cooperate with every writer, but when they start asking questions about things that caused my first marriage to end in divorce and all that, I back off. To me, it's just not news.

But I told Rick just about everything I could about when I was growing up and how my father helped me and all that. He should have plenty for a story.

Oh, well, I'll just have to wait and see.

★   ★   ★

When we called up Andy McGaffigan from Denver on July 23, we figured he'd be able to help our pitching staff, which is hurting right now with Joe Price and Frank Pastore on the disabled list.

Tonight, Andy pitched his first complete game in 24 major league starts and was outstanding. We beat the Astros, 5-2.

McGaffigan used to be a short reliever, a long reliever and a spot starter. Now he understands he's a starter and he's got confidence.

Nick Esasky—I played him in left field for the second time (the first time being Sunday)—hit a tape-measure homer in the fourth to put us ahead 3-2. It was a two-run shot.

This was a good win because now we're 53-46, with the Dodgers coming to town tomorrow night for four games starting with a doubleheader. (Los Angeles, atop the N.L. West, leads San Diego by 4½ games and Cincinnati by five games.)

Rose poses with his mother, LaVerne, at an August 3 wedding reception for his niece, Robin.

FRIDAY, AUGUST 2 .... ROSE 0 FOR 4

If somebody would've told me I'd get no hits tonight, I wouldn't have believed him.

I seldom have had better batting practice. I was hitting the ball hard to all fields and felt good. I was in a groove.

But in the first game of a double-header against the Dodgers, I went 0 for 4 and we lost, 5-3. This is one of the things I'll never understand about baseball. Swing the bat so good in BP, then come up empty in the game.

We had some chances to win the first game, but were unable to capitalize.

Ron Robinson pitched pretty good, but made a costly mistake. We were down only 2-1 in the fifth inning, but Robinson got a slider up to Pedro Guerrero and he hit it out (with two men on base). Pedro's on a tear—it was his 24th homer. And he came

FIRST GAME								
Los Ang.	ab	r	h	rbi	Cincinnati	ab	r	h	rbi
Duncan, ss	4	0	0	0	Milner, cf	5	0	1	0
Cabell, 3b	4	1	1	0	Venable, lf	2	0	1	1
Bailor, 3b	0	0	0	0	Stuper, p	0	0	0	0
Landreaux, cf	4	2	2	1	Kr'chicki, ph	1	0	0	1
Guerrero, lf	5	1	1	3	Franco, p	0	0	0	0
Brock, 1b	2	1	1	0	**Rose, 1b**	4	0	0	0
Marshall, rf	4	0	2	0	Parker, rf	4	0	1	0
Scioscia, c	4	0	1	1	Bell, 3b	4	0	1	0
Sax, 2b	4	0	2	0	Oester, 2b	4	0	0	0
Hershiser, p	1	0	0	0	Foley, ss	3	1	1	0
Russell, ph	1	0	0	0	Bilardello, c	3	0	1	1
Niedenfuer, p	0	0	0	0	C'cepcion, ph	1	0	0	0
					Robinson, p	1	0	0	0
					Hume, p	0	0	0	0
					Redus, ph-lf	3	2	3	0
Totals	33	5	10	5	Totals	35	3	9	3

Los Angeles ....0 1 1   0 3 0   0 0 0—5
Cincinnati ....0 0 1   0 1 0   1 0 0—3

Los Angeles	IP.	H.	R.	ER.	BB.	SO.
Hershiser (W. 12-3) ...	7	8	3	2	1	1
Niedenfuer (Save 9) ...	2	1	0	0	0	2

Cincinnati	IP.	H.	R.	ER.	BB.	SO.
Robinson (L. 5-3)	4⅓	7	5	5	3	4
Hume	⅔	1	0	0	0	0
Stuper	2	2	0	0	0	1
Franco	2	0	0	0	1	1

Game-winning RBI—Scioscia.
E—Duncan, Hershiser, Sax. DP—Los Angeles 2, Cincinnati 2. LOB—Los Angeles 8, Cincinnati 7. 2B—Cabell, Foley, Bell. HR—Landreaux (8), Guerrero (24). SB—Redus 2, Cabell. SH—Hershiser. SF—Venable. HBP—By Robinson (Hershiser), by Franco (Landreaux). PB—Bilardello. T—2:38. A—40,236.

back in the second game to hit his 25th, but that one didn't cost us.

I didn't play in the second game because they pitched a lefthander, Rick Honeycutt.

I've talked a lot about Jay Tibbs and the ability he has. When we left spring training, he was my No. 2 starter. He just never got his act together, so we had to send him to Denver on July 9.

I told reporters last year that he could pitch, I told them the same thing this spring and I said it again when I sent him out.

Well, we brought him back and I started him tonight in the second game. He just went through one of those periods for several weeks where he was confused and his confidence was shot. Hitters go through that, and pitchers go through it, too.

I was a little troubled this afternoon when I learned that Tibbsie had driven all the way from Denver rather than fly.

I know this really concerned Bill Bergesch, our vice president and general manager, because of the fatigue factor. How can a guy drive from Denver to Cincinnati and not be tired?

Once Jay told me about the trip, I stopped being so concerned. He drove to just outside Louisville on Thursday and got 10-12 hours sleep, then finished the trip this afternoon. That was only a two-hour drive. I could tell when he came to the ball park today that he wasn't tired.

Once he got out on the mound I could see from the first pitch that he was throwing differently. He had a different kind of confidence, too. He was throwing and not shying away from anything.

Jay gave us a split by beating the Dodgers, 5-2. They got only five hits off him and he went nine innings. The last time he won a game for us was June 2 against St. Louis.

He was relieved when we sent him to the minors because he was able to get his stuff back together. Tonight, he pitched a tremendous game.

With the strike deadline approaching, it was obvious to me that Dodgers Manager Tommy Lasorda was trying extremely hard to win a doubleheader. Except for changing catchers and pitchers, he put the same lineup out there in the nightcap that he had in the first game.

After the game, I went home, fed my horses and had a little dinner. I also had to make some important phone calls. More about that tomorrow.

SATURDAY, AUGUST 3 .... ROSE 0 FOR 4

This turned out to be a busy day.

Carol had to get up early and go downtown to model some clothes in a Rosie Reds fashion show at the Hyatt Regency.

I had to be at a local television studio a few hours later to tape a segment for this weekend's "Face the Nation" on CBS. Sunday's program is about the possibility of a strike.

The strike deadline is before the Tuesday games, which are all at night.

When I do a national TV show such as "Face the Nation," I go to the network's affiliate in Cincinnati and sit by myself in the studio. It's all done by satellite. Lesley Stahl was in Washington and I couldn't see her, but I could hear her questions in a little earplug.

She asked a lot about my thoughts on a strike and if I was worried about not being able to get Ty Cobb's record.

I told her the same thing I've been saying since the August 6 date was set. I can't worry about something I cannot control. I honestly do not feel there will be a strike. I'm on the union's side because of all it has done for me and other players.

It took only about 30 minutes to tape the interview, then my co-author and I stopped for lunch. Our wives joined us.

I mentioned some phone calls I had to make late last night. We're very close to getting catcher Bo Diaz from the Philadelphia Phillies.

Los Ang.	ab	r	h	rbi	Cincinnati	ab	r	h	rbi
Duncan, ss	4	0	0	0	Milner, cf	3	0	1	0
Cabell, 3b	4	0	0	0	**Rose, 1b**	4	0	0	0
Bailor, 3b	0	0	0	0	Parker, rf	4	0	0	0
Landreaux, cf	4	0	0	0	Bell, 3b	2	0	0	0
Guerrero, lf	4	1	1	1	Esasky, lf	2	0	0	0
Mald'ado, lf	0	0	0	0	C'cepcion, ss	3	0	1	0
Brock, 1b	3	0	0	0	Oester, 2b	3	0	0	0
Marshall, rf	3	0	1	0	Bilardello, c	2	0	0	0
Scioscia, c	3	1	1	1	Venable, ph	1	0	0	0
Sax, 2b	3	0	1	0	Van Gorder, c	0	0	0	0
Welch, p	2	0	0	0	Soto, p	2	0	0	0
					Kr'chicki, ph	1	0	0	0
Totals	30	2	4	2	Totals	27	0	2	0

```
Los Angeles ..................0 0 1  0 0 0  0 0 1—2
Cincinnati........................0 0 0  0 0 0  0 0 0—0
```

Los Angeles	IP.	H.	R.	ER.	BB.	SO.
Welch (W. 7-1)...........	9	2	0	0	3	5

Cincinnati	IP.	H.	R.	ER.	BB.	SO.
Soto (L. 10-12)..........	9	4	2	2	1	7

Game-winning RBI—Scioscia.
E—None. DP—Los Angeles 1. LOB—Los Angeles 3, Cincinnati 3. 2B—Marshall, Milner. HR—Scioscia (5), Guerrero (26). SH—Welch. T—2:07. A—38,474.

What I had to do Friday night—actually, it was early this morning—was call Phillies advance scout Hank King, an old friend and longtime Phillies batting-practice pitcher, and talk to him about some players who might be included if there's a deal.

If we get Bo, he could make a big difference. I'm not sure we'll be able to pull off the deal before the strike deadline, though. It's my understanding we'll have to wait until after that to see what happens.

Bill Giles, the Phillies' president, told Bill Bergesch that San Diego also wants Diaz.

★ ★ ★

Tonight's game was one of those that was decided by a matter of inches. It also was the kind of game that hurts.

The Dodgers beat us, 2-0. Bob Welch gave up only two hits and I didn't get either one of them. I did come close in the sixth inning—and that's what I mean by a matter of inches.

Mike Scioscia, their catcher, hit a homer in the third inning and it was 1-0.

In the sixth, Eddie Milner hit a double to right field. I came up and hit what looked like a sure gapper to left-center. Kenny Landreaux (the Dodgers' center fielder) made a running catch on the play—if he doesn't get to the ball, we're tied and I'm on second base.

Pedro Guerrero hit his 26th homer in the ninth off Mario Soto and that's how it ended. Mario gave up only four hits, but two of them were out of the park.

So, we're six games back now and must win tomorrow to get a split in this series.

★ ★ ★

Before the game, Joe Price, our player rep, had a meeting with the team to bring us up to date on negotiations in New York.

Joe told us that Don Fehr (acting executive director of the Major League Players Association) is going to make a proposal tomorrow on the pension contribution.

Instead of holding out for $60 million, the players are going to come down to about $40 million with the understanding that the difference will go to teams that are financially in trouble.

We'll just have to see what happens. The clock is ticking.

SUNDAY, AUGUST 4..................... DID NOT PLAY

Last night brought back a lot of memories.

After the game, my co-author, his wife Pat, Carol and I drove to the area of Cincinnati where I grew up to attend the wedding reception of my niece, Robin. She's the daughter of my sister Jackie.

Jackie has remodeled—and she lives in—the house on Braddock Street overlooking Anderson Ferry where Mom was born and my two sisters, my brother and I grew up.

The reception was held in a hall just across the street from the railroad tracks where I used to play as a kid.

Nearby is a concrete wall—I used to throw stones at that wall. We'd make a mark on it and see who could hit the bull's-eye. Down the road a little bit is a refinery. I remember a night when I was a kid that it caught on fire. Flames were shooting into the sky. They had fire hoses spread across the railroad tracks when a train came and cut the hoses in half.

On the way to the hall, we passed Pete Rose Park. I used to play in that park, and several years ago it was renamed in my honor.

The whole family was at the reception and Robin looked beautiful.

My mother, LaVerne, was there. So was my older sister Caryl and Jackie, mother of the bride. David and his wife Judy came a little later.

They had a disc jockey up on the stage playing music and we couldn't keep Mom off the dance floor. She's 70 and has had a lot of surgery over the years, but she kicked off her shoes and wore out some of my younger relatives. She did the twist, the shimmy and everything else. It's easy to see where I get my athletic ability.

When people asked Mom when she's going back to her home near Tampa, she said: "It's up to Peter. I'm staying here until he gets those hits (for the record). There's no way I'm going to miss that."

        ★   ★   ★

Before the game today, we had our annual players-children game.

Tyler is only 10 months old, but Carol brought him. He had a Reds uniform with "ROSE 14" on the back. He got one at-bat. I held him under my left arm and he helped me swing the bat righthanded. I can't tell yet whether he's going to be a switch-hitter.

After the kids played, they went into the wives' lounge. They had ice cream and little cakes shaped like baseballs.

        ★   ★   ★

As for the game that really counted, I didn't play. I went to my youth program. I started Tony Perez—he's 43—at first base and he had a big game. Doggie homered in the fourth inning and singled home Dave Parker with the winning run in the eighth. We beat the Dodgers, 5-4, and split the four games with them.

We're now five games back.

Afterward, I had to rush home so John Iacono of Sports Illustrated could get some pictures around the house for the issue that's going to come out about August 14 (and be dated August 19).

After that was done, I had to drive back downtown to appear on a television show on Ted Turner's WTBS.

Frankly, I'm beat.

AUG.

SUN	MON	TUE	WED	THU	FRI	SAT
				1	2	3
4	⑤	6	7	8	9	10
11	12	13	14	15	16	17
18	19	20	21	22	23	24
25	26	27	28	29	30	31

Magic No. **25**

Rose took time off from his hectic chase August 4 for a little child's play. The occasion was the Reds' annual players-children game and 10-month-old Tyler was dressed appropriately.

MONDAY, AUGUST 5 .... ROSE 1 FOR 4

It's not very often you walk into a baseball clubhouse after a win and see so many unhappy faces.

We beat San Diego, 8-7, tonight and I got a single in the eighth inning to move within 24 hits of breaking the Ty Cobb record. By winning, we took a firm hold on second place, five games behind first-place Los Angeles. The Padres are in third place, seven games out.

We're in great shape to make a run at the Dodgers, but the news from New York is not at all encouraging. Unless there's some kind of a miracle within the next 18 hours, there's going to be a strike.

The owners and the players' association are hung up on the salary arbitration issue. The owners want to put a cap on arbitration awards, but there's no way the players are going to go for that.

The strike wouldn't start until just before tomorrow night's games, so I'm still optimistic something can be worked out. Peter Ueberroth, the commissioner, has ordered both sides to resume talks tomorrow morning. That's encouraging. I've said all along he will play an important role behind the scenes. At least he's not letting the talks break off like they did in 1981.

One of the reporters mentioned to me that President Reagan could halt a strike, perhaps, by invoking the Taft-Hartley Act. I said I'd call him if somebody could get his number. He's called me before.

During that strike in 1981, I returned here from Philadelphia and worked out every day. I took batting practice and tried to stay sharp.

If there is a strike and it isn't settled in a hurry, I'm going to have workouts for all Reds players who stay in this area. I'll find a place and buy the equipment myself. In '81, some players let themselves get out of shape and never recovered when we started playing again. I don't want that to happen.

Marge Schott, my owner, told Joe Kay of the Associated Press that this has been a tough year on me—trying to pull the team together and at the same time going for the Cobb record.

She's probably right, but I don't believe in pressure. Even though I am backing the players, she says she's not going to turn her back on me.

We're both hopeful there can be a settlement as quickly as possible. There won't be any bitterness.

Everybody's wondering if I'll get paid. Marge says she hasn't thought about that, but I know if I continue to work for the club in some capacity, I'll get paid.

My thought right now is that I'll scout our farm teams at Class AAA Denver and Class AA Vermont.

I'll stay busy, you can count on that.

As for the Cobb record, I'm not going to go home and feel sorry for myself. The record will come—if not this year, then next year.

What bothers me most is having our momentum interrupted. We've got something going here. We've got a chance to win the West.

★   ★   ★

Dave Parker had four hits tonight, including two doubles and a three-run homer. He's batting .303 and has 80 runs batted in—the most RBIs in the National League.

If we win this division, Parker's going to be the MVP. What he did tonight, he's been doing all year long. He's our leader; he's the guts of our batting order. He reminds me of myself, but he hits home runs. He has a lot of fun playing the game. I'll tell you, he's a manager's dream. You just put his name in the lineup and let him go.

San Diego	ab	r	h	rbi	Cincinnati	ab	r	h	rbi
Bumbry, cf	4	0	1	0	Milner, cf	5	1	2	1
Bevacqua, ph	1	0	0	0	Rose, 1b	4	1	1	0
Lefferts, p	0	0	0	0	Parker, rf	5	2	4	3
Templeton, ss	5	2	3	1	Bell, 3b	2	1	0	0
Gwynn, rf	4	1	2	1	Esasky, lf	4	1	1	1
Garvey, 1b	5	1	2	1	C'cepcion, ss	4	0	1	1
Brown, pr	0	0	0	0	Oester, 2b	3	2	2	1
Nettles, 3b	5	0	2	1	Van Gorder, c	3	0	1	1
Kennedy, c	3	1	0	1	Franco, p	0	0	0	0
Martinez, lf	5	1	1	0	Power, p	0	0	0	0
Flannery, 2b	2	1	1	1	McG'figan, p	0	0	0	0
R't'r, ph-2-cf	1	0	0	0	Foley, ph	0	0	0	0
Hawkins, p	1	0	0	1	Stuper, p	0	0	0	0
Stoddard, p	1	0	0	0	Venable, ph	1	0	0	0
Davis, ph	1	0	0	0	Buchanan, p	0	0	0	0
Jackson, p	0	0	0	0	Cedeno, ph	1	0	0	0
R'rez, ph-2b	1	0	0	0	Robinson, p	0	0	0	0
					Bilardello, c	1	0	0	0
Totals	39	7	12	7	Totals	33	8	12	8

San Diego ....0 4 0 0 3 0 0 0 0—7
Cincinnati ....0 1 3 3 1 0 0 0 x—8

San Diego	IP.	H.	R.	ER.	BB.	SO.
Hawkins	2*	7	4	4	3	1
Stoddard	2	2	3	3	1	3
Jackson (L. 0-2)	3	2	1	1	0	1
Lefferts	1	1	0	0	0	0

Cincinnati	IP.	H.	R.	ER.	BB.	SO.
McGaffigan	2	6	4	4	1	1
Stuper	1	0	0	0	0	1
Buchanan	1⅔	3	3	3	2	1
Hume (W. 2-3)	⅓	0	0	0	0	0
Robinson	2	1	0	0	1	0
Franco	1⅔	2	0	0	0	2
Power (Save 19)	⅓	0	0	0	0	0

*Pitched to four batters in third.

Game-winning RBI—Van Gorder.

E—None. DP—San Diego 1. LOB—San Diego 9, Cincinnati 7. 2B—Martinez, Nettles, Parker 2, Esasky, Oester. HR—Parker (21). SB—Templeton, Concepcion, Milner, Oester. SF—Oester, Van Gorder. T—2:54. A—24,622.

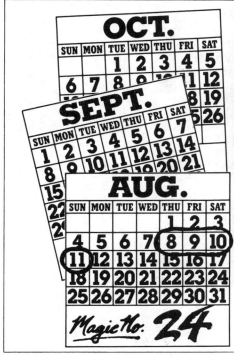

News of a strike settlement and the acquisition of Bo Diaz from the Phillies greeted Rose when he woke up August 7.

THURSDAY, AUGUST 8 .... ROSE 2 FOR 7

I was still in bed yesterday morning when I got the call from New York saying that a tentative settlement had been reached in the strike (which went into effect Tuesday and forced postponement of that night's major league schedule as well as Wednesday's games).

It was the best news I've heard in a long time.

A little later, Bill Bergesch called to say we're getting Bo Diaz from the Phillies. He's the catcher I've been looking for since spring training.

To get Bo, we sent the Phillies infielder Tom Foley, catcher Alan Knicely (now at Denver) and a yet-to-be-named player. We also got a young lefthanded pitcher by the name of Greg Simpson in the deal.

With Bo coming over, I sent catcher Dann Bilardello back to Denver, but I told him he'll be back on September 1.

I'm excited about the end of the strike and also about getting Bo Diaz.

The only thing I don't like right now is missing two home games with San Diego. We'd been playing well and showing a lot of optimism and enthusiasm.

I played with Bo in Philadelphia and I remember that great year he had in 1982 after we got him from Cleveland. He hit .288 and drove in 85 runs.

He's happy to be coming here because he knows he's going to get to play. He's had some knee problems, but I'm not worried about that.

Like Bill Bergesch said, the Phillies say Bo's healthy and they're an honorable club. We believe them.

Getting Bo is not a rap at the three catchers we've used—Bilardello, Dave Van Gorder and Knicely. But this trade is a lot like the one for Buddy Bell. Wayne Krenchicki and Nick Esasky were doing a good job for us at third base, but we're a better team with Buddy. I know we'll be a better team with Bo.

We're bringing up Tom Runnells, a switch-hitter, from Denver to be our backup infielder, filling the spot Foley handled.

With the strike over and the trade completed, we flew to Los Angeles last night. A lot of the wives were looking forward to this West Coast trip; I brought Carol along.

★　　★　　★

Tonight, I got two hits. My bunt single in the top of the 13th inning gave us a 6-5 win. We're now just four games behind L.A. and have three more games in this series.

As I've said many times, if a bunt will help the team, I'll go for it.

Cincinnati	ab	r	h	rbi	Los Ang.	ab	r	h	rbi
Milner, cf	5	0	1	0	Duncan, ss	6	2	3	0
Rose, 1b	7	1	2	1	Cabell, 3b	4	0	2	2
Robinson, p	0	0	0	0	Bailor, 3b	2	0	0	0
Parker, rf	6	1	2	0	Landreaux, cf	5	0	0	1
Bell, 3b	4	1	0	0	Brock, 1b	6	0	0	0
Esasky, lf	5	1	1	0	Marshall, rf	5	0	1	0
Oester, 2b	5	1	2	2	Matuszek, lf	2	1	1	0
C'cepcion, ss	6	0	0	1	Maldonado, lf	0	0	0	0
B. Diaz, c	5	0	1	1	Howell, p	0	0	0	0
Redus, pr	0	0	0	0	Russell, ph	1	0	0	0
Van Gorder, c	1	0	0	0	Niedenfuer, p	0	0	0	0
Soto, p	2	0	0	0	Whitfield, ph	1	0	0	0
Venable, ph	1	0	1	0	C. Diaz, p	0	0	0	0
Hume, p	0	0	0	0	Scioscia, c	2	1	0	0
Price, p	0	0	0	0	Yeager, ph-c	2	0	0	0
Kr'chicki, ph	1	0	0	0	Sax, 2b	5	0	0	0
Franco, p	0	0	0	0	Hershiser, p	2	0	0	0
Perez, ph	1	0	0	0	Reynolds, lf	3	1	1	0
Power, p	0	0	0	0					
C'deno, ph-1b	1	1	1	0					
Totals	50	6	11	5	Totals	46	5	8	3

Cincinnati	200	000	030	000	1—6	
Los Angeles	100	030	100	000	0—5	

Cincinnati	IP.	H.	R.	ER.	BB.	SO.
Soto	6	6	4	4	1	2
Hume	⅔	2	1	1	0	1
Price	⅓	0	0	0	0	0
Franco	2	0	0	0	0	2
Power (W. 4-2)	3	0	0	0	0	1
Robinson (Save 1)	1	0	0	0	1	1

Los Angeles	IP.	H.	R.	ER.	BB.	SO.
Hershiser	6⅓	4	2	2	5	2
Howell	1⅔	3	3	1	0	1
Niedenfuer	3	2	0	0	1	4
C. Diaz (L. 2-1)	2	2	1	1	0	2

Game-winning RBI—**Rose**.
E—Cabell, Sax, Scioscia. DP—Los Angeles 2. LOB —Cincinnati 12, Los Angeles 5. 2B—Cabell, Parker 2. SB—**Rose**, Duncan, Milner, Redus, Cedeno. HBP—By Soto (Matuszek); by Niedenfuer (Milner). WP—Hume. Balk—Soto. PB—B. Diaz. T—4:14. A—37,479.

With Cesar Cedeno on third base in the 13th, and two down, their third baseman, Bob Bailor, was playing behind the bag. The bunt was there, so I took it and it turned out to win the game for us.

I liked this game because it's never easy to win in Dodger Stadium. After seven innings, we were down 5-2, but we battled back.

★　　★　　★

Just before tonight's game, we put Joe Price back on the active list— he says he's ready to pitch after giving his arm a good rest—and we placed Bob Buchanan (elbow pain) on the disabled list. (Price proceeded to pitch one-third inning of relief against the Dodgers.)

★　　★　　★

You think it's tough (attention-wise) being a big-leaguer? How would you like to be Frank Sinatra?

I was talking to Ol' Blue Eyes before the game tonight. He was sitting in the first row behind our dugout, and he had people coming up to him most of the night. It was tough for him to watch the game.

FRIDAY, AUGUST 9 .... ROSE 1 FOR 4

Before going to Dodger Stadium for this evening's game, I went to a television studio today and taped the "Steve Sax Show."

Steve, of course, is the Dodgers' second baseman and plays the game real hard. He tells people he approaches baseball like I do, which is a compliment.

Speaking of TV, we're on an important West Coast trip, playing two of the teams we've got to beat to win our division, and none of the games is going to be telecast back to Cincinnati.

Marge Schott, our owner, told Bill Bergesch she's really upset about the situation.

When it looked like there was going to be a strike, WLWT-TV decided to show some of our games against the Dodgers and Padres during our last homestand. That means the games originally scheduled on this trip will not be shown.

Broadcaster Marty Brennaman told me he heard the station has received hundreds of calls.

Cincinnati	ab	r	h	rbi	Los Ang.	ab	r	h	rbi
Milner, cf	4	0	0	0	Duncan, ss	4	1	1	0
Rose, 1b	4	0	1	0	Cabell, 3b	4	1	3	0
Parker, rf	4	0	3	0	Guerrero, lf	3	1	1	3
Bell, 3b	4	0	0	0	Marshall, rf	4	0	1	0
Esasky, lf	3	1	1	1	Brock, 1b	4	0	0	0
Oester, 2b	4	0	0	0	Mald'nado, cf	3	0	0	0
C'cepcion, ss	4	0	1	0	Yeager, c	4	0	1	0
B. Diaz, c	4	0	1	0	Sax, 2b	3	0	0	0
Browning, p	3	0	1	0	Welch, p	3	0	0	0
Venable, ph	1	0	0	0					
Totals	35	1	8	1	Totals	32	3	7	3

Cincinnati ....0 1 0 0 0 0 0 0 0—1
Los Angeles ....3 0 0 0 0 0 0 0 x—3

Cincinnati	IP.	H.	R.	ER.	BB.	SO.
Browning (L. 9-9)	8	7	3	3	2	4

Los Angeles	IP.	H.	R.	ER.	BB.	SO.
Welch (W. 8-1)	9	8	1	1	2	2

Game-winning RBI—Guerrero.
E—Duncan, Oester, Bell. LOB—Cincinnati 9, Los Angeles 7. HR—Guerrero (28), Esasky (11). Balk—Welch. T—2:14. A—44,935.

My job is to play and manage this team. I don't want to get involved in things like television, but what this shows me is how much interest there is in the Reds this year. It's a good sign.

★   ★   ★

When the strike became official on Tuesday, the Dodgers' Pedro Guerrero flew home to the Dominican Republic. The strike was over so quickly, he couldn't get back to Los Angeles in time for last night's game and Tommy Lasorda was burning. After all, Guerrero is as responsible as anybody for the Dodgers being in first place.

According to the newspapers, Guerrero is being docked a day's pay— about $7,700.

Well, Guerrero got back today and played tonight—and I wish he hadn't. He hit his 28th homer with two on and we got beat, 3-1.

Nick Esasky hit a homer for us off Bob Welch, who has beaten us twice in seven days. He's won seven straight games.

I'll tell you one thing, until Guerrero cools off, we're going to have trouble catching the Dodgers. In each of his last five games against us, he's hit a home run.

I got one hit, a single. I now need 21 to beat the Cobb record with 56 games to go.

Dave Parker got three hits in four at-bats. The only time he didn't get a hit was in the first inning, after I singled to left field.

This was just one of those games. With two out in the fourth inning, Tom Browning was safe on a bunt single and Eddie Milner walked.

I then hit a rope right back to Welch. The ball hit off his leg and bounced right down. All Welch had to do was pick up the ball; he threw me out easily. If the ball bounces away from Welch and Parker gets to bat there, who knows.

So, we're 57-49 and five games back of L.A. and a half-game ahead of San Diego.

SATURDAY, AUGUST 10 .... DID NOT PLAY

Before I went to Dodger Stadium this afternoon, I lectured on hitting to about 200 kids at the Joe Torre Baseball School. I really enjoy this type of appearance.

While I was talking, I got to thinking about what an advantage a boy has when he's the son of a major leaguer.

That is, of course, if the boy is interested in baseball and wants to play in the big leagues someday.

My son Petey started coming to the ball park with me when he was hardly old enough to walk.

This may sound crazy, but one of the reasons I decided to leave the Reds as a free agent after the 1978 season was because Dick Wagner (then the Reds' president) had what I thought was an unreasonable rule. Sons of players weren't allowed on the field before games.

I said then that Petey wanted to be a big-league player and he needed the experience. Wagner wouldn't let the boys shag fly balls or anything else in the afternoon. I didn't like that rule. The Phillies said, sure, Petey could work out before games.

He's 15 now—he'll turn 16 on November 16—and I'm very proud of him.

I think the big advantage he has is being able to come to the ball park almost every day. I can see him hit in the cage, or I can hit him ground balls during batting practice.

Petey is pretty much of a listener and he catches on quickly, which makes it a lot easier for him. Plus, he's willing to do different things, to make sacrifices.

Petey learns fundamentals just sitting on our bench during a game. He hears the players talking all through the game. When a mistake is made, he sees it firsthand, then hears the coaches or the players talking about it.

He's a lot better hitter right now than I was when I was his age.

He swings just from the left side. My father and my uncle (Buddy Bloebaum) made me a switch-hitter when I was 9, but I've never seen the need to do this with Petey.

He's never had any problem hitting lefthanders. I've never felt there was any sense in becoming a switch-hitter just for the sake of being able to say you're a switch-hitter.

We have a good relationship. I see him play whenever I can, but make it a practice not to discuss the game with him in front of any of his teammates. I'll get him alone and go over it with him. I'll come down hard on him when he does something wrong, but nobody knows that except him and me.

Petey is learning to play the game the right way. He knows there are no shortcuts, and I'm convinced he's willing to pay the price. He's the only 15-year-old on his American Legion team.

★   ★   ★

We lost tonight, 2-1, to Fernando Valenzuela.

We had some shots at Fernando, but every time we hit a ball hard, we hit it at somebody.

I didn't play.

I have to say I was impressed with Jay Tibbs, even though he lost. He gave up only seven hits in six innings.

Before, if Tibbs had given up two runs in the first inning (as he did tonight), he might have fallen flat on his face.

SUNDAY, AUGUST 11.................. DID NOT PLAY

I went to Dodger Stadium early this morning because on Sundays, whenever he asks me, I do a talk show with Bud Furillo over Los Angeles radio station KABC.

I've been doing it for years and enjoy it. One thing I'm learning from this type of thing is that people seem to have a different opinion of me this year.

There are not too many negative things now. Even people who didn't like me are sort of pulling for me. You find this out on talk shows like this one.

I'm getting asked a lot why I'm not starting myself against lefthanders. (Rose, yet to start against a lefthander in 1985, has five straight hits against lefthanded pitching and is now 10 for 35, .286, versus lefthanders this season.)

When I played last year for Montreal, I didn't start against many lefthanders. I did early, but not late. When I came back to Cincinnati on August 17, I just decided to keep it that way.

During spring training this year I never had any doubt that Tony Perez would make our ball club, but he was primarily going to be my best pinch-hitter. I let him start at first base early in the season (beginning in the second week of May) and he did well against lefthanders, so I continued to use him against them.

As long as I continue to do my job against righthanders and he does his against lefthanders—including today's game, Doggie is batting .328 overall with 25 runs batted in—there should be no qualms about first base.

★　　★　　★

Jerry Reuss did a number on us today as the Dodgers won, 4-0.

We just couldn't do anything with him. We got just six hits and Doggie had two of them.

We start a four-game series in San Diego tomorrow and I'm thinking about making some lineup changes.

I just don't like the way we're playing offensively. The pitching hasn't been that bad, but it's tough for a pitcher to go out there thinking if he allows two or three runs he's going to get beat.

I can't understand this team because it seems like it's never just one guy who goes into a hitting slump, it's the whole club.

I'm thinking of giving Davey Concepcion a couple days off. He's had just three hits in his last 31 at-bats.

I might move Ron Oester (rested today) to shortstop and let the "kid," Tom Runnells, who made his major league debut last night and got his first two big-league hits today (while starting at second base), play second.

Runnells is an interesting person. He proves determination is worth it. He's 30 years old and this is the first time he's made it to the big leagues. It took him 30 years to get his first major league hit and two innings to get his second (Runnells singled in the seventh inning and again in the ninth).

★　　★　　★

Because Carol is here and not permitted to travel on the team bus, we hired a limo for the trip to San Diego.

It was a beautiful ride, just her and me. The route, Interstate 5, runs along the Pacific Ocean. Real picturesque. We went by San Clemente, where Richard Nixon used to live, and we went past Oceanside, which gives you a great view of the ocean. And we saw the Del Mar racetrack, which is not too far south of La Costa, the famous golf and tennis resort.

— 165 —

Manager Rose often depends on the advice of his righthand man, George Scherger.

MONDAY, AUGUST 12 .... DID NOT PLAY

There was a story in the newspapers today saying Cesar Cedeno is demanding a trade.

This really surprised me because while I know Cesar is unhappy over not playing much, he's never said anything to me or Bill Bergesch about a trade. Nothing.

As soon as he got to San Diego/Jack Murphy Stadium this afternoon, Cesar came into my office. He knew I had seen the story and wanted to let me know he had never said some of those things.

He said he would never demand a trade because there are two months left in the season and he can be a free agent in November.

He told me his words were misunderstood. Sure, he's complained about not getting to play, but that's all. I can understand where he's coming from about playing—about his desire to play—because of the free-agent thing. He's hitting .243 and wants a chance to get his average up. But I have to play the guys who are hot.

★   ★   ★

When I started looking ahead yesterday to resting my team captain, Davey Concepcion, my plan was to move Ronnie Oester to shortstop and play Tom Runnells, the rookie, at second.

I talked this over with my coaches and changed my mind because I know how well Ronnie can play second.

Still, a lot of people forget Oester was a shortstop in the minor leagues and the only reason he was moved when he came up was because of

Concepcion.

I'm eager to see what Runnells can do up here, so the next two nights will provide more of a chance. He'll be at shortstop.

The thing about Davey is that when he isn't swinging good, he lets it bother his fielding. In the early part of the season, he was one of my hottest players. He had his average up in the .280s, but since then it has fallen nearly 40 points (to .248).

Davey came out to the stadium early today and took a lot of batting practice. I watched him for a while and thought he was swinging good. The rest will do him some good.

★　　　★　　　★

We got beat tonight, 2-0, by the Padres. Mario Soto was pitching real good until the sixth inning when he gave up the two runs. Garry Templeton got a hit, Tony Gwynn walked and Steve Garvey doubled both of them home.

I didn't play tonight and still need 21 hits to break the record.

I'm concerned. We've lost four in a row at a time when we cannot afford to lose. After we beat the Dodgers on Thursday night, we were only four back. Now, we're eight back and in third place.

TUESDAY, AUGUST 13 .... ROSE 1 FOR 4

Bill Bergesch, vice president and general manager of the Reds, called my coaches and me to a meeting in his suite at the Town & Country Hotel today at noon.

Everything we've worked so hard for this season could go down the drain if we continue to lose. But our four-game losing streak isn't the reason Bill called the meeting.

Bill likes to have the guys in and talk to them every once in a while. That's all it amounted to. He wanted opinions of the coaches and me, and he wanted to know if there's anything he could do to help us play better.

A lot of teams have coaches' meetings like this once every two road trips. Bill recently took over this job (running the Reds' front office), and you have to remember this is his first road trip since Bob Howsam retired. I think he likes to keep the communications open between the coaches and the manager.

Cincinnati	ab	r	h	rbi	San Diego	ab	r	h	rbi
Milner, cf	4	0	1	0	Dilone, cf	3	0	0	0
Runnells, ss	4	0	0	0	Templeton, ss	5	0	2	0
Rose, 1b	4	0	1	0	Gwynn, rf	5	0	1	0
Parker, rf	4	1	1	1	Garvey, 1b	4	0	0	0
Esasky, lf	4	1	1	0	Bevacqua, 3b	4	0	2	0
Bell, 3b	4	1	1	0	Bumbry, pr-lf	0	0	0	0
Diaz, c	4	0	1	0	Martinez, lf	4	0	3	0
Oester, 2b	4	0	1	1	Fl'n'ry, pr-2b	0	0	0	0
Browning, p	2	0	1	1	R'ster, 2b-3b	4	1	1	0
Franco, p	1	0	0	0	Bochy, c	3	1	1	2
					Hoyt, p	1	0	0	0
					McR'nolds, ph	1	0	0	0
					Lefferts, p	0	0	0	0
					Ramirez, ph	1	0	0	0
					Jackson, p	0	0	0	0
					Brown, ph	1	0	0	0
Totals	35	3	8	3	Totals	36	2	10	2

Cincinnati ....0 0 0   3 0 0   0 0 0—3
San Diego......................0 0 0   0 0 2   0 0 0—2

Cincinnati	IP.	H.	R.	ER.	BB.	SO.
Browning (W. 10-9) ...	6*	7	2	2	3	8
Franco (Save 4)..........	3	3	0	0	0	3

San Diego	IP.	H.	R.	ER.	BB.	SO.
Hoyt (L. 13-7)............	4	7	3	3	0	2
Lefferts	2	1	0	0	0	1
Jackson......................	3	0	0	0	0	2

*Pitched to one batter in seventh.

Game-winning RBI—Parker.

E—Bell. DP—Cincinnati 1. LOB—Cincinnati 6, San Diego 10. 2B—Bevacqua, Royster. HR—Parker (22), Bochy (5). SB—Milner 2. SH—Browning. T—2:37. A —22,582.

We went over all the personnel. I make the decisions about who plays. What he wanted to talk about mostly was the attitude of the players and stuff like that.

I honestly don't think anybody's got a bad attitude, but I think a lot of the guys aren't playing the way they should be. Davey Concepcion, Buddy Bell and Bo Diaz were 5 for 53 collectively on this West Coast trip before tonight's game.

You worry about anybody who's not hitting, but you don't put the finger on them. We've scored just three runs in our last 41 innings and only two of those were earned. We haven't scored in our last 22 innings, and in our last 34 innings we have had just two extra-base hits.

What really troubles me is that we're losing despite getting such good pitching. In our last 45 innings before tonight's game, we've given up only 44 hits and the opponents have scored just 16 runs.

Before the strike, everybody was concerned about our pitching.

★　　★　　★

There's nothing like a victory to lighten everybody's load.

Dave Parker came through for us again tonight and we beat the Padres, 3-2, ending the four-game losing streak. The Cobra homered on the first pitch in the fourth inning off LaMarr Hoyt, breaking a scoreless tie. We got two more runs in that inning.

I went 0 for 3 batting lefthanded, but got a hit off Craig Lefferts, a lefthander. That was my sixth straight hit righthanded and put me over .300 against lefthanded pitching. I hit a 3-2 pitch to right field.

That hit got me down to 20 needed to break the record.

This was an important victory for us because the Dodgers just aren't losing. They haven't lost since we beat 'em Thursday night. If we hadn't won tonight, we'd have fallen nine back.

WEDNESDAY, AUGUST 14............ DID NOT PLAY

I don't usually go to the racetrack on the day of a game. But the Southern California weather was beautiful this afternoon, and I thought it would be nice to go to Del Mar. A longtime friend from Los Angeles took Carol and me to the track.

Del Mar is located about 20 miles north of San Diego up Interstate 5. It's a nice little track; they have a great jockey colony there.

It was a good break, very relaxing. Jim Kaat and Tom Browning also were there but didn't go up with us.

After the races, I did an interview with Ira Berkow of the New York Times. He's doing a series of articles on me as I go after the Ty Cobb record.

Today, we talked about Pete Rose the manager.

I told him about how I work with George Scherger, my bench coach.

Scherg and I work out a game plan in advance, almost like they do in football. I know which pitchers I'm going to use in certain situations, whether it's short relief, middle relief or long relief, and which pinch-hitters I'm going to use.

I think what George Scherger does so well is make me aware of my options. He tells me what they are and I select the one I want. I flash all the signs; I make all the pitching changes. Kitty knows who we want warmed up in a certain situation and, as my pitching coach, he gets them ready.

When I take a pitcher out, it's up to me to select the guy I want based on the opposing batting order coming up.

I also know who I'll substitute in other situations.

I think my managing philosophy is to keep the players happy. You can't always do this because some are going to get upset when they're not playing. But I try to keep everybody relaxed and treat men like men.

I told the players the first day I got here that if they've got a problem, come in and see me. If anything, I've probably been too patient with some of my players, especially pitchers.

★   ★   ★

My attempt to give everybody a good shot is one of the reasons I started Cesar Cedeno in center field tonight. We got beat, 4-1, by the Padres, and it was another tough loss. The Dodgers won again, so we're nine back now.

I put Cesar in center because I'm going to give him a shot to see if he can get his act together. Of all the players on this ball club, he has the most at stake because he's on the last year of his contract. We have six, seven weeks to go and if he can come alive like he did the last six, seven weeks of the 1984 season, he's looking at another contract here.

Cesar had a chance earlier this season and he didn't take advantage of it. I don't think there's been an outfielder on this ball club, with the exception of Duane Walker (traded to Texas in the Buddy Bell deal), who can honestly say I didn't give him a good chance.

But if Cesar continues to hit .240 or so, he's going to have a tough time getting a contract. (Cedeno was 0 for 3 tonight.)

Jay Tibbs pitched another good game tonight, but we couldn't do anything with Dave Dravecky.

★   ★   ★

Before tonight's game, Bill Bergesch got a call from Larry Bowa's agent. Bowa was released by the Cubs on Monday and will retire if he doesn't hook on with a contender.

While Bowa (a major league shortstop for 16 years) doesn't clear waivers until next Monday, there's a chance we might be interested in him for the rest of the year. It's something we're kicking around.

THURSDAY, AUGUST 15................ ROSE 0 FOR 3

This might have been the most important game on the trip. At least so far.

I went hitless in three at-bats today against San Diego, but had two walks. One walk came in the eighth inning after Eddie Milner had tripled in Ron Oester, who had reached base on an error. Milner's hit put us ahead 3-0.

After I walked, the count went to 3-2 on Dave Parker (who had hit a two-run homer in the first inning). I then stole second and Milner stole home, and the double steal made it 4-0. That turned out to be a big run because the Padres tied us with four runs in the ninth inning.

We won, 5-4, in the 10th when Doggie (Tony Perez) drove in Oester with a pinch-hit single with two out.

To start the 10th, Padres Manager Dick Williams brought in Gene Walter, a young lefthander. Oester got an infield single and Tom Runnells bunted him over to second. I sent Cesar Cedeno up to bat for Milner and he bounced to first.

That got me to the plate with a man on third and two out.

Williams walked me because I had taken Parker out of the game earlier, so he wasn't coming up next. The Cobra had a little muscle pull near his tail bone and it was bothering him.

I sort of expected Williams to put me on because Max Venable, a lefthanded hitter, was due up next.

I brought in Doggie to bat for Venable and they called for Roy Lee Jackson, a righthander. Doggie gets his hit up the middle and we win.

— 169 —

We didn't want to lose three out of four to San Diego like we did to L.A. The victory got us back ahead of the Padres in second place. (Cincinnati is 59-53, .527, while San Diego is 60-54, .526; both clubs trail Los Angeles by nine games.)

At this stage of the season, you can't worry about first place if you don't have second place.

Andy McGaffigan pitched great. Gave up just four hits in eight-plus innings and struck out eight. What happened was he walked Garry Templeton to start the ninth and Tony Gwynn got a single to left. That's when I brought in Teddy Power and they went on to tie.

★   ★   ★

I won't get to see Carol for about a week. After the game, she flew back to Cincinnati; she just couldn't stay away from Tyler any longer.

While she was jetting back home, we were flying to Houston for three games with the Astros before going to Pittsburgh.

Cincinnati	ab	r	h	rbi	San Diego	ab	r	h	rbi
Milner, cf	4	2	2	1	Templeton, ss	4	1	1	0
C'deno, ph-rf	1	0	0	0	Gwynn, rf	5	1	2	0
Rose, 1b	3	0	0	0	Garvey, 1b	4	0	0	1
Parker, rf	3	1	1	2	Kennedy, c	5	0	0	0
Venable, rf	0	0	0	0	Nettles, 3b	4	1	1	1
Perez, ph	1	0	1	1	Martinez, lf	4	0	1	1
Redus, pr-cf	0	0	0	0	Brown, pr-lf	0	1	0	0
Bell, 3b	5	0	0	0	McR'nolds, cf	4	0	3	1
Price, p	0	0	0	0	Flannery, 2b	3	0	0	0
Esasky, lf	4	0	0	0	Show, p	2	0	1	0
C'cepcion, ss	4	0	0	0	Lefferts, p	0	0	0	0
Power, p	0	0	0	0	Stoddard, p	0	0	0	0
Franco, p	0	0	0	0	Bevacqua, ph	1	0	0	0
Hume, p	0	0	0	0	Bumbry, ph	0	0	0	0
Kr'chicki, 3b	0	0	0	0	Royster, ph	1	0	0	0
Diaz, c	4	0	0	0	Walter, p	0	0	0	0
Oester, 2b	4	2	2	0	Jackson, p	0	0	0	0
McG'figan, p	2	0	0	0					
Runnells, ss	0	0	0	0					
Totals	35	5	7	4	Totals	37	4	9	4

Cincinnati ....2 0 0   0 0 0   0 2 0 — 5
San Diego ....0 0 0   0 0 0   0 0 4 — 4

Cincinnati	IP.	H.	R.	ER.	BB.	SO.
McGaffigan	8*	4	2	2	1	8
Power	⅔	3	2	2	1	0
Franco (W. 10-1)	⅓†	2	0	0	0	0
Hume	⅔	0	0	0	0	0
Price (Save 1)	⅓	0	0	0	0	1

San Diego	IP.	H.	R.	ER.	BB.	SO.
Show	7⅓	5	4	2	2	4
Lefferts	⅔	0	0	0	0	1
Stoddard	1	0	0	0	0	0
Walter (L. 0-1)	⅔	1	1	1	1	0
Jackson	⅓	1	0	0	0	0

*Pitched to two batters in ninth.
†Pitched to two batters in tenth.

Game-winning RBI—Perez.

E—Flannery, Templeton. DP—Cincinnati 1. LOB—Cincinnati 5, San Diego 6. 2B—McReynolds, Nettles, Martinez. 3B—Milner. HR—Parker (23). SB—**Rose**, Milner. SH—McGaffigan, Runnells. SF—Garvey. WP—Lefferts, Power. T—3:03. A—19,973.

★   ★   ★

You know, we're 5-5 in our last 10 games and have lost three games in the standings to the Dodgers. They have won seven in a row and are 8-2 in their last 10 games.

When a team's that hot, there's just no way to pick up ground.

L.A. is going up to San Francisco for the weekend and I think the Giants will cool them off. For as long as I can remember, the Giants have played the Dodgers tough.

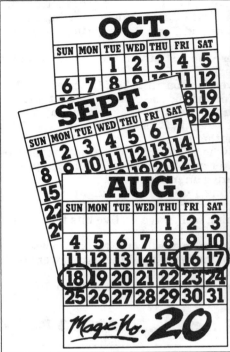

Longtime friend and team-mate Tony Perez still provides the big hit when needed.

FRIDAY, AUGUST 16 .... DID NOT PLAY

I cannot understand what motivates some people.

When Carol got home last night from San Diego, our baby sitter told her somebody pulled up some of our new shrubbery and tossed it in the swimming pool.

The sitter said that another time some young boys called her nasty names and opened the gate with the intention of letting our horses out.

I don't need that kind of stuff right now. We have a pretty good idea who the boys are, but it's difficult to prove anything. The best thing might be for me to get some guard dogs. That should keep them away.

★　　★　　★

The Astros beat us tonight, 5-4. It was our sixth loss on this road trip (in nine games) and we're now in third place, 10 games behind the Dodgers.

Somebody suggested this might be the low point of the season for the Reds and me.

I don't think about low points. What I'm trying to figure out is a way to get my righthanded batters hitting against lefthanders. That's the problem.

We've lost five straight games that opposing lefthanders have started. There was Bob Knepper tonight (righthanded reliever Dave Smith got the victory) and, going backward, Dave Dravecky, Mark Thurmond, Jerry Reuss and Fernando Valenzuela.

I'm feeling a little helpless because I don't start against lefthanders. I haven't started against one all season. (The Reds have faced lefthanded starting pitching 33 times this year, with Cesar Cedeno starting at first base in the first three of those games and Tony Perez getting the call in the last 30 games.)

It's one of those situations where the last guy in the world you could ever blame would be Doggie (Perez).

Doggie got a hit tonight and overall is batting .339. In the games he's started in my place at first base (including one contest against a right-hander), he's hitting .361 (39 hits in 108 at-bats). Doggie's getting a hit or two virtually every game—he's hit safely in 27 of his 31 starts—and Dave Parker is getting his hits against lefthanders.

The problem is that the guys who are leading off aren't getting on base and the guys who follow Parker and Doggie aren't doing anything. Because of this, we're not getting any run production.

I'm sitting in the dugout knowing I've had six straight hits against lefthanders, but the situation hasn't been right for me to hit.

Mario Soto, who has been pitching well, gave up five hits tonight and three of them were homers.

After hitting a game-tying homer in the ninth, Nick Esasky then misjudged a fly ball in the bottom of the inning and the Astros went on to win.

Ten games out? The Dodgers are going to come back down. I'm convinced of that. Just wait.

SATURDAY, AUGUST 17 .... ROSE 3 FOR 4

Today was an anniversary for me. It was just a year ago that I returned to Cincinnati as the Reds' player-manager.

It's a date I'll never forget. I got two hits, drove in two runs and we beat the Cubs, 6-4.

Tonight, I got three hits and drove in two runs and Davey Concepcion hit a grand slam as we beat Houston, 8-0. This was my first three-hit game since I was 3 for 4 against Montreal on July 27.

This game was important because for the first time in over a week, we picked up ground on the Dodgers. They got beat by San Francisco, 5-2, this afternoon.

I got two of my hits off Joe Niekro and the third, a double down the

Cincinnati	ab	r	h	rbi	Houston	ab	r	h	rbi
Milner, cf	3	1	0	1	Doran, 2b	3	0	0	0
Rose, 1b	4	1	3	2	Dawley, p	0	0	0	0
Parker, rf	4	0	0	0	Tolman, rf	1	0	1	0
Venable, rf	1	0	0	0	Garner, 3b-2b	4	0	2	0
Bell, 3b	4	1	0	0	Bass, cf	4	0	0	0
Esasky, lf	5	1	2	1	Cruz, lf	4	0	0	0
C'cepcion, ss	3	1	1	4	Mumphrey, rf	3	0	0	0
Diaz, c	4	0	0	0	DiPino, p	0	0	0	0
Oester, 2b	4	2	3	0	Davis, 1b	3	0	0	0
Browning, p	3	1	0	0	Thon, ss	3	0	1	0
					Mizerock, c	3	0	1	0
					Niekro, p	1	0	1	0
					Madden, p	0	0	0	0
					Rivera, ph-3b	2	0	0	0
Totals	35	8	9	8	Totals	31	0	6	0

| Cincinnati | | 4 | 0 | 0 | 1 | 1 | 2 | 0 | 0 | 0—8 |
| Houston | | 0 | 0 | 0 | 0 | 0 | 0 | 0 | 0 | 0—0 |

Cincinnati	IP.	H.	R.	ER.	BB.	SO.
Browning (W. 11-9)...	9	6	0	0	0	4

Houston	IP.	H.	R.	ER.	BB.	SO.
Niekro (L. 9-10)........	5⅓	8	8	7	4	3
Madden	⅔	0	0	0	0	1
Dawley	1	0	0	0	0	1
DiPino.........................	2	1	0	0	0	1

Game-winning RBI—Concepcion.
E—Milner, Oester, Mizerock. DP—Cincinnati 3. LOB —Cincinnati 6, Houston 4. 2B—Esasky, **Rose.** HR—Concepcion (7), Esasky (13). SH—Browning. SF—Milner. WP—Niekro. PB—Mizerock 2. T—2:07. A—22,703.

right-field line, came against a lefthander, Frank DiPino. The hit off DiPino was my seventh straight against lefthanders.

I've always said that anybody who plays in this league for a number of years should know the pitchers well.

I always "write down" in the back of my mind everything a pitcher throws. I've never been a guess hitter.

The second time up tonight, though, Niekro fooled me.

As many times as I've faced him (during Niekro's 16 seasons in the National League), he's never thrown me a slow curveball. With him, it's fastball-slider-knuckleball. I always file the pitches away by the speed he throws them—one, two, three, etc.

Joe had me 2-2 in the second inning, then shook off the catcher a couple times. I didn't think he'd throw me a knuckleball. What he threw was a real slow jug. It actually bounced and I swung at it. I was totally fooled because I didn't know he had that pitch.

The next time I face him, I'll have that slow curveball filed away in the back of my mind.

However, I don't think he'll try that next time.

A couple weeks ago (July 30) in Cincinnati, Nolan Ryan struck me out twice. He threw me a couple of real good straight changeups. In the first inning of that game, I sort of backed out and looked out at him and laughed. He smiled back at me because he knew I didn't know he had that pitch.

I'm going to face Ryan again tomorrow and it will be interesting to see if he throws the changeup again. I doubt he will.

I can't really explain how much I enjoy getting three hits, and it's not just because I now need only 17 to break the Cobb record. You like to get hits when they help you win. Hits are all part of run production.

My adrenaline was really flowing tonight. The more offensive-minded you get, the more pumped up you get.

I know how many hits I need for the record, but I don't have any mental countdown. I know the closer I get, the more revved up I'll get because, if nothing else, I can hear the people.

What's helping me right now are the fans. It seems like everywhere we've gone on this road trip the people are rooting for me. They want my team to lose, but they're rooting for me to get a base hit.

SUNDAY, AUGUST 18..................... ROSE 2 FOR 4

The Houston Astros are a strange ball club. I don't quite understand them. They've got good players, but don't win like I think they should.

Tonight, we beat them, 8-3, and it was another big victory. For the second day in a row, the Dodgers lost to the Giants in an afternoon game and we played at night.

So, when we took the field, we knew we'd cut L.A.'s lead to eight games if we won. A loss would have left us 10 back.

I got two hits and I need only 15 to break Ty Cobb's career record of 4,191 hits. I'll probably do it in the next couple of weeks, but I'm setting no date.

My second hit tonight was off Jeff Calhoun, a lefthander. That was my eighth straight hit batting righthand-ed. I'm 13 for 38 from that side, good for a .342 average (compared with

Cincinnati	ab	r	h	rbi	Houston	ab	r	h	rbi
Milner, cf	5	1	1	1	Doran, 2b	4	2	2	0
Rose, 1b	4	2	2	1	Puhl, rf	5	1	1	0
Parker, rf	4	2	1	1	Walling, 3b	2	0	1	1
Bell, 3b	3	0	1	1	Garner, ph-3b	2	0	1	0
Esasky, lf	4	0	2	2	Cruz, lf	3	0	2	1
Redus, pr-lf	0	1	0	0	Mumphrey, cf	3	0	0	0
C'cepcion, ss	4	1	1	1	Davis, 1b	4	0	0	0
Diaz, c	4	0	0	0	Bailey, c	4	0	0	0
Oester, 2b	3	0	0	0	Thon, ss	4	0	0	0
Tibbs, p	1	0	0	0	Ryan, p	2	0	0	0
Venable, ph	1	1	1	0	Smith, p	0	0	0	0
Price, p	0	0	0	0	Tolman, ph	1	0	0	0
Cedeno, p	1	0	0	0	Calhoun, p	0	0	0	0
Franco, p	1	0	0	0					
Totals	35	8	9	7	Totals	34	3	7	3

Cincinnati .... 0 0 0   0 0 4   0 4 0—8
Houston .... 0 0 0   0 2 0   1 0 0—3

Cincinnati	IP.	H.	R.	ER.	BB.	SO.
Tibbs (W. 6-13).........	5	5	2	0	3	4
Price........................	1	0	0	0	0	1
Franco (Save 5).........	3	2	1	1	2	2

Houston	IP.	H.	R.	ER.	BB.	SO.
Ryan (L. 8-11)...........	7⅓	7	7	7	4	7
Smith........................	⅔	1	1	0	1	0
Calhoun....................	1	1	0	0	0	0

Game-winning RBI—Bell.
E—Oester, Davis, Bailey, Cruz, Doran. DP—Houston
2. LOB—Cincinnati 5, Houston 10. 2B—Puhl, Cruz. 3B
—Doran, Parker. SB—Venable, Redus. SF—Walling.
T—2:43. A—14,216.

the .167 mark Rose had after his first 30 at-bats against lefthanders this season).

But getting back to the Astros. They're eight games under .500 (54-62) and in fourth place—15 1/2 games behind the Dodgers.

Bill Doran, their second baseman, has a tremendous amount of talent. Glenn Davis gives them a solid first baseman with power. Left fielder Jose Cruz is one of the better players in the league, one of the most underrated. I've always liked another one of their outfielders, Kevin Bass. And center fielder Jerry Mumphrey is very consistent.

Outfielder Terry Puhl is a good player; he wore us out with his bat (hitting .526) in the 1980 N.L. Championship Series when I was with Philadelphia.

Mark Bailey is one of those guys who's going to be a good-hitting catcher.

They've got good starting pitchers—Joe Niekro, Bob Knepper, Mike Scott, Nolan Ryan. Dave Smith is having a good bullpen year.

It just doesn't make sense why Houston's not up there in the standings.

I've got a hunch they've got too many players of similar capabilities. They've got a bunch of base-hit players, the kind they used to need in the Astrodome before they moved the fences in last winter.

But with the fences in, they need more guys who can hit the ball out of the park. You can't have a ball club with all home run hitters, and you can't have one with guys who hit just singles, doubles and triples.

Ryan struck me out the first time up tonight, but he didn't use that changeup he got me with in Cincinnati. I got a base knock to center off him in the sixth inning (a hit that drove in a run as Cincinnati scored four times).

I've been taking as much batting practice as I can and I'm not the least bit tired. I'm planning to take some BP tomorrow in Pittsburgh on the off-day.

I was telling broadcaster Marty Brennaman the other day that it was a year ago when I started hitting so well. After I rejoined the Reds and until the end of the season, I hit .365. I wish I could do that again.

I think I'm a better hitter with an incentive, like trying to help this team do something. I like to rise to the occasion.

And we're in this Western Division race now, with 47 games to go. We cannot afford a letdown.

We had a long flight to Pittsburgh after the game. It was almost 4 o'clock in the morning when I finally got to sleep because after I got to my room, I watched "Ghostbusters" on TV.

Now that's one funny flick.

★　　★　　★

The issue of Sports Illustrated containing the big article about me is out.

Overall, I have no complaints with the story. Writer Rick Reilly didn't dwell on some of the subjects I thought he might.

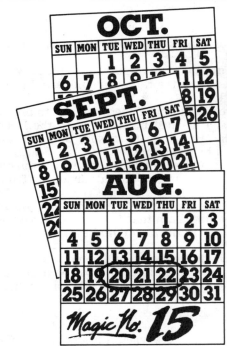

Bob Friend, the Pirates pitcher off whom Rose got his first hit in 1963, presented 4,192 roses to the Reds manager August 21 on Pete Rose Night in Pittsburgh.

TUESDAY, AUGUST 20 .... ROSE 0 FOR 3

Monday afternoon, coaches Billy DeMars and Tommy Helms threw some batting practice for five or six of us at Three Rivers Stadium.

Buddy Bell wanted to come out, but since he's been working so hard, I told him to take the day off.

It was a beautiful day and Three Rivers is a nice park to hit in. When I looked around yesterday, it was sad to think the Pirates might be leaving here. That would be a shame for all of baseball if it happens.

After the workout, I did about 50 minutes over the phone with Bob Trumpy for his WLW radio show in Cincinnati. We talked about pitchers. I still think Juan Marichal was the best I ever faced and that in his prime Sandy Koufax threw as hard as anybody I've ever seen.

Bill Bergesch called after that. We've decided we can't find room for Larry Bowa on our roster. We just can't work it out, and we've been told he is going to sign with the Mets for the rest of this season. I think he'll be

Cincinnati	ab	r	h	rbi	Pittsburgh	ab	r	h	rbi
Milner, cf	5	0	2	0	Orsulak, cf-lf	4	1	1	0
Rose, 1b	3	0	0	0	Ray, 2b	4	0	3	1
Parker, rf	4	0	0	0	Madlock, 3b	3	0	1	1
Bell, 3b	3	1	0	0	Th'mpson, 1b	3	1	2	1
Esasky, lf	3	1	1	0	Brown, rf	3	0	0	0
C'cepcion, ss	4	0	2	0	Pena, c	3	0	0	0
Diaz, c	3	0	1	1	Gonzalez, lf	3	0	0	0
Venable, ph	1	0	0	0	Wynne, cf	0	0	0	0
Oester, 2b	4	0	1	0	Khalifa, ss	3	1	1	0
Soto, p	2	0	0	0	Reuschel, p	2	0	0	0
Kr'chicki, ph	1	0	0	0					
Hume, p	0	0	0	0					
Perez, ph	1	0	0	0					
Totals	34	2	7	1	Totals	28	3	8	3

Cincinnati ....0 1 0   0 0 0   0 0 1—2
Pittsburgh ....1 0 0   1 1 0   0 0 x—3

Cincinnati	IP.	H.	R.	ER.	BB.	SO.
Soto (L. 10-14)..........	6	7	3	3	1	4
Hume	2	1	0	0	0	0

Pittsburgh	IP.	H.	R.	ER.	BB.	SO.
Reuschel (W. 9-6)	9	7	2	0	3	8

Game-winning RBI—Thompson.
E—Madlock, Thompson, Ray. DP—Cincinnati 1, Pittsburgh 1. LOB—Cincinnati 8, Pittsburgh 4. 2B—Orsulak, Milner. HR—Thompson (11). SH—Reuschel. SF—Madlock. T—2:17. A—7,827.

able to help that team, especially considering that Ron Gardenhire, their backup shortstop, has a bad leg.

★　　　★　　　★

Marge Schott, owner of the Reds, wants me to work it out so I break the Cobb record at home.

I would like to do it at home, but that's not important to me now. If we were mathematically eliminated from the race, it would be a different story. But we can win this division.

If we go away on a four-day road trip and I need two hits to break the record, I couldn't prolong that. I learned in 1964 (when the Reds dropped out of a first-place tie on the last day of the season) that you can win a pennant by one game or lose it by one game.

I know the people of Cincinnati would really like to see me get the hit there, but I also think the people of Cincinnati would rather see the Reds in the playoffs.

I know we're eight games out entering tonight's play, but my job as manager of the Reds is to try to field the team that I think will have the best shot at winning. And if having me in the lineup makes it a stronger team, I'm going to be in there.

I don't have a timetable, but I think the record will come in a couple of weeks. And, honestly, it will be hard to do it during our next homestand (August 23-September 1). We go on the road for a week after that.

★　　　★　　　★

We got beat by the Pirates and Rick Reuschel tonight, 3-2, and I went hitless in three at-bats.

There was some irony to this game because when Reuschel was looking for a job last winter, he called me. I talked with him and was thinking about giving him a tryout, but decided I had too many young pitchers. I talked with Bob Howsam and he said we didn't want to take a chance on Reuschel (a onetime 20-game winner with the Cubs).

I told Reuschel tonight that he wasn't the same pitcher I saw in Chicago last summer. His fastball was a yard and a half longer. I guess it was just a case of his arm getting stronger and him getting into shape.

I knew Rick Reuschel was a good hitter, I knew he was a good fielder, a good runner and had a good move to first base. He probably does more things than any pitcher in the league. I thought he had to have that good sinker to be successful. Rick didn't have it last year (when he was 5-5 for the Cubs with a 5.17 earned-run average), but he has it back now.

Reuschel—he's 36 years old—gave us just seven hits and went nine innings.

The Dodgers won, so we're now nine games back with 46 to go. We've got our work cut out for us.

WEDNESDAY, AUGUST 21............. ROSE 1 FOR 6

The Pirates honored me before tonight's game and it was a strange kind of thing.

When we got to the ball park on our first day here, there was a letter on my desk telling me and Reds publicist Jim Ferguson that the Pirates were going to have a Pete Rose Night. They apologized for not getting permission and for not telling us about it in advance.

Bob Friend, off whom I got my first major league hit in 1963, presented me with a floral arrangement of 4,192 red and white roses. They showed a real good video of my career on the TV board in center field, and the first 10,000 fans coming into the stadium got red roses.

I talked to Friend at home plate and he thanked me for helping make him part of history. We didn't get a chance to talk at length because he was late arriving.

Personally, I don't mind doing something that is going to help a team like the Pittsburgh Pirates. Somebody told me this was one of their largest crowds of the season (the turnout of 17,198 ranks as Pittsburgh's fifth-best figure of 1985).

Their third baseman, Bill Madlock, came up to me and said: "You're really packing 'em in, Pete."

He was being sarcastic, but when they're used to getting 6,000 or 7,000 fans and they get 17,000, it's not too bad.

We won the game, 8-5, and the Dodgers beat Philadelphia. I got only

Cincinnati	ab	r	h	rbi	Pittsburgh	ab	r	h	rbi
Milner, cf	3	2	2	1	Gonzalez, lf	5	1	2	1
Rose, 1b	6	0	1	2	Ray, 2b	4	1	0	0
Parker, rf	5	1	1	1	Madlock, 3b	2	0	0	0
Bell, 3b	5	0	0	0	Morrison, 3b	0	0	0	0
Esasky, lf	4	1	2	2	Brown, rf	5	1	3	1
Redus, pr-lf	0	1	0	0	Th'mpson, 1b	5	1	2	1
C'cepcion, ss	5	0	1	0	Pena, c	3	0	1	1
Diaz, c	3	0	0	0	Khalifa, ss	3	0	1	1
Franco, p	1	1	1	0	Wynne, cf	3	0	0	0
Oester, 2b	4	2	4	0	Almon, ph-cf	1	0	0	0
Browning, p	1	0	0	0	Walk, p	1	0	0	0
Venable, ph	1	0	0	0	Lezcano, ph	0	0	0	0
Hume, p	0	0	0	0	DeLeon, p	0	0	0	0
Van Gorder, c	1	0	0	1	Kemp, ph	1	1	1	0
					Clements, p	0	0	0	0
					Mazzilli, ph	1	0	0	0
					Guante, p	0	0	0	0
					Scurry, p	0	0	0	0
Totals	39	8	12	7	Totals	34	5	10	5

Cincinnati .... 0 0 3   1 0 2   0 0 2—8
Pittsburgh .... 1 0 0   2 0 0   2 0 0—5

Cincinnati	IP.	H.	R.	ER.	BB.	SO.
Browning (W. 12-9) ...	5	7	3	3	2	3
Hume	1⅔	1	2	2	2	1
Franco (Save 6)	2⅓	2	0	0	1	0

Pittsburgh	IP.	H.	R.	ER.	BB.	SO.
Walk (L. 0-1)	4	8	4	4	1	4
DeLeon	3	1	2	1	1	4
Clements	1	1	0	0	1	2
Guante	⅔	2	2	2	3	0
Scurry	⅓	0	0	0	0	0

Game-winning RBI—Esasky.
E—Bell, DeLeon. DP—Cincinnati 1. LOB—Cincinnati 12, Pittsburgh 9. 2B—Khalifa, Brown, Thompson, Kemp. 3B—Milner. HR—Gonzalez (2), Esasky (14). SB—Concepcion. SH—Browning. SF—Khalifa. HBP—By DeLeon (Esasky), by Hume (Madlock). WP—Walk 2. T—3:13. A—17,198.

one hit in six at-bats and had my consecutive-hit streak against lefthanders ended at 8 for 8. Pat Clements and Rod Scurry (lefthanded relievers) both got me out.

Nick Esasky hit a two-run homer and I also drove in two runs.

Bob Walk, their starter, was tough for me. Anyone is tough for me who doesn't pitch consistently. I have trouble with that type of pitcher—you can't look for areas. Walk has good stuff, but he might throw one pitch behind your head, then one on the outside corner. Or he might throw one up and away, then down and in on the corner. He's got good movement on his ball and he's a battler. I thought because he was 16-5 at Triple-A Hawaii this summer that he finally found his control.

I always thought J. R. Richard (the former Houston Astros star) was tougher to hit when he was wilder early in his career. Once he got his control, he wasn't that tough because you knew what he was going to throw.

I don't think Walk really knows what he's trying to do with the ball. He's not the type of guy who on a 2-0 or 3-1 count is going to give you a good pitch. You might get a ball over your head.

If he ever comes up with control, he's going to be tough. He had better control and better ideas about pitching in 1980 when he was with us in Philadelphia and started the first game of the World Series.

THURSDAY, AUGUST 22 .... ROSE 1 FOR 3

I got a call this morning from Bill Hayes, my marketing agent at Taft Merchandising. Hertz, the car-rental people, have made me an unusual offer.

When I break the Cobb record, they want to publish a full-page ad in the leading U.S. newspapers. The ad will say something about Hertz being No. 1 in car rentals and me being No. 1 in hits. Across the bottom will be copies of my baseball cards from the time I came up to the majors in 1963.

While they would pay me less than I usually get for something like this, the big thing is that I'd be able to get a free Hertz rental car whenever I need one for the rest of my life. That's pretty good.

We're going to do it.

★   ★   ★

Marty Brennaman, our radio announcer, and pitcher Tom Hume were movie actors yesterday. They were used as "extras" in a film being shot here in Pittsburgh. It stars Michael Keaton and is about an American auto assembly plant that is being shut down. One of the workers campaigns to get a Japanese company to relocate, and the city is saved.

Cincinnati	ab	r	h	rbi	Pittsburgh	ab	r	h	rbi
Milner, cf	4	0	2	0	Ors'lak, cf-lf	3	1	1	1
Rose, 1b	3	1	1	0	Ray, 2b	4	1	1	1
Parker, rf	3	0	1	0	Madlock, 3b	3	0	1	1
Esasky, lf	4	0	1	0	Wynne, cf	1	0	0	0
Kr'chicki, 3b	3	0	0	0	Th'mpson, 1b	4	0	0	0
Perez, ph	0	0	0	1	Brown, rf	4	0	2	0
C'cepcion, ss	4	0	0	0	Pena, c	3	0	0	0
Van Gorder, c	2	0	0	0	G'z'lez, lf-3b	4	1	1	0
Runnells, ph	0	0	0	0	Khalifa, ss	4	1	1	0
Diaz, c	0	0	0	0	Rhoden, p	3	1	2	1
Oester, 2b	4	0	0	0	Scurry, p	0	0	0	0
Tibbs, p	2	0	0	0					
Price, p	0	0	0	0					
Venable, ph	1	0	1	0					
Power, p	0	0	0	0					
Totals	30	1	6	1	Totals	33	5	9	4

Cincinnati ....0 0 0   0 0 0   0 0 1—1
Pittsburgh......................0 0 1   0 0 2   2 0 x—5

Cincinnati	IP.	H.	R.	ER.	BB.	SO.
Tibbs (L. 6-14)..........	6⅓	8	5	4	0	3
Price..........................	⅔	0	0	0	0	1
Power..........................	1	1	0	0	1	2

Pittsburgh	IP.	H.	R.	ER.	BB.	SO.
Rhoden (W. 8-13)......	8*	6	1	1	3	6
Scurry (Save 2).........	1	0	0	0	1	1

*Pitched to three batters in ninth.

Game-winning RBI—Rhoden.
E—Parker. LOB—Cincinnati 7, Pittsburgh 6. 2B—Khalifa, Parker. 3B—Ray. SB—Milner. SH—Orsulak. SF—Perez. WP—Tibbs. T—2:38. A—10,437.

I told Marty I knew he'd make it to the silver screen someday.

★   ★   ★

The Pirates beat us tonight, 5-1, and won two out of three in the series. It's difficult to believe this team has the worst record (37-80, .316) in the majors.

But the Pirates are playing loose and you know they've got some good pitchers. They were first in the National League in earned-run average last year. And they've been playing pretty good lately (with four victories in their last six games).

They've got Bill Madlock hitting and Jason Thompson getting on base a lot, and Johnny Ray is a good little player. Tony Pena is one of the best catchers in the league.

Rick Rhoden pitched a strong game for Pittsburgh tonight.

I got just one hit, which leaves me 13 short of breaking the record.

This was when we found out Pittsburgh had stolen our signs.

Eddie Milner was on first base and I had a 2-1 count. They pitched out and got Milner going to second. On the next pitch, I got a base hit to center field. You just don't pitch out 2-1 unless you've got the signs.

We had a chance in this game. We were down 5-0 in the ninth but loaded the bases with nobody out. Rhoden walked me on four pitches. Dave Parker then walked and Nick Esasky got a base hit to left (I didn't score because I had to hesitate to make sure the ball wasn't going to be caught).

The Pirates then brought in lefthander Rod Scurry. I let Doggie (Tony Perez) pinch hit for Wayne Krenchicki, and he got a line-drive sacrifice fly to score me. Scurry then pitched out of trouble for his second save of the season.

We go home now for our next 10 games. If we're going to gain on the Dodgers (who lead the Padres by seven games and the Reds by nine), this is a good time to do it.

When Cubs announcer Harry Caray commented on the air that Rose's son, Petey (above), was a good hitter but weak with the glove, the Reds manager took issue.

FRIDAY, AUGUST 23 .... ROSE 1 FOR 4

We had a good crowd tonight—more than 34,000—and we opened the homestand with a 3-2 win over the Cubs.

I got a bunt single off Jay Baller to start the rally that tied the score 2-2 in the third inning.

The bottom of the ninth inning was what everybody was talking about, though.

With Lary Sorensen pitching for Chicago, Ron Oester tripled to lead off the ninth. The ball bounced by Bobby Dernier in center field.

Most managers in this situation—a runner on third and nobody out—would walk the bases full, hoping to get a strikeout, ground ball or something to keep the run from scoring on a sacrifice fly.

I had Cesar Cedeno (pinch hitting

Chicago	ab	r	h	rbi	Cincinnati	ab	r	h	rbi
Dernier, cf	4	1	2	0	Milner, cf	3	0	0	0
Matthews, lf	4	0	0	0	Redus, ph-cf	1	0	0	0
Sandberg, 2b	4	1	1	1	**Rose, 1b**	4	1	1	0
Moreland, rf	4	0	0	0	Parker, rf	4	0	2	0
Cey, 3b	2	0	1	0	Esasky, lf	4	0	1	1
Owen, 3b	0	0	0	0	Kr'nchicki, 3b	2	0	0	0
Durham, 1b	3	0	1	1	Runnells, ss	0	0	0	0
Davis, c	3	0	0	0	C'pc'n, ss-3b	3	1	1	0
Dunston, ss	4	0	0	0	Van Gorder, c	4	0	1	1
Baller, p	2	0	0	0	Oester, 2b	2	1	1	0
Woods, ph	1	0	1	0	McGaf'gan, p	2	0	0	0
Meridith, p	0	0	0	0	Venable, ph	1	0	0	0
Lopes, ph	1	0	0	0	Franco, p	0	0	0	0
Sorensen, p	0	0	0	0	Cedeno, ph	1	0	1	1
Totals	32	2	6	2	Totals	31	3	8	3

```
Chicago ...................... 2 0 0   0 0 0   0 0 0—2
Cincinnati .................. 0 1 1   0 0 0   0 0 1—3
None out when winning run scored.
```

Chicago	IP.	H.	R.	ER.	BB.	SO.
Baller	6	6	2	2	3	2
Meridith	2	0	0	0	1	2
Sorensen (L. 3-5)	0*	2	1	1	0	0
Cincinnati	IP.	H.	R.	ER.	BB.	SO.
McGaffigan	6	5	2	2	3	6
Franco (W. 11-1)	3	1	0	0	1	1

*Pitched to two batters in ninth.

Game-winning RBI—Cedeno.
E—None. LOB—Chicago 8, Cincinnati 9. 2B—Dernier, Van Gorder, Cey. 3B—Oester. SB—Sandberg. SH—Concepcion, Dernier. WP—McGaffigan. T—2:28. A—34,283.

for reliever John Franco), Gary Redus and myself coming up.

The Cubs' manager, Jim Frey, considered his options and decided to pitch to Cedeno. CC lined a single off Sorensen for the winning run.

After the game, Frey paid me a great compliment.

"I considered walking the bases full," he told reporters, "but decided against it because of where the Reds were in their batting order. Two intentional walks would have brought up Mr. Pete Rose, who is going for baseball's all-time hits record. I didn't want to see him up there in that situation."

The Cubs had their fireballer, Lee Smith, warming up in the ninth, but they didn't bring him in to try to blow away Cedeno and Redus. Why? Because Smith had pitched in all three games of the series that the Cubs had just concluded in Atlanta.

In a case like that, you have to do what your pitching allows you to do. If you don't have a rested Lee Smith, it's tough. I don't know if I'd have tried to get Cedeno out or not.

We had them in a pressure cooker. If you get Cedeno out and you walk Redus to try to get me to hit into a double play, Redus is going to steal second base on the first pitch.

Then, the Cubs would have faced a guy going for 4,200 hits, or Dave Parker (up next), an MVP candidate.

Frey's decision made sense, really.

Oester did a fine job in this game. I'll tell you one thing, outside of Parker, he's been our most consistent player. He's done everything we've asked of him. He's a battler. No question about it.

You wouldn't need many players if you had 'em like Oester and Parker.

SATURDAY, AUGUST 24.............. DID NOT PLAY

I signed autographs from noon to 3 p.m. today at a sports memorabilia show.

Harry Caray, the Cubs' broadcaster, asked me how I could go to something like this when I'm in the middle of the Cobb thing.

Well, to tell the truth, I enjoy going out and rapping with the fans. Plus, I get a few dollars for the appearance. Today's outing wasn't too bad because I knew I wouldn't be playing tonight (against Cubs left-hander Steve Trout).

★   ★   ★

Don Zimmer, one of the Cubs' coaches, was talking to me today about Buddy Bell. Don was Bell's manager at Texas in 1981 and for a good portion of 1982.

Zimmer told me not to worry about the fact Buddy's not hitting (entering tonight's game, Bell has a .204 average with the Reds).

"Pete, you ought to try Buddy as your No. 2 hitter sometime," Don said. "He's as good a second-place hitter as there is. I wouldn't be a bit surprised if he's the league's All-Star third baseman next year. I don't care what he's hitting now. He's not a superstar, but he's a tremendous player.

"He plays hurt, he plays hard and he plays every day. He does a lot of little things that add up to wins. He gets baserunners over, he plays good defense, knocks in runs, is on time, works hard and is dedicated. He's just a good player who's really going to help your organization."

Milwaukee Brewers scout Dave Garcia, a coach at Cleveland when Buddy played there and later manager of the California Angels and then the Indians, also had some interesting things to say. He told me Bell is the best hit-and-run man he's ever seen.

★　　　★　　　★

I didn't play tonight, so I felt a little helpless as we got beat, 4-0. It was another well-pitched game by Mario Soto (who gave up one run, unearned, in seven innings), but Steve Trout and the Cubs' bullpen pitched a little bit better.

I was surprised Trout threw as well as he did because he just came off the disabled list after having elbow problems.

The Cubs said they were going to let Trout throw only 50 pitches and that's how many he'd thrown when he came out after the fourth inning. We had a couple of chances, but just couldn't do anything.

I told the guys after the game to forget it, but to come back strong tomorrow.

We've got to start winning some series to gain on people. That's the only way we're going to get back into this thing. This cat-and-mouse game isn't going to get it.

Realistically, I just don't know how good our chances are at this stage of the season. With 42 games to go, we're in third place and nine games back. We've got to have help from some of the other teams and we don't seem to be getting that.

So, if we can't win the division, we've got to bust our tails for second place. Right now, San Diego is 2 1/2 games ahead of us. If you can't be No. 1, you gotta try to take No. 2. I think it's going to be hard to beat us out of third (fourth-place Houston trails the Reds by seven games).

I just want all my players to keep trying to go up the ladder. That's all you can do. Hell, we can still win it because we're under double figures in games behind.

SUNDAY, AUGUST 25.................. DID NOT PLAY

When we were in San Diego 10 days ago, I went down to breakfast at the hotel one morning and Jerry Kapstein, an agent, was waiting for Davey Concepcion.

I've known Jerry a long time and he's a good friend. Jerry handles Concepcion, who's interested in getting a contract extension.

I told Jerry to tell Davey to start getting that edge back by working hard. He's getting lazy again. When he works hard, he's a helluva player. He's 37, but I don't care how old he is. When he doesn't work hard—take his ground balls or take batting practice right—he's not as good a player.

Davey has to keep preparing himself. When he does that, he has good range afield and good quickness in his bat. But when he just goes through the motions, so to speak, he's not effective. I see that trend with him when we don't play well. I've said it before and I'll say it again, Davey is not a good player on a bad team. Some players can't play on bad teams, some can't play on good teams.

He's used to winning and the team doing well.

Jerry talked with Davey after I left and I think it helped. Davey has really been playing well lately. We won over the Cubs, 5-3, today and he had two hits.

This was a good game for us because after I rested Bo Diaz for three straight nights and Buddy Bell for two (Thursday and Friday), they came back and helped us win. Bo's double off the left-field wall in the sixth inning drove in a run and broke a 3-3 tie. Buddy knocked in a game-tying run in the fifth with a double.

I have to give our owner, Marge Schott, a lot of credit. She stuck her neck out and backed Bill Bergesch and me 100 percent when we went after Bell and Diaz. We told her they can help us and she went with our judgment. Even though they've been slow to get started, she hasn't said a word. To me, that's a good owner.

★   ★   ★

Mario Nunez, my friend from Tampa, flew up yesterday and is going to spend a few days with me.

Mario's wife was watching our game on Chicago's WGN-TV the other day and heard Harry Caray remark that my son Petey is a good hitter but not a good fielder.

Today, Harry asked me to go on the pregame show and that's the first thing I mentioned.

"Where did you hear Petey is a poor fielder?" I asked.

I think I caught Harry by surprise because he didn't know what to say. I went on to tell him how good a fielder I think Petey is. He said he got some bad information.

★   ★   ★

After the game, Carol and I went over to Marge Schott's home, which is not very far from our house. Each year, Marge holds an outing at her place that benefits Cincinnati's Children's Heart Association. A lot of players donate gloves, bats and other things that are raffled off. Marge has held these outings for a number of years.

After that, we joined three other players and their wives for the Tina Turner concert at the Riverfront Coliseum.

Believe it or not, this is the first live concert I've ever attended. I enjoyed every minute of it. Dave Parker got the tickets and we were in the third row.

I've never seen anything like this. Tina really worked hard—before long, she was soaking wet. There were 12,000 people in the arena and 11,000 of them were on their feet.

Tina reminded me of an athlete. She worked so hard.

I'll guarantee you, if I ever get the chance again, I'm going to see her show.

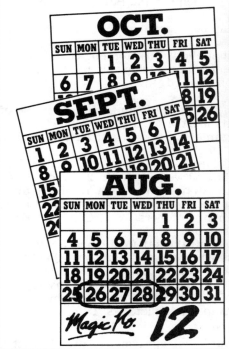

Despite the media crunch, Rose finds time for his fans. Rose (above) autographs a ball for young Montreal outfielder Mitch Webster before a July game against the Expos.

MONDAY, AUGUST 26 .... ROSE 1 FOR 4

This just might have been the toughest media day I've had since this Cobb stuff started.

After I got up this morning, I drove over near to where I grew up in Western Hills and got a haircut. There's a barber there who's been working on this mop for a long time.

I also picked up my black Porsche. I've had some work done on it, including getting a telephone installed.

I think the phone will be useful, like when I leave the stadium after night games. I can call Carol at home and tell her I'm on my way.

Once I got inside my office today, it was a mob scene. It seems like everybody and his brother wanted something. There were balls and pictures and a lot of other things to autograph.

Then came the rush of media.

An interview with NBC took almost an hour. CBS also was waiting to do a long interview, and a television reporter from Tampa had flown up to do a tape.

St. Louis	ab	r	h	rbi	Cincinnati	ab	r	h	rbi
Coleman, lf	4	0	1	0	Milner, cf	2	0	0	0
McGee, cf	4	0	1	0	**Rose, 1b**	4	0	1	0
Herr, 2b	3	0	0	0	Parker, rf	4	0	1	0
Porter, c	4	1	1	0	Esasky, lf	4	0	0	0
Van Slyke, rf	3	1	2	0	Bell, 3b	4	0	0	0
L'drum, ph-rf	1	0	0	0	C'cepcion, ss	4	0	0	0
Pendleton, 3b	4	1	2	1	Diaz, c	2	0	2	0
Jorgensen, 1b	2	0	0	0	Oester, 2b	3	0	1	0
Smith, ss	3	0	0	1	Tibbs, p	2	0	0	0
Cox, p	2	0	0	0	Venable, ph	1	0	0	0
					Price, p	0	0	0	0
Totals	30	3	7	2	Totals	30	0	6	0

St. Louis..........................0 3 0   0 0 0   0 0 0—3
Cincinnati........................0 0 0   0 0 0   0 0 0—0

St. Louis	IP.	H.	R.	ER.	BB.	SO.
Cox (W. 14-7)	9	6	0	0	3	1

Cincinnati	IP.	H.	R.	ER.	BB.	SO.
Tibbs (L. 6-15)...........	8	6	3	2	3	4
Price.............................	1	1	0	0	0	1

Game-winning RBI—Pendleton.
E—Pendleton, Diaz. DP—St. Louis 2, Cincinnati 1. LOB—St. Louis 5, Cincinnati 6. 2B—Van Slyke. SH—Cox, Smith. T—2:16. A—28,071.

Newspaper columnists from Philadelphia and Baltimore showed up and wanted some time.

I finally had to tell CBS it would be impossible to do their thing, but promised to make time tomorrow.

Jon Braude, the Reds' assistant publicity director, got a call from the White House today. They're trying to set up a telephone call from President Reagan when I break Ty Cobb's record.

★　　★　　★

St. Louis beat us tonight, 3-0. I got a first-inning infield single off Danny Cox, which leaves me 11 hits short of topping the Cobb record.

You can be aggressive in this game, but there's a difference in being aggressive and being reckless.

Take the fifth inning.

Eddie Milner led off with a walk, and we had the No. 2, 3 and 4 hitters coming up. You don't steal in that situation unless you're pretty much guaranteed you'll make it. Cox has a good move to first, and Darrell Porter isn't the worst thrower among catchers. Well, Cox kept Eddie close to the bag and Porter threw him out.

In the seventh, Bo Diaz hit a ball off the left-field fence and was out trying to get a double. Vince Coleman made a good play, but I don't think there's a left fielder in the league who wouldn't have thrown him out.

Jay Tibbs pitched a fine game for us. It's strange, but my top two starters leaving spring training—Mario Soto and Tibbs—are now tied for the league lead in losses with 15. (Soto has 10 victories, Tibbs six.)

★　　★　　★

The day was tough enough, but I was no sooner in my office than Ron Robinson picked that moment to complain about pitching only twice since the strike.

His timing was terrible. The writers were coming in and he was shouting at me about burying him.

I told him all he has to do is look at what the starters have done since the strike—not one has failed to go at least five innings.

Nothing is stopping these guys from pitching batting practice or throwing on the side to stay sharp.

The day was topped off when a sportscaster asked me if I might reconsider not starting against lefthanders because of all the media coming in.

I couldn't believe that question. I told him the media doesn't have anything to say about when I play. All the fans have to do is look in the newspaper and when a lefthander is pitching, don't count on me playing.

TUESDAY, AUGUST 27 .... DID NOT PLAY

I had to be up early today because Jonathan Meyersohn, a producer for the "CBS Evening News," and his crew came to the house a little before 11 o'clock.

They shot some tape around the house that is going to be edited for a segment on the nightly show that is anchored by Dan Rather.

Jonathan asked me just to do what I'd normally do this time of the day at home.

"Well, to tell you the truth, if you weren't here, I'd still be sleeping," I told him. "Carol and Tyler would be asleep, too."

The CBS crew took some shots of Carol and me feeding Smoogie, which is what I call Tyler. I think this boy is really a ham. Every time the lights went on, he smiled and tried to talk. When the lights went out, he was quiet.

People keep asking me how I am able to handle all these requests—all the TV crews and newspaper photographers who want to come out to the house.

I must admit that sometimes they're a little pushy and this bothers me, but for the most part I just go with the flow. These people have a job to do and it's up to me to cooperate with them every way I can.

After the taping, I went downtown for a baseball luncheon.

I represented the Reds at the Insiders' Club affair, along with Bill Bergesch, Buddy Bell and Jim Ferguson. The Cardinals sent Ozzie Smith and Kip Ingle, their assistant public-relations director. Jim O'Toole, who was a 19-game winner for the Reds when they won the pennant in 1961, also was there. Jim pitched in my first major league game in 1963.

I told the audience I think St. Louis is the best team in the National League right now, maybe in the majors.

An interesting subject came up at the luncheon. Somebody asked if I've always worn No. 14. The answer is no. When I went to spring training in 1963, I was a non-roster player and was assigned No. 27. The day before the first regular-season game of '63, after I had made the team, I was given No. 14 because I was a second baseman and Fred Hutchinson, the manager, wanted all his infielders to wear low numbers.

Before me, Don Zimmer wore No. 14 with the Reds. Zimmer joined the team in May 1962, then was traded the following winter. Like me, he attended Western Hills High School here in Cincinnati. (Tommy Harper wore No. 14 when he opened the '62 season as the Reds' third baseman, but newcomer Harper was soon dispatched to the minors.)

I broke up the luncheon group after saying that I really wasn't worried about Buddy Bell's slow start at the plate since being traded here. I added, "But, for heaven's sake, Buddy, please start hitting!"

★　　★　　★

We lost to the Cardinals tonight and fell 10 games behind the Dodgers, which made it bad enough. Even more upsetting was that we lost after coming from behind in the seventh inning on Cesar Cedeno's two-run single. My reliever, Teddy Power, couldn't hold the lead. He gave up three runs in the eighth and St. Louis won, 6-4.

St. Louis is executing as well as any team in baseball. I hope our guys learned something watching them.

WEDNESDAY, AUGUST 28.............. ROSE 2 FOR 6

Jim Kaat, my pitching coach, had breakfast this morning with Whitey Herzog, the St. Louis manager. Kitty pitched for Whitey when the Cardinals won the World Series in 1982.

Whitey said he might be interested in getting Cesar Cedeno from us. The Cardinals' first baseman, Jack Clark, is on the disabled list and Whitey is looking for some help.

I think we'd probably trade Cesar to them because I'm not sure we're going to sign him next year. There aren't that many opportunities for him here, and he's earning about $700,000.

Bill Bergesch, our vice president and general manager, has been in

St. Louis, where the owners ratified the new labor agreement today. I'm going to tell him the Cardinals are interested in Cesar and let him take it from there.

★   ★   ★

I had a meeting at 1 o'clock this afternoon with my attorney, Reuven Katz, and Bill Hayes, my marketing agent. We went over a lot of the final plans for ventures we're getting involved in relating to breaking the Cobb record.

We were all surprised that United Press International came out with a book about me (titled "4192!") before I even got the record. We knew nothing about it. What would happen if, for some reason, I don't get the record? Good question.

★   ★   ★

Tonight's game was a great one. I walked with the bases loaded in the 12th inning and we beat St. Louis, 7-6. It took us 4 hours and 13 minutes to get the job done, but I think this is a game we might look back on.

The Cardinals scored six runs off Mario Soto in the third inning and

St. Louis	ab	r	h	rbi	Cincinnati	ab	r	h	rbi
Coleman, lf	4	1	0	0	Milner, cf	3	0	2	1
McGee, cf	6	1	3	2	Redus, ph-cf	2	0	0	0
Herr, 2b	6	1	1	0	Power, p	0	0	0	0
Porter, c	3	1	1	0	Perez, ph	0	0	0	0
Van Slyke, rf	2	1	0	1	**Rose, 1b**	6	0	2	2
L'drum, ph-rf	3	0	1	0	Parker, rf	6	1	1	0
Pendleton, 3b	6	0	2	2	Esasky, lf	6	1	2	0
Jorgensen, 1b	5	0	2	0	Bell, 3b	4	0	0	0
Smith, ss	6	1	2	1	Franco, p	0	0	0	0
Andujar, p	2	0	1	0	Cedeno, ph-cf	2	0	0	0
Worrell, p	0	0	0	0	C'cepcion, ss	5	2	3	0
DeJesus, ph	1	0	0	0	Diaz, c	4	1	2	1
Forsch, p	0	0	0	0	Browning, pr	0	0	0	0
Dayley, p	0	0	0	0	Van Gorder, c	1	0	1	0
Harper, ph	1	0	0	0	Oester, 2b	5	1	3	2
Lahti, p	0	0	0	0	Soto, p	0	0	0	0
Horton, p	0	0	0	0	Robinson, p	1	0	0	0
					Runnells, ph	1	0	0	0
					Stuper, p	0	0	0	0
					Venable, ph	1	1	1	1
					Price, p	0	0	0	0
					Kr'chicki, 3b	2	0	0	0
Totals	45	6	13	6	Totals	49	7	17	7

```
St. Louis ............................ 006   000   000   000—6
Cincinnati .......................... 000   006   000   001—7
```
Two out when winning run scored.

St. Louis	IP	H.	R.	ER.	BB.	SO.
Andujar	5⅓	8	6	6	3	2
Worrell	1⅔	1	0	0	0	0
Forsch	⅓	1	0	0	0	0
Dayley	1⅔	1	0	0	0	0
Lahti (L. 2-2)	2°	6	1	1	1	2
Horton	⅔	0	0	0	2	0

Cincinnati	IP.	H.	R.	ER.	BB.	SO.
Soto	2⅓	4	6	6	4	3
Robinson	2⅔	3	0	0	0	1
Stuper	1	2	0	0	0	1
Price	1	1	0	0	1	2
Franco	3	1	0	0	0	3
Power (W. 5-4)	2	2	0	0	1	0

°Pitched to two batters in twelfth.

Game-winning RBI—**Rose.**

E—None. DP—St. Louis 3. LOB—St. Louis 11, Cincinnati 14. 2B—Pendleton, Concepcion, Parker, Esasky, Venable. SB—Porter, Smith, Coleman. SH—Andujar, Jorgensen. HBP—By Andujar (Concepcion). T—4:13. A—21,049.

were still up 6-0 in our sixth, but we tied them in that inning and our relief pitching did a super job until we scored in the 12th.

I had two hits, which leaves me nine short of breaking the Cobb record.

Joaquin Andujar started for St. Louis and although I didn't get any hits off him, I've seen him throw harder. I think he hurt his left (non-pitching) hand when he slid into third base in the sixth inning.

Joaquin is a very competitive pitcher. You don't win 20 games two years in a row if you're not. (Andujar took a 20-7 record into tonight's game after posting a 20-14 mark last season.)

I think Mario was overthrowing tonight. You don't usually see him walk four guys and not make it through the third inning.

My walk in the 12th inning off Rick Horton came on a 3-1 pitch.

On the first pitch of that at-bat, I faked a bunt and I would have bunted had the pitch been a strike. Third baseman Terry Pendleton was playing behind the bag, and he started backpedaling when Horton went into his windup. The last month or so I've been very successful with that righthanded bunt.

I got to thinking about a base hit in that situation because if I'd gotten three hits tonight, getting the record here over the weekend would have been possible. But a walk won the game for us and that was the important thing.

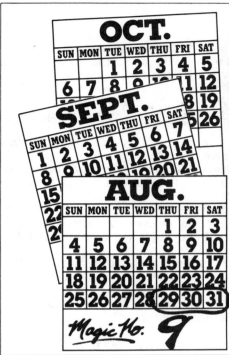

Former Reds pitcher Joe Nuxhall often throws batting practice before heading to the broadcast booth.

THURSDAY, AUGUST 29................. ROSE 1 FOR 3

Before Bob Howsam retired as the Reds' president, he asked me if I would speak to the Cincinnati Rotary Club sometime late in the season. This is the date we chose.

They told me that today's crowd was the largest of the year for the Rotary Club.

I just talked about the Reds and how the city is becoming excited about the team again.

After that, I went to the Multimedia studios for something I've never done before. It was neat. I was interviewed by sportscasters in cities such as New Orleans, Tampa, Miami, Salt Lake City, Atlanta, Charlotte, N.C., and Orlando, Fla.

I sat in a studio and, via satellite, each sportscaster got a separate interview that lasted about six minutes. They asked an assortment of questions and the whole thing took only a little over an hour. It was great for me because it wasn't like 10 TV stations asking for separate interviews.

Pittsburgh	ab	r	h	rbi	Cincinnati	ab	r	h	rbi
Almon, lf	4	0	0	0	Milner, cf	5	1	1	0
Gonzalez, 2b	4	0	1	0	Parker, rf	2	2	1	1
Morrison, 3b	4	0	1	0	Esasky, lf	4	0	0	0
Brown, rf	4	0	2	0	Bell, 3b	3	1	3	5
Th'mpson, 1b	3	0	0	0	Rose, 1b	3	2	1	0
Pena, c	4	0	2	0	C'cepcion, ss	3	0	1	0
Khalifa, ss	4	0	0	0	Diaz, c	4	0	1	0
Orsulak, cf	3	0	1	0	Oester, 2b	3	0	0	0
DeLeon, p	1	0	0	0	Browning, p	4	0	1	0
Lezcano, ph	1	0	0	0					
Scurry, p	0	0	0	0					
Totals	32	0	7	0	Totals	31	6	9	6

```
Pittsburgh ..................... 0  0  0   0  0  0   0  0  0—0
Cincinnati ..................... 0  0  3   0  3  0   0  0  x—6
```

Pittsburgh	IP.	H.	R.	ER.	BB.	SO.
DeLeon (L. 2-15)	7	9	6	6	7	4
Scurry	1	0	0	0	0	1

Cincinnati	IP.	H.	R.	ER.	BB.	SO.
Browning (W. 14-9) ...	9	7	0	0	1	4

Game-winning RBI—Parker.
E—Browning, Bell. DP—Pittsburgh 2, Cincinnati 2. LOB—Pittsburgh 7, Cincinnati 8. 2B—Parker, Bell. HR—Bell (2). SH—DeLeon. T—2:22. A—18,789.

★   ★   ★

I mentioned yesterday that the Cardinals were interested in obtaining Cesar Cedeno.

They must have been talking about it after Wednesday night's game because Cesar asked me when I got to the clubhouse if there was going to be a trade. The Cardinals' Joaquin Andujar told him there was a chance.

It wasn't until batting practice tonight that Bill Bergesch called me aside and said the deal was made. We're getting minor league outfielder Mark Jackson, considered one of the Cards' bright young prospects, in the trade.

With Cedeno leaving, I'm bringing up Eric Davis from Denver immediately. He'll be in uniform tomorrow night.

We also had to make another roster move. Joe Price (more elbow problems) is going on the disabled list and Bob Buchanan, who's been on the DL since August 8, is coming off.

★   ★   ★

We took advantage of the momentum we created Wednesday night by beating the Pirates, 6-0, tonight. Buddy Bell had a homer and five RBIs.

The Pirates have now lost 18 straight games on the road—four shy of tying the major league record (held by the 1890 Pittsburgh club and the 1963 New York Mets).

Tom Browning, our most effective pitcher of late, threw a seven-hit shutout. He's 14-9 and has a good chance to win 20.

FRIDAY, AUGUST 30 .... ROSE 0 FOR 2

I didn't get up until about 12:30 today because I had a tough night sleeping. We had severe thunderstorms in the early morning hours and the burglar alarm kept going off.

I had some eggs and bacon, then went to Riverfront Stadium.

Hal McCoy of the Dayton Daily News is revising a scrapbook of Pete Rose photos originally published about 10 years ago. He stopped by my office and we talked about captions for some of the new pictures.

McCoy is with the same newspaper as Si Burick, who's in the writers' section of baseball's Hall of Fame.

Pittsburgh	ab	r	h	rbi	Cincinnati	ab	r	h	rbi
Orsulak, cf	4	0	0	0	Milner, cf	4	0	2	0
Ray, 2b	4	0	1	0	**Rose, 1b**	2	0	0	0
Madlock, 3b	4	0	0	0	Parker, rf	4	0	1	0
Th'mpson, 1b	3	0	0	0	Esasky, lf	3	0	1	0
Brown, rf	3	0	1	0	Bell, 3b	3	0	0	0
Pena, c	3	0	0	0	C'cepcion, ss	4	0	0	0
Gonzalez, lf	3	0	2	0	Diaz, c	4	0	1	0
Khalifa, ss	3	0	0	0	Oester, 2b	4	1	3	0
Reuschel, p	3	0	1	0	Tibbs, p	3	0	0	0
					Venable, ph	1	0	1	1
Totals	30	0	5	0	Totals	32	1	9	1

Pittsburgh .... 0 0 0   0 0 0   0 0 0—0
Cincinnati .... 0 0 0   0 0 0   0 0 1—1
One out when winning run scored.

Pittsburgh	IP.	H.	R.	ER.	BB.	SO.
Reuschel (L. 10-7)	8⅓	9	1	1	3	5

Cincinnati	IP.	H.	R.	ER.	BB.	SO.
Tibbs (W. 7-15)	9	5	0	0	0	3

Game-winning RBI—Venable.
E—Thompson. DP—Pittsburgh 1, Cincinnati 1. LOB —Pittsburgh 3, Cincinnati 10. 2B—Milner, Gonzalez, Oester, Venable. SH—**Rose.** T—2:00. A—21,253.

Bruce Schoenfeld of the Cincinnati Post wants me to list and then discuss with him my 10 most memorable hits. I haven't finalized my list yet.

Compared with the first part of the week, today was fairly light in terms of media attention and the like.

★   ★   ★

If we're going to make a run at the Dodgers, we've got to beat teams like the Pirates. And that's what we've done the last two nights.

We had a super game tonight. I didn't get any hits, but Ron Oester came through again for me.

Jay Tibbs and Rick Reuschel had a scoreless battle going when Ron doubled off Bill Madlock's glove at third base with one out in the ninth.

I then sent up Max Venable to bat for Tibbs. Max hit a double to left-center and we won, 1-0.

We're now 30-14 in one-run decisions (the best mark in the league), and we have three straight victories. The winning streak and two straight losses by Los Angeles have gotten us back into the race. (The Dodgers now lead San Diego by seven games and Cincinnati by 7½.)

This was an important victory for Tibbs. He gave up only five hits and it was his first shutout of the year.

SATURDAY, AUGUST 31 .... ROSE 0 FOR 4

It looks like it might be Chicago.

I didn't get any hits tonight against Pittsburgh's Bob Walk and I still need eight hits to pass Ty Cobb. So, it's not very likely I'm going to get the record in St. Louis. After playing the Pirates again tomorrow at Riverfront Stadium, we play three games in St. Louis beginning Monday, have an off-day on Thursday and then play three games in Chicago starting on Friday.

There's a chance I'll break the record at Wrigley Field. If not, we come back to Riverfront on September 9 for the start of a four-game series against San Diego (games one and four of the Padres series will make up the August 6 and August 7 games postponed by the strike).

Pittsburgh	ab	r	h	rbi	Cincinnati	ab	r	h	rbi
Orsulak, cf	4	2	2	0	Milner, cf	4	0	0	0
Gonzalez, 3b	4	1	2	1	**Rose, 1b**	4	0	0	0
Ray, 2b	4	1	2	1	Parker, rf	4	0	0	0
Th'mpson, 1b	4	0	1	1	Esasky, lf	3	0	1	0
Brown, rf	4	1	1	0	Bell, 3b	4	0	1	0
Pena, c	4	1	1	3	C'cepcion, ss	3	0	1	0
Kemp, lf	4	0	0	0	Diaz, c	3	0	1	0
Khalifa, ss	3	0	0	0	Oester, 2b	3	0	1	0
Walk, p	4	0	0	0	McGaffigan, p	1	0	0	0
					Runnells, ph	1	0	0	0
					Hume, p	0	0	0	0
					Kr'chicki, ph	1	0	0	0
					Power, p	0	0	0	0
Totals	35	6	9	6	Totals	31	0	5	0

Pittsburgh.....................4 0 0   0 0 1   1 0 0—6
Cincinnati.....................0 0 0   0 0 0   0 0 0—0

Pittsburgh	IP.	H.	R.	ER.	BB.	SO.
Walk (W. 1-1)	9	5	0	0	2	7

Cincinnati	IP.	H.	R.	ER.	BB.	SO.
McGaffigan (L. 1-2)...	6	7	5	5	1	4
Hume	2	2	1	1	0	2
Power	1	0	0	0	0	2

Game-winning RBI—Ray.
E—None. DP—Pittsburgh 1, Cincinnati 1. LOB—Pittsburgh 3, Cincinnati 6. 2B—Gonzalez, Ray, Diaz, Bell. HR—Pena (8). SB—Orsulak 2. T—2:04. A—28,656.

I'm toying with the idea of sitting myself down against Bob Forsch on Tuesday night in St. Louis. Maybe I'll let Doggie (Tony Perez) start against Forsch because he always hits him well.

★   ★   ★

The Pirates were due to win after losing 19 straight games on the road—and that's what they did tonight. Bob Walk shut us out, 6-0.

This was a tough loss because the Phillies beat Los Angeles for the third straight time. I've been saying somebody would come along and beat the Dodgers three in a row, but I'm surprised it happened in Dodger Stadium.

Tonight, we just ran into a pitcher who had a great game. Walk's got a major league arm, a major league breaking ball. Everything was working for him.

When you run into a guy who's going like that, you just hope your man pitches as good of a game. Our man (Andy McGaffigan) didn't. He gave up four runs in the first inning, with three of the runs coming on a homer by Tony Pena.

Andy threw well in the second, third and fourth innings. He's had trouble early at times. I don't know if he's not ready when he gets out there or what it is. If you're going to get behind, the first inning is the time to do it—but not by four runs.

SUNDAY, SEPTEMBER 1 .... ROSE 2 FOR 4

When I arrived at Riverfront Stadium at about 10:30 a.m. today for our 2:15 p.m. game, I got a double dose of bad news.

Dave Parker said he wouldn't be able to take batting practice because he had the flu. Then, trainer Larry Starr said Davey Concepcion couldn't play because he has a pulled muscle under his knee.

Luckily, Parker was able to start and he ended up getting the game-winning RBI.

On another front, Jim Ferguson, our publicity director, said there could be as many as 300 media people in attendance when I get within a hit or two of the Cobb record. Fergie suggested that beginning tomorrow night in St. Louis, we use an interview room rather than my office after the game. That will make it easier for everybody, me included.

Pittsburgh	ab	r	h	rbi	Cincinnati	ab	r	h	rbi
Ors'lak, cf-lf	3	1	0	0	Milner, cf	3	0	0	0
Lezcano, ph	1	0	0	0	Perez, ph	1	0	1	0
Kemp, lf	4	0	2	0	R'd's, pr-cf-lf	0	1	0	0
Wynne, cf	0	0	0	0	Rose, 1b	4	0	2	1
Ray, 2b	3	0	0	1	Parker, rf	4	0	1	1
Th'mpson, 1b	3	0	0	0	Esasky, lf	4	0	0	0
Brown, rf	2	1	1	0	Franco, p	0	0	0	0
Pena, c	4	0	2	1	Bell, 3b	4	0	0	0
Morrison, 3b	4	0	1	0	Oester, 2b	3	0	0	0
Khalifa, ss	4	0	0	0	Diaz, c	2	1	2	1
Rhoden, p	3	0	0	0	Runnells, ss	2	0	0	0
Scurry, p	0	0	0	0	Venable, ph	1	1	1	0
Robinson, p	0	0	0	0	C'cepcion, ss	0	0	0	0
Mazzilli, ph	0	0	0	0	Soto, p	1	0	0	0
					Power, p	0	0	0	0
					Davis, cf	0	0	0	0
Totals	31	2	6	2	Totals	29	3	7	3

```
Pittsburgh......0 0 1  0 0 0  0 1 0—2
Cincinnati......0 0 0  0 0 0  0 3 x—3
```

Pittsburgh	IP.	H.	R.	ER.	BB.	SO.
Rhoden	7⅓	4	2	2	1	4
Scurry (L. 0-1)	0*	3	1	1	0	0
Robinson	⅔	0	0	0	0	1

Cincinnati	IP.	H.	R.	ER.	BB.	SO.
Soto (W. 11-15)	8	6	2	2	4	8
Power	⅓	0	0	0	1	0
Franco (Save 8)	⅔	0	0	0	0	0

*Pitched to three batters in eighth.

Game-winning RBI—Parker.
E—Brown. LOB—Pittsburgh 8, Cincinnati 5. 2B—Brown, Pena. HR—Diaz (3). SH—Soto 2. SF—Ray. Balk—Soto. T—2:32. A—30,062.

★ ★ ★

We were down 2-0 today but scored three runs in the eighth inning to win, 3-2.

We're now 6½ games behind the Dodgers, who lost their fourth straight to the Phillies.

Before today's game, Mike Schmidt called from L.A. to wish me luck. Herbie's swinging pretty good now. He said the Phillies are playing well, and I think he's happy for us that the Phils were able to beat the Dodgers.

I had two hits today, meaning I'm just six short of breaking the record. My hit in the eighth drove in the tying run and also caused some controversy.

When I swung, the ball hit the dirt in front of home plate, then took a high bounce over Jim Morrison's head at third base.

Chuck Tanner, the Pittsburgh manager, argued that the ball hit my foot. He even got the ball and stuck it in his pocket.

The Pirates' catcher, Tony Pena, told the writers I yelled that the ball hit my foot. When reporters asked about that, I told them Tony doesn't understand English very well.

While I got two hits, I'm not hitting the ball as hard as I'd like. I told all the media after the game that I'm definitely going to rest on Tuesday against St. Louis' Bob Forsch. Tony Perez will play.

★ ★ ★

Bill Bergesch invited Carol and me up to his box at Riverfront to watch some of the Bob Hope show that followed our game.

Our flight to St. Louis was at 8:30 p.m. I'm going to miss Tyler and Carol, but Carol is going to bring Tyler to Chicago on Wednesday night. She's also going to bring Petey.

I honestly feel when I come back home, I'll bring the record with me.

Dave Parker's two-run homer September 2 helped the Reds beat the Cardinals.

MONDAY, SEPTEMBER 2 .... ROSE 0 FOR 3

Maybe I am pressing a little bit.

The reason I say that is because I'm really swinging good in batting practice, hitting seeds. But it's not carrying over to the games.

I was 0 for 3 tonight (in a 5:35 p.m. game), but I'll take 0 for 3 anytime when we win and that's what we did. We beat Joaquin Andujar and the Cardinals, 4-1, at Busch Stadium.

Tom Browning pitched another great game and Dave Parker hit a two-run home run, his first homer since August 15.

Browning is now 15-9 and has won six games in a row.

I've had only three hits in my last 16 at-bats. And I've been hitless in three of our last four games.

Cincinnati	ab	r	h	rbi	St. Louis	ab	r	h	rbi
Milner, cf	5	1	1	0	Coleman, lf	3	0	1	0
Venable, lf	4	0	1	1	Smith, ss	4	0	0	0
Rose, 1b	3	1	0	0	Herr, 2b	4	0	1	0
Parker, rf	3	2	2	2	Cedeno, 1b	4	0	1	0
Bell, 3b	4	0	1	1	McGee, cf	4	1	2	1
C'cepcion, ss	4	0	1	0	Landrum, rf	3	0	1	0
Diaz, c	4	0	1	0	Pendleton, 3b	3	0	1	0
Oester, 2b	4	0	1	0	Nieto, c	3	0	0	0
Browning, p	3	0	1	0	Andujar, p	1	0	0	0
Franco, p	0	0	0	0	DeJesus, ph	1	0	0	0
					Worrell, p	0	0	0	0
					Harper, ph	1	0	1	0
					Campbell, p	0	0	0	0
Totals	34	4	9	4	Totals	31	1	8	1

Cincinnati	0	0 1	0 0 2	0 1 0—4
St. Louis	0	0 0	0 0 0	1 0 0—1

Cincinnati	IP.	H.	R.	ER.	BB.	SO.
Browning (W. 15-9) ...	6⅔	4	1	1	3	5
Franco (Save 9)..........	2⅓	4	0	0	1	1

St. Louis	IP.	H.	R.	ER.	BB.	SO.
Andujar (L. 20-8).......	6	6	3	3	2	2
Worrell	2	2	1	1	0	1
Campbell	1	1	0	0	0	0

Game-winning RBI—Venable.
E—None. DP—Cincinnati 3, St. Louis 1. LOB—Cincinnati 6, St. Louis 7. 2B—Concepcion, Milner, Venable, Cedeno, McGee, Parker, Bell. HR—Parker (24), McGee (8). SH—Franco. T—2:15. A—29,026.

This was a big game for us. The Padres got bombed by the Mets, 12-4, so we moved past San Diego into second place. We're 6½ games back of the first-place Dodgers and could've been 5½, but L.A. beat Montreal, 5-4, in 11 innings.

I did something in the first inning tonight that I haven't done for a long, long time.

We had a rookie umpire by the name of Gerry Davis working behind the plate. When he called me out on strikes on a 2-2 pitch, I slammed my bat to the ground and shouted at him.

It's tough enough to play at this time of day, with the shadows and the twilight. All you want is a good effort from the umpire.

When I get two strikes, I want the cat to bear down a little bit. The pitch was outside.

★　　★　　★

During the postgame press conference—we've set up interview sessions for a half-hour before and after each game—Jim Ferguson announced that whenever I break the record, there's going to be the least amount of interruption possible in the game. I want it that way because I don't think it's fair to opposing pitchers to take 15 or 20 minutes.

Of course, the best thing would be to come up in a tie game in the bottom of the ninth inning, a runner at second and two out and get the base knock. But then I'd have to go out and retrieve the ball myself.

Dick Young of the New York Post made a great point at the press conference. Before responding to what he said, I went over and shook his hand.

Dick said that chasing this Cobb record surely couldn't compare—as far as pressure is concerned—to 1978 when I had the 44-game hitting streak. He's 100 percent right. This record will happen.

Pressure would be needing one hit with one at-bat left in my career. With that hitting streak in '78, I had to get a hit every day.

★　　★　　★

Before the game, I asked Dave Parker about all the media.

I wondered if he'd gotten any vibes about it being a distraction for the team, or if the players are perturbed.

"No way," he said. "The guys are liking it. What they don't understand is how you're able to handle it so well."

TUESDAY, SEPTEMBER 3 .... DID NOT PLAY

I had an interesting talk with Bob Broeg, longtime sports editor and columnist for the St. Louis Post-Dispatch, before tonight's game. He's retired now, but still writes a column.

I've known Bob, a member of the writers' wing at baseball's Hall of Fame, since I was a rookie. When I learned he was good friends with Stan Musial, I began to pick his brain.

I once asked Bob what it took to reach certain plateaus in hitting—1,000 hits, 2,000 hits, etc. His answer was simple: You cannot afford to let down—even with an at-bat that means nothing.

I've probably had the ability to bear down as much as anybody in the history of the game, but I don't think I can honestly say that I have been able to do it in all 13,746 (official) at-bats of my major league career. I'd like to think I have, but sometimes you don't because it's raining, or 30 degrees, or maybe 110 degrees, or you have a headache, or something else.

But I bear down more than anybody—maybe it's because I have to.

Bob asked me, of people who've passed away, who I'd most like to have with me when I break the Cobb record. That was easy—my father;

Fred Hutchinson, who was my first big-league manager; and Mike Ryba, a former manager in the Reds' system and a onetime major league player, coach and scout.

Mike had a big influence on me. When I was a minor-leaguer in the Cincinnati camp during spring training of 1963, I took Mike's advice and stuck around for a Reds game even though I wasn't on the roster. That's the exhibition game I got into in the late innings and collected two doubles—it was my big break.

But who's to say these people won't be with me when I break it. I think they will.

★   ★   ★

Dave Parker asked to talk to me privately today.

Dave has been subpoenaed as a witness in the baseball-related drug trial in Pittsburgh.

This has been bothering Dave, and I think it's one of the reasons he's been in a hitting slump (entering this series, Parker had been in a 12-for-62 tailspin). Parker told me a couple weeks ago he was concerned about the reaction fans might have to this.

Tommy Helms, my coach, has been helping Dave over this hurdle. Parker has really turned his life around and he's got nothing to hide. I'm proud of Dave, and I told him not to worry about anything that might come out of the trial.

★   ★   ★

The Cardinals beat us, 6-4, tonight.

I didn't play, but I made more moves as manager than I have in any game since I took over. It was fun.

In the top of the seventh, when we scored two runs to tie 4-4, Whitey Herzog (St. Louis manager) used five pitchers, which tied a National League record. I used a pinch-runner and four pinch-hitters in the inning, including a pinch-hitter for a pinch-hitter. Parker blooped a double to left field that knocked in two runs, but St. Louis came back in the bottom of the inning with two more runs.

As far as I'm concerned, my moves (in the seventh) worked because we tied the game. I did it without getting confused; I had everybody ready.

I made a big mistake, though, and I'm surprised somebody didn't pick it up.

In the late maneuvering, I put the pitcher (Ron Robinson) in the seventh slot in the batting order and I put my catcher, Dann Bilardello, in the fourth spot.

I was trying to hide the pitcher as far back as I could, but I shouldn't have done it that way. If somebody had gotten on in the ninth and Dave Parker gets a hit, Bilardello is the hitter instead of the pitcher. And if I had needed to hit for Bilardello, then the only guy left who can catch is Pete Rose. I should have reversed them, so I could have used a pinch-hitter for the pitcher.

WEDNESDAY, SEPTEMBER 4 .... ROSE 1 FOR 3

On my way to Busch Stadium this afternoon, I was asked to stop by the Stan Musial statue outside the ball park. It was for a picture for one of the Cincinnati newspapers.

That got me to thinking back to the day (September 29) in 1963 when I was a rookie and Musial got the last two hits of his big-league career against the Reds in the final game of the season.

Fred Hutchinson (then the Reds' manager) told me to pay close attention because I was watching history being made. (Musial's hits were his 3,629th and 3,630th in the National League; Rose went 3 for 6 that afternoon and had 170 N.L. hits at that point.)

I never dreamed that day I would eventually pass Musial's N.L. hits record (in 1981) and be close to Ty Cobb's all-time major league mark today.

★   ★   ★

I have great respect for athletes in other sports. I probably watch more pro football and college basketball on television than anybody.

Cincinnati	ab	r	h	rbi	St. Louis	ab	r	h	rbi
Milner, cf	3	0	1	0	Coleman, lf	4	1	2	0
Redus, ph-lf	2	1	1	0	Dayley, p	0	0	0	0
Venable, lf	3	0	1	0	Worrell, p	0	0	0	0
Es'sky, ph-1b	1	0	0	0	McGee, cf	4	0	0	0
Rose, 1b	3	0	1	0	Herr, 2b	2	0	0	0
Davis, pr-cf	0	1	0	0	Van Slyke, rf	3	1	1	0
Parker, rf	4	1	3	2	Porter, c	4	0	0	0
Bell, 3b	2	0	1	0	Pendleton, 3b	4	2	2	1
C'cepcion, ss	3	0	0	1	Jorgensen, 1b	3	0	2	1
Diaz, c	4	0	1	0	Smith, ss	3	0	1	1
Oester, 2b	4	0	2	0	Kepshire, p	1	0	0	0
McGaf'gan, p	2	0	0	0	Braun, ph	1	0	0	0
Kr'chicki, ph	1	0	0	0	Landrum, lf	0	0	0	0
Robinson, p	1	0	0	0					
Totals	33	3	11	3	Totals	29	4	8	3

Cincinnati ....0 0 0   1 0 0   0 2 0—3
St. Louis ....1 0 0   1 0 0   0 0 2—4
None out when winning run scored.

Cincinnati	IP.	H.	R.	ER.	BB.	SO.
McGaffigan	6	5	2	2	4	3
Robinson (L. 5-4)	2*	3	2	1	0	0

St. Louis	IP.	H.	R.	ER.	BB.	SO.
Kepshire	7	8	1	1	2	5
Dayley	⅓	3	2	2	0	1
Worrell (W. 1-0)	1⅔	0	0	0	1	3

*Pitched to three batters in ninth.

Game-winning RBI—Jorgensen.
E—Concepcion. DP—St. Louis 3. LOB—Cincinnati 7, St. Louis 6. 2B—Van Slyke. HR—Parker (25). SB —Coleman 2, Herr, Jorgensen. SH—Kepshire. SF— Concepcion. T—2:33. A—25,425.

So, I felt honored when several of the St. Louis (football) Cardinals came by to get some balls and other things autographed.

★   ★   ★

The writers keep talking about how I've accomplished a lot in baseball without much natural ability.

Now wait a minute.

You don't play the game as long as I have without some ability.

They say I couldn't run. Well, I had to be able to run to get all the doubles I have (738). They say I couldn't throw. Well, I had to have a pretty good arm because when I was an outfielder, I tied for the league lead in assists a couple of times.

Natural ability? Yeah, I think I've always had natural ability to hit a baseball. You know, hand-and-eye coordination. And I've been durable.

★   ★   ★

I got a single down the right-field line tonight, which leaves me five hits short of breaking the Cobb record. That knock off reliever Ken Dayley (Rose's 11th hit in his last 15 at-bats against lefthanders) kept the eighth inning alive as we moved ahead of the Cardinals 3-2.

Then we handed it to them.

Andy Van Slyke led off the Cardinals' ninth with a double and Terry Pendleton then hit a ball to Davey Concepcion at shortstop.

I think Davey took his eye off the ball, because it bounced off his glove for an error.

Van Slyke took off for third as the ball was hit—a bad baserunning mistake. He got away with it. He'd have been out if Davey fields the ball.

Davey then tried to get Van Slyke, who was heading for home, at the plate—and made a poor throw. Pendleton advanced to second. Mike Jorgensen then singled home Pendleton and the Cards won, 4-3.

Rose acknowledges the cheers
of Chicago fans after getting
hit No. 4,191 on September 8.

FRIDAY, SEPTEMBER 6 .... ROSE 2 FOR 5

Our open date yesterday here in Chicago came at a perfect time. It gave me a chance to relax and get away from the daily questioning about the Ty Cobb record.

Carol and her mother brought Tyler to Chicago and they arrived Wednesday. Petey and my daughter Fawn also came in for the three games with the Cubs.

I had a relaxing afternoon yesterday at the races, then I watched a couple of baseball games on TV at night.

I thought about having a little workout, but decided against it because the guys needed a day off. I know I did.

★　　★　　★

I went to Wrigley Field early today and I must say the adrenaline is really beginning to flow. I was a little sluggish early in batting practice, but hit the ball good in the last couple of rounds.

Cincinnati	ab	r	h	rbi	Chicago	ab	r	h	rbi
Milner, cf	5	2	2	2	Hatcher, cf	4	0	0	0
Rose, 1b	5	1	2	2	Dunston, ss	4	0	0	0
Parker, rf	4	0	3	1	Sandberg, 2b	4	1	3	0
Esasky, lf	4	0	0	0	Moreland, rf	3	1	0	0
Venable, lf	0	0	0	0	Cey, 3b	4	1	1	3
Bell, 3b	5	0	0	0	Durham, 1b	4	1	1	1
C'cepcion, ss	4	0	2	0	J. Davis, c	4	0	0	0
Diaz, c	4	1	2	0	Bosley, lf	4	1	1	1
Oester, 2b	3	2	1	0	Botelho, p	0	0	0	0
Soto, p	4	1	0	0	Perlman, p	1	0	0	0
					Woods, ph	1	0	1	0
					Patterson, p	0	0	0	0
					Owen, ph	1	0	0	0
					Meridith, p	0	0	0	0
Totals	38	7	12	7	Totals	34	5	7	5

```
Cincinnati ......................1 4 0   0 2 0   0 0 0—7
Chicago .........................0 1 0   3 0 0   0 0 1—5
```

Cincinnati	IP.	H.	R.	ER.	BB.	SO.
Soto (W. 12-15)	9	7	5	5	1	10

Chicago	IP.	H.	R.	ER.	BB.	SO.
Botelho (L. 1-3)..........	1⅔	7	5	5	1	2
Perlman......................	3⅓	4	2	2	0	3
Patterson...................	2	1	0	0	0	2
Meridith......................	2	0	0	0	0	2

Game-winning RBI—Parker.
E—None. LOB—Cincinnati 7, Chicago 3. 2B—Parker. 3B—Milner, Sandberg. HR—**Rose** (2), Durham (16), Cey (18), Oester (1), Bosley (7). HBP—By Botelho (Esasky), by Meridith (Parker). PB—J. Davis. T—2:36. A—17,026.

We ended up beating the Cubs, 7-5, but my batting-practice hitting didn't carry over to the first inning.

The Cubs' Derek Botelho threw me just three pitches and struck me out. I had some words with umpire Bob Engel. I thought the third pitch was low and I shouted, "I hope you give my pitcher (Mario Soto) that pitch."

We scored four runs in the second inning and two of them came across when I hit a homer to right field. It was only my second home run of the year (both have been at Wrigley Field). If the wind hadn't been blowing out, it wouldn't have been a homer.

I hit it on a 3-2 pitch. Just before I swung, their catcher, Jody Davis, said, "What do you think we're going to throw you now?"

I looked at him and said, "Jody, I really don't give a damn."

I got a fastball.

Usually, Cubs fans in the bleachers throw back home run balls hit by the other team—that's what they did when Ronnie Oester hit his two-run shot in the fifth.

But the ball I hit wasn't returned.

Ironically, it turned out that the guy who got the ball has been a Reds fan since the mid-1970s and says I'm his idol. He said the ball went over his head, but it must have bounced back. During all the confusion, he looked down and the ball was sitting on the concrete in front of his seat.

After the homer, the Wrigley Field fans gave me a standing ovation. I know I distracted from Dave Parker's at-bat, but when they started chanting "Pete, Pete," I went out of the dugout and waved to them. I think that's the first time I've ever done that on the road—maybe ever.

I also got a single in the sixth inning off reliever Reggie Patterson, which leaves me three hits short of breaking the record.

★　　★　　★

We had a crazy kind of press conference after the game. They had me standing on the on-deck circle and the media gathered around. Fans in the stands were close to the field, and they were yelling and cheering.

Milt Richman, longtime columnist for United Press International, thinks I should retire as a player after I get the record. He said Hank Aaron told him there was an enormous letdown after he broke Babe Ruth's career home run record.

I disagree that there will be a letdown. Henry didn't have the things on his mind that I do now when he broke the Ruth record. He wasn't in charge of a team chasing the Dodgers.

Milt interviewed one of my coaches, Tommy Helms, about my situation. Helms asked him why I should retire and Milt said because I will embarrass myself.

Tommy told him about all the little things I do to help the team.

"We're a better team when Pete's out there," he said. "If we had a 22-year-old stud who can hit 40 home runs, maybe Pete wouldn't play. But we don't."

SATURDAY, SEPTEMBER 7 .... ROSE 0 FOR 4

Today was a scorcher. The temperature in Chicago reached 99 degrees and it was humid.

The weather got to me in batting practice. I got sicker than a dog and had to go in and take a cold shower. I guess I didn't realize how hot it was because, as usual, I wore a sweat jacket at practice. Larry Starr, our trainer, said that's probably why I got sick.

I felt OK once the game started, but I didn't get any hits. Down 9-3 after seven innings, we rallied in the ninth but still lost to the Cubs, 9-7, at Wrigley Field. This was a tough one because the Dodgers beat the Mets with a run in the ninth inning. So, we trail L.A. by 8½ games again.

I grounded out once, struck out twice and lined to the pitcher. On the liner, which came in the sixth inning, Jay Baller stuck up his glove in desperation and caught it. Actually, the ball caught him.

A little later, Baller said, "Thanks for waking me up today, Pete."

In the ninth inning against Lee Smith, I got a walk and ended up scoring when Dave Parker hit the fourth grand slam of his career.

Cincinnati	ab	r	h	rbi	Chicago	ab	r	h	rbi
Milner, cf	5	1	1	1	Dernier, cf	4	1	1	1
Rose, 1b	4	1	0	0	Matthews, lf	4	2	2	2
Parker, rf	5	3	3	5	Speier, 3b	1	0	0	0
Esasky, lf	5	0	2	1	Sandberg, 2b	3	1	1	0
Bell, 3b	4	0	1	0	Moreland, rf	3	0	0	0
C'cepcion, ss	3	0	0	0	Cey, 3b	3	2	1	2
Diaz, c	4	1	1	0	Lake, c	0	0	0	0
Oester, 2b	4	1	2	0	Durham, 1b	4	1	2	3
Browning, p	2	0	1	0	Davis, c	4	0	0	0
Runnells, ph	0	0	0	0	Sorensen, p	0	0	0	0
Franco, p	0	0	0	0	Smith, p	0	0	0	0
Hume, p	0	0	0	0	Dunston, ss	4	1	2	0
Buchanan, p	0	0	0	0	Eckersley, p	1	1	1	1
Stuper, p	0	0	0	0	Baller, p	1	0	0	0
Kr'chicki, ph	1	0	0	0	H'tcher, ph-lf	1	0	0	0
Totals	37	7	11	7	Totals	33	9	10	9

Cincinnati .... 1 0 0   1 0 1   0 0 4—7
Chicago .... 1 1 0   1 0 0   6 0 x—9

Cincinnati	IP.	H.	R.	ER.	BB.	SO.
Browning	6	4	3	3	2	4
Franco (L. 11-2)	⅓	4	4	4	0	0
Hume	⅓	0	1	1	1	0
Buchanan	⅓	1	1	1	0	0
Stuper	1	1	0	0	0	0

Chicago	IP.	H.	R.	ER.	BB.	SO.
Eckersley	4	4	2	2	0	2
Baller (W. 1-3)	3	3	1	1	2	2
Sorensen	1	1	0	0	0	0
Smith	1	3	4	4	1	0

Game-winning RBI—Dernier.
E—None. LOB—Cincinnati 6, Chicago 5. 2B—Bell, Parker, Esasky, Dunston. HR—Eckersley (1), Milner (1), Parker 2 (27), Cey (19), Matthews (10), Durham (17). SB—Dernier, Sandberg. SH—Runnells, Hatcher. HBP—By Browning (Dernier). T—2:31. A—30,300.

The Cobra has been on fire lately. On this trip, he's 13 for 20. He's had four doubles, four homers and driven in 13 runs. That slump is certainly behind him.

It now looks like I'm going to break the Cobb record against San Diego back in Cincinnati next week. I'm not going to start Sunday against the Cubs or Monday night against the Padres because both teams are scheduled to start lefthanders.

Not getting any hits today cost my team because Parker follows me to the plate. When you consider the way Dave's swinging—he had two homers and a double today—had I been on base more, we might have won.

No matter what anybody says, I wasn't trying to save any hits for Cincinnati.

In the second inning, umpire Paul Runge called me out on strikes. I turned to him and said, "Are you trying?"

He said: "My very best."

I walked away, but I didn't think he had a consistent strike zone. I feel umpires have a tough job and seldom criticize them, but if a guy's going to call a low ball a strike, he shouldn't call one up around the letters a strike, too.

I've struck out six times on this trip and four of them have been called third strikes. I honestly don't think all of those called third strikes were strikes at all. Oh, well.

★　　★　　★

I had an interesting thing happen to me before today's game.

The official scorer approached me and asked if it mattered whether hit No. 4,192—should I have a shot at it here—was a "clean" base hit.

I said, "Well, hell no. If I hit a ball off the shortstop's glove in the hole, it's a base hit. I just don't want to put you through a lot of pressure—you call 'em the way you want to call 'em. Don't ask me. You do your job and I'll try to do mine."

He was a young man and was very nice about it.

★　　★　　★

Reporters have asked me about the drug trial in Pittsburgh. Lonnie Smith (a former teammate at Philadelphia) mentioned my name and several others in regard to "supposedly" taking amphetamines, but he had no factual evidence.

This relates to a 1981 Reading, Pa., investigation during which all players who testified were exonerated. (In '81, the former team physician for the Phillies' Class AA farm club in Reading was accused of illegally distributing amphetamines to seven Phillies players. Charges later were dropped.)

SUNDAY, SEPTEMBER 8 .... ROSE 2 FOR 5

Throughout my career, I've always gone to the ball park figuring I was going to play. Even on days I haven't been in the lineup, it's been my practice to prepare mentally for the game.

So, when I learned that lefthander Steve Trout had fallen off his bicycle Saturday night and that the Cubs were going to start a righthander today, it didn't bother me in the least.

I got to Wrigley Field early and saw Trout shagging fly balls in center field—something he always does the day he pitches. I didn't know anything was up at that point.

I sat in the bullpen for about a half-hour talking to Sarge (the Cubs' Gary Matthews), and Billy Connors (Chicago's pitching coach) came over. Connors didn't say anything about Trout.

We had a little pregame press conference and, after that, I was on my

Cincinnati	ab	r	h	rbi	Chicago	ab	r	h	rbi
Milner, cf	5	1	2	1	Dernier, cf	5	1	2	0
Rose, 1b	5	1	2	1	Matthews, lf	3	1	0	0
Parker, rf	4	0	1	0	Woods, lf	1	0	0	0
Esasky, lf	5	1	0	0	Sandberg, 2b	5	1	1	0
Power, p	0	0	0	0	Moreland, rf	5	2	3	3
Bell, 3b	4	1	1	3	Cey, 3b	3	0	2	1
C'cepcion, ss	4	0	1	0	Speier, 3b	0	0	0	0
Van Gorder, c	3	0	1	0	Durham, 1b	4	0	1	1
Kr'chicki, ph	1	0	1	0	J. Davis, c	4	0	1	0
Redus, pr	0	0	0	0	Hatcher, pr	0	0	0	0
Bilardello, c	0	0	0	0	Lake, c	0	0	0	0
Oester, 2b	4	1	2	0	Dunston, ss	4	0	3	0
Tibbs, p	1	0	0	0	Patterson, p	1	0	0	0
O'Neill, ph	1	0	0	0	Sorensen, p	0	0	0	0
Stuper, p	0	0	0	0	Bosley, ph	0	0	0	0
Runnells, ph	1	0	1	0	Lopes, ph	1	0	0	0
Hume, p	0	0	0	0	Smith, p	0	0	0	0
Buchanan, p	0	0	0	0					
V'nable, ph-lf	1	0	1	0					
Totals	39	5	13	5	Totals	36	5	13	5

Cincinnati .... 0 0 1　0 3 0　0 0 1—5
Chicago .... 3 0 2　0 0 0　0 0 0—5

Game called because of darkness after nine innings.

Cincinnati	IP.	H.	R.	ER.	BB.	SO.
Tibbs	3	6	5	5	2	3
Stuper	2	3	0	0	0	0
Hume	2⅓	4	0	0	0	0
Buchanan	⅔	0	0	0	0	0
Power	1	0	0	0	0	0

Chicago	IP.	H.	R.	ER.	BB.	SO.
Patterson	5	8	4	4	1	2
Sorensen	3	2	0	0	0	1
Smith	1	3	1	1	0	3

E—J. Davis. DP—Cincinnati 2. LOB—Cincinnati 8, Chicago 8. 2B—Dernier. 3B—Moreland. HR—Bell (3). SB—Parker, Milner. SH—Patterson, Sorensen. Balk—Tibbs. T—2:42. A—28,269.

way to do an "NFL Today" TV segment when coach Billy DeMars said Trout wasn't pitching. Billy said the Cubs were going with a righthander, Reggie Patterson. That meant I was going to play.

A lot of thoughts went through my mind. I could catch Ty Cobb with two hits and pass him with three. If I did tie or break the record today, though, Carol and Tyler wouldn't be here to see it. My daughter Fawn had driven back to Cincinnati. Reuven Katz, my attorney, left after Saturday's game. No one, not even me, thought I'd be playing today.

Reds Owner Marge Schott, who has been so supportive all season, wasn't here either. Neither was the baseball commissioner.

In the first inning, I singled to left-center off Patterson.

I grounded out in the third inning, but in the fifth I tied Cobb's record of 4,191 career hits when I singled to right field on a 3-2 pitch.

The fans—the crowd was 28,269—were wonderful. They gave me standing ovations every time I came up. And in the fifth, they stood for about five minutes cheering and applauding. It was a great feeling.

On the on-deck circle, Dave Parker was clapping, too. Finally, I took off my batting helmet and acknowledged the crowd.

While I stood on first base, I don't know exactly what went through my mind. I just thought I got a good hit; I hit the ball hard.

Patterson told reporters he thought about coming over and congratulating me, but decided against it because he was too concerned about pitching to Parker. He also paid me a great tribute, saying I was the greatest player who ever played this game.

My big knock was important because it got a three-run inning started. Buddy Bell accounted for the runs with a homer and we closed within a run (5-4) of the Cubs.

I had a lot of mixed emotions after that because I batted two more times. Parker and some of the other guys told me to save the record-breaker for home.

I went up to bat in the seventh and ninth innings with a lot on my mind. But I'll tell you right now, I can't go into the batter's box and not try to get a hit.

The hardest ball I hit all day was in the seventh when I grounded out against Lary Sorensen. I had visions of that ball taking a bad hop over the shortstop's head and me getting the record that way.

Honestly, that time up I was looking for a walk. I was down in a crouch as low as I've been in my whole career. In that situation (the Reds still were down by a run and Rose was leading off the inning), a walk was as good as a hit. I hit a rope.

The rain started falling in the bottom of the eighth and the game was halted. The delay lasted 2 hours, 3 minutes.

When the game was finally resumed and I came up in the ninth, we had just tied the score on Eddie Milner's single.

Now, there were runners on first and second and nobody out. Lee Smith was pitching and I think it was the darkest time of the day.

I can't ever remember going to the plate when guys on my own team didn't want me to get a hit. But I believe that was the case when I followed Milner to the plate in the ninth.

I never thought about bunting—I haven't bunted in that situation all year. If I do that, I take the bat out of Parker's hand (by setting up an intentional-walk situation).

As it turned out, I swung and missed on a 2-2 pitch. And we failed to score again in that inning.

After the Cubs went down in the ninth, the umpires suspended the game because of darkness. (The National League later announced that the contest will stand as a 5-5 tie, with all individual statistics being officially recorded. If the game is needed to determine the outcome of either divisional race, it will be made up in its entirety after the end of the regular season.)

The long day wasn't over. Our flight to Cincinnati was delayed for three hours.

Then there was all the media awaiting us when we arrived back home. Every TV station wanted me to go on live and talk about hit No. 4,191—and I did. But I was dead tired.

Rose salutes a jubilant Cincinnati crowd after collecting his record-breaking hit on September 11.

MONDAY, SEPTEMBER 9 .... DID NOT PLAY

Everyone knew I wasn't going to play tonight, but we still had 29,289 fans at Riverfront Stadium. And they were revved up.

When I came out to argue a call with first-base umpire Dutch Rennert in the seventh inning, I got a standing ovation.

Davey Concepcion singled home the winning run in the ninth and we beat the Padres, 2-1.

I had an edgy-type, wrong feeling most of the game, though. In the first inning, Doggie (Tony Perez) overcharged a ball at first base, dived for it and it went for a hit. The fans started yelling, "Pete, Pete, Pete."

That kind of stuff—calling for me to replace Doggie—can hurt the team. The excitement over the Cobb record should be used to help us, not create problems.

Concepcion was teasing me all night. He kept saying we were going to have the winning run in scoring position late in the game, he'd be due up and that he then would call a timeout and say, "I want you to hit for me."

I said, "Davey, I'm not hitting for you. If you've got that man in that winning situation, you better knock him in." He did.

★   ★   ★

An ironic thing is going to happen tomorrow night.

Mario Soto won't be able to start because of a bad foot, so I'm going with "True Creature," Ron Robinson.

Remember back in early June when I told about how Ron was the last man I had cut in spring training and that he didn't want me to get the record until he got back?

Well, not only did we recall Ron in mid-May, but now the "Creature" will pitch on the night when I might get hit No. 4,192.

Robinson probably won't be able to sleep tonight.

TUESDAY, SEPTEMBER 10.............. ROSE 0 FOR 4

Tonight was going to be the night —but I didn't get the big knock. I went 0 for 4.

Worse yet, the Padres beat us, 3-2, and the Dodgers moved 9½ games ahead of us by sweeping a double-header from Atlanta.

We had a crowd of 51,045 at Riverfront Stadium and I guess I disappointed a lot of people who wanted to see me break the record.

Besides our fans, Commissioner Peter Ueberroth was here. So was National League President Chub Feeney. And, of course, there was all the media.

I really thought I would get it tonight, but I swung the bat good only once—in the eighth inning, when I lined out to left fielder Carmelo Martinez on a 1-0 pitch from San Diego's second pitcher, a rookie named Lance McCullers. McCullers was throwing a lot harder than the Padres' starter, LaMarr Hoyt (who, coming off shoulder problems, was making his first start since August 18).

I was really bearing down in the eighth because that was an important situation. There was one out and we had the tying run on second.

The other three times up, all against Hoyt, I might have been a little overanxious. I went for some pitches I shouldn't have.

My first time up, the count went to 3-1 and I should have taken the walk. I kept saying to myself, "You've got to be patient."

But, I swung at "ball four"—the pitch was up—and I popped to shortstop Garry Templeton.

In the fourth, I flied out to left field on the first pitch. And on a 2-1 pitch in the sixth, I again popped out to Templeton at short.

Hoyt told reporters pretty much what I would have guessed.

"I gave him some good pitches to hit," said Hoyt, the first of three straight righthanded Padre starters we'll be facing (lefthander Dave Dravecky opened the series for San Diego), "and he didn't swing at them. Then, he swung at some bad ones."

★ ★ ★

When I got back to the house tonight, I kept thinking that situation in the eighth inning was a perfect time for a double. Knock in the tying run and have the crowd get all involved.

I'll tell you one thing, I just can't picture myself going 0 for 4 tomorrow night. No way.

San Diego	ab	r	h	rbi	Cincinnati	ab	r	h	rbi
Templeton, ss	5	1	4	1	Milner, cf	3	0	0	0
Gwynn, rf	5	1	2	0	Rose, 1b	4	0	0	0
Garvey, 1b	3	0	1	1	Parker, rf	4	0	2	0
Nettles, 3b	4	0	0	1	Esasky, lf	4	1	0	0
Bochy, c	4	0	0	0	Bell, 3b	4	1	1	2
Martinez, lf	4	0	0	0	C'cepcion, ss	4	0	0	0
McR'nolds, cf	4	0	0	0	Diaz, c	3	0	0	0
Flannery, 2b	4	1	2	0	Oester, 2b	3	0	1	0
Hoyt, p	2	0	0	0	Robinson, p	1	0	1	0
Bumbry, ph	0	0	0	0	Franco, p	0	0	0	0
McCullers, p	0	0	0	0	Venable, ph	1	0	1	0
Lefferts, p	0	0	0	0	Power, p	0	0	0	0
Brown, ph	1	0	0	0					
Gossage, p	0	0	0	0					
Totals	36	3	9	3	Totals	31	2	6	2

San Diego.....................2 0 0 0 0 0 1 0 0—3
Cincinnati.....................0 0 0 2 0 0 0 0 0—2

San Diego	IP.	H.	R.	ER.	BB.	SO.
Hoyt (W. 14-8)	6	5	2	2	0	2
McCullers	1⅔	1	0	0	0	2
Lefferts	⅓	0	0	0	0	0
Gossage (Save 22)	1	0	0	0	0	1
Cincinnati	IP.	H.	R.	ER.	BB.	SO.
Robinson (L. 5-5)	6⅓	7	3	3	2	1
Franco	1⅔	0	0	0	1	1
Power	1	2	0	0	0	0

Game-winning RBI—Templeton. E—Diaz, Concepcion. LOB—San Diego 9, Cincinnati 4. 2B—Templeton, Parker. HR—Bell (4). SH—Robinson, Milner. WP—Franco. T—2:11. A—51,045.

San Diego	ab	r	h	rbi	Cincinnati	ab	r	h	rbi
Templeton, ss	4	0	0	0	Milner, cf	5	0	0	0
Royster, 2b	4	0	1	0	**Rose, 1b**	3	2	2	0
Gwynn, rf	4	0	1	0	Parker, rf	1	0	1	0
Garvey, 1b	4	0	0	0	Esasky, lf	3	0	0	2
Martinez, lf	3	0	0	0	Venable, lf	0	0	0	0
McR'nolds, cf	3	0	1	0	Bell, 3b	4	0	1	0
Bochy, c	3	0	1	0	C'cepcion, ss	4	0	1	0
Bevacqua, 3b	3	0	1	0	Diaz, c	3	0	1	0
Show, p	2	0	0	0	Redus, pr	0	0	0	0
Davis, ph	1	0	0	0	Van Gorder, c	0	0	0	0
Jackson, p	0	0	0	0	Oester, 2b	3	0	1	0
Walter, p	0	0	0	0	Browning, p	4	0	1	0
					Franco, p	0	0	0	0
					Power, p	0	0	0	0
Totals	31	0	5	0	Totals	30	2	8	2

```
San Diego.......................0 0 0   0 0 0   0 0 0—0
Cincinnati......................0 0 1   0 0 0   1 0 x—2
```

San Diego	IP.	H.	R.	ER.	BB.	SO.
Show (L. 9-10)...........	7	7	2	2	5	1
Jackson......................	⅓	1	0	0	1	0
Walter........................	⅔	0	0	0	0	2

Cincinnati	IP.	H.	R.	ER.	BB.	SO.
Browning (W. 16-9)...	8⅓	5	0	0	0	6
Franco......................	⅓	0	0	0	0	0
Power (Save 20)........	⅓	0	0	0	0	0

Game-winning RBI—Esasky.
E—Show. DP—San Diego 1, Cincinnati 1. LOB—San Diego 4, Cincinnati 11. 2B—Browning, Diaz, Bell. 3B—**Rose.** SB—Gwynn. SF—Esasky. T—2:17. A—47,237.

I got the big knock (hit No. 4,192) tonight—a single off San Diego's Eric Show in the first inning. The Cobb record is mine.

I also got a triple and a walk and scored both of our runs as we beat the Padres, 2-0. I ended the game by making a diving stop on a Steve Garvey grounder. The whole thing was like a movie script.

I picked out a different bat tonight, one that was a little lighter. I was whipping it pretty good in batting practice and decided to go with it.

After Eddie Milner fouled out in the first inning, I came up. I looked up at the clock and it was almost 8 o'clock.

Show's first pitch was a ball. I fouled off the next one and he came back with something inside, making the count 2-1.

Show then threw a slider and I lined it to left-center. It was 8:01 p.m.

I don't have enough paper to talk about the vibrations that the 47,237 fans put through my body.

I can't describe my emotions because I couldn't control them after I got to first base. I would have been all right if the fans hadn't kept cheering for so long (seven minutes).

When you're out there (on first base) and don't have anything to do, you start thinking about what has happened in your life and what led to everything. A lot of history went through my mind.

Obviously, my relationship with my father was foremost. I fought it off (breaking into tears) a couple of times. I thought about all the times he was sitting up there in the stands watching the games. I thought about the times when I was a little boy and he took me to Crosley Field.

I started thinking about people I wished were here but weren't—my father; my Little League coach, Red Grothaus; my uncle Buddy (Bloebaum), who got me my first contract with Cincinnati; and my first manager in the major leagues, Fred Hutchinson. They've all passed away.

Everything they taught me to do and taught me to work for, I've accomplished. And none of them was here to see it. You don't think about that at first. You think about the fans' response. But when you stand on first base for so long, things add up.

At first, I wiped a few tears away, then I couldn't control them. Tommy Helms (first-base coach) was the only one close by and I embraced him. Then my son Petey came out.

I'm glad Petey came out because I needed a crutch about then.

Petey didn't say a word, but I said: "Don't worry about this, son, you'll beat my record." He kept everything back—he didn't cry.

I'm glad I have the record. I'm also happy it was a well-played game —and that we won.

Enthusiasm and Desire Helped Rose Blossom Into a Superstar

Pete Rose, a puzzled look coming over his face, thought about the question for several seconds.

"First time I heard Ty Cobb's name mentioned?" he said, repeating the question. "I don't know. Maybe when I was a kid, but I don't know. My dad and I used to talk about great baseball players and Ty Cobb's name probably came up. I just don't know."

Rose says he often talked about Cobb with the late Waite Hoyt, a Hall of Famer and Cobb playing contemporary (for about a decade) who used to broadcast Cincinnati Reds games.

"That was much later," Rose said. "Waite told me Cobb was the meanest man he ever met in a fight. Cobb was a great hitter, but the thing that's always surprised me is I don't ever remember reading much about his defensive ability. I know other players like me a little bit better than they liked Cobb."

In 23 big-league seasons, Rose has become one of America's most prominent and respected professional athletes. When he shattered Cobb's major league career hits record of 4,191, the calendar said he was 44 years old. In reality, he was 44 going on 16—or 12.

When Peter Edward Rose first became a professional baseball player in 1960, people didn't believe he was for real. Brash and cocky, Rose possessed a contagious enthusiasm for the game. He ran out walks, never stopped talking and hustled his way through every task that confronted him.

A quarter century later, he has not changed. And people still question if he's for real.

A man 44 still wearing knickers and sliding on his belly?

Rose, in fact, is a champion to millions of middle-aged fantasizers throughout America. Years ago he gave up the boyish crew cut and, yes, there are more inches around the middle and the hair is graying, but Pete Rose is still Pete Rose.

"At times, he's a little boy," said Rose's wife, Carol. "There's a serious side to him, but he refuses to let anything depress him. No matter what the situation, he manages to keep his spirits high. He likes people around him to be happy. When he's with our little boy, Tyler, you wouldn't believe he's the same Pete Rose you see on the baseball field."

Pete Rose has always been fascinated by numbers and by competition. He says they go hand in hand, but without consistency they are meaningless.

"Most longevity records are hard to break," Rose said. "Players don't think about playing that long—Cobb got his 4,191 hits in 24 seasons. He retired in 1928. It took me 23 seasons. Owners don't want to pay players that long now. I think it will be pretty hard to break my record."

Rose's record is a tribute to longevity, determination, hustle and the fun of playing a game that no longer is enjoyed that much by many of its briefcase-carrying participants.

"Peter has never stopped being a little boy at heart," said his mother, LaVerne Noeth, 70. "His father was just like that. He played semipro football until he was in his 40s and if I hadn't threatened him with divorce, he probably would have played even longer."

Pete's beloved and macho father, Harry Francis Rose, died 15 years ago.

Rose's mother, whose second husband, Robert Noeth, died in 1984, refers to the father as Pete, the son as Peter.

LaVerne and Harry had four children—Caryl, now 48; Jackie, 46; Pete, 44, and Dave, 36. The family lived on Braddock Street in Cincinnati, on a hill overlooking Anderson Ferry and the Ohio River. Jackie recently remodeled the house and lives there now.

"Peter's father always stressed consistency," Rose's mother said. "I remember when Peter was a little boy. He would get four hits and come up to his father, obviously proud. I would be waiting in the car and want to cry. Each night before Peter would go to sleep, his dad would make him swing a bat nearly 100 times, first from the right side and then from the left side.

"His father is the reason he has been such a great player. He just kept pushing him, but at the same time he made playing sports fun. I know that is why Peter has maintained the enthusiasm all these years. And he is teaching his son, Petey, the same way."

If Rose had decided to take up the piano, he would have been good because, above everything else, he believes in practice.

"You have to have fun at what you do to get the most out of it," Rose said. "The way you become good at anything is to practice. My father taught me how to practice and to have fun. That's why I still go to the ball park so early, that's why I have so much fun taking extra batting practice. But the one thing I learned at an early age was to practice the things you are not good at. Not many people do that. If you're weak at

After going to spring training as a non-roster player in 1963 and making the Reds' roster, Rose introduced his father Harry (left) to Manager Fred Hutchinson (right).

fielding, you should take ground balls. If you're weak at hitting, you should practice hitting. Most people practice what they do best."

Pete's mother says he was only 2 years old when his father, a banker, bought him a glove, bat and ball.

"They went out in the backyard and from that time on, Peter loved sports," she said. "His dad would be tired from working all day at the bank, but Peter would beg him to play with him and he did. While he was young, he was a mama's boy, but as he got older he spent all his time with his father. Most boys his age were interested in other things as they were growing up. Not Peter. All he cared about was sports.

"He didn't go to dances and other things at school. He didn't even like girls. I'll tell you something else, though, he was a spoiled brat, a little stinker. He never got in trouble, but always got his own way except with his father."

Rose was driven by his father, but their relationship was the ultimate.

On December 8, 1970, Pete's father left work early because he was ill. When he entered the house above the river, he started up the steps to the second floor, but fell forward. He was dead of a blood clot in the heart.

People in Cincinnati still say it was the most devastating blow Rose has suffered. After the funeral, Pete would drive to the house to pick up his mother, nicknamed Rosey, but refused to enter the house.

"The only time I can remember crying after I grew up was when my dad died," Pete said.

Rose was not a good student. His marks were not high enough for him to pass his sophomore year at Western Hills High School in Cincinnati. Officials asked him to go to summer school, but his father wouldn't have it. "No," said Harry Rose. "If you do that, you won't be able to devote the whole summer to baseball."

So he made Pete repeat the 10th grade.

Rose was a second baseman with the Tampa Tarpons of the Florida State League in 1961.

"My father was in the Cincinnati Reds clubhouse only once," Rose said. "That was a day when he posed for a picture with me for Sports Illustrated. And the only time he would wait for me outside the clubhouse was when he wanted to have me meet someone—or chew me out.

"He was a great football player. He had poor eyes because of all the detail work he had to do at the bank, but he was excellent. He was a tough man. He had more guts than any two guys I've ever known. He played until he was 42.

"He was mild-mannered, a nicer man than I am. I have done some things he would not be too proud of. There are three things in my life I never saw: I never saw my dad smoke, take a drink of hard liquor or argue with my mom.

"But my dad got to see me win batting titles, play in All-Star Games and in the World Series. I think I repaid him.

"He was always pushing me. He was never satisfied with what I achieved. He is the reason I always give 110 percent. He is the reason I run as hard as I can to first base. He would never let me ease up. He once called me aside and said, 'Peter, you always have to give 110 percent. The guy you're playing against, see, may be giving 100 percent. So, if you're just giving 100 percent, too, no one will win.' "

Rose played his final minor-league season in 1962 for Macon of the Sally League.

Pete said he always felt like he had something to prove.

"I used to walk around the streets of Cincinnati and people would come up to me and say, 'You'll never be half the athlete your father was.' It used to hurt, but it made me determined. Now, they come up to me and say, 'You're your father all over again.'"

Dave Bristol, a former Reds manager (1966-69), says he has never known a young man more influenced by a parent.

"Pete never hesitated to voice his affection for the man who took him by the hand and virtually led him to the major leagues," Bristol said.

Although Rose says football was equally important to him in high school, his father always dreamed of the day his son would play for the hometown Reds. They'd go to Crosley Field (longtime home of the Reds) together, sit in the bleachers, and talk about the intricacies of baseball.

"It started when I was about 6," said Pete, reflecting on his father's desire to see him play in the majors. "And believe me, I couldn't have done it without him. He was always there when I needed his guidance and support. One of the first things he ever said that impressed me was, 'If you don't win, you haven't accomplished anything.'

"Even when my dad went to work at the bank, he never walked when he could run. I'm grateful his hustle rubbed off on me."

Skeptics said young Pete would never make the majors. He was too small and lacked natural ability.

"Everybody on my father's side of the family matured late," Pete said. "My dad was only 150 pounds when he was 20 and I was only 155 when I was 19. Nobody was much interested in signing me, but I wanted to play for the Reds. I grew up in Cincinnati, so my uncle, Buddy Bloebaum—he was my mom's brother and a bird-dog scout for the Reds—talked them into signing me because he knew I would mature. He's dead now—he died two years after my father. He was a good minor league player, especially after he learned to switch-hit. He told my father I should learn the same thing, so that's why I had to swing the lead-weighted bat every night. That also helped build up my arms and chest.

"I'd start out (swinging) 10 times each way, righthanded and lefthanded. I'd increase the number until I got to say 20 swings, then start all over again at 10. That's what made my arms big and helped me get the bat out in front all the time."

Rose had an offer to attend the University of Tennessee on a football scholarship when he finished at Western Hills, but his father and Bloebaum wanted him to play for the Reds.

"We went to Crosley Field to talk to Phil Seghi, who was the farm director at the time," Pete said. "They gave me $7,000 as a signing bonus and set it up so I got another $5,000 if I went on the major league roster and lasted 30 days. There was no time limit on that—any year I made it and lasted 30 days, I got the extra $5,000."

The signing was in 1960.

Rose batted .277 for Geneva, N.Y., of the New York-Penn League that first summer, then hit .331 at Tampa of the Florida State League in 1961. His 30 triples for Tampa led the league.

"I was making $400 a month that year ('61) and I owned two pairs of pants and three pairs of socks," he said. "But those were the good ol' days. We won the league championship and the owner wanted to do something for us. He bought us all Zippo lighters. And I don't smoke!"

With Macon of the Sally League in 1962, Rose hit .330, and in the Florida Instructional League that fall he impressed the late Fred Hutchinson, who was the Reds' manager.

During the winter, Hutchinson kept telling people that if he had any guts he'd stick Rose on second base in 1963 and forget about him.

The incumbent second baseman was Don Blasingame, a Cincinnati favorite and a starter for the Reds' 1961 National League champions.

In March of '63, not yet 22 and with just 2½ seasons of professional experience, Rose found himself in the Reds' spring-training camp at Tampa. He was not on the major league roster, however.

But on a steamy-hot Sunday afternoon at Al Lopez Field, Rose stood out against the Chicago White Sox in a game he wasn't even supposed to play. With that performance, he was on his way to the majors.

"I wasn't on the game roster that day and I could have gone home if I had wanted," Rose recalled. "Mike Ryba, who was managing in the Reds' system then, suggested I stick around."

As the day progressed, Hutchinson inserted Pete as a pinch-runner and kept him in the game. The Reds won in extra innings, with Rose contributing two doubles.

"That got me to the big leagues," Rose said. "Hutch gave me another chance to play and I got some hits."

Later in the spring, the Reds were playing the New York Yankees. In his first at-bat, Pete drew a walk. And as he has done since he was 9 years old, he dashed to first base.

Yankee stars Whitey Ford and Mickey Mantle began riding Rose, yelling, "Hey, you, Charlie Hustle." Reporters heard the remark and the nickname stuck.

"In those days, clubs barnstormed north and I was still with the team (despite being on a minor league roster) when we played in Indianapolis the day before the National League opener," Pete recalled. "Three hours before the game the next day, I signed a major league contract for $7,000 and I thought I was a millionaire." And by July 1, Blasingame had been sold to the Washington Senators.

Pete, 0 for 11 in his first three big-league games, got his first hit in the

The Pete Rose look (left), which has changed considerably in recent years, originated in 1963, Rose's rookie season. By 1970, Cincinnati's Big Red Machine was taking form with a cast that included (below, right to left) Manager Sparky Anderson, Rose, Bobby Tolan, Tony Perez, Johnny Bench, Lee May, Bernie Carbo, Tommy Helms and Woody Woodward.

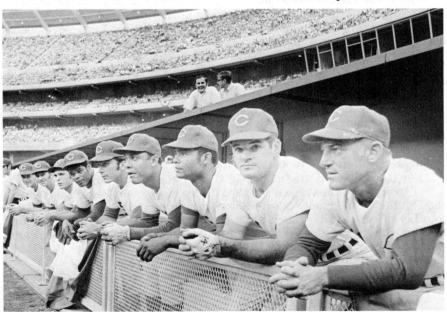

majors on April 13, 1963, a triple off Pittsburgh's Bob Friend. It was the first of 170 hits for Rose that season, a year in which he batted .273 and was named the National League's Rookie of the Year.

Rose's first 16 years in the majors were spent with the Reds, with whom he played in four World Series, including what might be the most exciting Series of all time—Cincinnati's dramatic seven-game victory over Boston in 1975. In that Series, Rose was voted the Most Valuable Player.

He won National League batting titles in 1968, 1969 and 1973. He was the N.L.'s MVP in 1973, and in 1978 he helped provide baseball with one of its most exciting seasons.

On May 5, 1978, Rose singled off Montreal's Steve Rogers for his 3,000th major league hit. Then, from June 14 through July 31, he established a modern National League record by hitting in 44 consecutive games. Atlanta's Larry McWilliams and Gene Garber ended that streak on August 1.

Sadly for Reds fans, 1978 appeared to be Rose's last season with Cincinnati. After failing to reach an agreement on a new contract with the Reds, Rose became baseball's most celebrated free agent of that time before signing with the Philadelphia Phillies.

Ironically, the Reds fired Sparky Anderson, who had managed the club to World Series titles in 1975 and 1976, a week before Rose joined the Phils.

Anderson has fond memories of his years (1970-1978) with Rose.

"I'll tell you one thing," said Anderson, who guided the Detroit Tigers to a World Series championship in 1984, "he took the very least amount of ability and he's going to walk into the Hall of Fame on the first ballot. If that isn't a credit to a human being, I don't know what is.

"He's not like some of the guys who had great ability and never made a major league team. They had ability, but not the heart and the guts.

"I was with the guy for nine years and I can say this without any doubt in my mind. He is the greatest single competitor I have ever been associated with in my life. Pete Rose will kill you. Oh, I don't mean he will hurt somebody, but he goes out there with one thing on his mind—to beat you. You can't ask for anymore than that. That's what this game is all about."

Rose insists that without Anderson, the Reds would not have attained the levels they did in the mid-1970s.

"Sure, we had a great team," Pete said, "but Sparky wasn't the only manager in the 1970s to have great players. We had great players, but he knew how to handle them. He's a communicator and keeps his players happy. He's got great rapport. He's like a psychologist."

For Rose, leaving the Reds after the '78 season was not easy.

"I took a lot of heat from the fans for leaving," said Rose, who helped the Phillies to their only World Series crown in 1980. "It's amazing the number of people who called me a traitor—they called my kids traitors in school. Here's a guy who slid on his belly for 16 years for them and played just as hard as he could for them and all of a sudden the Reds decided they didn't want him anymore and he's the villain.

"But how can one guy, even Pete Rose, take on an organization like the Cincinnati Reds? No way."

While with the Reds, Rose had hit .300 or higher 13 times, won three batting titles, made 12 All-Star teams, compiled nine 200-hit seasons, put together the electrifying 44-game hitting streak and collected 3,164 career hits.

But the conservative Reds, who were paying Rose $370,000 a year, refused to give him $450,000 for two or three years, so Pete—who would turn 38 soon after the opening of the '79 season—went the free-agent route. He was chosen by 13 teams in the re-entry draft of November 3, 1978, then admittedly was shocked at how much some of baseball's richest owners were willing to pay for his services.

Little did Rose know that within six years he would be back with the Reds as their player-manager, charged with pumping new life and spirit into what had become a troubled franchise.

At the time, though, there was some bitterness—and hurt.

"I used to sit and wonder why Dick Wagner (then the Reds' president) didn't like me because I know one thing about Dick Wagner: He likes gamers. He likes people who work hard, and he likes people who play every day. Now, sure I did some things off the field he didn't like, but he did things I didn't like.

"One thing is for sure. When I was on the field, I produced. And from that standpoint, I didn't quite understand. I did anything the Reds ever asked me to do. Go here, promote 'em here, go there, go to the Caribbean —anything the Reds wanted me to do, I did. I guess that was just their way of saying thanks. Thanks, but no thanks.

"From what I understand, they did the same thing to Joe Morgan— just forced him out (after the 1979 season). They didn't give him a contract; they didn't even draft him. At least they drafted me. I was the first free agent they ever drafted. Wagner did a lot of things that just didn't make sense at the time, but that's all water over the dam now. I'm back here and I'm happy."

From the Reds' standpoint, of course, you could have argued that Rose, at 37, and Morgan, at 36, quite possibly were near the end of the line, productivitywise. However, Rose is still going strong in 1985 and Morgan, a key player for Philadelphia in its '83 stretch drive to the N.L. East title, played in the majors through '84.

"I guess what disappointed me most about leaving the Reds then," Rose said upon further reflection, "was the fact I never had an opportunity to talk to the team's owners at the time, Mr. and Mrs. (Louis) Nippert. They are really nice people, down-to-earth people. It didn't make sense to me people that smart and that rich could let something like that happen without ever saying yes or no . . . or, wait a minute, we'd better talk. They just gave Dick Wagner all the authority."

Rose told friends how much he wanted to play in Philadelphia, but when the bidding war started, it seemed unlikely the Phillies would be able to compete with the likes of Atlanta's Ted Turner, Kansas City's Ewing Kauffman, Pittsburgh's John Galbreath or St. Louis' August Busch.

Just when it appeared the Phillies were out of the sweepstakes, some behind-the-scenes wheeling and dealing, a $600,000 commitment from a television station and Rose's desire to remain in the National League to pursue numerous records turned the tide.

The contract the Phils worked out was one of the least-complicated ever given a superstar. It paid Pete $905,000 in 1979, $805,000 in 1980,

$705,000 in 1981 and $810,000 in 1982.

The background to Rose's leaving Cincinnati is intriguing, as are the circumstances around his return.

Relations between Rose and Wagner became strained as early as 1977 when Pete signed a two-year contract for $370,000 per season.

In the spring of 1978, Reuven Katz, Rose's longtime friend and attorney, who incidentally has always been a Cincinnati Reds fan, approached Wagner and said he thought it would be fitting to work out an agreement guaranteeing that Rose would end his career in Cincinnati. On May 21 of that year, the Reds would honor Pete for becoming the 13th player in major league history to achieve 3,000 hits. Katz thought it would be a coup to announce a new contract that day and he suggested a non-guaranteed agreement of about $400,000 a season for two or three years.

"It could have lasted as long as the Reds wanted it to," Katz remembered. "If, in management's opinion, Pete failed to make the team some spring, he could be dropped and not owed any extra money."

Wagner refused to consider the proposal. After the season, Rose was offered approximately $450,000 for two years. Earlier in the year, he would have taken it and remained in Cincinnati. But after the 44-game hitting streak and with hints of what Pete might get as a free agent, the contract was turned down.

There was some casual negotiation after that, but little movement by the Reds. Before the re-entry draft, letters were written to some teams, advising them not to draft Rose because he had no intentions of playing for them.

Soon after, the Reds made a goodwill tour of Japan.

Rose returned the day before Thanksgiving and had his final session with the Reds. Then, on the morning of November 27, he started the barnstorming that would take him to Atlanta, St. Louis, Kansas City and Philadelphia.

As Rose and Katz prepared to board a plane that Monday morning, the attorney turned to Pete and said: "Get ready for the most exciting week of your life."

Atlanta was first.

The flamboyant Turner offered Rose $1 million a year for four years and $100,000 a year for the rest of his life.

"All I want to do is keep you here a couple of years until the Reds get rid of Dick Wagner so you can return to Cincinnati where you belong," Turner said.

After Atlanta, there were stops in Kansas City and St. Louis on the same day.

Although the Kansas City offer was not the most exotic, it was the one Rose almost chose over Philadelphia's.

"I'll give you a four-year contract with options for the fifth and sixth years," Kauffman said. "I know your dad played football until he was over 40 and I know you have a shot at Ty Cobb's hits record. I'd like to see you get it in a Kansas City uniform."

The Kansas City salary figure was slightly less than what the Braves offered but, with certain clauses, would have pushed the total to $1 million a year. In addition, Kauffman offered Rose some investment opportunities.

Rose and Katz visited Busch in a St. Louis hospital where the Cardinals owner was to have surgery the next morning. Busch's yearly salary offer was less than the previous two, but Pete was invited to work for Anheuser-Busch as a spokesman for the brewery and, after his career ended, he would get his own beer distributorship.

The Pirates' offer was less than the first three, about $400,000 a season, but Galbreath, who owns Darby Dan Farm, knew Rose loved horse racing and tried to entice him that way. He offered to set up Rose in the horse-breeding business. Pete would receive two brood mares and the stud service of the Darby Dan Farm's top stallions.

"It could have been the best offer," Rose said, "but I would have had to wait too long to see what would happen. If I had been a millionaire, I might have taken it."

The final stop was Philadelphia, and everyone thought Rose would climax his whirlwind week by signing with the Phillies. Instead, a news conference was called to announce that the Phils were out of the running.

"It was crazy," Pete said. "I felt sick. I wanted to play for the Phillies all along, but their offer was $2 million less than the Kansas City and Atlanta offers. I was willing to take less money to play with them, but not that much less."

Phillies President Bill Giles, club vice president at the time, devised the creative financing of a new Rose contract package, with the television station kicking in what amounted to at least $600,000.

The Phillies' new offer was made on the morning of December 3, 1978.

"I wasn't dead set on the National League," Rose said, "but when the offers got to where they were pretty close in dollars, I wondered if it was worth taking the difference and giving up a shot at Stan Musial's all-time National League hits record of 3,630."

Two days later, he signed with the Phillies. And the relationship was excellent—until 1983.

Rose, more than anyone else, taught the Phillies how to win. They defeated Houston in the 1980 N.L. Championship Series en route to their World Series conquest of Kansas City. And the Phils beat Los Angeles in the 1983 playoffs before losing to Baltimore in the World Series.

To Rose, winning the '80 World Series and parading down Broad Street the following day were his most memorable moments in Philadelphia.

But June and August nights in 1981 were more meaningful, especially to baseball historians.

On June 10, 1981, at Veterans Stadium against Houston's hard-throwing Nolan Ryan, Rose singled in his first at-bat for hit No. 3,630. Righthander Ryan struck out Pete in his next three times up.

Rose then had to wait two months to break Musial's 18-year-old record because the 50-day players' strike interrupted the season.

Play was resumed on the night of August 10. Rose went after the record against St. Louis at Veterans Stadium, with 60,561 fans hoping to see history made.

The first three times up, Rose failed.

The chants and cheers so prevalent early in the game were not as loud or as enthusiastic when Rose came to the plate leading off the bottom of the eighth inning. Mark Littell's first pitch was over the heart of the plate. Rose took a deep breath, patted his fire-engine-red helmet and took a couple of practice swings before Littell's next delivery.

Littell fired an inside fastball. Rose swung hard. The ball shot between third baseman Ken Oberkfell and shortstop Garry Templeton and bounced into left field. The waiting was over. Rose had become the most prolific hit-maker in National League history.

As 3,631 colored balloons climbed above the south Philadelphia stadium and fireworks scorched the humid night's sky, Musial loped from his box seat to first base to congratulate Rose. Musial, who had retired after the 1963 season with 3,630 hits, was beaten to first by young Petey Rose, who was serving as batboy for the historic occasion.

"I told Petey when I went to the plate I felt like I was going to get a hit," Rose said. "When I took the weight off my bat, I handed it to him. He was feeling down a little. He said, 'If you don't get it tonight, you'll get it tomorrow.'

"I said to him, 'Watch this time. I'm gonna get the hit.' I was just trying to pick his spirits up, like my dad used to do for me. He's just a little boy and worries a lot about things like this.

"Earlier, I didn't feel I had much pop in my bat. I had driven my new car back from the All-Star Game in Cleveland the previous night and it took over eight hours. I didn't think it would tire me out, but maybe it did. Then, I forgot that some men were coming to work on the den in my new townhouse. I didn't get much sleep at all.

"So, in the eighth, I took a lighter bat up there because I wasn't swinging the heavy one very well. . . ."

Rose collected his historic hit at 10:34 p.m. At 10:47, after Rose had scored (the Phils had a two-run inning but lost, 7-3), the fans were still caught up in the emotional moment. The chanting continued and did not stop until Pete came out of the dugout and waved a white towel to the fans.

"Petey was the first one out there to first base," Rose said, "and I was surprised at that. He said, 'Nice going, Pop.' And I gave him the ball. So it worked out nice. I got goose bumps listening to the fans yelling my name.

"I thought about a lot of things at that moment. I thought back to 1963 when I played against Stan Musial in his final game. I never dreamed that one day I would be getting a hit in 1981 to break his record. I sat on the dugout step with Fred Hutchinson (in '63) and he told me to pay close attention at Musial. He told me I was watching history being made."

There was supposed to be the traditional congratulatory call from the President of the United States during the postgame news conference, but this turned into one of baseball's most hilarious moments.

As the enormous media mob gathered around Rose in an interview room, a red telephone on the podium rang. President Ronald Reagan was calling.

In fact, Reagan called three times before he finally got through.

Each time Rose picked up the phone and each time an unidentified voice asked who was speaking.

"It's a good thing it isn't a missile on the way," Rose quipped after the second call failed.

Another time, he said: "We can put a man on the moon, but I can't get

Rose posed for photographers in 1978 with Tommy Holmes, who formerly held the modern National League consecutive-game hitting streak record. Pete had just hit in his 38th straight game to break Holmes' mark en route to his 44-game streak.

a call from President Reagan."

Again, the phone rang.

"Hello," Reagan said.

"Hello," Rose responded.

"Pete Rose?"

"Yes, sir!"

"This is Ronald Reagan."

"How you doing?" Rose asked as the media crowd broke up.

"I don't know," Reagan said. "I'll tell you, I've had trouble getting this line. I think I had to wait longer than you did to break the record."

"We were going to give you five more minutes and that was it," Rose cracked.

Said Reagan: "We've been having some trouble here getting through and I just wanted to call and congratulate you. I know how you must feel and it's great."

Said Rose: "Well, thank you very much. I know you are a baseball fan and we appreciate your taking time out to call us here in Philadelphia. I know all the fans appreciate it and Pete Rose the 2nd appreciates it, too."

Said Reagan: "I can tell you, you are right about my being a fan and as a matter of fact, I was a sports announcer broadcasting major league baseball long before I ever (laughter from the President) . . . I ever had any kind of job like I have now. But this is really a thrill and I know how everyone must feel about it after the long dry spell waiting for the season to get back under way. You've really brought it back in style."

Rose hung up the phone, cracked a joke, then said he was going to think about Ty Cobb's all-time record of 4,191 hits.

"People are worried I may not have a chance to break that because I missed 55 games during the strike," Pete said. "Well, if I get that close, I think I will find a way to get it. I'm not going to think back and worry about the strike. After all, I could have missed 55 games with an injury."

Several hours after the game, Rose was still discussing the events of the night.

"When I got to first base, Keith Hernandez (St. Louis first baseman) said something to me," Pete mused. "I told him, 'This is something, isn't it?' And he said, 'Yeah, it's great, but it should have happened in Cincinnati.' He said he couldn't believe the Reds let me leave that town. But these people in Philadelphia have done more for me than I could ever expect. That's why I tried to acknowledge all of them. It was the most awesome thing that has ever happened to me individually."

Rose's first four years in Philadelphia were a success for both the Phillies and the veteran player.

After playing second base, the outfield and third base for the Reds, Rose made himself one of the best first basemen in the majors with the Phillies.

In '79, although the Phillies failed to win the East Division for the first time in four years, Rose batted .331 and collected 200 or more hits for a record 10th time.

He showed teammates how to rise above personal problems by hitting in 23 straight games after Karolyn, his wife of 15 years, filed for divorce.

He admitted that not being able to spend as much time with Petey and daughter Fawn bothered him, but that once in uniform he could not let those things affect his play.

"My philosophy has always been if I have problems off the field, why should I kick that onto the fans?" he reasoned. "Why should I kick that onto my teammates? Success eliminates a lot of problems. You understand what I mean? If you're having problems somewhere and you're hitting .220, you've got a lot of problems. But if you're hitting .300 and playing well, you don't have as many problems. It's like a singer. If he has a problem and has a million-dollar record on his hands, it's a lot easier to have the problems."

During Rose's tenure in Philadelphia, he convinced All-Star third baseman Mike Schmidt he could become the National League's MVP. Schmidt won the award twice.

When Rose signed with the Phillies, he was given a four-year contract, with the club holding an option for the fifth year.

In the spring of 1982, Katz began negotiations with Giles on an extension (which also led to a boost in salary for Rose in '82). In April, an agreement was signed that was interpreted as a lifetime contract. Rose received $1.1 million in '82 and $1.2 million in 1983 (with a similar sched-

Though Rose is known for his intensity, he seldom has been in-volved in open warfare. One such occasion occurred in Game 3 of the 1973 National League Championship Series when his hard slide at second base upset Mets shortstop Bud Harrelson and resulted in a fight.

ule for the remaining years).

The Phillies, however, built in an escape clause. They had to renew the contract by November 1 each year, or buy it out for an additional $500,000.

And the Phils exercised their option after the 1983 season, giving Rose his release.

But 1983 became a disaster of sorts long before the farewell.

Five days before spring training ended at Clearwater, Fla., in '83, Manager Pat Corrales and General Manager Paul Owens summoned Pete for a closed-door meeting.

They asked him if he would play right field because recently signed free agent Tony Perez, a former Rose teammate in Cincinnati, was swinging a hot bat and would add to the offense if inserted into the lineup at first base.

Being the ultimate team player, Rose agreed.

Privately, Pete knew it wasn't the best decision for him. When he returned to his spring-training residence that day, he was worried. And for several weeks after that, his right shoulder and arm ached so much from all the practice throws he was making from right field that he couldn't sleep at night.

With the Reds, Rose had been an outstanding second baseman before moving to the outfield, where he played almost flawlessly in right and left. When Anderson wanted to put George Foster in left field and asked Pete to take over at third base, Rose agreed. That single move—which made Foster an everyday player—proved crucial in the Reds' emergence as one of baseball's all-time great teams.

First base was logical in Philadelphia, and it was a position Pete hoped he would play for the rest of his career.

Although Rose will never admit it publicly, moving to right field for Philadelphia was a difficult adjustment.

The Phillies were quick to point out that without Perez in the lineup in the early going, they might not have won the '83 N.L. East title. Perez drove in 23 runs in Philadelphia's first 26 games.

During the early weeks of the season, Pete shuffled between first base and right field, not knowing where he'd be playing from day to day.

Later, when his batting average stayed below .250, Rose became a part-time player. For the first time in his storybook career, he went to the park each day not knowing his status.

Late one night during a drive from New York's Shea Stadium to Philadelphia, Rose shed his macho shield. He was depressed.

"For the first time in my life I've lost some of my confidence," he said. "You know when MY confidence is messed up, something's wrong."

For most of September, Rose sat on the bench and watched Len Matuszek, a major contributor in the Phillies' divisional title run, play first base. Perez had gone into a prolonged slump weeks earlier and was used mostly as a pinch-hitter.

When the Phillies clinched their fifth division championship in eight years on September 28, Rose, the man who repeatedly had shown the way for Phils, was not in the lineup.

The toughest moment came in the 1983 World Series.

With the Series against Baltimore tied at a game apiece, Pete was benched for Game 3. It was the most embarrassing episode of his career.

The Phillies no longer needed Pete Rose. The door was slammed shut. The Orioles won Games 3, 4 and 5, sewing up the Series crown. (Pete was back in the lineup, however, for Games 4 and 5.)

Rose, appearing in his sixth postseason classic, had never watched a World Series game from the bench. Petey had flown in from Cincinnati and arrived at Veterans Stadium for Game 3 a few minutes after Owens, who had replaced Corrales as manager in mid-July, broke the news to Pete.

Rose always has had a way of reaching back for something extra in important games—and that made the sit-down all the harder to take.

"I thought about all that," Rose said. "I was cool. I went back into the Pope's (Owens') office and told him I had batted against Mike Flanagan (Baltimore's starter in Game 3) in three different spring-training games. I had gotten some hits off him.

"I learned one thing. The manager doesn't have to give you a reason why you're not playing. He makes out the lineup. He's the boss. I didn't argue. You can't argue with the manager."

Katz, in Philadelphia for the World Series, was numb.

"I was surprised," the attorney said. "But there have been a lot of surprises this year. That's one of the wonderful things about baseball; it's unpredictable."

The decision everyone in Philadelphia expected—that Rose would not be back in 1984—was made official at a news conference on October 19. Giles had tears in his eyes when he made the announcement, but said it was agreed there would be a parting because Rose would not accept the Phillies' proposal that he become a part-time player.

"When you mess with my pride, when you back me up against the wall with my pride, somebody's going to be in trouble," Rose said. "Just wait."

The wait was long and frustrating.

After three restless months without a team, Rose signed a one-year contract with the Montreal Expos on January 20, 1984.

Expectations were high that Rose would be able to work the same miracles with the Expos that he had performed in Cincinnati and Philadelphia.

Nearing age 43, Rose refused to realize how perilously close he was to the end. He kept saying he did not sign with Montreal just for a chance to chase Cobb's record.

"For those who think I can't play anymore, Montreal gave me a contract and they're a pretty good team," he said. "There's nothing I can do about the date I was born. I wish people would forget how damned old I am. I don't feel old, I don't act old and medical experts have told me my body isn't old.

"I led the league in hits (in 1981) at age 40, and nobody said anything about me being washed up. The people of Montreal should hope I get 202 hits (the number needed entering the '84 season to surpass Cobb's mark) because, if I do, I'll produce for this team. I'm going to get the record. I'm not worried about that. If I don't get it this year, I'll get it next year."

When Rose came to grips with the reality of his release from Philadelphia, he decided that his off-season conditioning should include considerably more than playing tennis with Katz.

He spent the winter on a strength and flexibility program with Reds trainer Larry Starr. He reported to spring training in excellent shape.

Expos Manager Bill Virdon decided to use Rose in left field, with Al Oliver at first base. Even when Oliver was traded to San Francisco in spring training, Rose remained the left fielder.

"They keep asking me what I bring to this team," Pete said. "The only thing I know of is, it's the same thing I bring wherever I go—a positive attitude, a confident attitude, a love for the game and a burning desire to win. I'm just a player who is going to try to do his job.

"Montreal has always had a great team—on paper. It's just a matter of understanding what they have to do to win. Leadership can do only so much. Any player can help with his contribution. If I do well, that's where the leadership will come out."

Rose opened the '84 season needing just 10 hits to become only the second player in major league history to reach 4,000. He hoped to reach the milestone during a three-game series in Cincinnati against the Reds, beginning April 9.

Rose moved within range by collecting five hits in the Expos' first five games of the season. He proceeded to collect two hits in the first game of the Reds series, a 9-6 loss to Cincinnati, then reduced the figure to one with two more hits in another defeat, 8-6.

The Expos and Reds were matched in an afternoon game on Wednesday, April 11. It would be a big day for Rose—regardless. In a small ceremony at Katz's home that morning, Rose married Carol June Woliung.

Pete, with a devilish smile on his face, was in high spirits as he drove from his new Indian Hill home to the Katz residence.

"How many guys get married in the morning, then go out and get their 4,000th hit?" he asked.

"Nobody I know of," his companion said.

The stereo in his turbo-powered Porsche was on full blast, but after a few seconds of Barbra Streisand's "The Way We Were," Rose changed stations.

"Not a very good song for a guy who's getting married," he said.

To avoid the rush of media, the wedding was kept a secret. In fact, one rumor had the couple getting married in West Palm Beach, Fla., before spring training ended.

It didn't take the world long to know once Pete arrived at Riverfront Stadium. He was wearing a blue suit, and it was hard to miss the rose in the lapel.

It would have been a perfect script had he gotten his 4,000th hit that sunny afternoon. He would have done it in his hometown, against his beloved Reds and on the day of his wedding.

The Expos won, 9-3, but Rose walked four times and grounded out in five trips to the plate.

So, for Mr. and Mrs. Pete Rose and the Montreal Expos, it was on to Canada for the Expos' home opener against another former Rose employer, the Philadelphia Phillies, in Olympic Stadium on, of all dates, Friday, April 13.

Rose reached the 4,000-hit mark when he lashed a fourth-inning double to right field off Philadelphia's Jerry Koosman en route to a 5-1 Montreal victory. He was accorded a three-minute standing ovation by the crowd of 48,060.

"Sure, it's a milestone," Rose said that day, "but in a sense all the hits are the same to me. Baseball is a game of peaks and valleys. This was a high peak for me."

Overall, Rose's tenure in Montreal was less than successful. He injured his foot chasing a fly ball in left field against Philadelphia and later had an injury in his right forearm. Eventually, Virdon put Rose on first base, but his playing time was not steady.

On July 26, the Expos obtained first baseman Dan Driessen from Cincinnati. Virdon said Rose would become a pinch-hitter and occasional starter.

"When you make a move, someone pays a price," Virdon said. "You always have to think that when your club has a chance to shore up, when someone is available, you have got to do it.

"This is nothing against Pete. Pete has done a good job. There had to be some sentiment about his chase of Cobb. But an even tougher thing about benching Pete is he's such a good guy."

Rose refused to say he was bitter.

"I'm not going to sit there with my head between my legs," he said when reporters questioned his reaction. "I've always been able to understand my role and accept it. You have enough grumblings everywhere you go. You don't need someone like me to sit over there and grumble. Everyone wants to play. If they don't want to play, you don't want them in the dugout."

Rose had started two-thirds of the Expos' games. And when he didn't start, he served as the team's top pinch-hitter.

But several hours after Driessen arrived, Rose called Katz.

"See if there is a team out there that might need me down the stretch," Rose told Katz. "I want to play."

A few days later, Katz attended the wedding of a client, Reds pitcher Jeff Russell. During the reception, Katz mentioned the subject of Pete Rose returning to Cincinnati to Reds President Bob Howsam.

"My first conversation was very casual," Katz said. "At least the suggestion was made and I made a mental note that day to pursue it."

There were several subsequent conversations. Howsam seemed interested in Rose returning as manager, but he was cold on a playing-manager role.

"I think he had serious doubts Pete could still play," Katz said.

On Sunday, August 12, after the Chicago Cubs had defeated the Expos, 7-3, Rose called Howsam from Montreal.

"We talked for nearly two hours; I should have called collect," Pete said. "He wanted me as manager, but I told him why I thought I could help as a player-manager.

"I had had a lot of talks with Billy DeMars (Expos batting coach who now has a similar role with Cincinnati) and Virdon. I asked them if they thought I could still hit. They said I could. Why should I give up something I can still do? Regardless of what you heard or read, I did not want to play every day. That's what I had to convince Mr. Howsam. I was exhausted when I got off the phone, but I think he believed me."

The next day Rose and the Expos flew to San Francisco for a three-game series in Candlestick Park. Meanwhile, Katz, Howsam and Expos President John McHale started two days of lengthy negotiations.

One of the first things McHale did was ask Katz if Rose would be interested in becoming a player-manager with the Expos.

Katz said no.

Howsam flew to Philadelphia for the summer baseball meetings on the night of August 14 and met with McHale. Howsam agreed to send second baseman Tom Lawless to the Expos for Rose. The deal was cast.

Howsam had planned to fire Manager Vern Rapp on the morning of August 16, an open date on the Reds' schedule, then hold a full-dress news conference during which Rose would appear.

Instead, a rumor of Rose's impending appointment hit the news wires on the afternoon of August 15 and before nightfall, Reds General Partner William J. Williams confirmed it.

Rose, who had not even told his wife ahead of time, flew all night in Williams' private jet from California and appeared at what Reds vice president Jim Ferguson termed the biggest news conference he'd seen in 25 years of covering or working for the team.

A huge headline in the Cincinnati Enquirer told it all: PETE COMES HOME.

So, after nearly six years in exile, the city's favorite son was back, becoming the first playing manager in the major leagues since Don Kessinger filled that role with the Chicago White Sox in 1979.

With Montreal, Pete had played in 95 games, batting .259 and collecting 72 hits.

"Rose is returning mainly to be the manager, and also pinch hit and fill in a few times," Howsam said. "What I expect from him is what I always expect from a manager—to work hard and lead a winning team.

"Vern Rapp has made every effort to do an outstanding job from the standpoint of getting everything he could out of his players. He was not as successful as we would have liked (the Reds were 51-70 under Rapp), so we'll see if another approach might do something."

Even before the news conference, there was a demand for tickets for the Reds' weekend games at Riverfront Stadium against Chicago. The town was abuzz.

When Rose addressed the media assembled in temporary seats on the infield, he was 129 hits short of Cobb's record and the obvious question was how often he would play.

"As of today, Nick Esasky is the first baseman," Rose said. "I plan to play periodically, and something I've learned to do over the last couple of years is pinch hit. Do I have a fair chance of catching Ty Cobb as a pinch-hitter? No way."

Rose, wearing a Reds jacket and cap on the hot afternoon, insisted that pursuit of Cobb's record would take a back seat to his managing the Reds.

Howsam, sitting close by, smiled.

"I will never and never have put the record ahead of what the team's trying to accomplish," Rose said. "There again, the record would be great for me. I happen to be probably the only player ever to have a chance of breaking that record. But it's not the utmost thing in my career, in my life. I won't jump off a bridge if I don't get the record. I'm talking about the record because you guys brought it up.

"I can still play, but not every day. And I don't care how much playing time I get. If I'm going to break the record, I'm going to break the record. If the man upstairs sees it in his heart to have me break the record, I'll break it. I'm not worried about it."

The news conference lasted more than an hour.

Later, Pete, his wife Carol, and a friend left Riverfront.

En route to a restaurant for dinner, Rose turned to his friend and said: "You know how difficult it was for me to say I couldn't play every day? That hurt."

By coincidence, Pete's mother—whose second husband (Bob Noeth) had died 12 days earlier—was visiting son Dave from her home near Tampa, Fla., when the announcement was made.

Dave, his wife Judy, their three children and LaVerne Noeth stopped by Rose's Indian Hill home to welcome him back.

"Bob and I would sit and talk about Peter returning to Cincinnati," LaVerne said. "He would say, 'Someday Pete will be manager of the Cincinnati Reds. I'll bet you anything you want on that.' Too bad he couldn't be here tonight.

"And too bad Peter's dad wasn't here. When I heard the news, I cried and so did my two daughters."

Much later, Pete and his friend talked baseball late into the night.

"Wadda you think of Jim Kaat as my pitching coach?" Rose asked. "You got his phone number back in Pennsylvania?"

The call was placed, but Kaat's wife said he was at the Meadowlands, attending harness racing.

"I'll get him tomorrow," Rose said.

Seven days later, Kaat was appointed pitching coach, replacing Stan Williams.

As the clock approached midnight on August 16, Rose was trying to decide whether he should pencil his name into the next day's lineup.

"You have to," his friend advised. "I don't think all those people were standing in line today for tickets so they could see Pete Rose take the lineup card to home plate before the game. They want to see you get some hits and slide on your belly. That's what they want to see."

Rose smiled. "Yeah, that's what they want to see."

Cincinnati's favorite son did not disappoint the festive crowd of 35,038—the largest attendance at Riverfront since opening day.

It was a triumphant return.

With the crowd on its feet, Rose lined a run-scoring single in his first at-bat and before the standing ovation had quieted, he raced to third and slid into the bag on his stomach on outfielder Bob Dernier's two-base throwing error.

In the seventh, he doubled to left field and again thrilled the crowd with a dramatic, although unnecessary, head-first slide. The Reds won, 6-4.

The return of Peter Edward Rose was official.

With players exhibiting new spirit and demonstrating how much they enjoyed playing for Rose, the Reds finished 19-22 under him. They were 15-12 in September.

Rose played in 26 games for Cincinnati, batting .365 (35 for 96) and recording seven three-hit games.

That left him with 4,097 hits, 95 short of breaking Cobb's record.

Rose takes a break from his busy routine to discuss baseball with co-author Hal Bodley.

Hal Bodley

Hal Bodley, baseball editor of USA Today, has known and covered Pete Rose since 1963, Rose's rookie year in the major leagues. The two became close friends when Rose left the Cincinnati Reds after the 1978 season and signed as a free agent with the Philadelphia Phillies, a team that Bodley covered while a columnist for the Wilmington, Del., News-Journal newspapers and a correspondent for The Sporting News.

Bodley was with the Wilmington News-Journal from 1960 to 1982, and his "Once Over Lightly" column was syndicated by Gannett News Service from 1977 to 1982. He has won numerous regional and national writing awards, being selected Delaware Sportswriter of the Year 12 times, and is past president of the Associated Press Sports Editors Association.

Rose and his wife Carol were best man and maid of honor in 1981 when Bodley and the former Patricia Jean Hall were married.